THE BAR CODE BOOK

THIRD EDITION

Reading, Printing, Specification, and Application
of Bar Code and Other Machine Readable Symbols

Roger C. Palmer

THE
BAR CODE
BOOK

Third Edition

Reading, printing, specification, and application of bar code and other machine readable symbols.

Roger C. Palmer

Helmers Publishing, Inc.
174 Concord Street
Peterborough, New Hampshire 03458

Helmers Publishing, Inc.
174 Concord Street
Peterborough, New Hampshire 03458

Printed in the United States of America
ISBN 0-911261-09-5

CONTENTS

PREFACE

This publication is designed to be an authoritative information resource for both beginning and experienced bar code users. Most chapters can stand alone, thereby allowing casual readers to focus on particular topics of interest without necessarily covering all of the preceding chapters. The book should prove to be a useful text for an introductory college or university course on automatic identification.

The appendices contain complete specifications for many of the bar code symbologies, derivations of several relationships that are commonly used in bar code systems, and other useful information.

Bar code is just one of several automatic identification technologies. This field is rapidly evolving, making it difficult to create a text that is totally up-to-date in all aspects. This publication reflects the state of the art as of early 1995. Inevitably, more advanced equipment and applications will be introduced as time progresses; I hope the material contained herein will provide a sound basis for the future.

ACKNOWLEDGMENTS

Many people contributed to the publication of this book. In particular, I would like to acknowledge the contributions and assistance provided by David C. Allais, Michael W. Callahan, Lowell A. Klaisner, David Armstrong, and Sprague Ackley. I would also like to thank Jackie MacMillan and Bobbie Yates for their word processing assistance. Technical editing was provided by Carl Helmers of Helmers Publishing, Inc.

Introduction

Bar code is a technology that has received much publicity in the past few years. Widely implemented in the retail marketplace, it is rapidly gaining increasing visibility in a broad range of diverse applications.

A conventional bar code is a machine readable symbol consisting of a series of parallel, adjacent bars and spaces. Predetermined width patterns are used to represent actual data in the symbol. A simple bar code symbol is illustrated in Figure 1-1.

Figure 1-1: Simple Bar Code Symbol. A bar code symbol consists of a series of varying-width parallel bars and spaces. One of a number of encodation schemes is used to represent information by the width of the bars and the spaces between the lines.

Bar code can be thought of as a printed version of the Morse code, with narrow bars representing dots, and wide bars representing dashes. To read the information contained in a bar code symbol, a scanning device—such as a light pen—is moved across the symbol from one side to the other, as shown in Figure 1-2. As the scanning device is moved across the symbol, the width pattern of the bars and spaces is analyzed by the reading equipment and the original data is recovered. Some scanning devices do not require the operator to provide the scanning motion: an electronic scanning system or arrangement of moving optical elements allow the symbol's bars and spaces to be sequentially examined automatically. More advanced equipment uses machine vision technology to "take a picture" of a symbol and decode the information directly.

Figure 1-2: Scanning. Scanning is the act of acquiring the information encoded in a bar code symbol. A common scanning device for bar code symbols has an active spot that is moved through the symbol from one side to the other, crossing every bar and space. The reader technologies accomplish this through various manual, mechanical and electronic means.

Although this book's title refers to "bar code," we will broaden the scope to include other forms of optical symbols that are specifically designed for reading by machine means.

Bar code is an automatic identification technology. It allows real-time data to be collected accurately and rapidly. But bar code by itself does not solve problems. The combination of bar code with appropriate computer hardware and application software creates the potential for improving performance, productivity, and ultimately, profitability.

This book provides a thorough background of the technology of bar coding. It reviews applicable equipment and outlines selection criteria. It also presents information on techniques and approaches to system integration and examines several applications in a broad range of industries.

Data Entry Techniques

Computers have become an integral part of almost all business operations. They are actively used for planning, controlling, producing, and analyzing most aspects of commerce. The ever-decreasing cost and size of computers has allowed them to penetrate a wide variety of businesses, institutions, agencies, and even homes.

A piece of computer hardware by itself is not exceptionally useful. In order to be productive, a computer must be equipped with software suitable to the particular application. The effectiveness of the computer hardware/software system is a function of the input data that is provided to it. In order to maximize the benefit from a computer, timely (ideally, real-time) and accurate data is required.

There are many data collection techniques that can be used with computers.

2.1 Manual Methods

The traditional method of entering data into a computer system has involved manually keying in information (using a keyboard) that has been gathered on sheets of paper. Studies show that the error rate with this technique is approximately 1 error for every 300 characters entered. Obviously, every data transaction requires that a human operator be involved.

Manual keying does not provide real-time data entry, since the data being entered usually reflects events that occurred in the past. Because data is often gathered first on paper sheets and then transcribed via keyboard, several opportunities for making data errors exist.

2.2 Automatic Methods

To offset the disadvantages of manual entry methods, several automatic data entry technologies have been developed. In this usage, "automatic" refers to the fact that a single entry event can result in the capture of a stream of data (from a single character to dozens of characters). In this definition of automatic data capture, a human operator may or may not be a part of the actual entry data event.

In evaluating automatic identification techniques, there are two important parameters which must be considered. The first is substitution error rate (SER), often referred to as the "error rate." This term describes the probability that a given scanned character contains an error. The number of errors to be expected in a given application is equal to the substitution error rate times the number of characters scanned.

The second parameter is the first read rate (FRR). This term (expressed as a percentage) refers to the probability that an attempt to capture data (a "scanning attempt") will result in data being captured on the first attempt. As an example, if 1000 symbols are to be scanned using a system with a 75 percent first read rate, then approximately 1333 scanning attempts will be required. For a given technology, there is usually a strong inverse relationship between first read rate and the substitution error rate.

The other criteria to consider in reviewing different technologies are:

1. Is the data "printed," or is it recorded in some other fashion? Information can be machine read using several different approaches: optical, mechanical, electrical, or magnetic. Printed data is simple and economical since the same printing process can also be used to create human readable text and graphics.

2. Can the object be "scanned" at a distance or in the presence of motion?

3. Does the automatic identification technology permit modification of the recorded data? The ability to record as well as read information offers the greatest flexibility, but may introduce concerns about data integrity.

Punched Cards

Developed in 1890, punched cards are one of the oldest forms of automatic identification. Keypunching data into a card is obviously a manual process, but the ability to batch read a stack of cards into a data processing system confirms that this is an automatic identification technology.

Punched card use has declined rapidly since the early 1970s.

Mark Sense

Mark sense involves the presence or absence of printed marks in fixed locations on a document. The marks are equivalent to the punched holes in tabulating cards. The principle of mark sense has been broadly applied to the automatic scoring of students' tests.

Mark sense was successfully used in material handling and warehouse sortation prior to the widespread acceptance of bar code.

Mark sense is a transitional technology between punched cards and modern bar codes. The black marks on a mark sense document bear a one-to-one relationship with the holes in a punched card. When the cost of processing electronics declined dramatically, it became more practical and versatile to line up the marks in a single row, thereby forming a bar code.

Optical Character Recognition

Traditional optical character recognition (OCR) uses a highly stylized printed font. The two most common fonts are OCR-A and OCR-B, as shown in Figure 2-1.

OCR fonts can be printed by several different techniques and are readable by humans as well as machines. When used to read pages of OCR-printed text, an automatic page scanner can quickly capture all of the data, while exhibiting an

A B C D E

Figure 2-1: Optical Character Recognition (OCR). OCR is a stylized, printed font that is recognizable by both humans and machines. OCR is two-dimensional, requiring acquisition and analysis of raw data over an area rather than over a single line as is the case with bar code. Imperfections in the symbol have a significant impact on the acquisition of OCR coded information.

error rate of 1 character out of approximately every 10,000 scanned.

When traditional OCR is used to label products or documents, a hand-operated scanner is employed. Some operator skill is required, and the first read rate can easily be less than 50 percent. If good quality labels are used, careful operators who have received suitable training can achieve a first read rate of 80 percent or more.

Unlike bar code, OCR is a two-dimensional technology. An OCR scanner examines both vertical and horizontal features of the printed characters during the decoding process, therefore requiring control of print quality in both axes.

Recent developments in font-independent scanning equipment have been made possible by advances in recognition algorithms and the decreasing cost of computing, but this technology has not yet had much impact on automatic identification applications. The primary market for this technology has shifted: font independent OCR is now primarily used as an entry technique for word processing and desktop publishing systems.

OCR was selected as the standard automatic identification technology by the National Retail Merchants Association (NRMA) in the mid-1970s. Many retail stores installed OCR equipment, but its use declined in the 1980s because of:

- Low first read rate with semi-skilled operators

- Lack of an automatic omnidirectional OCR scanner for checkout counters

- High substitution error rate compared to bar code

- Heavy inroads made by bar code technology.

The NRMA subsequently revised its initial technology recommendation and now supports the use of bar code in retail applications.

One OCR application that is growing is passport control. Several countries print specific identification data in a prescribed position in passports, using the OCR-B font. Fixed-position specialized scanners are then used at border control points to collect data from these Machine Readable Passports (MRP).

Machine recognition of hand-printed or written text entered on digitizing screens has received a lot of recent publicity due to the newly-developing market for Personal Digital Assistants (PDAs), but the FRR and SER leave a lot to be desired.

Magnetic Ink

Magnetic ink character recognition (MICR) is the technology commonly employed in the marking of U.S. bank checks (see Figure 2-2).

Photo by Roger C. Palmer

Figure 2-2: MICR. MICR (Magnetic Ink Character Recognition) is an automatic data entry technique that uses a stylized font printed with magnetic ink. A major application area of MICR is the encoding of information on checks and bank drafts for use in the clearing and sorting process.

A highly stylized font is printed with an ink that has magnetic properties. Although the information could be read optically, MICR characters are decoded with fully automatic magnetic scanners. As in all magnetic technology, the reading equipment makes contact with the characters to be read.

This technology is well entrenched in the banking industry, having been used for many years. At the time MICR was introduced for bank checks, this was the only technology available for automatic entry of the account data. Because of the special ink and complex reading equipment, MICR is not used or suitable for general purpose applications outside of banking.

Magnetics

It is possible to encode a great deal of information onto a magnetic stripe, similar to the one found on the back of most credit cards. Information is stored as a series of regions with differing magnetization, just like computer tapes or floppy disks. Data can be written to or changed on a magnetic stripe, adding flexibility to an information system.

Magnetic stripes have not been widely adopted for general tracking applications because of:

- The unavailability of noncontact scanning equipment

- Environmental considerations

- The inability of conventional printing methods to encode magnetic information

- Higher labeling costs compared to optical technologies that use images printed onto paper substrates.

Voice Recognition

Equipment is available that can "understand" spoken speech. This technology is well suited for certain manned applications (like baggage sortation) where operators need both hands free. Voice recognition, however, does not fit our definition of automatic identification: part numbers will have to be spoken character by character. Furthermore, in the mid-1990s, commercially available equipment must often be "trained" for each operator and has a limited vocabulary. The operator is an integral part of the data capture process and is the main cause of all errors. The continuing evolution of electronic processors is resulting in progress toward the ultimate goal of speaker-independent recognition of connected speech, but there is a long way to go yet.

Machine Vision

Machine vision systems are used in many manufacturing companies to sort, to inspect, or to measure products automatically. They consist of a high-resolution television camera (or equivalent) interfaced to a computer via signal processing circuitry. Considerable software complexity is involved in most machine vision systems. This equipment is usually custom-tailored for each application.

In order to differentiate between physically similar objects, some form of optical marking is still required. This can take the form of conventional characters or a series of arbitrary marks. A machine vision system can perform automatic identification via bar code or OCR symbols, but its primary function is inspection and sortation.

A later chapter in this book will describe "Area Scanning," which is a specialized bar code scanning technique with many similarities to machine vision.

Radio Frequency Identification

Automatic identification systems using radio frequency (RF) can read data from tags that are not even optically visible to the system. A radio signal is transmitted toward the tag, and it responds with a radio signal that is modulated with information stored in the tag. One of the initial applications involved the tracking of livestock, but many applications in transportation and manufacturing have subsequently developed.

Tags can be preprogrammed with data, or they can allow the data to be changed in response to commands modulated onto the interrogating radio signal. Most programmable tags require an internal battery; nonprogrammable tags usually derive their operating power from the interrogating beam.

The tags are fabricated either from conventional integrated circuit technology or as a surface acoustic wave (SAW) device. The SAW technology makes a very simple and potentially low-cost device, but capacity is low and the data must be preprogrammed into the tag during fabrication.

RF identification uses two different frequency ranges: either very low frequency (below 300KHz), or very high frequency (above 200 MHz). The high-frequency systems allow longer ranges and higher data rates, but the costs are also higher. Low-frequency systems allow more casual tag orientation.

The simplest tag is one that contains only a single bit of information. This is sometimes used in security applications or as an anti-shoplifting device. In industrial applications, RF tags often can contain several thousand bits of information.

A read/write RF tag containing a large amount of data can be considered as a portable database. When permanently attached to a valuable asset or vehicle, it can maintain a complete service or configuration history.

RF tags can also be used to find items that may be difficult to locate. A large warehouse can be pre-wired with a quantity of overhead RF interrogators connected to a control unit. The control unit can sequentially address the RF interrogators, and determine the approximate location of all the tags in the warehouse, as well as read the data stored in them.

RF identification systems offer significant advantages in many applications where the cost of the RF tag can be justified. Note that this description applies to RF used in tags for RF identification, as opposed to RF communication.

RF is also used for communication in certain types of real-time, portable bar code readers.

Smart Cards

Smart cards are often packaged in a form factor similar to plastic credit cards. A smart card contains nonvolatile memory, a controller, and some type of security control scheme. Some smart cards employ electrical contacts to read and write data between the card and the reader, while other designs are contactless, using electrostatic or magnetic coupling. Most current applications for smart cards involve financial, security, or medical data, and the card is normally carried by an individual. Contactless smart cards are in many ways similar to short range RF tags: one differentiator is that smart cards are usually carried by personnel, whereas RF tags are normally attached to objects.

Touch Memory

Touch memory has many similarities to contact-type smart cards. The actual memory device looks like a small "button style" camera battery: it is a round metallic case with one electrical contact in its center and another contact ring around its periphery. Figure 2-3 illustrates an example.

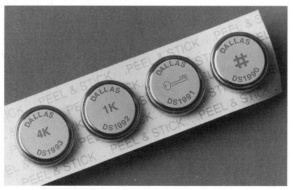

Figure 2-3: Touch Memory. A touch memory device has two electrical contacts and contains nonvolatile electronic memory.

A touch memory has internal nonvolatile electronic data storage. Data can be written to or read from the device using a probe-like device that is touched to the unit, thereby establishing electrical connection with the contacts.

Bar Code

As described in the Introduction (Chapter 1), a conventional bar code symbol consists of an array of parallel bars and spaces of differing widths. Information is

Figure 2-4: Bar Code. With conventional bar code symbols, information is encoded in the widths of the bars and spaces of the pattern. The bar height allows redundancy by providing many possible scanning paths, only one of which needs to be without imperfections. Bar code is an optical technique because information is scanned using light that reflects off dark or light regions of the symbol. Conventional bar code data capture is a one-dimensional character recognition technique since data need only be acquired from the widths of lines and spaces along a line scanning path.

encoded into the width patterns.

Bar code symbols can be printed at low cost with a wide variety of printing techniques, and the overall symbol can be uniformly scaled up or down to suit particular requirements. Conventional bar code is considered a single dimensional technology—only the widths of the bars and spaces contain information. The height of these elements can be considered as a measure of the bar code symbol's data redundancy.

Bar code systems can offer very high data security; the substitution error rate often can be better than 1 error in 1 million characters. The first read rate is usually better than 80 percent, and many automatic scanners increase the perceived scanning success rate to almost 100 percent.

The most visible application is in the supermarket industry, where bar code has been used since the early 1970s. Bar code is now the de facto automatic identification technology in a wide range of industries.

2.3 Choice of Data Entry Technology

Table 2-1 summarizes the key features of each of the described data entry techniques. The statistics in this table reflect the assumption that a human operator was going to capture the data on a label attached to a carton. The data entry times include allowances for an operator to pick up the scanning device, orient it if necessary, and move it to the label. (See page 10.)

Compared to the other automatic identification techniques outlined in Table 2-1, bar code stands out as an attractive technology. It is inexpensively printed by a variety of techniques and offers high data security. A wide variety of reading equipment is available to suit all imaginable applications.

Bar code and human-readable text are often printed together, so little additional cost is associated with the inclusion of a bar code symbol. A single beam scanned through a conventional bar code symbol can extract all of the information. This inherent simplicity has led to the availability of effective yet low cost handheld scanners and high-performance fixed scanners that can read bar code symbols from a distance of several feet on objects moving hundreds of feet per minute.

Because of these advantages, bar code has become the dominant automatic identification technology.

Table 2-1

COMPARISON OF DATA ENTRY TECHNIQUES

	Time to Enter A 20 Character Data Field*	Substitution Error Rate	Size of Label** (20 Characters)	Cost of Label	Cost of Reading Equipment	Advantages	Disadvantages
Manual Keying	10 Seconds	High	0.4" × 2.2"	Low	Low	Low initial equipment costs.	Requires human operator. Poor speed and error rate. Poor flexibility.
OCR	4 Seconds	Medium	0.5" × 2.5"	Low	Medium	Can be read by humans.	Poor error rate. Inflexibility of reading equipment.
MICR	Normally Machine-Scanned	Medium	0.5" × 2.5"	Medium	High	Can be read by humans.	Expensive. Inflexibility of reading equipment.
Magnetic Strip	4 Seconds	Low	0.4" × 1.0"	Medium	Medium	Large amounts of data can be encoded. Data can be changed.	Affected by magnetic fields. Requires contact. Inflexibility of reading equipment.
Voice Recognition	20 Seconds	High	0.4" × 2.2"	Low	High	"Hands off" operation.	Requires human operator. High error rate. Equipment must be "trained" for different operators.
Machine Vision	Normally Machine-Scanned	Depends on Marking Technique	Variable	Variable	Very High	Can be part of inspection system.	Expensive. Not suited for general applications.
Radio Frequency	2 Seconds	Low	1.0" × 1.5" × 0.2"	High	High	Label does not need to be visible.	Expensive labeling.
Bar Code	4 Seconds	Low	0.6" × 2.5"***	Low	Low	Flexibility of printing and reading equipment.	

* Assumes the use of a human operator.
** Assumes the smallest size of label that is suitable for general application.
*** Assumes the use of a single row of bar code.

3

History of Bar Code

One of the very first patents that disclosed some of the basic bar code concepts was issued to J. T. Kermode et al in 1934. This patent described a card sorter, but discussed the use of an arrangement of four parallel lines as an identification scheme to differentiate objects. In 1935 D. A. Young received a patent on a card sorting machine that also used an arrangement of parallel optical marks for identification purposes.

Retail applications drove the early technological development of bar coding, but industrial applications soon followed. We will first trace the retail roots.

Wallace Flint, son of a Massachusetts grocery wholesaler, wrote his 1932 Master's thesis at Harvard on a system for automating supermarket checkout counters. Flint's proposed system used flow racks and punched cards to automatically dispense products to customers. The proposal was economically unfeasible, but this was the first time that the benefits of an automated checkout had been completely documented. Forty years later, Flint was the vice president of the National Association of Food Chains, and he actively supported the standardization effort that led to the Universal Product Code and its associated symbology.

In the late 1940s, Joe Woodland and Berny Silver were investigating technical approaches that would allow prices of grocery items to automatically be read at the checkout stand. Several approaches were pursued, with developments culminating in the filing of U.S. Patent 2,612,994 in 1949.

The Woodland and Silver patent describes a circular printed pattern with the appearance of a miniature archery target. This format is often referred to as a bull's-eye code. The concentric rings of the target are, however, simply bars and spaces curved into a circular form. Conceptually, bull's-eye coding and bar coding are the same. Technology and retail economics were still not ready for bar code, but twenty years later Joe Woodland, then an IBM engineer, was part of the team that developed the precursor to the U.P.C. bar code symbol.

In the late 1950s and early 1960s, several inventors proposed the construction of stylized human-readable characters that would look like bar code to the automatic scanner but appear like numerals or letters to a person. Typical of these inventors was Girard Feissel, who filed a U.S. Patent in 1959 depicting the numerals 0 through 9, each constructed from seven parallel bar segments. Unfortunately, such arrangements are more difficult for machines to read than true bar code and less pleasant for humans to read than traditional type fonts.

Serious efforts toward developing a standard for automating the supermarket point-of-sale began in 1968. RCA developed a bull's-eye symbol and scanner that operated in a Kroger store in Cincinnati for an 18-month period beginning in 1972. This test store provided much valuable data for cost benefit analysis and system refinement. Meanwhile, in mid-1970 a grocery industry ad hoc committee was formed under the chairmanship of R. Bert Gookin to select a standard code and symbol for that industry. This ad hoc committee subsequently established guidelines and formed a symbol selection subcommittee to select an industry standard symbol. Proposals were solicited from interested manufacturers of computers and point-of-sale equipment. Seven equipment manufacturers responded with proposed symbols, several of which are illustrated in Figure 3-1.

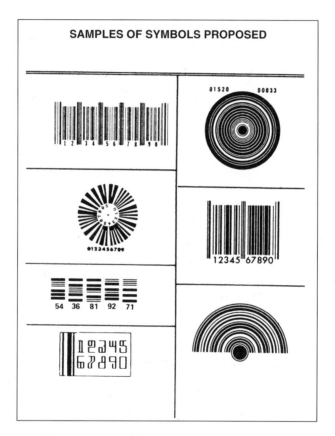

Figure 3-1: Proposed Symbols. Bar code technology has its roots in the late 1960s and early 1970s. At the time of the definition of the grocery industry's U.P.C. (Universal Product Code) symbology in the early 1970s, many proposals from different organizations were examined. Some of the originally proposed bar code symbologies are shown here.

A massive symbol evaluation was undertaken including laboratory tests by Battelle Memorial Institute, printing tolerance tests assisted by the Graphic Arts Technical Foundation, printability tests by participating grocery manufacturers, and store tests of complete working systems. This effort concluded with selection of the U.P.C. symbol as the industry standard on April 3, 1973. This final symbol closely resembles the one that had been proposed by IBM.

The early success of U.P.C. in U.S. and Canadian supermarkets encouraged foreign, particularly European, interest in the system. This interest led to the adoption of the EAN (European Article Numbering) code and symbol in December 1976.

In 1970, a small company called Charecogn Systems delivered a system to the U.S. Department of Agriculture that was designed to read circular bar codes known as Sunburst Codes. This symbology was also proposed for retail applications, but the currently used U.P.C. symbol prevailed. The Sunburst Code was used for several years by the Ohio Milk Board.

Industrial applications of bar code can be traced back to the early 1960s. In 1962 E. F. Brinker of Westinghouse Air Brake filed a patent that described a bar code attached to the side of a railroad car. In the late 1960s, North American Railroads adopted a system invented by Sylvania that used retroreflective red, blue, and white bars; 95 percent of U.S. freight cars had been labeled by the time the system was abandoned in 1974 because of poor performance due to insufficient training, maintenance, and equipment investment.

Several companies pursued warehouse and related applications following the initial railroad experience. In 1971 the Plessey Company developed a bar code and reading system for library checkout. Codabar was developed by Monarch Marking Systems in 1972. This symbology continues to be used in blood collection applications as well as in its original library usage.

Prior to 1974, bar codes could only encode numeric digits plus a few special characters. In 1974, Dr. David C. Allais of Intermec Corporation developed Code 39, the first commercial alphanumeric bar code symbology.

During the 1970s, bar coding became increasingly practical and economical with the advent of low-cost electronics—microprocessors in particular—and the availability of smaller, lower cost lasers. Inventors in many companies devised their own bar code symbology and associated scanning equipment. This resulted in the proliferation of several dozen different bar code symbologies with no commonly accepted standards. In the 1980s adoption patterns and standardization activities sharply narrowed the field. In retail applications, the U.P.C./EAN symbol was pervasive. On the industrial side, Code 39 became clearly dominant, but Interleaved 2 of 5 continued to enjoy reasonably broad usage. Several other symbologies continued to be used in specific applications.

During the 1970s, as bar code became technically and economically more viable, the U.P.C. retail system provided stability and acted as a stimulant for industrial acceptance. This acceptance has given rise to standardization of bar code symbologies and specifications. Military Standard 1189 (Code 39) was adopted in January 1982. This was closely followed by ANSI Standard MH10.8M in 1983 covering Code 39, Interleaved 2 of 5, and Codabar. The U.P.C. Shipping Container symbol (Interleaved 2 of 5) was adopted in 1984. The Automotive Industry Action Group in the same time frame standardized on Code 39 and developed a well thought out format for its shipping container label. In the same year the health industry established its HIBC standard (Code 39). Other industries including paper, aluminum, electronics, telecommunications, and furniture developed their own standards using Code 39.

The early 1980s brought two attempts to reduce the amount of space required for a bar code symbol. Code 128 was introduced by Ted Williams of Computer Identics in 1981, and Code 93 was introduced by Dr. David C. Allais in 1982. Use of these symbologies allowed labels to be approximately 30 percent shorter than if Code 39 was used. Very few applications are presently using Code 93. Since 1990, Code 128 has enjoyed increasing popularity, and it is reasonable to predict that its adoption could rival that of Code 39 by the late 90s.

In the late 1980s, the U.S. Postal Service embarked on a program to widely deploy its Postnet symbol throughout their system. Today this unique symbol is commonly used on U.S. letter and flat mail.

In late 1987, Dr. David C. Allais introduced Code 49, a nonconventional symbology that offers significant density advantages over more traditional bar code symbologies. One year after the announcement of Code 49, Ted Williams introduced a similar multirow symbology called Code 16K. In 1990, Symbol Technologies announced PDF417, a multirow symbology offering higher capacity.

In 1992, Ted Williams developed Code One, a novel "checkerboard style" 2-D (two-dimensional) matrix symbology with a special integral target incorporating conventional bar code characteristics. This was the world's first public-domain 2-D matrix symbology.

In 1993, the United Parcel Service (UPS) company introduced MaxiCode, a unique 2-D matrix symbology that they had developed internally for their parcel tracking systems.

As these various standards evolved, manufacturers and users saw the need for greater precision, technical refinement, and uniformity. Responding to this need, the Automatic Identification Manufacturers (AIM), a trade organization, chartered its Technical Symbology Committee to come up with a family of AIM Uniform Symbol Specifications (USS). These were developed and published for Code 39, Interleaved 2 of 5, Codabar, Code 93, Code 128, Code 49, Code 16K, PDF417, and Code One. This committee has now been asked to develop a USS for MaxiCode, DataMatrix, and possibly some other previously proprietary area symbologies.

4

Symbologies

Conventional bar codes are usually thought of as parallel arrangements of varying width bars and spaces, but this definition fails to include some of the postal schemes which use variable height bars. In order to account for these two diverse forms of bar code, we will use the following two definitions:

- Width-modulated symbol: A parallel arrangement of varying-width bars and spaces.

- Height-modulated symbol: A parallel arrangement of varying-height bars.

"Symbology" is the term used to describe how information is encoded into the physical attributes of the bars and spaces. In other words, it is the set of rules for a particular type of bar code.

Bars are normally thought of as the darker elements of the symbol, whereas spaces are the lighter.

Imagine a symbology based on Morse code. Dots could be represented by narrow bars, and dashes could be wide bars. The resulting patterns are shown in Figure 4-1. Although easy to visualize, this symbology is not practical because there would be a different number of bars in each character, making decoding difficult. This "Morse bar code" would make inefficient use of label area because only the black parts of the symbol contain meaningful data. Use of this symbology would result in many data errors due to printing defects, because many of the character patterns can be transposed into other character patterns by the addition or deletion of one or more elements.

Symbology is analogous to language. When humans communicate via the spoken or written word, any language can be used provided that both parties agree to and are proficient in the choice. The same concept follows in bar code: depending on the data to be communicated, several different symbologies can be used. Communication obviously cannot occur unless the reading and printing equipment use a compatible symbology. This is an important consideration because dozens of different bar code symbologies have been developed since the basic technology's inception.

It is important in the subsequent discussions to differentiate between the terms "code" and "symbol." Code refers to the actual data contained: it can be a part number, serial number, transaction code, or other type of data. Symbol refers to the actual arrangement of parallel bars and spaces that encode the data. In this respect,

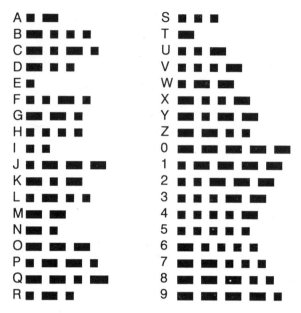

Figure 4-1: Morse Code Symbology. It would be possible to design a bar code symbology based on the Morse code, but it would be very prone to errors due to the varying character width and structure.

it is somewhat unfortunate that the term "bar code" was adopted, because it only leads to confusion over the precise meaning of the terms.

4.1 Symbology Configurations

We have already introduced the concept that bar code symbols don't necessarily always encode information based on patterns of bar widths. We will now examine the general configuration of a variety of printed symbol types.

Linear Symbologies

A linear bar code symbology is a single row of bars and spaces. It may use either width modulation or height modulation to encode the data: examples of both are

Figure 4-2: Linear Bar Code Symbols. A single row of parallel bars and spaces encodes information into either width or height patterns.

shown in Figure 4-2. Linear bar code symbologies are the most common form in use today.

Circular Symbologies

Various circular symbologies have been proposed over the years. These either use varying width concentric circles or arcs, or circular arrangements of linear symbologies or segments thereof. Examples are shown in Figure 4-3.

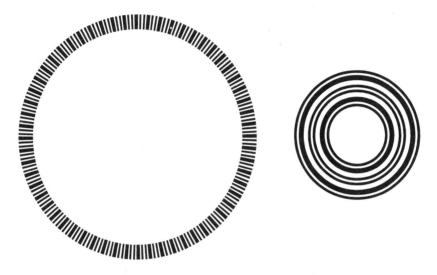

Figure 4-3: Circular Symbologies. Varying width concentric circles or circular configurations of linear symbologies are used.

2-D Stacked Symbologies

A 2-D (two-dimensional) stacked bar code symbology uses multiple rows of width modulated bars and spaces. Each row is the same physical length and looks just like a conventional linear symbology. The adjacent rows touch each other and may include separator bars for delineation. Figure 4-4 shows three examples of 2-D stacked symbologies. Note that it is impractical to have a stacked symbology that uses height modulation.

2-D Matrix Symbologies

A 2-D matrix symbology encodes information into a two dimensional pattern of data cells. The data cells can have different colors (usually black or white) and shapes (squares, dots, or polygons), and may be separated by space containing no information. Over the years, a wide variety of 2-D matrix symbologies have been developed. Figure 4-5 illustrates some of these.

Unlike stacked symbologies, a 2-D matrix symbology is printed and read with

Figure 4-4: 2-D Stacked Symbologies. Multiple rows of linear bar codes are stacked together to form a single symbol.

equipment having similar resolution in the vertical and horizontal axes. These symbologies are sometimes referred to as area symbologies.

4.2 Characteristics of a Symbology

Before further examining symbologies, it is appropriate to understand the characteristics and parameters that will be reviewed for each code.

Character Set

The term "character set" describes the range of data characters that can be encoded into a given symbology. Some symbologies can encode only numbers and are therefore termed "numeric" symbologies. Other symbologies can encode alphanumeric information, while others support the entire 128 unique codes of the ASCII-128 character set. Still others allow arbitrary binary data to be encoded, or offer a range of user-defined character messages.

Symbology Type

Width-modulated bar code symbologies fall into two general categories: discrete and continuous.

In a discrete code, each character can stand alone and can be decoded independently from the adjacent characters. Each character is separated from its neighbor by loosely toleranced intercharacter gaps, which contain no information. Every character has a bar on each end. See Figure 4-6.

Figure 4-5: 2-D Matrix Symbologies. A two dimensional array of data cells encodes the message data.

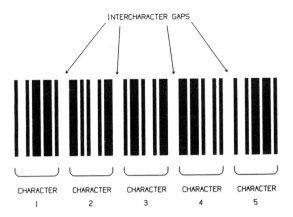

Figure 4-6: Discrete Symbology. In a discrete bar code symbology, every character stands alone and is separated from its neighbor by an intercharacter gap. The width of the intercharacter gaps carries no information. In the decoding process, each character is treated individually.

A continuous symbology has no intercharacter gaps. Every character begins with a bar and ends with a space, as shown in Figure 4-7. The end of one character is indicated by the start of the next character.

Because the intercharacter gaps are loosely toleranced, a discrete code can be printed by a variety of different techniques. A discrete code can easily be produced by a printer such as a movable font device, that prints an entire character at one time.

Since there are no intercharacter gaps, a continuous symbology requires less symbol length to encode a given amount of data. Partially offsetting this density advantage is the fact that the range of available demand printing technologies is slightly more restricted for continuous codes than it is for discrete symbologies.

The relative data security of width-modulated symbologies is unaffected by the fact that they are either discrete or continuous.

At this time, there are only two height-modulated symbologies: Postnet and 4-State. Both use a constant space width throughout the symbol and do not have intercharacter gaps.

Number of Element Widths

In a width-modulated bar code symbol, data is conveyed in the widths of the bars and spaces. Two basic types of bar codes exist: those that employ only two element widths (wide and narrow), and those that employ multiple widths.

In a two-width symbology, the ratio between wide and narrow element widths is called N. N is typically allowed to vary over some range (usually from 2.0 to 3.0), but must be constant for a given symbol. As N gets larger, the allowable printing tolerance also increases. If a bar code is printed within published specifications ("in spec"), data security is not compromised for smaller values of N.

In a multiple-width symbology, bars and spaces can assume several different width values. Most multiple-width symbologies are modular, meaning that the length of a character is subdivided into a predetermined number of modules, and a bar or space width is always an integral number of modules.

Multiple-width symbologies are usually continuous and are often decoded using edge-to-similar-edge algorithms. This technique involves the measurement of distances between similar edges of adjacent elements rather than the measurement of actual element widths.

Figure 4-8 shows that the T_1, T_2, T_3, T_4, and P measurements will remain constant if all elements grow or shrink uniformly. Since many bar code printing problems involve uniform ink spread, this decoding technique offers potential advantages for symbologies where the edge-to-similar-edge distances are unique for each character. If printed in spec, multiple-width symbologies can be just as secure as two-width symbologies.

Continuous symbologies with multiple element widths and a constant number of elements in each character are called (n,k) codes, where n refers to the number of modules in a character width and k to the number of bars (and spaces). Assuming that all patterns start with the same element (usually a bar), the total number of possible patterns in an (n,k) code can be determined from the expression:

$$\frac{(n-1)!}{(2k-1)!(n-2k)!}$$

Table 4-1 gives the number of unique patterns in an (n,k) code for a variety of values of n and k.

Table 4-1
(n, k) UNIQUE PATTERNS

n	k				
	1	2	3	4	5
2	1	0	0	0	0
3	2	0	0	0	0
4	3	0	0	0	0
5	4	4	0	0	0
6	5	10	1	0	0
7	6	20	6	0	0
8	7	35	21	0	0
9	8	56	56	8	0
10	9	84	126	36	1
11	10	120	252	120	10
12	11	165	462	330	55
13	12	220	792	792	220
14	13	286	1287	1716	715
15	14	364	2002	3432	2002
16	15	455	3003	6435	5005
17	16	560	4368	11440	11440

Six (n,k) symbologies are described in this chapter: U.P.C./EAN (7,2); Code 93 (9,3); Code 128 (11,3); Code 49 (16,4); Code 16K (11,3); and PDF417 (17,4).

Fixed or Variable Length

Some symbologies by their very structure encode only messages of a fixed length. Other symbologies should only be used in a fixed-length environment because of

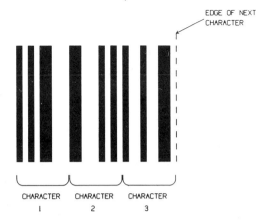

Figure 4-7: **Continuous Symbology**. In a continuous bar code symbology, there are no intercharacter gaps. Every character begins with a bar and ends with a space. Some form of termination pattern starting with a bar must provide the last "edge of next character" for the symbol's last character.

data security considerations, while some can be used to encode true variable length data.

X and Z

X is the term used to describe the nominal (or intended) width of a bar code symbol's narrow elements (both bars and spaces). When examining an unknown symbol, it is common to measure and compute the average width of the symbol's narrow elements: this, strictly speaking, is not X, but is instead referred to as Z. By convention, both X and Z are expressed in mils (thousandths of an inch).

2-D matrix symbologies do not have bars (other than the reference patterns in some symbologies). Here, X refers to the nominal dimension (height, width, or diameter) of the smallest data cell.

Figure 4-8: **Edge-To-Similar-Edge Measurements**. In the process of decoding a bar code symbol, the measurement of edge-to-similar-edge distances by the scanner becomes the raw data. The T-distances remain constant in the presence of uniform bar growth or shrinkage. This example shows four such T-distance measurements.

Density

Bar code symbologies differ in the amount of data that can be encoded in a given unit of length. In order to allow meaningful comparisons, the value of X (width of a narrow bar or space) needs to be considered when examining relative densities.

Note that density is normally specified only for the data characters. The overall length of a symbol needs to include start/stop characters, quiet zones, and any check characters.

The concept of density can be expanded to address the area efficiency of a symbology. This concept is covered later in the chapter.

Self-Checking

A symbology is termed self-checking if a single printing defect will not cause a character to be transposed into another valid character in the same symbology.

Start Character, Stop Character

A start character is a particular pattern of bars and spaces that is placed at the beginning of a symbol to indicate to the scanner where the symbol begins; it sometimes also indicates the scanning direction. A stop character is a pattern placed at the end of a symbol for marking the end of the data characters; it sometimes is also used to indicate the scanning direction.

Check Character

A check character is a character (or characters) placed in a predetermined position in a symbol, whose value is based on some mathematical relationship of the other characters in the symbol. It is used by the scanner for validating that the correct data has been decoded. If the check character can only assume numeric values (the numbers 0 through 9), it is often called a check digit.

Error Correction

As an extension of check characters, some symbologies include additional characters that can actually be used to correct decoding errors or fill in missing data. These error correction characters are mathematically based on the data characters. There are several different forms of error correction that have been developed: the two most common types are Reed Solomon and Convolution codes. In general it takes two error correction characters to correct a single data character error.

Bi-directional

A bi-directional symbology is one that can be decoded by scanning either left to right or right to left. Almost all conventional symbologies in use today are bi-directional. As an extension of this concept, a later part of this chapter will discuss 2-D matrix symbologies which can be read in any orientation.

Self-Clocking

Scanners need reference information in order to have a means of measuring the relative positions of the edges of all the elements. Some older symbologies actually included a separate clock track, as shown in Figure 4-9. This is inefficient, and modern symbologies are designed in such a way (the "self-clocking" property) that scanners do not require a separate clock track to recover the width information.

Figure 4-9: Clocked Symbology. A clock track is read in conjunction with a separate data track.

4.3 Width-Modulated Linear Symbologies

Width-modulated linear symbologies are the oldest and most common form of bar code.

4.3.1 U.P.C.

The Universal Product Code (U.P.C.) has been successfully employed in the retail industry in the United States and Canada since 1973. U.P.C. is a coding system as well as a symbology; it is designed to uniquely identify a product and its manufacturer. It is important to differentiate between the U.P.C. coding scheme and the U.P.C. symbology.

The actual U.P.C. code is a 12 digit code: the first 6 digits represent the manufacturer of the labeled item, the next 5 digits are a unique product identifier code and

Figure 4-10: U.P.C. Version A Symbol Encoding the Data "01234567890". A typical U.P.C. Version A symbol consists of two halves representing a total of 12 numeric digits. The two six-digit halves are surrounded by left, center and right guard patterns. The left half uses the character set A encodations of digits and the right half uses character set C encodations of digits (see Figure 4-12). The first numeric digit is the number system character, which with the next five digits, is the U.P.C. manufacturer's code. The first five digits of the right half of the pattern are the product code digits and the final digit is the check character, used for error detection. Although U.P.C. is a continuous symbology, the left and right halves of the pattern can be independently decoded.

the twelfth digit is a check character, based on the previous 11 digits of data. The first digit of the 6 digit field is also the number system character.

U.P.C. is a fixed length, numeric, continuous symbology using four element widths. There are two versions of the U.P.C. symbol: Version A, which encodes 12 digits, and Version E which encodes six digits. A variable length version known as U.P.C. Version D was originally defined, but it was never used, and it has been dropped from the official specification. Figure 4-10 illustrates the data arrangement in a Version A symbol.

The first digit of a U.P.C. Version A symbol represents the number system as well as being part of the manufacturer's identification. Number systems '0', '6', and '7' are assigned with the five digits to identify the manufacturer; others have special uses as shown in Table 4-2.

Table 4-2
U.P.C. VERSION A NUMBER SYSTEM ASSIGNMENTS

Number System Digit	Application
0	92,000 manufacturer identification numbers 8,000 locally assigned numbers
1	Reserved
2	Random weight consumer packages
3	Drug Products
4	In-store marking without format
5	U.P.C. coupons
6	100,000 manufacturer identification numbers
7	100,000 manufacturer identification numbers
8	Reserved
9	Reserved

The final digit is a check digit whose value is mathematically based on the first eleven digits encoded in the symbol. A weighting scheme (the weighting alternates between 1 and 3) is used in its calculation, so that the check digit also protects against transposition errors if the data is manually entered. The check digit calculation is shown in Appendix A1.

A U.P.C. Version A symbol is physically arranged into halves. The first six digits and the second six digits are separated in the U.P.C. Version A symbol by two center guard bars. The two symbol halves are then enclosed by two left guard bars and two right guard bars. The various guard bars can be thought of as start/stop patterns.

The actual data is encoded as two bars and two spaces within seven modules. As described previously, this is a (7,2) code, which has 20 unique patterns where every pattern starts with a bar and ends with a space. Taking a "mirror image" of these patterns, we end up with 20 additional patterns that begin with a space and end with a bar. All twenty of the patterns that start with a bar and end with a space,

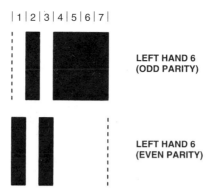

LEFT HAND 6
(ODD PARITY)

LEFT HAND 6
(EVEN PARITY)

Figure 4-11: U.P.C. Version A Encoding of the Digit "6". A different pattern is used for the left and right halves of the U.P.C. symbol. Here we show how the "6" is represented for both locations. The scale enumerates the seven modules contained in the fixed width U.P.C. character pattern.

together with half of the "mirror image" patterns are used in the overall U.P.C./ EAN system, making a total of 30 unique patterns. Bar and space widths may be 1, 2, 3, or 4 modules wide. Figure 4-11 illustrates the pattern for "6" encoded for either the left or right half of the symbol.

Encoding differs for the left and right halves of the Version A symbol, as shown in Figure 4-12. The left hand digits use patterns from character set A, and the right hand digits use patterns from character set C. Version E symbols are encoded using specific patterns from the A and B character sets.

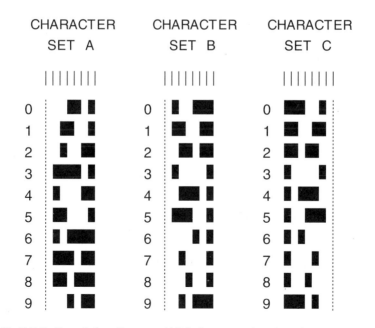

Figure 4-12: U.P.C. Encoation Patterns. U.P.C. is a numeric only code, containing 12 digits in Version A, or 6 data digits in Version E. The 30 unique patterns are shown here as graphic symbols drawn to scale.

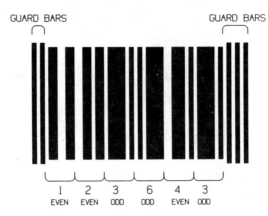

Figure 4-13: U.P.C. Version E Symbol. U.P.C. Version E is an eight digit variation of the U.P.C. symbology used only with number system "0." It is intended to be used to label small items. In this example, the number system 0 data 12300-00064 (2) has been compressed to the shorter numeric code (0) 123643 (2). The last data digit in this example (the 3) indicates the type of compression. Guard bars precede and follow the six data digits. See Appendix A2 for decode rules. The character set of the encodation follows the pattern shown to encode the check character "2." Because of the data compression process used, a Version E symbol is often referred to as a zero-suppressed symbol.

The bar height of either half of a U.P.C. Version A symbol is greater than the width of the six digits, ensuring that at least one of two orthogonal scanning beams will be able to pass completely through each half of the symbol, thereby allowing omnidirectional scanning. The scanner can independently decode the left and the right halves of the symbol because an examination of the data's character set indicates which half was decoded. The guard bars are usually printed with greater length than other bars in the symbol in order to maximize the allowable scanning tilt angle.

The nominal X dimension employed in U.P.C. symbols is 13 mils. An allowable magnification factor of 0.8 to 2.0 results in a range of printable X values between 10.4 and 26 mils.

U.P.C. is intended to be decoded using the edge-to-similar-edge algorithm. Unfortunately, the encodation of digits 1 and 7 results in the same T distances. A similar problem exists with the digits 2 and 8. To avoid this ambiguity, a U.P.C. reader also needs to examine element widths when these problematic characters are encountered.

U.P.C. Version E has an implied system character of "0," six explicitly encoded data digits, and an implicitly encoded seventh digit (check character). It is suited for identifying products in small packages. The symbol layout is illustrated in Figure 4-13.

U.P.C. Version E (also known as the "zero-suppression version") allows manufacturers to encode a limited number of unique twelve digit product codes in six digits. The six digits are enclosed between two left hand guard bars and three right hand guard bars. The check character is encoded by the character set pattern of the six data digits. The check character (2), in Figure 4-13, is encoded using the pattern shown. The system character "0" is implied.

See Table 4-3 for the particular character set pattern used to encode specific check characters.

Table 4-3
CHARACTER SET PATTERNS—U.P.C.-E

U.P.C.-E Character Set Pattern

| | Character Location Number | | | | | Modulo Check |
1	2	3	4	5	6	Character Value
B	B	B	A	A	A	0
B	B	A	B	A	A	1
B	B	A	A	B	A	2
B	B	A	A	A	B	3
B	A	B	B	A	A	4
B	A	A	B	B	A	5
B	A	A	A	B	B	6
B	A	B	A	B	A	7
B	A	B	A	A	B	8
B	A	A	B	A	B	9

For labeling periodicals and paperback books, two supplemental encodings are provided: one encodes two digits, and one encodes 5 digits. These are used in combination with either a version A or version E U.P.C. symbol. The first bar of the supplemental symbol is separated by seven modules from the last bar in the main symbol.

4.3.2 EAN

The European Article Numbering system (abbreviated as EAN) is a superset of U.P.C. and was introduced about 1978. An EAN scanner can decode U.P.C., but some original U.P.C. scanner systems, developed prior to the introduction of EAN, cannot decode EAN.

EAN has two versions, EAN-13 and EAN-8, encoding 13 and 8 digits respectively. An EAN-13 symbol contains the same number of bars as U.P.C. Version A, but encodes a thirteenth digit from the character set pattern of the left hand six digits, in the same manner as the encoding of the check digit in a U.P.C. Version E symbol. This thirteenth digit, in combination with the twelfth digit, defines two flag characters that represent a country code. (EAN numbers the digit positions from right to left). For compatibility with U.P.C., flags 00 through 09 are reserved.

The flag character assignments are listed in Appendix S.

Character set patterns for the left half of EAN-13, with the exception of "0," are the reverse of U.P.C.-E. The character set patterns are shown in Table 4-4. EAN scanner software decodes a U.P.C.-A bar code by reading the character set pattern of the left half as all character set A and adds a "0" in front of the 12 digits decoded from the bars to provide the 13th digit (00 12345 67890 5). The check character calculation for EAN-13 ignores the left-most digit and is calculated in the same manner as U.P.C.-A.

Table 4-4

CHARACTER SET PATTERNS—LEFT HALF OF EAN-13

EAN-13 Character Set Pattern						First Country Flag Value
A	A	A	A	A	A	0
A	A	B	A	B	B	1
A	A	B	B	A	B	2
A	A	B	B	B	A	3
A	B	A	A	B	B	4
A	B	B	A	A	B	5
A	B	B	B	A	A	6
A	B	A	B	A	B	7
A	B	A	B	B	A	8
A	B	B	A	B	A	9

Table 4-4: Character Set Patterns for the Left Half of EAN-13. Character set A and character set B (See Figure 4-12) bar and space patterns are selected using the patterns shown. When a U.P.C.-A bar code is decoded by an EAN scanner, the software adds the 13th digit, a '0' and places it in front of the 12 digits of the U.P.C. code.

An EAN-8 symbol is structured in the same manner as a U.P.C. Version A, but with only four digits encoded in each half. An EAN-8 symbol encodes two flag digits, five data digits assigned for the product by the Country Coding Authority, and one check digit. An EAN-8 symbol is shown in Figure 4-14.

Each country has a coding authority (or numbering association) which assigns codes to manufacturers and maintains a central database. The Uniform Code Council, based in Dayton, Ohio, administers the U.P.C. system for the United States. In Canada, administration is carried out by the Product Code Council of Canada, based in Toronto, Ontario. The EAN system is under the overall direction of the International Article Numbering Association, based in Brussels, Belgium.

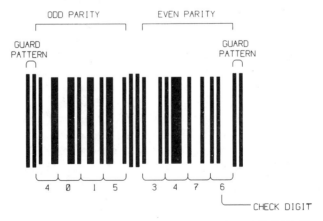

Figure 4-14: EAN-8 German (40) Symbol Encoding the Data "15347". EAN (European Article Numbering) is a super set of the original U.S. based U.P.C. coding scheme and has been adopted for the international marketplaces in over 56 countries. The EAN-8 symbol has eight digits including one check digit. The encodation patterns are identical to U.P.C. Version A (see Figure 4-12); like U.P.C., the symbol is divided into left and right halves with center, plus left and right guard patterns.

Each country using the EAN system maintains a separate Article Numbering Association.

U.P.C./EAN has proven to be extremely successful in the retail marketplace. Almost all retail channels use the coding system to access databases for item identification and price look-up. In normal usage, every decoded message from a retail scanner is verified against an in-store computer's data base before being acted upon. In this mode, a very high data security has been reliably demonstrated.

4.3.3 Interleaved 2 of 5

Interleaved 2 of 5 is a high-density, self-checking, continuous numeric symbology. It has been mainly used in the distribution industry.

Every Interleaved 2 of 5 character actually encodes two digits; one in the bars, and one in the spaces. There are five bars, two of which are wide and three of which are narrow. Similarly, there are five spaces in each character, two of which are wide and three of which are narrow. Each digit has its own unique 2 out of 5 arrangement, as illustrated in Figure 4-15. Note that W represents a wide element, and N represents a narrow element.

All of the odd-positioned data is encoded in the bars, and all of the even-positioned data is encoded in the spaces. Figure 4-16 illustrates this, encoding the data "38."

A complete Interleaved 2 of 5 symbol consists of the start code (two narrow bars and two narrow spaces), the data characters, and the stop code (one wide bar, a narrow space, and a narrow bar). Figure 4-17 is an example of this, encoding the data "1991".

(a)

0	NNWWN	5	WNWNN
1	WNNNW	6	NWWNN
2	NWNNW	7	NNNWW
3	WWNNN	8	WNNWN
4	NNWNW	9	NWNWN

(b)
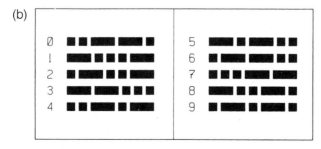

Figure 4-15: Interleaved 2 of 5 Encodation Patterns. Interleaved 2 of 5 is a continuous, numeric symbology, consisting of pairs of digits. The first digit of each pair is encoded in the widths of bars. The second digit of each pair is encoded in the widths of the spaces between the bars. Each digit has two wide elements and three narrow elements encoded as narrow (N) or wide (W) in the table (a). The complete encodation table for the bar form of the digits is shown at (b).

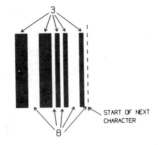

Figure 4-16: Interleaved 2 of 5 Symbol Encoding the Data "38". The interleaving of digits is shown here for the character code "38." The widths of the bars encode (see Figure 4-11) the digit 3. The widths of the spaces encode the digit 8. As a continuous symbology, the start of the first bar of the next character (or stop code) is needed to determine the width of the last space in each two-digit pair.

Unfortunately, a partial scan (i.e., a scanning path that does not include both quiet zones) has a high probability of decoding as a valid, but shorter Interleaved 2 of 5 symbol. This is due to the simple nature of the start and stop patterns: an examination of Figure 4-15 will show that a partial scan of several of the Interleaved 2 of 5 patterns could produce a start or stop code. Because of this problem, Interleaved 2 of 5 is best used in a fixed-length application, with all reading equipment programmed to accept messages only of the correct length. Shorter data can be padded with leading zeros.

Interleaved 2 of 5 is often used with a modulo 10 check digit in the final position in order to improve data security. The use of a check digit by itself is not sufficient to prevent the partial scan problem. Note that the total number of digits encoded in an Interleaved 2 of 5 symbol must be even: if the message to be encoded has an odd length, it is customary to add a leading zero.

In many environments, several different Interleaved 2 of 5 symbol lengths may exist. In order to minimize system problems due to accidental partial scans of the longer symbols, protection stripes (commonly called bearer bars) should be used. Bearer bars prevent a partial scan from being decoded as a valid Interleaved 2 of 5 symbol (see Figure 4-18).

To prevent the partial scan problem, the bearer bars must touch the top and bottom of all of the data bars. Minimum width of a bearer bar should be 3X. A partial

Figure 4-17: Interleaved 2 of 5 Symbol Encoding The Data "1991". This is a complete symbol showing the start pattern, 4 digits, and the stop pattern. Because interleaving is done with successive pairs of digits, this symbology must always encode an even number of data digits; odd length patterns are conventionally padded with a zero digit.

Figure 4-18: Interleaved 2 of 5 Symbol with Bearer Bars. Partial scans of Interleaved 2 of 5 symbols do not necessarily produce an error condition. The introduction of bearer bars helps prevent errors due to partial scans. When the scanning path leaves the symbol through either top or bottom it crosses the bearer bar, thereby resulting in an invalid start/stop code.

scan of the symbol will now penetrate one or more bearer bars, and the resulting apparent arrangement of wide and narrow elements will not bear any resemblance to a start or stop code, thereby preventing an erroneous decode.

An Interleaved 2 of 5 symbol has only two element widths, wide and narrow. N is the symbol used to describe the ratio between the widths of wide elements and narrow elements. N can have any value between 2.0 and 3.0 for a given symbol, but should be larger than 2.2 if X (the nominal narrow element width) is less than 20 mils.

Despite the partial scan problems, Interleaved 2 of 5 has been successfully employed in many applications that can benefit from its high density. When printed with an X value of 7.5 mils and an N of 2.2, Interleaved 2 of 5 can encode 18 characters per inch. Interleaved 2 of 5 is the highest density conventional bar code symbology for numeric messages less than 10 digits long.

4.3.4 Codabar

Originally developed in 1972, Codabar today is used in libraries, blood banks and certain air parcel express applications.

Codabar is a self-checking, discrete symbology having 16 characters in its set: the numbers 0 through 9, and the $: / . + - characters. There are four different start/stop codes, allowing some useful information to be conveyed in these overhead characters.

The most peculiar aspect of Traditional Codabar is that the widths of the bars and spaces to be printed can take on 18 different values, depending on the particular character. There are many different explanations as to how this came about, but the most probable is that these multiple widths were generated to give a constant character width, and then empirically fine tuned to give best performance with the pre-microprocessor reading equipment that was available in 1972.

All Codabar characters are constructed from four bars and the three intervening spaces. Ignore the 18 different widths for a moment, and consider that all elements are either wide or narrow. Codabar uses three different character encoding schemes:

1. The 0 through 9 digits and the $ and - characters are each printed with one

Figure 4-19: Codabar Number "7" Character. Codabar is a discrete symbology with four bars per digit encoded. The digit "7" shown here has one wide bar and one wide space.

wide bar and one wide space. All other elements are narrow. Figure 4-19 shows the number "7."

2. The four special start/stop characters : / . + are encoded with three wide bars and no wide spaces. An example of the "/" character appears in Figure 4-20.

3. The four start/stop characters (a, b, c, d) are encoded with one wide bar and two wide spaces. Figure 4-21 shows the "b" start/stop character.

Figure 4-22 describes the encoding of the 20 different Codabar characters; Figure 4-23 is a Codabar symbol encoding the data "$12345" and using the "a" start code and "b" stop code.

When used by the blood bank industry, Codabar implements a concatenate feature. Two adjacent symbols will be concatenated by the reader into a single message if one symbol uses a "d" stop character and the other begins with a "d" start character and they are both scanned with a single scanning motion. This ensures that the two symbols are on the same blood collection bag, because the reader's software checks that the apparent symbol spacing is very close (usually within 0.75").

As mentioned before, a peculiarity of Traditional Codabar symbology is the large number of printed element widths. When printed at its highest density, the Codabar character set employs the dimensions shown in Table 4-5.

Figure 4-20: Codabar "/" Character. This character has four bars with three spaces separating them. This character is represented as three wide bars, one narrow bar and no wide spaces.

Figure 4-21: Codabar "b" Start/Stop Character. Codabar uses start/stop characters to frame records of multiple data characters The "b" start/stop character is shown here. As in Figure 4-19, this character has four bars with three spaces separating them. There are three narrow bars, one wide bar, two wide spaces, and one narrow space.

Table 4-5
CODABAR ELEMENT WIDTHS (mils)

6.5	13.6	17.9
8.0	14.7	18.6
9.3	14.9	19.4
10.0	16.1	19.6
10.1	16.7	24.3
10.4	17.2	24.4

When printed in this fashion, every character is the same width. Many of the published dimensions differ by only a few ten thousandths of an inch, which is obviously insignificant when typical printing tolerances are considered. In practice, most Codabar printers use many fewer dimensions.

Many people are using a variant of Traditional Codabar symbology known as Rationalized Codabar. This is the symbology described in USS-Codabar (published by AIM). Rationalized Codabar is totally compatible with Traditional Codabar and just as secure, despite having a slightly higher density.

Figure 4-22: Codabar Encodation Patterns. Rationalized Codabar encodes 20 different characters composed of the 10 numeric digits, the graphics - $: . + and the start/stop codes a, b, c, d. Several examples from this table are found in Figures 4-19 to 4-21, and 4-23.

a$12345b

Figure 4-23: Codabar Symbol Encoding the Data "$12345". Each Rationalized Codabar symbol consists of a start code, one or more data characters, and a stop code. Here we show the data "a$12345b." Additional data can be encoded in the actual choice of start and stop codes.

Rationalized Codabar uses only two element widths: wide and narrow. As in Code 39, N defines the width ratio between nominal wide elements and nominal narrow elements, and X defines the width of a nominal narrow element. Because of the symbology's structure, there are two different character widths (Figures 4-22 and 4-23 were printed using Rationalized Codabar).

The allowable printing tolerance is defined as a function of the values of X and N.

4.3.5 Code 39

Code 39 was the first alphanumeric symbology to be developed. This symbology is widely used in non-retail bar code applications. It is a discrete, self-checking, variable length symbology that can readily be printed by a variety of technologies. It is sometimes referred to as "3 of 9 Code."

Every Code 39 character has five bars and four spaces, making a total of 9 elements. Of these nine elements, three are wide and six are narrow, making Code 39 a two-width code. Figure 4-24 shows the letter "I" in Code 39.

Figure 4-25 illustrates Code 39's encodation patterns—each of Code 39's 43 characters has a unique arrangement of three wide elements and six narrow ones.

A Code 39 symbol begins and ends with an asterisk (*), which is this symbology's start/stop code. Figure 4-26 is an example of a Code 39 symbol encoding the data message "CODE."

Each character is separated from its neighbor by a loosely toleranced intercharacter gap that contains no information. Because of the mirror image relationship between the start/stop character and the letter "P," an upper limit is specified for the intercharacter gap width in order to prevent short reads, especially in the case of partial scans.

Figure 4-24: Code 39 Character "I". This pattern is a typical Code 39 character encoded according to the pattern for "I" shown in Figure 4-25. The "1" and "0" notations show how the typical Code 39 pattern may be represented as a sequence of nine binary bits in a computer memory.

Figure 4-25: Code 39 Encodation Patterns. Code 39 encodes 44 different alphabetic, numeric, and graphic characters. Every character encodation has three wide elements and six narrow elements out of nine total elements, hence the name. Code 39 is a discrete symbology: each character encoded starts and ends with a bar; no information is contained in the width of the spaces between characters. The asterisk (*) is reserved for use as the start/stop code. Symbols may be any practical length. Error detection at a character level follows from the high degree of redundancy in the Code 39 encodations.

Although there are only 43 data characters in Code 39's character set, it is possible to encode all 128 ASCII characters using Code 39's Full ASCII feature. If a reader is in its Full ASCII mode, the symbols $ / % and + are used as precedence codes with the 26 letters as shown in Table 4-6.

Table 4-6
CODE 39 FULL ASCII CHART

ASCII	CODE 39	ASCII	CODE 39	ASCII	CODE 39	ASCII	CODE 39
NUL	%U	SP	Space	@	%V		%W
SOH	$A	!	/A	A	A	a	+A
STX	$B	"	/B	B	B	b	+B
ETX	$C	#	/C	C	C	c	+C
EOT	$D	$	/D	D	D	d	+D
ENQ	$E	%	/E	E	E	e	+E
ACK	$F	&	/F	F	F	f	+F
BEL	$G	!	/G	G	G	g	+G
BS	$H	(	/H	H	H	h	+H
HT	$I	)	/I	I	I	i	+I
LF	$J	*	/J	J	J	j	+J
VT	$K	+	/K	K	K	k	+K
FF	$L	'	/L	L	L	l	+L
CR	$M	–	–	M	M	m	+M
SO	$N	.	.	N	N	n	+N
SI	$O	/	/O	O	O	o	+O
DLE	$P	0	0	P	P	p	+P
DC1	$Q	1	1	Q	Q	q	+Q
DC2	$R	2	2	R	R	r	+R
DC3	$S	3	3	S	S	s	+S
DC4	$T	4	4	T	T	t	+T
NAK	$U	5	5	U	U	u	+U
SYN	$V	6	6	V	V	v	+V
ETB	$W	7	7	W	W	w	+W
CAN	$X	8	8	X	X	x	+X
EM	$Y	9	9	Y	Y	y	+Y
SUB	$Z	:	/Z	Z	Z	z	+Z
ESC	%A	;	%F	[	%K	{	%P
FS	%B	<	%G	\	%L			%Q
GS	%C	=	%H	]	%M	}	%R
RS	%D	>	%I	↑	%N	~	%S
US	%E	?	%J	–	%O	DEL	%T,%X %Y,%Z

Note that in order to interpret pairs of characters as the equivalent ASCII character in Table 4-6, the reader must be in the Full ASCII mode, otherwise the two characters from each pair are just decoded separately. This ambiguity based upon reader configuration and/or history is an inconvenience in some applications.

Breaking up long bar code messages into two or more shorter symbols for ease of reading is sometimes advantageous. If the first data character of a Code 39 symbol is an encoded space character, the bar code reader appends the information contained within the symbol (excluding the leading space character) to its buffer. This operation continues for all symbols that contain a leading space character. When a Code 39 symbol is read that does not contain a leading space character, the data is appended to the reader's buffer, and the entire buffer is transmitted and cleared for new data.

Code 39 is self-checking (a single printing defect cannot cause a substitution error) and is normally not used with a check character. An optional modulo 43 check character is defined for use in specific applications that require exceptional

Figure 4-26: Code 39 Symbol Encoding the Data "CODE." A typical Code 39 symbol begins with a start code (the "*" in Figure 4-25) and ends with the same code as a stop code. An arbitrary number of characters (four shown here) comprises the data of the record.

data security. The Health Industry Business Communications Council (HIBCC) has adopted the use of this check character for health care applications. As a general policy, the use of Code 39's check character is encouraged, especially if the print quality is less than optimum.

4.3.6 Code 128

Code 128 was introduced in 1981 as a very high-density alphanumeric symbology. Since 1990, it has seen increasing adoption in a variety of applications. It is a variable length, continuous symbology with multiple element widths.

Each Code 128 character has 11 modules which may be either black or white. Each character has three bars and three spaces; this is therefore an (11,3) code. Each character begins with a bar and ends with a space. Figure 4-27 shows a Code 128 character.

| 1 | 2 | 3 | 4 | 5 | 6 | 7 | 8 | 9 | 10 | 11 |

Figure 4-27: Code 128 Character. Code 128 is a continuous symbology. Each character contains three bars and three spaces in an overall length of 11 modules.

Code 128 has 106 different printed character patterns. Each printed character can have one of three different meanings, depending on which of three different character sets is employed. Three different start characters tell the reader which of the character sets is initially being used, and three shift codes permit changing character sets inside a symbol.

Character set C consists of the 100 two-digit pairs 00 through 99. This allows the effective density of Code 128 to be doubled when printing all numeric data. Figure 4-28 illustrates the character patterns and the three character sets.

CODE A	CODE B	CODE C	VALUE		CODE A	CODE B	CODE C	VALUE
Space	Space	00	0		V	V	54	54
!	!	01	1		W	W	55	55
"	"	02	2		X	X	56	56
#	#	03	3		Y	Y	57	57
$	$	04	4		Z	Z	58	58
%	%	05	5		[	[	59	59
&	&	06	6		\	\	60	60
'	'	07	7		]	]	61	61
(	(	08	8				62	62
)	)	09	9		_	_	63	63
*	*	10	10		NUL	`	64	64
+	+	11	11		SOH	a	65	65
,	,	12	12		STX	b	66	66
-	-	13	13		ETX	c	67	67
.	.	14	14		EOT	d	68	68
/	/	15	15		ENQ	e	69	69
0	0	16	16		ACK	f	70	70
1	1	17	17		BEL	g	71	71
2	2	18	18		BS	h	72	72
3	3	19	19		HT	i	73	73
4	4	20	20		LF	j	74	74
5	5	21	21		VT	k	75	75
6	6	22	22		FF	l	76	76
7	7	23	23		CR	m	77	77
8	8	24	24		SO	n	78	78
9	9	25	25		SI	o	79	79
:	:	26	26		DLE	p	80	80
;	;	27	27		DC1	q	81	81
<	<	28	28		DC2	r	82	82
=	=	29	29		DC3	s	83	83
>	>	30	30		DC4	t	84	84
?	?	31	31		NAK	u	85	85
@	@	32	32		SYN	v	86	86
A	A	33	33		ETB	w	87	87
B	B	34	34		CAN	x	88	88
C	C	35	35		EM	y	89	89
D	D	36	36		SUB	z	90	90
E	E	37	37		ESC	{	91	91
F	F	38	38		FS	|	92	92
G	G	39	39		GS	}	93	93
H	H	40	40		RS	~	94	94
I	I	41	41		US	DEL	95	95
J	J	42	42		FNC3	FNC3	96	96
K	K	43	43		FNC2	FNC2	97	97
L	L	44	44		Shift	Shift	98	98
M	M	45	45		Code C	Code C	99	99
N	N	46	46		Code B	FNC4	Code B	100
O	O	47	47		FNC4	Code A	Code A	101
P	P	48	48		FNC1	FNC1	FNC1	102
Q	Q	49	49		START (Code A)			103
R	R	50	50		START (Code B)			104
S	S	51	51		START (Code C)			105
T	T	52	52		STOP	STOP	STOP	
U	U	53	53					

Figure 4-28: Code 128 Encodation Patterns. Code 128 encodes the full 128 character ASCII character set using three alternate character sets, A, B and C. Each set includes shift codes and start codes to control which set is to be used. Thus a given character pattern can have several meanings, depending on the character set currently in use.

Using character set A, Figure 4-29 shows the data "CODE 128" encoded. Because this example has mixed alphanumeric data, character set A must be used. Note that a two-module wide termination bar is added to the stop character, making it 13 modules long. Every Code 128 symbol includes a check character, which is the modulo 103 sum of the value of each character multiplied by a weighting sequence.

A second Code 128 sample symbol, Figure 4-30, illustrates the use of double density numeric mode. The message is "1234 abcd." The symbol starts by using character set C and can therefore encode the digits 1234 in only two data characters. A shift character then instructs the reader to move to character set B, which is used for the remainder of the symbol. Alternatively, the entire message could have been encoded using character set B, but the symbol would have been longer by one character.

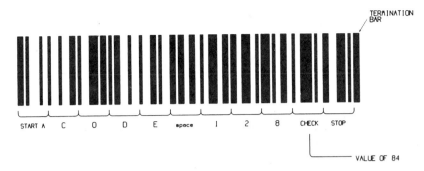

TERMINATION BAR

START A   C   O   D   E   space   1   2   8   CHECK   STOP

VALUE OF 84

Figure 4-29: Code 128 Symbol Encoding the Data "CODE 128". Each Code 128 symbol contains data framed by a start symbol, check digit, and a stop symbol. The data portion can be of arbitrary length. The start pattern selects the initial character set, in this case, A (See Figure 4-28). The check digit is calculated according to the method described in the text.

By the use of a function code character, Code 128 offers a concatenation feature allowing two or more messages to be decoded and transmitted as one.

A variant of Code 128 is used in retail distribution applications for serialized carton tracking. This is referred to as UCC-128 (Uniform Code Council-128), and uses the standard Code 128 character set, except that every symbol begins with a Start C character, followed by a Function Code One character. EAN-128 is similarly used in distribution applications outside of North America.

TERMINATION BAR

START C   12   34   SHIFT TO CODE B   space   a   b   c   d   CHECK   STOP

VALUE OF 56

Figure 4-30: Code 128 Symbol Encoding the Data "1234 abcd". The shift codes of Code 128 allow alternation between the three character sets A, B, and C. Reading from left to right, the information begins in character set C with the start code selection. In character set C, the two codes "12" and "34" are followed by the code meaning "shift to character set B." The rest of the message is encoded using character set B. The message ends with the check digit code followed by the stop code.

4.3.7 Code 93

Code 93, introduced in 1982, was specifically designed to provide a high density complement to Code 39. Given autodiscriminating reading equipment, the two symbologies can be freely mixed in a system with no change to a host computer's software.

Code 93 is a variable length, continuous symbology employing four element widths. Each Code 93 character has nine modules that may be either black or white. Each character contains three bars and three spaces, as shown in Figure 4-31. Each character begins with a bar and ends with a space. This is a (9,3) code—

Figure 4-31: Code 93 Character. Code 93 is a continuous symbology. Each fixed-length character contains three bars and three spaces in an overall length of nine modules.

hence the name. Code 93 has 47 characters in its character set, as shown in Figure 4-32.

The start/stop code is represented by the symbol ▢, and the four unique circle codes, Ⓢ, ⑳, ⊘, and ⊕, are used as precedence characters to unambiguously represent all 128 ASCII characters in a similar fashion to Code 39's Full ASCII feature. Because the special "circle codes" are used for the Full ASCII feature, the ambiguity problem present with Code 39 is eliminated. Figure 4-33 is a Code 93 symbol encoding the message "CODE 93".

In Code 93 the start and stop codes are the same, except that a termination bar is added to the stop code to indicate the end of the final space. Code 93 is not self-checking, but is able to offer high data security through the use of two modulo 47 check characters that are referred to as "C" and "K." These two check characters are neither transmitted by the reading equipment nor printed in the human-readable interpretation.

Like Code 39, Code 93 includes a multiple read feature that allows concatenation of successive symbols that contain a leading space character.

Because the data character sets of both symbologies are the same, and because neither the start/stop codes nor the check characters are transmitted by the reader, Code 93 can be introduced into a system using Code 39 without changing any system software when an autodiscriminating reader is used.

Both Code 128 and Code 93 were developed because of a perceived requirement for higher data densities than that offered by Code 39. In order to compare this attribute, we first examine the theoretical modular density. We have already observed that Code 128 and Code 93 characters employed 11 and 9 modules respectively. In its highest density configuration (N = 2, intercharacter gap = 1X), Code 39 uses 13 modules, as shown in Figure 4-34.

Figure 4-34 is not a true comparison of densities because it neglects the overhead characters and assumes that Code 39 uses an N of 2.0. To better understand the differences, let's examine two examples of complete symbols, shown in Table 4-7. A constant X dimension of 10 mils will be assumed, and Code 39 will employ an N of 2.2.

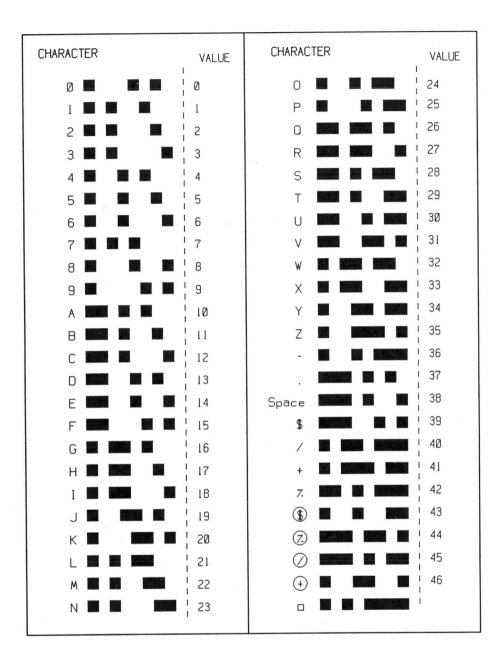

Figure 4-32: Code 93 Encodation Patterns. Code 93 defines 48 unique patterns including a stop code. Shift codes (shown here as ⑨, ⑩, ⑪and ⊕) are used to extend this basic character set (see Table E-1). By this means, Code 93 can unambiguously represent all 128 ASCII characters as a series of two character sequences.

Figure 4-33: Code 93 Symbol Encoding the Data "CODE 93". The Code 93 symbols consist of a start code, followed by an arbitrary length data region, followed by two check characters and a stop character. The "C" and "K" check characters are computed according to an algorithm that is part of the Code 93 specification, as detailed in Appendix E.

Table 4-7
COMPARISON OF CODE LENTHS

	Message = "TESTING 123"	Message = "123456 ABC"
Code 39 Length	1.76″	1.62″
Code 128 Length	1.56″	1.12″
Code 93 Length	1.36″	1.27″

From these examples it can be seen that Code 128 is the densest linear symbology for data that contains long strings of numbers, whereas Code 93 is the densest linear symbology for random alphanumeric messages.

4.3.8 Other Linear Symbologies

Most present-day general applications make use of U.P.C./EAN, Code 39, or Code 128. Interleaved 2 of 5 and Codabar are both established industry standards and also have their supporters. Several other linear symbologies exist and need to be mentioned for the sake of completeness. In each case, the developers have tried to optimize the compromise between the following conflicting but desirable goals: a large character set, high density, generous printing and decoding tolerances, and ease of printing with a variety of techniques.

2 of 5 Code

The 2 of 5 Code has its origins in the late 1960s. It has been used for warehouse sortation systems, photofinishing envelope identification, and sequentially numbered airline tickets.

Simple and straightforward, all information in a 2 of 5 Code is contained in the width of bars, with the spaces only separating individual bars. Bars may be either wide or narrow, where the wide bar is conventionally three times the width of the narrow bar. Spaces may be any reasonable width but are typically equal to the narrow bars. Narrow bars are identified as a 0 bit and wide bars as a 1 bit. The encoding convention is given in Figure 4-35 and a complete symbol is shown in Figure 4-36.

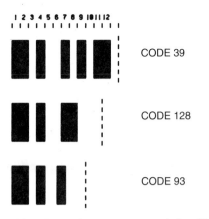

Figure 4-34: Modular Densities. Bar codes are constructed of multiple modules that can be either bar or space. For example, the nine elements of Code 39 total 13 modules in width (if the wide-to-narrow ratio is 2.0 and the intercharacter gap is 1X). Here we compare the number of modules required to represent the fixed-length character level codes in several symbologies using the same minimum element width, X.

The code structure is easily remembered by associating the bar positions from left to right with weighting factors 1, 2, 4, 7, and parity. Exceptions to this are zero, start, and stop.

The 2 of 5 Code is discrete and self-checking. When the wide-bar-to-narrow-bar ratio is 3:1 and the spaces equal one unit, each data character requires 14 units of length including the gap between characters. If the wide-to-narrow ratio were reduced to 2:1, each character would still require 12 units. This relatively low density (larger number of units per character) is the primary disadvantage of 2 of 5 Code compared to other numeric symbologies.

The start and stop characters have sometimes been shortened to 00 for the start code and 10 for the stop code. This arrangement is the same as used for Interleaved 2 of 5 described in Section 4.4 above. Another variation has been to use narrow printed marks separating white spaces of variable width. In this case the encoding is simply reversed so that the spaces carry meaning and the bars act as separators. These variations require specially programmed readers.

Code 11

Code 11 was developed in early 1977 to satisfy specialized requirements for a very high-density discrete numeric bar code. The most extensive application of Code 11 has been labeling telecommunications components and equipment.

The name Code 11 is derived from the fact that 11 different data characters can be represented in addition to a stop/start character. The character set includes the ten digits and the dash symbol.

Each character is represented by a stand-alone group of three bars with two included spaces (Figure 4-37). Three different bar widths and two space widths are used. Although Code 11 is discrete, it is not self-checking because a single printing defect can transpose one character into another valid character. Data security is obtained by using one or (preferably) two check digits.

Analysis suggests that Code 11, using only one check digit, has roughly four

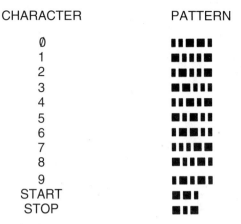

CHARACTER	PATTERN
0	▮▮▮▮▮
1	▮▮▮▮▮
2	▮▮▮▮▮
3	▮▮▮▮▮
4	▮▮▮▮▮
5	▮▮▮▮▮
6	▮▮▮▮▮
7	▮▮▮▮▮
8	▮▮▮▮▮
9	▮▮▮▮▮
START	▮▮▮
STOP	▮▮▮

Figure 4-35: Code 2 of 5 Encodation Patterns. In Code 2 of 5 data is only carried in the bar widths. The space widths are uniform, nominally equal to the narrow bar width. As illustrated here, Code 2 of 5 patterns define the ten numeric digits, a start and a stop code.

times the error probability of Code 39. When Code 11 is used with the recommended two check digits, it becomes more secure than either Code 39 (without a check character) or Codabar.

Plessey Code (Pulse Width Modulated)

Plessey Code was developed by the Plessey Company in England with formal specifications first dated March, 1971. Plessey Code was used in early library applications. A variation of Plessey Code and the associated scanning equipment was provided by Plessey to the ADS Company, and this variation is known as Anker Code. Anker Code was used in European point-of-sale systems before the advent of EAN. The basic encoding principle in Plessey Code was used by MSI Data Corporation to construct its MSI bar code, sometimes known as Modified Plessey Code. The primary application for MSI Code is marking of retail shelves and subsequent scanning with portable devices for inventory reordering.

In Plessey Code each character consists of four bars and the adjacent four spaces. Each bar/space pair contains one information bit. Zero bits consist of a narrow bar followed by a wide space, while One bits consist of a wide bar followed by a narrow space. For Plessey and Anker Code the zero bit is approximately a one-unit bar followed by a four-unit space. With these relationships each character consumes 20 units of width, which yields lower density than is typical for a numeric symbology. The complete Plessey symbol includes a start character, some number

Figure 4-36: Code 2 of 5 Symbol Encoding the Data "12345". A typical Code 2 of 5 symbol is illustrated here. Code 2 of 5 was an early bar code symbology that has been largely supplanted by the denser Interleaved 2 of 5 Code.

Figure 4-37: Code 11 Character. Code 11 offers high density, but it is not self-checking. In order to provide acceptable data security, one or two check digits are used with each symbol.

of data characters, an eight-bit cyclic check, a termination bar, and usually a reverse start character.

In MSI code the zero bit is a one-unit bar followed by a two-unit space and the one bit is a two-unit bar followed by a one-unit space. Complete four bit characters are thus 12 units wide, which is large for a numeric symbology. The MSI symbol includes a start pattern, data characters, one or two check digits, and a stop pattern.

The generic name for the Plessey Code family is "pulse width modulated." These symbols are continuous and are not self-checking. Usually used in a fixed-length format, the character set is limited to the ten digits plus six additional characters. Pulse width modulated symbols offer no important technical advantage over the more modern symbologies.

Matrix 2 of 5

Matrix 2 of 5 Code is a variation of Code 11 devised by the Nieaf Company in the Netherlands. It is limited to the ten digits and start/stop character.

Discrete but not self-checking, Matrix 2 of 5 is used with a single modulo 10 check digit. Compared with Code 11 (using two check digits) and the other industrial symbologies, Matrix 2 of 5 is somewhat more subject to substitution errors and offers no particular advantage.

Nixdorf Code

Nixdorf bar code was introduced in Europe by the Nixdorf Computer Company in the early 1970s. The largest area of application was department store point-of-sale systems. The sponsorship for Nixdorf Code has been confined to the Nixdorf Company, and the rapid adoption of EAN is likely to supersede the use of Nixdorf Code.

Nixdorf bar code is numeric, discrete, and self-checking, but the symbol also uses a check digit. Each character consists of three bars and the two contained spaces. Three different bar widths are used (1 unit, 2.25 units, and 3.75 units).

Delta Distance A

The concept of Delta Distance A (DDA) Code was introduced by McEnroe and Jones of IBM in 1971. Delta Distance A is a discrete, extended numeric (16 total characters) symbol. Characters are composed of six narrow bars with variable width spaces between the bars. The motivation behind Delta Distance A was to devise a symbology with relatively small but constant character printing area that could be printed with formed font type computer line printers. Sponsorship of Delta Distance A has been confined to IBM.

Ames Code
Since 1974 Ames Code has been printed on file folders by the Medical Records Systems Division of Ames Color File Corporation. Ames Code is a discrete, self-checking, numeric bar code that uses only the "2 of 7" characters of Codabar.

Meter Code
Sprague Ackley of Intermec introduced Meter Code in 1992 for use on "number wheel meters" (like a mechanical car odometer). Meter Code is a discrete code designed to work with black intercharacter gaps. Every data character begins with a space and ends with a space.

Bone Code
An unusual symbology called Bone Code was developed in 1992 by Sprague Ackley of Intermec for identifying fish from the hatchery where they originated. The width and color of a small series of growth rings in the small bone in a fish's ear is intentionally programmed by varying water temperature during the incubation period. A 2 of 5 pattern arrangement is used, and the data has been proven to be readable under high magnification.

Miscellaneous
A fair number of lesser known linear symbologies have been applied by individual sponsoring companies. These include: AGES, AS-6, AS-10, Calra Code, F2F, Fujitsu, Norand (version of F2F), RTC, Toshiba, and Telepen. A forthcoming book entitled *Encyclopedia of Machine-Readable Codes* by Ben Nelson, of Markem Corporation, will provide details on the more than 190 symbologies that have been developed this century.

4.4 Height-Modulated Linear Symbologies

The postal industry has spawned two linear symbologies that encode information into arrays of variable height bars. The bar and space widths are constant and fairly loosely toleranced. These nonconventional symbologies were apparently developed in response to the need to print variable bar code data directly onto the surface of envelopes at very high speeds. Because the bar codes are sprayed on with in-line ink jet printers as the envelopes rapidly fly by, it is very hard to precisely control bar widths. To allow information to be reliably encoded under these less than ideal circumstances, approaches were developed to use bar height modulation rather than width.

4.4.1 Postnet
Postnet is widely used by the U.S. Postal Service. It is a clocked technology (see also Figure 4-9) in which a scan through the bottom of the bars provides a timing track. An example of a Postnet symbol is shown in Figure 4-38.

Postnet is a numeric symbology that uses five bars and four spaces for each encod-

---

Figure 4-38: Postnet Symbol. Postnet encodes information by modulating the height of constant width bars.

ed digit. A constant width and spacing of the bars is used throughout the symbol. In a given character, two of the bars are tall and the remaining three are short.

4.4.2 4-State Code

Unlike the U.S., most countries' postal codes are alphanumeric. In response to the need for an alphanumeric bar code that could be printed on the fly at high speeds, the British Post Office (BPO) developed a height modulated symbology called BPO 4-State Code.

Figure 4-39: 4-State Symbol. The height modulation method includes descending as well as ascending bars.

4.5 2-D Stacked Symbologies

2-D (two-dimensional) stacked symbologies were developed in an attempt to reduce the area typically consumed by conventional linear bar code symbols.

In order to allow for easy alignment of scanning equipment with the centerline of linear symbologies, most standards require a bar height of at least 15 percent of a symbol's length. As more data is encoded into a symbol, the overall length increases and the bars must be made correspondingly taller. Therefore, the symbol's area increases as the square of the message length. Recognizing this, Dr. Dave Allais proposed breaking up long symbols into a series of shorter linear symbols and stacking them up into a multi-row arrangement. The row length is short, and therefore the bar height can be short, reducing the overall symbol area.

This novel arrangement of stacked linear symbol segments proved to be a very useful concept, and four stacked symbologies have been introduced using the idea. Each symbology has used a different method of handling the three main issues to be addressed:

• How to keep track of the rows.

• How to handle scan lines that cross between rows.

• How to detect and/or correct localized errors.

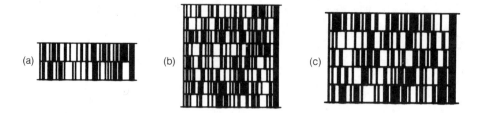

Figure 4-40: Code 49 Symbols. A Code 49 symbol contains two to eight rows. The number of rows used depends on the amount of data and the compression possible using methods described in the text.

4.5.1. Code 49

Code 49 was introduced by Intermec in late 1987 as a symbology uniquely suited to labeling small objects. It is the first "stacked" bar code symbology. A Code 49 symbol contains from two to eight adjacent rows, each separated by a one-module separator bar. See Figure 4-40 for examples of two-row and eight-row symbols.

Each row contains four "words" encoded in a (16,4) format. Each row has a start code and a stop code, as illustrated in Figure 4-41.

Figure 4-41: Code 49 Row. Here we show a Code 49 row standing alone in a form similar to other bar code symbols presented in this book. Each row is 70 modules long and contains four words.

Each row contains 18 bars and is 70 modules long. A quiet zone of at least one module is required on the right side, and at least 10 modules on the left side. These parallel rows of data also include parity information indicating the row number. The bottom row also encodes the number of rows in the symbol and contains the symbol check characters.

A Code 49 symbol's rows can be scanned in any order. The reader keeps track of the row numbers and the number of rows to expect. A "good read" beep is not sounded until all of the rows have been captured, but a click is sounded whenever a new row is scanned (unless it has already been scanned).

The number of rows required is determined by the number of characters to be encoded, as outlined in Table 4-8.

Table 4-8
CODE 49 CAPACITY

Number of Rows	Number of Alphanumeric Characters	Number of Numeric Characters
2	9	15
3	16	26
4	23	38
5	30	50
6	37	61
7	42	70
8	49	81

As mentioned earlier, each row encodes four (16,4) words. Each word encodes two characters from the Code 49 character set outlined in Table 4-8. Each character is assigned a corresponding value.

Table 4-9
CODE 49 CHARACTER SET

Character	Value	Character	Value
0	0	P	25
1	1	Q	26
2	2	R	27
3	3	S	28
4	4	T	29
5	5	U	30
6	6	V	31
7	7	W	32
8	8	X	33
9	9	Y	34
A	10	Z	35
B	11	—	36
C	12	.	37
D	13	space	38
E	14	$	39
F	15	/	40
G	16	+	41
H	17	%	42
I	18	↑ (shift 1)	43
J	19	↑↑ (shift 2)	44
K	20	F1 (function 1)	45
L	21	F2 (function 2)	46
M	22	F3 (function 3)	47
N	23	ns (numeric shift)	48

Based on the characters encoded, each word can have a value from 0 to 2400. The word value is determined by adding the value of the character in the right half of the word to 49 times the value of the character in the left half of the word.

Because each word contains two characters, there are eight characters per row. Each word may be encoded in the (16,4) structure with either an odd or an even parity. The row's parity pattern indicates the row number and identifies the last row.

For symbols with fewer than seven rows, the final row contains two check words that are based on a weighted sum of all of the other characters in the symbol. Symbols with seven or eight rows have three check words in the final row.

The last character in every row provides a row check. Its value is equal to the Modulo 49 sum of the character values.

The next-to-last character in the last row is used to indicate the number of rows in the symbol and a symbol mode. The mode value (from 0 to 6) determines whether the symbol will be interpreted in a multiple read mode (allowing several Code 49 symbols to be concatenated). Other modes include starting in either numeric or alphanumeric mode or with an implied leading single-shift or double-shift character.

Numeric mode allows five digits to be encoded into three alphanumeric characters, providing higher density for long strings of numeric data. The numeric shift character is used to go into or out of numeric mode.

ASCII characters beyond the basic Code 49 character set are encoded as a character pair. The first character of the pair is either a Shift 1 or a Shift 2 character. Table 4-9 describes the pairings for all 128 ASCII characters.

As in most bar code symbologies, Code 49's bar height can be varied to suit the application requirements. Taller bars will allow greater ranges of scanner tilt angles and additional vertical redundancy. For laser-based scanning, a minimum bar height of at least 8 modules is normally specified for Code 49.

4.5.2 Codablock

Identcode-Systeme introduced a scheme variously referred to a Codablock or MLC-2D which combined short Code 39 symbols into a multi-line structure with row identifiers and separator bars. Users had been employing multiple Code 39 symbols with identifiers and reading them with specially programmed readers for many years, but MLC-2D is the first attempt to actually publish a method for doing this. An example is shown in Figure 4-42.

Because the native symbology is Code 39, and because of the high overhead introduced with the MLC-2D structure, the density is quite low.

The ICS specification includes an example of an 18-character alphanumeric message implemented in four rows. The resultant symbol size is much larger than that of a Code 49 or Code 16K symbol encoding the same information.

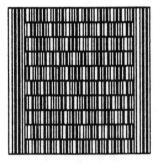

Figure 4-42: Codablock Symbol. Codablock uses multiple rows of Code 39 and includes additional characters to identify rows.

Table 4-10
CODE 49 ASCII CHART

ASCII	CODE 49	ASCII	CODE 49	ASCII	CODE 49	ASCII	CODE 49
Null	↑ Sp	Space	Sp	@	↑↑ 6		↑↑.
SOH	↑ A	!	↑ 6	A	A	a	↑↑ A
STX	↑ B	"	↑ 7	B	B	b	↑↑ B
ETX	↑ C	#	↑ 8	C	C	c	↑↑ C
EOT	↑ D	$	$	D	D	d	↑↑ D
ENQ	↑ E	%	%	E	E	e	↑↑ E
ACK	↑ F	&	↑ 9	F	F	f	↑↑ F
BEL	↑ G	!	↑ 0	G	G	g	↑↑ G
BS	↑ H	(	↑ —	H	H	h	↑↑ H
HT	↑ I	)	↑ .	I	I	i	↑↑ I
LF	↑ J	*	↑ $	J	J	j	↑↑ J
VT	↑ K	+	+	K	K	k	↑↑ K
FF	↑ L	,	/	L	L	l	↑↑ L
CR	↑ M	–	–	M	M	m	↑↑ M
SO	↑ N	.	.	N	N	n	↑↑ N
SI	↑ O	/	/	O	O	o	↑↑ O
DLE	↑ P	0	0	P	P	p	↑↑ P
DC1	↑ Q	1	1	Q	Q	q	↑↑ Q
DC2	↑ R	2	2	R	R	r	↑↑ R
DC3	↑ S	3	3	S	S	s	↑↑ S
DC4	↑ T	4	4	T	T	t	↑↑ T
NAK	↑ U	5	5	U	U	u	↑↑ U
SYN	↑ V	6	6	V	V	v	↑↑ V
ETB	↑ W	7	7	W	W	w	↑ W
CAN	↑ X	8	8	X	X	x	↑↑ X
EM	↑ Y	9	9	Y	Y	y	↑↑ Y
SUB	↑ Z	:	↑ +	Z	Z	z	↑↑ Z
ESC	↑ 1	;	↑↑ 1	[	↑↑ 7	{	↑↑ $
FS	↑ 2	<	↑↑ 2	\	↑↑ 8	|	↑↑ /
GS	↑ 3	=	↑↑ 3	]	↑↑ 9	}	↑↑ +
RS	↑ 4	>	↑↑ 4		↑↑ 0		↑↑ %
US	↑ 5	?	↑↑ 5	—	↑↑ –	DEL	↑↑ Sp

4.5.3 Code 16K

Code 16K has a somewhat similar physical structure to that of Code 49, but up to 16 rows may be used without concatenating symbols. The data characters in each row are encoded using a "reverse video" (bars are white, spaces are black) implementation of standard Code 128 (11, 3) character patterns. Each row starts and ends with a unique start and stop character that can be used to identify the particular row and scan direction.

Two overall symbol check characters are used, but individual row check characters are not present. A single character in the first position of the first row is used to indicate the total number of rows and starting mode. An example Code 16K symbol is illustrated in Figure 4-43.

Each row is 70 modules long, and encodes five data characters. Code 128's "double density" mode is used for long strings of numeric information.

It is easier to implement Code 16K's decoding capability in a reader than it is Code 49's, especially if Code 128 software is already resident.

Figure 4-43: Code 16K Symbol. Code 16K uses multiple rows of "reverse video" Code 128, enclosed between special start and stop patterns.

Because of the larger number of rows permitted, Code 16K has a higher ultimate capacity than Code 49. As the number of rows increases, however, the bar height must be reduced if an approximately square symbol form factor is desired.

When printed with the same module size, both symbologies are the same overall length. The capacity of Code 49 and Code 16K, as a function of the number of rows and the data type, is compared in Table 4-11.

Table 4-11
CAPACITY COMPARISON OF CODE 49 AND CODE 16K

Number	Alphanumeric Data		Numeric Data	
of Rows	CODE 49	CODE 16K	CODE 49	CODE 16K
2	9	7	15	14
3	16	12	26	24
4	23	17	38	34
5	30	22	50	44
6	37	27	61	54
7	42	32	70	64
8	49	37	81	74
9	–	42	–	84
10	–	47	–	94
11	–	52	–	104
12	–	57	–	114
13	–	62	–	124
14	–	67	–	134
15	–	72	–	144
16	–	77	–	154

From Table 4-11, it can be seen that for symbols with two to eight rows, Code 49 offers a higher density than does Code 16K, but the advantage disappears for longer messages.

4.5.4 PDF417

Announced in 1990 by Symbol Technologies, PDF417 has similarities both with multi-row symbologies such as Code 49 and with area-based symbologies such as

Figure 4-44: Example of PDF417 Symbol. Three different character encodations are used, repeating every third row. This provides some tilt tolerance without the use of separator bars.

Vericode. No separator bars are used, thereby giving this symbology an area efficiency advantage over Code 49. Short bar heights are employed under the assumption that the decoding software will be able to handle the inevitable cross-row scanning paths that will occur. Figure 4-44 is an example of a PDF417 symbol.

Every symbol character uses 4 bars and 4 spaces in a 17 module length. This is a (17,4) structure which gives rise to the symbology's name. There are 929 symbol character values in each of three different character sets. The three different PDF417 character set encodations are called "clusters." A given row uses one specific character set, and the two adjacent rows use different character sets. The character set used is repeated for every third row. Because no row will use the same character set as its neighbor, the scanner is able to tell if a scanning path has crossed a row boundary without using separator bars such as those used in Code 49 and Code 16K. The number of rows and the row length is variable, allowing the symbol's aspect ratio to be adjusted for particular labeling applications.

PDF417 is normally printed with a very short bar height, based on the assumption that operator misalignment will be handled by reader software that is able to piece together partial scans of individual rows (this is commonly called "scan stitching"). A quiet zone is required above and below the symbol, as well as at the two ends.

PDF417 includes optional error correction characters. The use of these characters becomes more important as shorter bar heights are used. The number of error correction characters can be one of eight possible values from 2 to 512. It is recommended that the number of error correction characters should be at least equal to 10 percent of the number of data characters. If the maximum number of 512 error correction characters is used, it is possible to correct up to 256 errors.

Of the 929 possible character values, the first 900 are used to encode data, and the other 29 are used to change the data compaction modes or to perform other special tasks. There are three data compaction modes: "Text," "Numeric," and "Byte." The Text mode encodes two characters per symbol character, using four sub-modes: "Alpha," "Lower Case," "Mixed," and "Punctuation." The Numeric mode encodes almost three digits into one symbol character, and the Byte mode encodes up to six 8-bit bytes of digital data into five symbol characters.

Other data interpretations for special applications are possible with PDF417 through the use of a feature called Global Label Identifiers (GLIs). There are 811,800 possible values of the GLIs, which can be used for international character sets or user-defined interpretation in closed systems.

A concatenation scheme known as "Macro PDF417" allows up to 99,999 symbols to be linked into one large file. Another option known as "Truncated PDF417" allows even smaller symbols to be printed if the symbol quality is expected to be high: this variant replaces the right row indicator and stop character columns with a single 1-X stop bar.

This symbology has been positioned by its developer as a high-capacity symbology, rather than simply as a high density one. For shorter message lengths (up to perhaps 40 characters), PDF417 does not offer any density advantage over Code 49 or Code 16K, but the ultimate message capacity of a single PDF417 symbol can exceed 1000 characters (depending on data content). Further details on PDF417 are contained in Appendix H.

4.6 2-D Matrix Symbologies

2-D Matrix symbologies (sometimes called "Area Symbologies") are more complicated than linear or stacked symbologies and require more sophisticated printing and scanning equipment. Offsetting the additional complexity is the fact that area symbologies offer much higher densities than those provided by linear or stacked symbologies.

4.6.1 USD-5

USD-5, often referred to as "slug code," is designed to be scanned with machine vision equipment and was developed many years ago. This symbology is suited for short numeric messages primarily used in sortation applications. An example of a USD-5 symbol is illustrated in Figure 4-45.

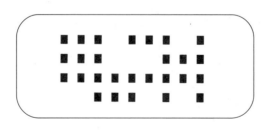

Figure 4-45: USD-5 Symbol. This older numeric symbology has similarities with punched cards.

USD-5 is similar to traditional punched cards that were commonly used for computer programming in the 1950s and '60s, except that optical marks are used instead of holes.

4.6.2 Vericode

This is a proprietary symbology based on a checkerboard arrangement of black and white squares contained within a square border pattern. Figure 4-46 illustrates an example of a Vericode symbol encoding 28 alphanumeric characters.

Figure 4-46: Vericode Symbol. This proprietary symbology uses a checkerboard arrangement of black and white square modules.

4.6.3 DataMatrix

DataMatrix has some similarities with Vericode. Each symbol has a unique perimeter pattern that is used for finding the symbol and determining its orientation. Two of the outside rows are solid, forming the letter "L", and the opposite two perimeter rows use an alternating black-white pattern which helps synchronize the decoding process. An example 22-character symbol is shown in Figure 4-47.

Figure 4-47: DataMatrix Symbol. This 2-D matrix symbology uses a unique perimeter pattern that helps the reading system determine the data cell locations.

Originally a proprietary symbology, it was announced in 1994 that DataMatrix would be placed in the public domain. Further technical details are located in Appendix J.

4.6.4 MaxiCode

MaxiCode, originally called DenseCode and then UPSCODE, is sometimes referred to as Hex Code. This symbology was developed by the United Parcel Service for automatic sortation and tracking of packages. It is a fixed length, alphanumeric symbology composed of an approximately square array of interlocking hexagons that surround a circular pattern. As originally conceived, the hexagons could be black, white, or gray, but MaxiCode is currently specified to only use black or white hexagons. Unlike other symbologies, MaxiCode specifies a fixed module size and symbol dimensions. An example is shown in Figure 4-48.

As disclosed in the patent, a MaxiCode symbol encodes a 596-bit message that includes substantial redundancy. United Parcel Service has indicated that it is willing to put MaxiCode into the public domain. Further details on the symbology are contained in Appendix K.

4.6.5 Code One

In 1992, Code One was introduced by Ted Williams as the world's first nonproprietary 2-D matrix symbology. A unique bar code-like pattern is located in the center of the symbol and is used to help scanning equipment locate the symbol, as well as indicating the size and data capacity. Actual message data is contained in an array of black and white square data cells.

Code One is an alphanumeric fixed length symbology, but several different symbol sizes are specified. Figure 4-49 shows several Code One examples.

Table 4-12
CODE ONE DIMENSIONS AND CAPACITY

Code One Version	Width (X)	Height (X)	Alpha-numeric Capacity	Numeric Capacity	Full ASCII Capacity
S-10	13	9	—	6	—
S-20	23	9	—	12	—
S-30	33	9	—	18	—
T-16	19	17	13	22	10
T-32	35	17	34	55	24
T-48	51	17	55	90	38
A	18	16	13	22	10
B	22	22	27	44	19
C	32	28	64	104	44
D	42	40	135	217	91
E	54	52	271	435	182
F	76	70	553	886	370
G	98	104	1096	1755	732
H	134	148	2218	3550	1480

Code One symbols include a substantial amount of error-correction capability, allowing data recovery from damaged symbols.

Further details on Code One are contained in Appendix I.

Figure 4-48: MaxiCode Symbol. Interlocking hexagons surround a "bulls-eye" locating pattern.

4.6.6 ArrayTag

In 1990 a small Canadian company called Array Tech Systems (a spin-off from the University of Victoria) introduced a 2-D matrix symbology known as ArrayTag. This symbology was originally octagonal in shape, but evolved into a hexagonal array of circular dots within a hexagonal border. The ArrayTag concept was originally developed for identifying logs in the forestry industry, but the symbology is certainly applicable to more conventional applications. Figure 4-50 is an example of an ArrayTag symbol.

Multiple hexagonal ArrayTag symbols can be nested together to increase data capacity. Because of the unique form of perimeter pattern in the outermost data row (analogous to the start/stop pattern in a linear symbology), no quiet zone is required, and area efficiency is high.

The symbology has been structured so that re-synchronization of the scanner occurs no less frequently than every 7 data cells. This attribute allows symbols to be successfully read in the presence of substantial optical distortion, such as that caused by labeling uneven surfaces, or scanning at oblique angles.

Figure 4-49: Code One. Because a particular version of Code One has a specified data capacity and number of cells, it is not necessary to use any quiet zones. A variety of data sets and compaction modes are provided to match particular applications. Table 4-11 gives the size (in modules) and capacity of the various Code One symbols.

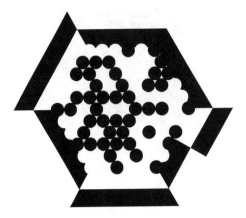

Figure 4-50: ArrayTag Symbol. This 2-D matrix symbology does not require any quiet zones.

4.6.7 Dotcode

Dotcode is a square matrix of circular dots. The symbology was originally developed by the Philips corporation of Eindhoven. The matrix can be any size between 6 x 6 and 12 x 12 dots. Certain dots must be in pre-specified positions in order to provide orientation and size information to the scanner. There are clear areas surrounding each dot which contain no information. An example of a 7 x 7 Dotcode symbol is shown in Figure 4-51.

4.6.8 LEB-code

Saab Automation developed a 2-D matrix type symbology that uses an array of rectangular data cells between two "checkerboard-like" fixed orientation pattern areas. Figure 4-52 shows an example of this symbology.

4.6.9 QR Code

At Scan-Tech Japan in 1994, the Nippondenso company introduced a 2-D matrix symbology that uses an array of square data cells and three fixed orientation targets. Figure 4-53 shows an example of a QR Code symbol.

Figure 4-51: Dotcode. A Dotcode symbol is a square matrix of round dots. Matrix size can be between 6 x 6 and 12 x 12 dots.

Figure 4-52: LEB-code. This symbology was announced in 1994 by Saab Automation.

Figure 4-53: QR Code. This 2-D matrix symbology was developed by Nippondenso.

4.6.10 Calra Code
Calra Systems in Tokyo developed a 2-D matrix symbology that is composed of groups of square blocks containing four data modules. These square blocks each encode one data character, and they are stacked in rows and columns to form the complete symbol.

4.7 Other Symbologies

Other symbologies have been developed that do not easily fit into the previously discussed categories of linear, stacked, height, or area symbologies.

4.7.1 Tema Code
In the early 1970s, Ray Stevens developed an interesting variant on a width-modulated linear bar code symbology that he called Tema Code. Figure 4-54 illustrates a Tema Code symbol.

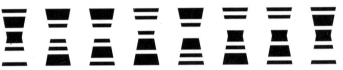

Figure 4-54: Tema Code. This symbology was designed so that it could be printed one character at a time using daisy wheel printers.

Tema Code's characters are arranged with their bars and spaces parallel to the length of the symbol. This is obviously a discrete symbology, and it was designed so that it could be printed using a daisy-wheel printer with a special print wheel. Because of the bar orientation, specialized scanning equipment must be used.

4.7.2 Sunburst Code
In the early 1970s, a company known as Charecogn proposed a radial circular symbology known as Sunburst Code for use in supermarket checkout applications. The grocery industry ad hoc committee was evaluating several symbols for this application (their efforts resulted in the adoption of the U.P.C. symbol), but the Sunburst Code was not given a field trial.

Figure 4-55: Sunburst Code. This radial circular symbology was proposed by Charecogn for POS applications.

An example of the symbology (as disclosed in U.S. Patent 3,636,317) is shown in Figure 4-55.

Each encoded character is represented by a specific sector of the symbol. Within a character, there are 8 modules which can be either black or white. Each character can have three or four bars and can start or end with a bar or space. Bars and spaces are either one or two modules wide.

4.7.3 Bull's-Eye Code

In 1971 the RCA corporation introduced a concentric circular bar code for use in supermarket checkout. The basic concept for concentric circular bar codes had been patented by Joe Woodland and Berny Silver twenty years earlier. Figure 4-56 shows one of the early RCA symbols.

Figure 4-56: Bull's-Eye Code. This concentric circular symbology was proposed by RCA.

When a slice is taken through this circular symbology, you are left with what appears to be a conventional width-modulated linear symbology. The bull's-eye code used multiple widths for both the bars and the spaces.

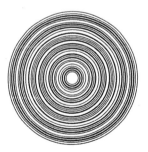

Figure 4-57: SureShot. This circular symbology uses Code 39 patterns.

In 1993, concentric circular symbologies were "re-invented" yet again, and a Canadian firm introduced what it calls SureShot, which is shown in Figure 4-57.

SureShot is basically identical to the 1970 vintage bull's-eye code, except that the thickness patterns of the black and white rings are based on Code 39 encodation.

4.7.4 DataGlyph

In the summer of 1994, the Xerox Corporation introduced a form of symbology that consists of a rectangular array of short bars that are canted either to the left or the right at 45 degrees. As an example, "/ \ \ /" represents the data 1001. When printed with small feature size, the individual detail quickly becomes lost to the human eye, and the symbol appears as a uniform gray background that is supposedly less obtrusive when printed on documents that are also designed to be used by humans.

4.7.5 Supercode

In late 1994, a so-called "packet" symbology called Supercode was proposed. This symbology is somewhat similar to 2-D stacked symbologies, but it allows the individual rows (they are called "packets") to be physically separated. A symbol consists of between 3 and 1024 packets. At the character level, a (16,4) structure is used.

4.8 Symbology Efficiencies

The performance of today's bar code systems is dependent, to a large extent, on the characteristics of the bar code symbologies that are used.

When developing or evaluating a general purpose bar code symbology, there are many desirable characteristics:

1. A large character set. Some applications can be satisfied with a simple numeric character set, but most users require an alphanumeric capability.

2. Easy to decode with high reliability.

3. Possible to decode using inexpensive scanning equipment.

4. Easy to print because of its simple physical structure and broad tolerances.

5. High data security, even if printed at the extremes of allowable printing tolerance.

6. High information density for a given minimum symbol feature size.

Unfortunately, some of these six requirements tend to be mutually exclusive. With very few exceptions, however, most symbologies in use today meet the first five requirements. We will now look in detail at the information density characteristics of bar code symbologies.

Figure 4-58: Code 39. This Code 39 symbol contains only a single data character and therefore conveys only 5.43 bits of information.

The information content of a message is measured in bits. We are dealing primarily with character-based systems and will assume that all characters in the set are equally probable. From information theory, the information content of a single character is defined as:

$$I = \log_2 C$$

where:

I = bits of information per character
C = size of the character set

As an example, if a message consists of a single character that can have one of 16 possible values, then the information content of this message is four bits. Table 4-13 illustrates I for a number of common values of C.

Table 4-13
INFORMATION CONTENT AS A FUNCTION OF CHARACTER SIZE

C	I (bits)
10	3.32 (U.P.C., Interleaved 2 of 5)
26	4.70
43	5.43 (Code 39 character)
47	5.56 (Code 93 character)
49	5.62 (Code 49 character)
103	6.69 (Code 128, Code 16K character)
256	8.0 (One 8-bit byte)
929	9.86 (PDF417 Codeword)
2401	11.23 (Code 49 Word)

The total information content of a multicharacter message is equal to:

$$\log_2 C^N$$
$$\text{or}$$
$$N \log_2 C$$

where:

C = size of the character set
N = number of characters in the message

In comparing the efficiencies of different one-dimensional symbologies, it is convenient to examine the linear efficiency, defined as:

$$\text{Linear Efficiency} = \frac{\text{bits of data in the symbol}}{\text{length of symbol in modules}} \times 100\%$$

Here, the term "modules" is the minimum feature size, or X dimension.

As an example, consider the Code 39 symbol with a single data character that is shown in Figure 4-58. This simple symbol contains 5.43 bits of information. If printed with a 2.5:1 wide-to-narrow ratio, each character will be 14.5 modules wide (including a one module intercharacter gap), and the overall symbol length will be 42.5 modules.

Looking just at a single character in this example, the gross linear efficiency is 5.43/14.5 = 37.4 percent. When the "overhead" characters are added (start/stop), the net linear efficiency is 12.8 percent. Obviously, net efficiency will increase for longer message lengths.

The gross linear efficiency of some commonly used one-dimension symbologies is shown in Table 4-14.

Table 4-14
GROSS LINEAR EFFICIENCY OF SOME
ONE-DIMENSION SYMBOLOGIES

	Gross Linear Efficiency
I 2/5 (printed at 2.5:1)	41.5%
Code 39 (printed at 2.5:1)	37.4%
Code 93	61.7%
Code 128	60.8%

As we have seen before, the *net* efficiency will vary, depending on message length. In Table 4-15, we examine two sets of examples, one encoding approximately 20 bits of data, and one encoding 100 bits.

Table 4-15

20 Bit (approx.) Message	Net Linear Efficiency	100 Bit (approx.) Message	Net Linear Efficiency
I 2/5 (3 characters)	35.3%	I 2/5 (15 characters)	40.1%
Code 39 (4 characters)	25.2%	Code 39 (19 characters)	34.0%
Code 93 (4 characters)	30.0%	Code 93 (18 characters)	50.2%
Code 128 (3 characters)	35.2%	Code 128 (15 characters)	50.9%

The above-described net linear efficiencies are impressively high, but it must be remembered that the efficiency is being measured along one axis only. A bar code symbol also occupies *height*, which encodes no additional information. Current one-dimensional bar code symbols use tall bars to allow for easy hand scanning and are therefore very inefficient in their use of area. In order to understand this characteristic, we will introduce a new term:

$$\text{Area Efficiency} = \frac{\text{bits of data in the symbol}}{\text{area of the symbol in square modules}} \times 100\ \%$$

To see how the concept of area efficiency works, we will examine the six character Code 39 symbol shown in Figure 4-59. The actual data encoded in this symbol is the message "ABCDEF".

Because Code 39 has 43 characters in its set, each data character conveys $\log_2(43)$ = 5.43 bits of information. This six character symbol therefore contains 6 x 5.43 =

127X

Figure 4-59: Area Efficiency. This Code 39 symbol encodes six characters and therefore conveys 32.6 bits of information. The physical area of the symbol is 2,413 square modules, and the area efficiency is 1.35%.

32.6 bits of information. If printed with a 3:1 wide-to-narrow element width ratio, the overall physical length of this symbol is 127X. Common practice (and industry standards) require a bar height of a least 15% of the symbol's length, or 0.15 x 127 = 19X in this example. The symbol therefore occupies an area of 19 x 127 = 2,413 square modules.

The area efficiency of this symbol is therefore:

$$\text{Area Efficiency} = \frac{\text{bits of data}}{\text{area in square modules}} \times 100\%$$

$$= \frac{32.6}{2,413} \times 100\% = 1.35\%$$

The figure of 1.35% does not sound very high at all and leads one to believe that there are probably other, more efficient ways of encoding information into a machine-readable symbol. As message lengths get longer, the symbol's physical length also increases, and the bar height must be increased to maintain the 15% height requirement. As message lengths increase, the area efficiencies of linear symbologies such as Code 39 actually decreases as illustrated in Table 4-16.

Table 4-16		
AREA EFFICIENCIES		
6 characters		20 characters
Code 39 (at 3:1)	1.35%	0.59%
Code 93	2.67%	1.57%
Code 128	2.77%	1.38%
I 2/5 (at 3:1)	3.80%	1.24%

As mentioned above, the apparent low efficiencies of these linear width-modulated symbologies are primarily a function of the requirement to maintain a 15% bar height. If the bar height was reduced to 5% of the symbol's length, these area efficiencies would triple! Unfortunately, shorter bar heights make it harder to manually scan symbols using either wands, linear CCD scanners, or single line laser scanners.

SCANNING
ANGLE RANGE

Figure 4-60: Scanning Angles. The range of possible scanning angles is a function of the symbol's aspect ratio.

A common term used to describe linear width-modulated symbologies is "aspect ratio," which is simply the ratio of a symbol's bar height to the overall symbol length. A 15% bar height is equivalent to a 0.15 aspect ratio.

As aspect ratio is decreased, it becomes increasingly difficult to align the scanner (or its scanning path) with a symbol. Figure 4-60 illustrates the range of possible scanning angles.

Table 4-17	
Aspect Ratio	Range of Scanning Angles
0.05	5.7°
0.10	11.4°
0.15	17.0°
0.20	23.0°
0.25	28.0°
0.35	39.0°

The range of possible scanning angles is determined by the symbol's aspect ratio, as described in the following expression:

Range of Scanning Angles (in degrees) = 2 arctan (aspect ratio)

Table 4-17 tabulates the above expression for a variety of aspect ratios.

As stated before, many current industry standards for linear symbologies require an aspect ratio of at least 0.15. This results in a 17 degree range of scanning angles, which is well matched for wand scanning, but probably overly conservative for CCD or laser scanning.

Figure 4-61: Multiple Rows. By breaking a symbol into a series of shorter symbols, aspect ratios can be maintained while overall area is reduced.

CODE 16K

TESTING 12345 ABCDEF

CODE 49

TESTING 12345 ABCDEF

PDF417

TESTING 12345 ABCDEF

Figure 4-62: Comparison of Multi-row Symbologies: These three example symbols encode the same 20 character message and use the same X dimension.

For a constant aspect ratio, the area of a linear symbology increases roughly as the square of the encoded message length. Recognizing this, one way of improving area efficiency is to take a long message and encode it into a series of adjacent and associated short symbols. This concept is illustrated in Figure 4-61, where a single symbol is drawn to scale next to three symbols which are each one third of the length of the first symbol and maintain the same aspect ratio.

Looking at Figure 4-61, it can be seen that the total area of the multi-row implementation is only one third that of the single row symbol, despite the fact that the aspect ratio is maintained for each symbol. This is the basic concept that led to the development of the three multi-row symbologies: Code 49, Code 16K and PDF417. In order to be practical, the simple structure illustrated in Figure 4-61 would have to be supplemented by schemes to:

1. Keep track of the total number of rows and their sequence.

2. Prevent errors due to scan lines crossing from one row to another.

As discussed earlier in this chapter, the three multi-row symbologies use different approaches to address these issues. Both Code 49 and Code 16K use horizontal separator bars between the rows to inhibit the decoding of cross-row scans, whereas PDF417 uses three different character sets (called "clusters") that are switched between rows.

Both Code 49 and Code 16K are specified with a minimum bar height of 8X, although it is possible to use a smaller value if scanning equipment is used which can still provide an acceptable degree of alignment tolerance. PDF417 has a minimum specified bar height of 4X if no error correction is used, or 3X if the symbol is encoded with error correction characters.

For short message lengths, all three multi-row symbologies have similar efficiencies as illustrated in Figure 4-62.

For longer messages, PDF417 has higher area efficiency than Code 49 and Code 16K if minimum specified bar height is used. Table 4-18 compares the area efficiencies of the three multi-row symbologies for a variety of message lengths.

Table 4-18				
	20 characters	40 characters	200 characters	500 characters
Code 49[1]	4.3%	5.0%	—	—
Code 16K[(1)]	4.2%	4.7%	—	—
PDF417	5.5%[(2)]	6.9%[(3)]	12.6%[(4)]	15.4%[(5)]

Notes: (1) 8X row height.
(2) 4X row height, no error correction, 3 columns, 5 rows, TC mode, 4 shifts.
(3) 4X row height, no error correction, 4 columns, 7 rows, TC mode, 8 shifts.
(4) 3X row height, error correction level 3, 8 columns, 17 rows, TC mode, 40 shifts.
(5) 3X row height, error correction level 4, 16 columns, 21 rows, TC mode, 100 shifts.

ABCDEFGHIJK

CODE 39

ABCDEFGHIJK

CODE 49

ABCDEFGHIJK

CODE ONE

Figure 4-63: Comparison of Symbology Types. These three symbols all encode the data "ABCDE-FGHIJK" using the same X dimension. It is clear that the 2-D matrix symbology occupies much less label space (and is therefore much more efficient).

Note that the PDF417 symbols defined in generating Table 4-17 used either 4X or 3X bar height, while the Code 49 and Code 16K symbols were assumed to use a bar height of 8X, which is the minimum value allowed in their specifications. If the same row height had been used for all three stacked symbologies, PDF417 would have been less efficient than Code 49 or Code 16K.

Both linear and stacked symbologies have bars that are taller than one X dimension. This is done to ensure scannability with readily-available equipment such as handheld laser scanners (see subsequent chapters), which provide high resolution in an axis perpendicular to the height of the bars. In 1994, both handheld and fixed-mount scanners became available offering similar resolutions in the X and Y axes, thereby opening the door for true two-dimensional matrix symbologies. As discussed earlier in this chapter, 2-D matrix symbologies are much more efficient than linear or stacked symbologies as illustrated in Figure 4-63.

4.8.1 Density Comparison

From the previous discussion describing the concept of area efficiency, it can be understood that there are major differences between symbologies. For a given message, the required label size is highly dependent on the symbology used. In order to better understand the trade-offs, we will do a side-by-side comparison of a variety of different symbologies encoding three different messages lengths. The comparison will include only symbologies that are (or are in the process of becoming) public domain.

    Code 39

    Code 93

    Code 128

    Code 49

    Code 16K

    PDF417

    Code One

    DataMatrix

    MaxiCode

    ArrayTag

The comparison will be performed using three different message lengths of the repeating data "12345ABCDE12345ABCDE. . . ." The message lengths to be used are 20 characters, 50 characters, and 500 characters. The messages will be encoded into each symbology, and the area of the resulting symbol assuming an X dimension module size of 10 mils will be tabulated. Areas will be presented both for the symbol by itself and for the symbol plus any required quiet zone or clear area. Table 4-18 presents the data and lists detail notes.

In preparing the data for Table 4-18, the minimum bar height allowed by the particular symbology specification was used and recommended levels of error correction were included. Note that MaxiCode has a specified nominal cell size and therefore appears to be at an artificial disadvantage in this comparison. Areas for ArrayTag symbols were calculated based on the smallest rectangle that the cluster could fit into, and therefore are conservative.

	Table 4-19					
	AREA (SQUARE INCHES)					
	20 characters		50 characters		500 characters	
SYMBOLOGY	No Quiet Zone	With Quiet Zone	No Quiet Zone	With Quiet Zone	No Quiet Zone	With Quiet Zone
Code 39[1][2]	1.52	1.61	—	—	—	—
Code 93[1]	0.71	0.77	—	—		—
Code 128[1]	0.89	0.97	—	—	—	—
Code 49[3]	0.26	0.30	0.50	0.58	—	—
Code 16K[3]	0.26	0.30	0.64	0.74	—	—
PDF417	0.21[4]	0.28[4]	0.37[5]	0.46[5]	2.94[6]	3.14[6]
Code One	0.05[7]	0.05[7]	0.09[8]	0.09[8]	0.53[9]	0.53[9]
DataMatrix[10]	0.0723	0.105	0.144	0.208	1.123	1.618
Maxicode[11]	1.04	1.18	1.04	1.18	—	—
ArrayTag	0.05[12]	0.05[12]	0.12[13]	0.12[13]	0.86[14]	0.86[14]

Note:
(1) Bar height = 15% of symbol length.
(2) N = 2.5.
(3) Row height = 8X.
(4) Row height = 4X, no error correction, TC mode, 3 rows, 6 columns.
(5) Row height = 3X, error correction level 2, TC mode, 6 rows, 8 columns.
(6) Row height = 3X, error correction level 5, TC mode, 24 rows, 20 columns.
(7) Version B.
(8) Version C.
(9) Version F.
(10) Using ECC140 error correction.
(11) Nominal size (0.035 inch x 0.041 inch hexagons).
(12) A composite of 2 ArrayTags.
(13) A composite of 5 ArrayTags.
(14) A composite of 42 ArrayTags in a rectangular 6 x 7 arrangement.

The data presented in Table 4-19 clearly shows how the use of 2-D matrix symbologies can drastically reduce symbol size, especially for longer message lengths. Figures 4-64, 4-65, and 4-66 are scale representations of the symbols from the data in Table 4-18.

4.9 Legal Status of Symbologies

A symbology is nothing more than a set of rules or instructions describing how to make optically contrasting marks in such a fashion that information can be conveyed in a machine-readable form. With very few exceptions, equipment vendors have historically developed symbologies and placed them "in the public domain." Although the definition of "public domain" is to some degree subject to interpretation, it is generally recognized that manufacturers of printing and scanning equipment will not need to obtain licenses or pay royalties to the developer of a public domain symbology, and users will likewise not be financially encumbered.

A complete symbology specification will include information on how the developers intended that the encoded information be recovered during the reading process. This portion of the specification is commonly referred to as the "reference decode algorithm." Although the existence of patents may restrict scanner manu-

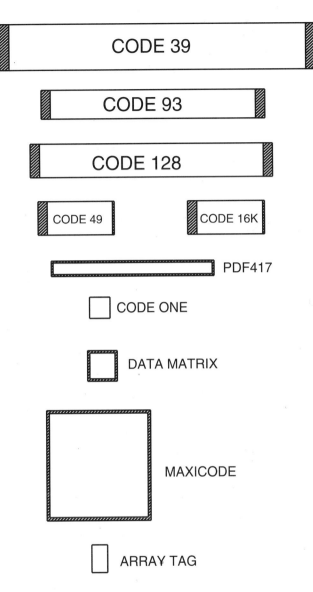

Figure 4-64: Symbology comparison. Using the data from Table 4-18, these symbols encode 20 characters, and use the same X dimension. The cross-hatched areas represent the minimum required quiet zones.

facturers from using particular hardware configurations, a public domain symbology should freely allow equipment developers to implement the reference decode algorithms without restriction.

This tradition of equipment vendors developing symbologies and placing them in the public domain for all to use served the automatic identification industry well for many years. There are many cases of competitive equipment vendors working together to ensure that a wide range of equipment was available to support newly developed symbologies and the users of this technology were the ultimate beneficiaries.

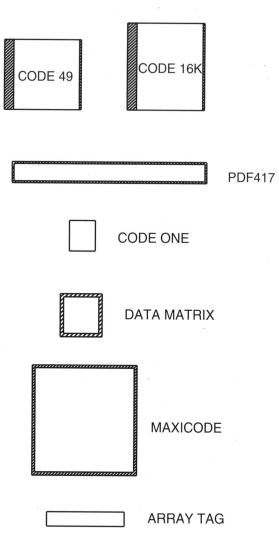

Figure 4-65: Symbology comparison. Using the data from Table 4-18, these symbols encode 50 characters, and use the same X dimension. The cross-hatched areas represent the minimum required quiet zones.

Outsiders to the automatic identification industry might find it odd that a symbology developer would actually assist a competitor in developing equipment, but this is one of the reasons that the bar code industry grew so rapidly during the 1980s, thereby benefiting all equipment suppliers as well as users.

A few small companies that did not have a continuing revenue flow from the sale of equipment developed symbologies with the express intent of licensing their use to both users and/or equipment manufacturers. These business efforts all proved to ultimately be less than successful.

As the 1980s drew to a close, the U.S. Patent Office showed an alarming tendency to grant patents for concepts that many believe were not truly novel, unique, and/or innovative. The courts sided with the patent holders, and equipment manu-

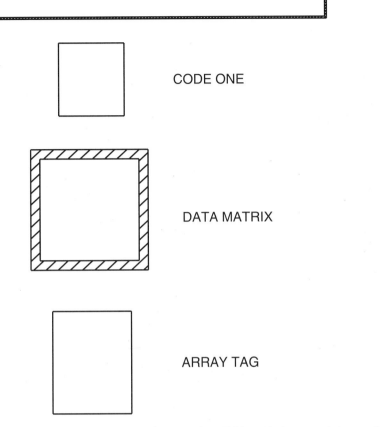

Figure 4-66: Symbology comparison. Using the data from Table 4-18, these symbols encode 500 characters, and use the same X dimension. The cross-hatched areas represent the minimum required quiet zones.

facturers embarked on an ever-increasing frenzy of patent applications in an effort to protect their ability to do business, and/or seek competitive advantage. One outcome of this unfortunate turn of events is the regrettable re-emergence of symbology developments that are proprietary in substance, if not in name. This trend continued into the nineties.

Users are cautioned to confirm the legal status of any new symbology that they may wish to employ.

4.10 Choosing a Symbology

Often, the choice of symbology is easy. If product is being shipped to supermarkets, it must be marked with U.P.C. or EAN; if it is being shipped to the U.S. Department of Defense, it must be marked with Code 39. If the product is a mailing label destined for a U.S. address, various postal discounts encourage the use of a Postnet symbol.

For internal applications where external standards do not apply, the user has many symbologies from which to choose. The final choice of symbology should take into consideration:

- Physical area available for the symbol

- Type of data to be encoded

- Amount of data to be encoded

- Type of printing equipment to be employed (and hence the practical lower limit of X)

- The scanning environment (is an operator involved, or is scanning to be completely automatic?)

- Special scanning considerations (depth of field, omnidirectionality, speed, etc.)

- Robustness of the symbology

- Availability of printing and scanning equipment.

Where space is available and messages are short, Code 39 or Code 128 are ideally suited: these symbologies are commonly used throughout the world, and relatively inexpensive printing and scanning equipment is readily available from a variety of sources.

If large amounts of data are to be encoded and/or label space is at a real premium, some form of a 2-dimensional symbol is called for. The use of a symbology that is completely in the public domain will inevitably result in a wider choice of equipment suppliers and lower ultimate cost.

It is always advisable to use as large an X dimension as practical for the available space, even if it means using a symbology that has higher area efficiency. This will make it easier to print and scan, and will result in higher depth of field (DOF).

Further details of many of the above described symbologies are contained in the appendices.

Bar Code Standards

Successful data collection systems require the use of bar code standards. There are three types of bar code standards: Print Quality, Symbology, and Application. Sources for these standards are listed in Appendix T.

5.1 Print Quality

Print Quality is the basis of all Symbology and Application Standards. Print Quality defines a bar code symbol measurement method. There is one Print Quality Standard recognized worldwide, and it is referenced in all Symbology and Application Standards, and it is supported by all verifier manufacturers. It is "ANSI X3.182 Guideline for Bar Code Print Quality," published by ANSI (American National Standards Institute).

5.2 Symbology Standards

Symbology Standards define the pattern of bars and spaces. There is one source of all common Symbology Standards that is recognized worldwide called AIM (Automatic Identification Manufacturers). Standards for Code 39 (3 of 9), Code 128, Interleaved 2 of 5 (ITF), Codabar, Code 93, Code 16K, Code 49, Code One, PDF417, and development support are available from AIM.

5.3 Application Standards

Application Standards are specific to individual activities. Application Standards specify a particular Print Quality Level based on ANSI X3.182 and a particular Symbology based on an AIM standard. Most Application Standards relate to the distribution of items in an open system. There is one umbrella "shipping label" standard recognized worldwide called "ANSI MH10.8M Bar Code Labels for Unit Loads and Transport Packages." Virtually all Application Standards are a subset of ANSI MH10.8M. Labels that comply with ANSI MH10.8M will be scannable in virtually all shipping environments.

Specific industries have developed standards that are a subset of ANSI MH10.8M, and they include the Auto Industry (AIAG), the Electronics Industry

(EIA), the General Distribution Industry (UCC), and the Health Industry (HIBCC). These and other standards sources are listed in Appendix T.

General Document Source

All documents are available through Global Engineering Documents by calling toll free in the U.S. and Canada (800) 854-7179 or internationally at (714) 261-1455.

Equipment Manufacturers

Many of the bar code symbologies were originally developed by bar code equipment manufacturers. These include:

INTERMEC	Code 39, Code 93, Code 11, Code 49
Computer Identics	Code 128
Laserlight Systems	Code 16K, Code One
Monarch Marking Systems	Codabar (traditional)
Symbol Technologies	PDF417

Identifiers

With the wide range of existing and proposed bar code application standards, the possibility of confusion is great. Many of the standards use the same symbology, increasing the possibility of accidental data misinterpretation.

If each data structure were uniquely identifiable by virtue of its length or content, there would be no problem. Unfortunately, it is not always possible to unambiguously recognize a given industry's symbol by a cursory examination of the data.

To address this problem, the Federation of Automated Coding Technologies (FACT) is developing a master data identifier reference listing. The data identifiers are a specific sequence of character(s) occurring in a preassigned position (usually the beginning) within a data structure. The term "flag characters" is sometimes used to describe data identifiers. As an example, any data structure beginning with a "+" and followed by an alpha character can presently be recognized as being coded as an HIBCC Primary symbol. As more associations use the FACT Data Identifier system as part of their coding structure, the possibility of data confusion will be reduced.

A partial listing (as of mid-1990) of the FACT data identifiers is provided in Appendix K.

5.4 Print Quality Standards

Symbology standards include limits on dimensional tolerances, spots, voids, edge roughness, reflectivity, and contrast. If these requirements were meticulously met, there would be no need for a separate print quality standard; the quality would be excellent, and system performance would not be compromised. A symbol's perceived print quality as observed by a scanner can vary, depending on the resolution of the scanner. A higher resolution scanning device will see localized imperfections that might not be discernible to a lower resolution device. Because of this resolution dependence, print quality standards usually specify the size and shape of the measuring aperture used for the evaluation.

Many of today's bar code applications are using symbols that deviate (usually unintentionally) from published printing standards in some respect or another. These symbols give a lower read rate and higher error rate than totally in spec bar code, but they may be adequate for certain applications or equipment.

In order to quantify these deviations in a fashion that will give predictable (but possibly lower than optimum) levels of performance, American National Standards Institute (ANSI) has just completed developing a bar code print quality standard. The ANSI document is entitled "Guideline for Bar Code Print Quality", and it categorizes symbols into grades from A to F. A symbol to be evaluated is subjected to a minimum of ten evaluation scans using a round aperture of specified diameter. The scans are equally spaced along the symbol's bar height, starting at a height of 10 percent, and ending at 90 percent, as illustrated in Figure 5-1 .

Figure 5-1: Evaluation Scans. In the ANSI Bar Code Print Quality Standard, a minimum of ten equally spaced scans are evaluated against specific criteria. Automatic bar code verifiers will evaluate several parameters for each scan to determine an overall symbol quality level.

The reflectance signal from each scan is evaluated and graded against specific criteria for contrast, modulation, decodability, and defects. An individual scan is then assigned a grade based upon the worst grade received in each of the evaluation categories. The overall symbol quality level is then calculated by numerically averaging the grades of each of the evaluation scans. All of this grading is meaningless unless the measuring aperture diameter and measuring wavelength are also specified. The appropriate measuring aperture to use is either specified by the particular application standard, or taken from Table 5-1.

Table 5-1
MEASURING APERTURE

X Dimension (mils)	Measuring Aperture Diameter (mils)	Number
4 < = X < 7	3	03
7 < = X < 13	5	05
13 < = X < 25	10	10
25 < = X	20	20

Using the ANSI approach, the overall symbol print quality is stated in the following format:

$$G/N/W,$$

where

    G = overall symbol grade
    N = measuring aperture number (see Table 5-1)
    W = nominal wavelength in nanometers

Note that a given bar code symbol may satisfy the requirements for several different grades, depending on the aperture chosen. For example, a single bar code symbol might have the following quality levels: D/03/630, C/05/630, B/10/630, A/20/630, F/20/900. This example is probably a symbol with an X dimension of over 16 mils that contains some spots, voids, and edge roughness and is printed with an ink that has little absorption at infrared wavelengths. The larger 20 mil aperture is able to average out the smaller defects, but the smaller apertures are sufficiently affected that the grade levels are reduced.

Each scan is made with a specified optical geometry. The observed reflectivity perceived with the measuring aperture is recorded as a function of the position of the aperture as it traverses along one of the scanning paths. Figure 5-2 illustrates a typical plot of the observed reflectance from an evaluation scan. This data is called a "Scan Reflectance Profile." Specific details of the ANSI methodology will be discussed in a subsequent chapter.

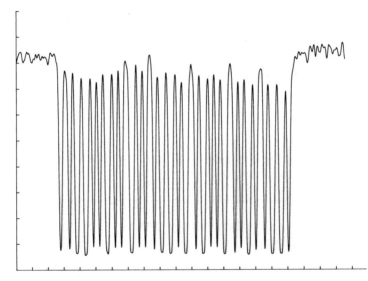

Figure 5-2: Scan Reflectance Profile. This is a plot of the localized symbol reflectivity as a measuring aperture is scanned across the symbol along a specific path.

Fundamentals of
Bar Code Reading

A bar code reader (sometimes referred to as a "bar code scanner") is a system used to extract the information that is optically encoded in a symbol and convert it into computer-compatible digital data. The decoded data can be transmitted directly to an attached computer, can be stored locally for later processing, or can interact with an application program that is resident in the reader system itself.

The reader will include some type of electro-optical system which is used as a transducer so that the particular characteristics of the optical symbol can be examined by the reader's processing electronics. A generalized block diagram of a bar code reading system is shown in Figure 6-1.

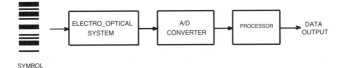

Figure 6.1: Generalized Bar Code Reading System.

The electro-optical system includes means for illuminating the symbol and provisions for determining how much light is reflected from specific areas of the symbol. The output from the electro-optical system is typically an analog voltage, and it is converted into a digital signal that the processor can handle by the block labeled "A/D Converter."

The output from the A/D converter can be a simple 1 bit signal representing "black" or "white" (in which case the A/D converter is called a "waveshaper" or "digitizer"), or it might have a resolution of several bits corresponding to shades of gray on the original image.

When scanning a linear symbology such as Code 39 or Code 128, a conventional bar code reader (as opposed to a vision-based system) has to perform seven basic functions:

1. Find the correct elements.

2. Determine the width of each of the bars and spaces or the edge-to-edge distances.

3. Quantize the element widths into a number of levels appropriate to the symbology being used (two for Code 39, Interleaved 2 of 5, and Codabar; four for U.P.C./EAN and Code 93; five for Code 128, etc.).

4. Ensure that the quantized element widths are consistent with all of the encodation rules for the symbology. Compare the pattern of quantized element widths to a table of stored values for that symbology and determine the encoded data.

5. If necessary, reverse the data order. The reading direction is determined by examining the start/stop characters.

6. Confirm that valid quiet zones exist at both ends of the symbol.

7. Confirm that any check characters are consistent with the decoded data.

The second step, that of element width measurement, is accomplished by the electro-optic system in combination with software running in the bar code reader's microprocessor. The next five steps are handled by software routines that implement a particular decode algorithm.

The tasks that a reading system needs to perform are more complex when a 2-D symbology is to be read.

6.1 Electro-Optical System

The electro-optical system is the part of the reader that actually scans the bar code symbol. The scanning operation is provided by the operator's hand motion, by an internal mechanical scanning system, by an electronic imaging device, or by movement of the symbol. The instantaneous electrical output is representative of the localized reflectivity of the symbol at the point that is being scanned. The description that follows refers initially to electro-optical systems that use a single scanning line. When the electro-optical system is a separate physical unit that is connected to the rest of the reading system, it is commonly referred to as an "input device."

These are usually active systems: they illuminate the symbol with light energy, then examine the amount of light reflected by a localized area of the symbol. The symbol's spaces will reflect more light than the bars.

Unless an image sensor such as a CCD is used, the electro-optical system sequentially analyzes a path of points passing through the symbol in a perceived scanning path.

The area of the symbol that is actually being examined at any given time is referred to as the "spot." The spot is not necessarily round in shape. For conventional bar code, the spot's dimension in an axis perpendicular to the long axis of the bars should be consistent with the width of the narrowest element to be scanned.

The spot is formed either by broadly collecting the light reflected from a tightly-focused illuminating beam (see Figure 6-2) or by flooding the symbol with light and using a tightly-focused aperture to collect the light (see Figure 6-3).

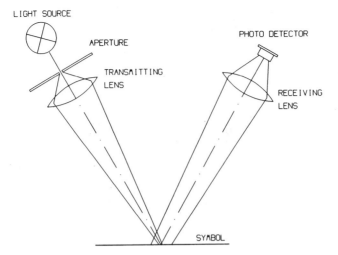

Figure 6-2: Focused Illuminator. Resolution is achieved by tightly controlling the diameter of the spot cast by an illuminating beam. The reflected light is received by a loosely-focused collection system.

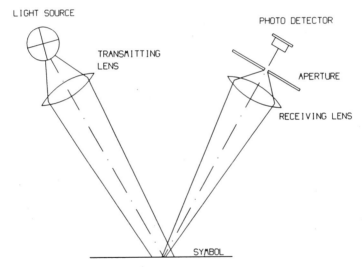

Figure 6-3: Focused Collector. Resolution is achieved by imaging a collector aperture. In this method, either ambient light or an illuminating light source floods a large area with light. The sensitive region of the scan is a tightly-focused spot that scans across the pattern.

The light reflected from the spot on the symbol is directed to a photodiode detector (or equivalent device), which generates a small electrical current that is proportional to the amount of light returned. An amplifier in the input device increases the signal from the photodiode to a usable voltage level. As the spot is moved in a path perpendicular to the long axis of the bars (this is commonly called scanning), the analog voltage from the amplifier varies. This is shown in Figure 6-4.

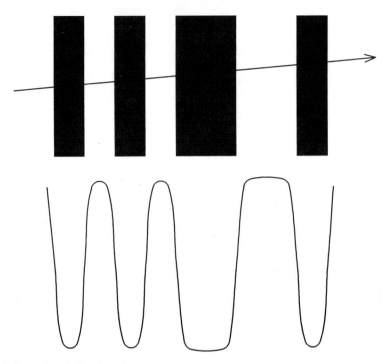

Figure 6-4: Scanning A Symbol. As the scanner beam crosses the bar code pattern, the analog voltage from the detector is proportional to the reflectivity observed by the scanning spot. Notice how the sharp edges of the bar pattern become rounded curves at the output of the detector.

The trace of the analog voltage from the amplifier is representative of the reflectivity of the symbol along the scanning path. If the spot diameter is much smaller than the symbol's narrow widths, the representation will be quite accurate. Practical scanning spots have finite diameters and do not have crisp edges. As an example, a cross section of a laser beam used for bar code scanning might look like the Gaussian curve shown in Figure 6-5.

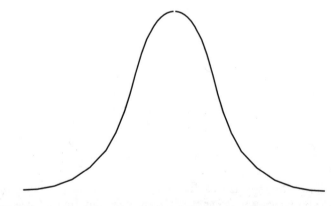

Figure 6-5: Intensity Cross Section of a Laser Beam. A cross section of a laser beam used for bar code scanning has a Gaussian intensity profile.

SYMBOL

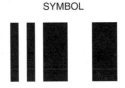

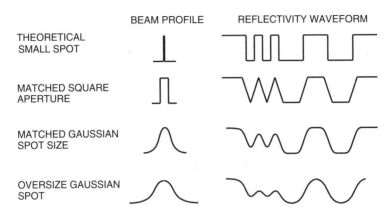

	BEAM PROFILE	REFLECTIVITY WAVEFORM
THEORETICAL SMALL SPOT		
MATCHED SQUARE APERTURE		
MATCHED GAUSSIAN SPOT SIZE		
OVERSIZE GAUSSIAN SPOT		

Figure 6-6: Effect of Beam Diameter. The resulting electrical signal from the scanning operation is the mathematical convolution of the symbols reflectivity profile and the scanning spot's intensity profile. The finer details in the symbol are attenuated as the spot diameter grows.

The analog signal measured at the output of the amplifier, referred to earlier, is the mathematical convolution of the reflectivity profile of the symbol along the scanning path and the intensity profile of the scanning spot. Depending on the diameter of the scanning spot relative to the symbol's dimensions, the electrical waveform may not be an accurate representation of the symbol's actual reflectivity profile. Figure 6-6 shows this effect. Those readers with a mathematical or engineering background will recognize that the high frequency components of the waveform are attenuated as the relative spot diameter gets larger.

Several different wavelengths of light have been used in bar code scanning. Wavelength is usually expressed in nanometers with the visible portion of the spectrum (those wavelengths that are visible to the human eye) extending from 750 nanometers to 450 nanometers.

Early bar code scanning only used infrared wavelengths in the 900 nanometer range; many contemporary devices operate at wavelengths near 633 nanometers, which is the wavelength emitted by a helium-neon (HeNe) laser.

Some printing techniques do not give adequate contrast in the infrared range, whereas other types of printing, particularly those using carbon-based inks, can give satisfactory contrast for all visible and infrared wavelengths.

The two most common scanning wavelengths are conveniently referred to as bands B900 and B633, corresponding to wavelengths in the 900 and 633 nanometer bands respectively. Because B900 wavelengths are not visible to the human eye, certain types of security badge applications make use of this wavelength. In some environments where labels will get contaminated with grease, oil, or blood, B900 may perform better than B633.

Some postal applications use either fluorescent or phosphorescent inks which emit light at a specific wavelength when illuminated by light at another specific wavelength (usually UV). This allows symbols to be read irrespective of whether they were printed on white paper, or directly on top of other conventional printing.

6.2 Analog-To-Digital Converter

The Analog-To-Digital Converter (A/D converter) is a circuit that takes the analog waveform produced by the scanning operation (commonly referred to as the "video" signal) and converts it to a digital signal that can be used by the reader's microprocessor.

In its simplest form, the A/D converter is a simple electrical comparator which compares the instantaneous value of the video signal to a fixed reference voltage or threshold. Whenever the video signal is above the threshold, the comparator produces a digital output indicating that the scanner's spot is currently on the white part of the symbol, and if the instantaneous value of the video signal is below the threshold, the comparator's digital output indicates that a bar is being examined. The output of the A/D converter is a single digital bit that can either be a binary "1" or a "0." This single bit A/D converter is commonly referred to as a "waveshaper" or "digitizer," and its operation is illustrated in Figure 6-7.

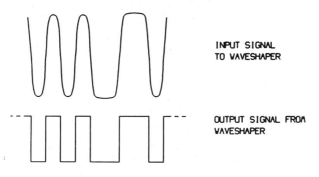

INPUT SIGNAL
TO WAVESHAPER

OUTPUT SIGNAL FROM
WAVESHAPER

Figure 6-7: Operation of a Waveshaper. The analog voltage (top) is converted to a digital signal by means of a waveshaper. The output of the waveshaper is a time-varying binary signal switching between either of two states (bottom).

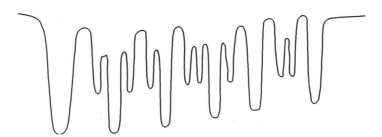

Figure 6-8: Typical Input Signal. This waveform shows the effect of marginal scanner resolution and an overall reflectivity gradient. Use of a fixed threshold to determine the edges between bars and spaces will result in less than optimum decoding performance.

The simplistic fixed threshold waveshaper described above would not give acceptable performance in a commercially viable scanner, because the circuit often has to cope with challenging signals such as the one in Figure 6-8.

Figure 6-8 shows the combined effect of marginal scanner resolution and an overall symbol reflectivity gradient. The ideal waveshaper response is also shown in the figure, and it is clear that a fixed threshold is inadequate for this purpose. In examining the waveforms in this example, it appears that an ideal waveshaper would simply declare the black/white transitions as those positions where the observed reflectivity is at the mid-point of the observed reflectivity of the adjacent "hill" and "valley" of the reflectivity plot. These positions are easy to determine after the fact, but are extremely difficult to quantify during the actual scanning process. A number of patents have been granted for ingenious electronic circuits that approximate the ideal waveshaper response. Some of the ideas used include:

1. Setting the threshold to a value that is offset from the last observed hill or valley by a predetermined amount.

2. Setting the threshold to the mid-point of the average bar and space reflectivity observed in the last scanned label.

3. Setting the threshold to the mid-point of the bar and space reflectivity observed in the first bar and space of the currently scanned label.

4. Setting the threshold to the mid-point of the reflectivity of the most recent bar and space.

5. Defining an edge as the position where the second derivative of the input waveform changes sign.

If waveshapers could see ahead to the next element's reflectivity, they could do a much better job of determining the edges of bars and spaces. The ever-decreasing cost of memory and microprocessors today makes it feasible to consider building a completely digital waveshaper that can provide the equivalent of this capability. Such a device would convert the video waveform into a large number of digital samples containing several bits of resolution, then storing these samples into successive locations in memory. After the samples have been stored, a microprocessor that is programmed with an appropriate algorithm examines the stored values, determines the sequence of bars and spaces, then extrapolates the location of the transitions between the elements.

6.3 Processor

All practical reading systems incorporate a processor of some type. Depending on the capabilities of the equipment, this could be as simple as a one-chip, 8-bit microprocessor, or it could be as complex as an array of high speed RISC devices.

In a conventional bar code reader, the electro-optical system's spot is scanned through the symbol either by the operator or by the motion of moving optical elements within the scanner itself.

In the presence of a uniform scanning velocity, it is easy to determine the relative widths of the actual bars and spaces by measuring the time that the electrical signal from the scanner spends at the voltages which represent either black or white respectively. In other words, with uniform velocity it is relatively easy to map from the time domain to the space domain.

In the presence of large or nonmonotonic acceleration, it is much more difficult to determine the bar and space widths from an examination of the scanner's electrical output signal. The ease and accuracy of this mapping is dependent on the particular software algorithms employed by the processor. Similar problems can be caused by optical distortion, such as that encountered when scanning symbols that are wrapped around circular objects.

The processors used in vision-based scanning systems (see Chapter 8) have a considerably more complex task to perform.

All bar code symbologies were designed with some type of decoding algorithm in mind. These are often published as part of the symbology specification and are referred to as "reference decode algorithms." The reference decode algorithm or an equivalent is programmed into the memory of the reader's microprocessor.

7

Attended Bar Code Scanners

This chapter will focus on conventional bar code scanning equipment where a symbol is read by moving a scanning spot through the bars and spaces of a width-modulated symbol. We will specifically review equipment that is intended to be used by an operator: unattended equipment is the subject of Chapter 8. Vision-based equipment can also be used to read bar code symbols and this is described in Chapter 9.

As shown in Figure 7-1, an attended bar code reader can be considered as consisting of two separate elements: the input device and the decoder. These two elements can reside in separate physical packages connected by a cable (or possibly by a wireless link), or they can be in a single unit.

Referring to Chapter 6, the input device includes the electro-optical system and the A/D converter, while the decoder is equivalent to the processor.

7.1 Input Devices

An input device determines the localized reflectivity as the spot moves through the symbol. As described in Chapter 6, light is directed toward the symbol and a photodetector determines how much is reflected by the spot. The output voltage

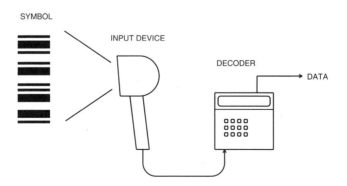

Figure 7-1: Attended Bar Code Reader. There are two distinct elements to a bar code reading system designed to be used by an operator. The input device scans the symbol in some way, translating reflectivity levels into an electrical signal. The decoder then converts this signal into the character data representation of the symbol's code.

of an input device can be either analog or digital. If the output is analog, a wave-shaper must be incorporated into the decoder unit. A complete block diagram of an input device in shown in Figure 7-2.

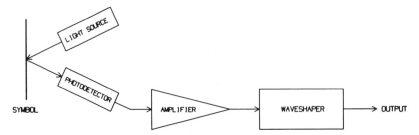

Figure 7-2: Input Device Block Diagram. An input device includes a source and detector of light, an amplifier, and a waveshaper. The output of the input device is fed to a decoder so that the data encoded in the symbol can be recovered.

Input devices fall into five different classifications depending on their scanning mechanism and physical format, as shown in Table 7-1. Each of these input devices will be discussed separately.

Table 7-1
Input Device Classification

	Fixed Beam	Moving Beam
Handheld	Contact	Noncontact
	Noncontact	
Fixed Mount	Noncontact	Noncontact

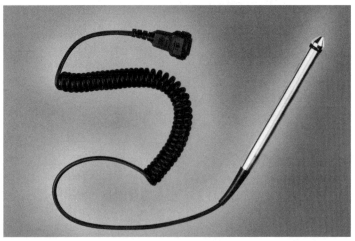

Courtesy of Welch-Allyn, Inc.

Figure 7-3. Typical Scanning Wand. Wands are the most common input device. The scanning action of a wand is produced by the motion of the operator's arm. The typical wand such as this one is set up for motion with the tip in contact with the symbol. Such contact wands may require protected symbols to prevent damage to the symbol from repeated scanning.

Handheld, Fixed Beam Contact Devices

As the name suggests, handheld, fixed beam contact devices physically touch the symbol that is being scanned. Most devices have some depth of field, allowing thin protective laminates to be employed. These devices do not include any mechanism for automatically providing the scanning motion. The device's beam is fixed with respect to its physical housing, and the scanning motion must be provided by the operator. These types of input devices are commonly referred to as "wands" or "light pens."

The tip that contacts the symbol is designed to minimize scratching and may be either plastic, steel, or a sapphire ball (see Figure 7-3). Wands generally operate by flood-illuminating the symbol, then creating the spot (often called "aperture") by focusing the received light path. A variety of spot sizes are usually available.

Some operator skill is required to use a handheld, fixed beam contact device, but the techniques are easy to learn. The most common mistakes made by inexperienced operators are:

- Scanning too slowly, resulting in a "jerky" motion.

- Stopping the scan before the quiet zone at the end of the symbol.

- Not starting the scan in the leading quiet zone.

- Scanning out past the ends of the symbol's bars.

Handheld, Fixed Beam, Noncontact Devices

Noncontact devices are able to scan symbols placed on soft or irregular surfaces and can scan through thick laminates or windows. Handheld, fixed beam, noncontact devices require that the operator manually provide the scanning motion: this involves somewhat more skill than a contact device because the operator must also maintain the unit at an appropriate distance from the symbol being scanned. Figure 7-4 shows a representative device, which is often pistol shaped.

Some devices use incandescent or LED light sources to illuminate the symbol

Courtesy of Intermec Corp.

Figure 7-4. Handheld, Fixed Beam, Noncontact Scanner. This type of scanner also relies on operator motion to scan the beam over the symbol. The focal point is several inches from the tip of the gun, so actual contact with the symbol is not needed.

and employ optical elements in the returned light path to define the spot size. Greater depth of field or working distance is typically obtained with a solid state laser diode defining the spot size in the transmitted beam. If a laser diode that emits in the infrared spectrum is used, a visible finder beam is included to aid in alignment with the symbol.

Handheld, Moving Beam Scanners

In a moving beam, handheld scanning device, the scanning motion is provided by an internal electromechanical system. Revolving polygons or oscillating mirrors are common implementations, although moving holograms are also practical scanning elements. The typical scan rate is approximately 40 scans per second. Because the scan rate is above 20 per second, the human eye's persistence of vision gives the impression that a continuous scan line, rather than a moving spot, is being projected.

Advantages of moving beam handheld scanning devices are that little operator skill is required and that suboptimum quality symbols benefit from a large number of scanning attempts in a short period of time.

Again, there are two general categories: focused illuminating beam with general receive optics, and flood illumination using focused receive optics.

The first handheld devices used Helium Neon (HeNe) laser tubes and the associated high voltage power supplies. Today, focused beam devices are typically designed with solid-state laser diodes. The HeNe lasers operate at 633 nanometers and are easily visible for aiming purposes. Most solid-state laser diodes operate at wavelengths of 660 to 670 nanometers, which is not as visible to the human eye as 633 nanometers, but units are becoming available with shorter wavelengths, increasing the perceived brightness. Figure 7-5 shows representative devices.

Courtesy of Symbol Technologies, Inc.   Courtesy of Intermec Corp.

Figure 7-5. Handheld, Moving Beam Scanners. Handheld, moving beam scanners usually employ either a helium-neon or solid-state laser as a light source. The scanning motion is provided by rotating or oscillating mirrors, polygons, or holograms inside the scanner. Operator aiming is facilitated either by a separately projected visible reference line, or by the last beam itself.

The flood illumination units (see Figure 7-6) use either visible light-emitting diode (LED) or incandescent light sources. Depth of field and working distance are typically less than focused beam units, and these products have never been commercially successful.

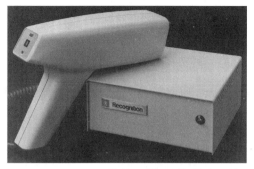

Courtesy of Recognition Equipment Inc.

Figure 7-6. Flood Illumination, Handheld, Moving Beam Scanner. A typical flood illumination moving beam scanner is shown here. The received scanning motion is provided by an internal oscillating mirror, which causes the imaged collection aperture to sweep through the symbol.

The scanner may incorporate a mechanism that intentionally causes the scanning line to wobble or oscillate vertically over a narrow range. This allows different areas of the symbol to be scanned on subsequent passes, and can sometime provide improved performance on marginal print quality symbols where only a few usable scan paths exist through a large population of symbol defects. This technique is equivalent to the scanner's examining an area of the symbol, rather than just a single scanning line, thereby making use of one of bar code's most useful attributes: its vertical redundancy.

The increased interest in 2-D symbologies has led to the development of handheld rastering laser scanners. The horizontal scan rate is much higher (about 400 scans/sec) than conventional laser scanners and a vertical scan rate of about 10 scans/sec is used. The amplitude of the two scan patterns is such that a rectangular area is covered that matches the typical form factor of a 2-D stacked symbol. A representative device is shown in Figure 7-7.

Courtesy of Symbol Technologies, Inc.

Figure 7-7: Rastering Handheld Laser Scanner. A fast horizontal scan rate and a slower vertical rate are optimized for reading 2-D stacked symbols.

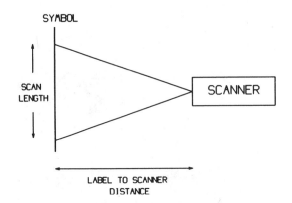

Figure 7-8: Scan Length. Scan length is the distance that the scanner's active spot travels along the direction perpendicular to the bars of a symbol. Scan length increases as scanner-to-symbol distance increases.

Depending on the actual scanning mechanism employed, there is a definite length associated with the scanning line. As a symbol is brought closer to the moving beam scanner, the scan line length becomes shorter, as illustrated in Figure 7-8.

The extreme ends of the scan line are often not usable, due to rapid beam acceleration in this area. The usable scan line length often defines how close a symbol can be read successfully by a moving beam scanner.

In 1990, the first handheld scanner with partial omnidirectional capability was introduced. A revolving mirror arrangement projects a series of scanning lines toward the symbol at differing angles. If adequate symbol bar height exists, at least one of the scanning lines will be able to cut all the bars and spaces, no matter what the symbol orientation is relative to the scanner. Unfortunately, a legal dispute regarding patent infringement resulted in the scanner being withdrawn from the marketplace.

The automated operation of handheld, moving beam scanners often encourages operators to adopt a cavalier usage style. Operators will initiate the scanning when clearly outside of the operational range of the unit, then move the device into the correct range, waiting for a beep. Unfortunately, this technique ensures that the decoding will occur with the worst possible signal-to-noise ratio, possibly resulting in data errors. To offset this, decoders that are interfaced to moving beam scanners may incorporate a "voting" algorithm, whereby data from two or more scans are compared before decoding is completed.

Rather than scanning the transmitted light beam, it is also possible to scan the received light path as a whole with modern electronic detectors. This type of scanner is often referred to as a CCD scanner because of the charge-coupled device (CCD) semiconductor technology used for the photodiode array sensor. A CCD scanner is able to do this without any moving parts. A stationary flood illumination scheme is employed, and an image of the bar code symbol is optically transferred to a linear array of multiple adjacent photodetectors. The array contains a sufficient number of photodiodes so that at least two photodiodes are covered by the narrowest element to be resolved. Figure 7-9 is a block diagram of a handheld scanning device using this technique.

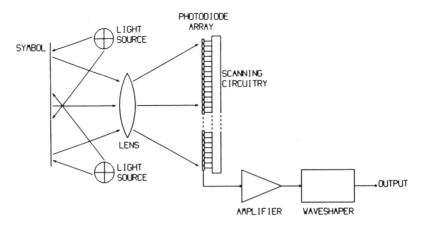

Figure 7-9: CCD Scanner Arrangement. The CCD scanner contains no mechanical moving parts. Flood illumination from a light source covers the whole symbol. Scanning is done electronically using the digitized image of a line through the symbol provided by the linear photodiode array. Electronic scanning can also be performed using video imaging systems (such as conventional TV cameras) as input devices.

The actual scanning motion is achieved by electrically scanning each of the individual photodiodes in a sequential manner. Because there are so many diodes, and they are very close together, the electrical output is a smooth waveform.

The actual spot size is determined by the size and shape of an individual photodiode in the array, together with the magnification properties of the optics. In order to freeze motion between the symbol and the scanner, the light source is often flashed between scans of the photodiode array.

Note that the effective photodiode spacing must be small enough that a minimum of two (preferably four) photodiodes are covered by the width of any of the symbol's narrow elements. Also, the maximum symbol length that can be read depends on the number of photodiodes in the array. Figure 7-10 illustrates a typical device. Depth of field is somewhat less than that achievable with a laser-based device, but advances are continuing in this area.

Courtesy of Welch Allyn/Data Collection Div.

Figure 7-10: Typical CCD Scanner. This example is a handheld unit. Although small and rugged, CCD scanners have less depth of field than laser-based units.

The previous discussion described linear arrays of photodiodes. It is also feasible to use a 2-dimensional area array of photodiodes to electronically scan a bar code symbol. The additional information derived from scanning all of the photodiodes can be used either to average out localized printing defects by using the vertical redundancy present in the symbol's bars, or may be used to provide true omnidirectional scanning, regardless of bar height. This technology is discussed further in Chapter 9.

Either CCD scanners or laser scanners could also be equipped with systems that increase the usable DOF by using moving optical elements that move the apparent "waist" or prime focal point either toward or away from the scanner. This can either be done in an open loop manner whereby the optimum scanning distance is continually and repetitively being changed in the hope that at least some of the scanning paths will be in focus, or a distance measuring means can be used to intelligently position the optics (this is called "autofocussing").

Card Scanners

Most people have experienced magnetic card scanning: all popular credit cards have a magnetic strip on the back that is read as the card is "swiped" through a slot reader or inserted into an automated bank teller machine. Equipment exists that can allow similar functionality with cards containing bar code symbols.

A slot reader, such as that shown in Figure 7-11, contains a simple electro-optical system that images a spot at a fixed location within a slot. As the operator moves a card containing a bar code symbol through the slot, the symbol's reflectivity differences are effectively scanned. The illumination is usually performed by LED or incandescent light sources, but it is certainly possible to construct a slot reader that uses a laser.

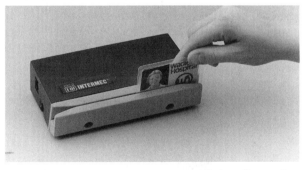

Courtesy of Intermec Corp.

Figure 7-11: Slot Reader. The operator "swipes" a card containing a bar code symbol through the unit's slot.

Slot readers only get one look at the symbol as it passes by, so good print quality is essential if high first read rates are required. These devices are often configured with nonsymmetric spots, usually in the shape of ellipses. The longer axis of the ellipse is aligned parallel to the symbol's bars. This "tall" spot is better able to extract meaningful information from a bar code symbol in the presence of printing defects.

Another type of device is a card insertion reader. Similar to a bank's automatic teller machine, the operator simply inserts the card to be read into an opening on the device, and a mechanical drive takes over to move the card past pre-positioned optical elements. In this device, the scanning speed and card orientation are quite controlled, making it possible to read either linear or 2-D stacked symbologies in either orientation (parallel to the long or short side of the card) if an appropriate imaging device is used.

Card readers are sometimes used at access control points in security systems. In order to prevent the duplication of the symbols contained on valid badges by means of a photocopier, it is possible to incorporate a plastic laminate on the badge which covers the symbol with a substance containing specific optical filtering capabilities. If the card reader's electro-optical system is designed to match the characteristics of the optical filter, there will be no problem reading the symbol even if it appears completely black to the human eye and is impossible to photocopy.

Wavelength

All input devices, whether fixed mount or handheld, respond to the optical reflectivity differences between a symbol's bars and spaces at a particular wavelength(s) of the light employed. Light is a form of electromagnetic radiation as are conventional radio waves, but light has a much shorter wavelength. It is conventional to express optical wavelengths in nanometers (1 nanometer is equal to 0.000000001 meter). Figure 7-12 illustrates the electromagnetic spectrum.

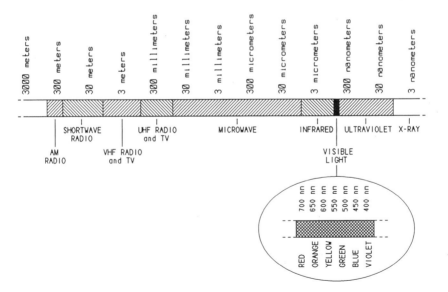

Figure 7-12: Visible Light Wavelengths Within The Electromagnetic Spectrum. Visible light is just one part of the overall electromagnetic spectrum. A specific location in the spectrum can be identified by stating either the wavelength or the frequency.

Input devices operate by illuminating the symbol with optical energy, then examining the amount of energy reflected back. The reflectivity of background material and printed bars varies at different wavelengths. The wavelength to which an input device responds is a function of the light source and the characteristics of any optical filters used. Although a single wavelength is usually quoted for a particular scanner, the equipment typically works in a band of wavelengths centered about the nominal. Some input devices are available with a choice of wavelengths (factory installed).

Bar code symbology and/or application standards specify the wavelength band(s) at which the specified optical properties are to be met. The two most commonly quoted bands have been traditionally referred to as B633, centered at 633 nanometers, and B900, centered at 900 nanometers. Some printing processes (especially those using carbon-based ink) can achieve contrast at both B900 and B633, although some thermally printed labels only have sufficient contrast at B633.

Figure 7-13 represents the reflectivity of the dark elements (as a function of wavelength) in an example printing process. An examination of this plot indicates that a symbol printed with this process would be unreadable at B900 but would be usable at B633. This is because the bars would be indistinguishable from the spaces if a scanner were to be operating at the infrared wavelengths of B900.

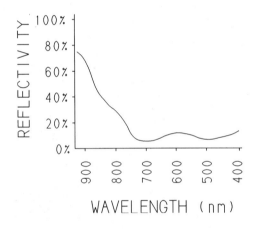

Figure 7-13: Example Reflectivity Plot. This example graph shows the reflectivity of a black bar as a function of the wavelength of the illumination. This plot illustrates that a scanner operating at 900 nm would not be able to differentiate between a bar and a space, but a 633 nm scanner would have no difficulty.

Having adequate symbol contrast at the wavelength employed by the input device is important. Before selecting a particular scanner or printing technique, make sure that there is a wavelength "match."

When looking at a symbol with the human eye, it is important to realize that the examination is being made over a broad range of wavelengths that may or may not include the wave length actually used by the input device. Normal ambient light is a mixture of different wavelengths. The human eye's response covers a range from about 750 to 450 nanometers, with a spectral sensitivity which approximates the plot in Figure 7-14.

Just because a symbol appears to have adequate contrast when viewed by eye, there is no guarantee that a scanner will be able to decode it, especially if the scanner operates at a wavelength that is outside the eye's range.

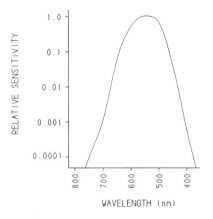

Figure 7-14: Sensitivity of the Human Eye. The eye's spectral sensitivity typically extends from 750 to 450 nanometers.

In general, input device wavelength falls into the following categories:

- Helium-neon Lasers: Devices employing HeNe lasers operate at 633 nanometers.

- Incandescent Light Sources: Scanners using incandescent light sources typically have a peak response (depending on the optional filter employed) in the 600 nanometer to 650 nanometer range.

Flash Lamps: Scanners with flash lamps usually have a peak response (depending on the filter) in the 550 nanometer to 650 nanometer range.

- Visible LEDs (light-emitting diodes): Visible LEDs used in wands and non-contact scanners have wavelengths in the 630 nanometer to 700 nanometer range.

- Infrared (IR) LEDs: IR LEDs used in wands and noncontact scanners have peak responses in the 850 nanometer to 920 nanometer range.

- Solid-state Laser Diodes: Until mid-1988, diode lasers were not readily available with wavelengths shorter than 780 nanometers. In late 1988, visible laser diodes operating at wavelengths in the 640 nanometer to 680 nanometer range began to be incorporated into bar code scanning equipment. Prices and wavelengths have both been falling. Input devices employing laser diodes operating near 630 nanometers are now available. As shown in Figure 7-15, eye sensitivity is much higher at 630 nanometers than at 680, thereby making it much easier to see the scanning beam with the newer units.

Specular Reflections
Because bar code scanning relies on the reflection of light from a symbol, we need to consider the two possible types of reflection that can occur at a label's surface: diffuse reflectance and specular reflectance.

Most people are familiar with the concept of specular reflectivity: this is the type of reflection that occurs on a mirror. High school physics courses teach that a beam of light reflected off a mirror is reflected at an angle such that the angle of reflection is equal to the angle of incidence, as shown in Figure 7-15.

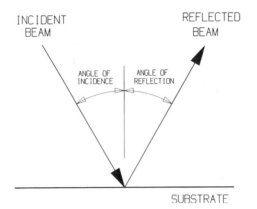

Figure 7-15: Specular Reflectivity. Specular reflection occurs from shiny surfaces and an incident beam is reflected intact.

Diffuse reflectance occurs from dull, matte, non-shiny surfaces such as paper. When a light beam is projected at a diffuse surface, the reflected light is radiated in a symmetric pattern. The energy reflected at a given angle is a function of the cosine of that angle (this is so-called Lambertian radiation). This concept is illustrated in Figure 7-16.

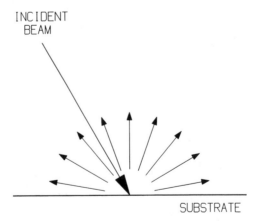

Figure 7-16: Diffuse Reflectivity. When light strikes a diffuse surface, it is reflected in all directions in amounts depending on the direction. The intensity of the reflected light at a given angle is proportional to the cosine of the angle (measured from a perpendicular to the surface). This is sometimes referred to as Lambertian radiation.

Ideally, bar code symbols would be printed on material possessing diffuse reflectivity characteristics. Within some range of angles to a line perpendicular to the symbol (typically 45 degrees), the input device would be assured of receiving back a reasonable amount of reflected light from the outgoing beam. If, however, a bar code symbol were printed on a perfect mirror, it would only be possible to read the symbol if the input device were perfectly perpendicular to the symbol, and then all of the outgoing light would be reflected back into the scanner, probably "blinding" it.

It is not typical to print bar codes on mirrors, but many materials and processes produce symbols with some appreciable specular reflectivity component. It will be difficult to scan these symbols if the input device is perfectly perpendicular to the symbol because the specular reflectivity will result in the bars looking just as reflective as the spaces. It is easy to identify symbols with a high specular component: hold up the symbol at a shallow angle, and see if you get bright reflections from the window or overhead lights. Clear, smooth laminates often produce strong specular reflectivity.

In order to avoid specular reflectivity problems, it is advisable to always orient the input device at an angle to the symbol. Ten or 15 degrees is a good angle for this purpose.

Resolution

The narrowest bar or space that an input device can resolve is a function of the spot size. The spot diameter (or width if an asymmetric shape is used) should ideally be no wider than the narrowest element of the symbol, although some devices do allow the use of a somewhat larger spot.

If the spot is considerably smaller than the symbol's narrowest element width, extraneous (but possibly allowable) printing specks, voids, and edge roughness might be misinterpreted as additional bars and spaces. To minimize this problem, it is desirable to match the input device's spot size to the narrow element width of the symbols employed.

A common problem is the use of a wide range of symbol densities in a given application. The spot size must be small enough to accommodate the narrowest element width that will be encountered. This means that the spot size will probably be too small for optimum performance on the symbols that have large X dimen-

Figure 7-17: Elongated Spot. Averaging along the bars is achieved by elongating the circular spot. This can reduce the effect of localized printing defects. In this diagram the effective spot shown is an ellipse. The elongated spot technique works best where the orientation of the symbol's bars is constrained to be parallel to the long axis of the spot.

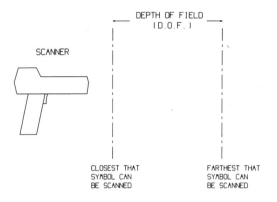

DEPTH OF FIELD
(D.O.F.)

SCANNER

CLOSEST THAT
SYMBOL CAN
BE SCANNED

FARTHEST THAT
SYMBOL CAN
BE SCANNED

Figure 7-18: Depth of Field. Depth of field defines the range of scanning distances that can be used for a given symbol's minimum element width, X. Depth of field is determined by the optical design of the scanner.

sions. To better handle a wide range of symbol densities, an elongated spot can be beneficially employed (see Figure 7-17). Such a spot aligned with its long axis parallel to the bars can provide averaging of some localized printing defects while maintaining the ability to operate with small element widths. Note that the spot needs to be aligned with bars. For this reason it is not suitable for use with wands but can be used with a moving beam or CCD device.

Depth of Field

Any noncontact input device has a certain range of distances over which a symbol can be successfully decoded. This range is called depth of field (DOF); see Figure 7-18.

The depth of field is a function of the symbol's X dimension. Larger values of X result in greater depth of field. This is similar to the depth of field effect in photography: larger objects appear to remain in focus over a wider range of camera-to-object distances than smaller objects.

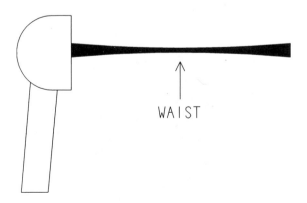

WAIST

Figure 7-19: Cross Section of a Scanning Beam. Every scanner has an effective scanning beam. The beam diameter is at a minimum at the waist of the beam. The beam diameter increases on both sides of the waist. Symbols with larger values of the minimum element width, X, can be read over a wider range of distances.

Laser Depth of Field: It is impossible to produce a light beam with constant diameter along its length: the beam diverges (the diameter increases) on either side of a minimum point, called the waist or focal point. This concept is illustrated in Figure 7-19, which is a cross section of a laser light beam from a noncontact laser scanner.

The diameter of the waist and its distance from the scanner are functions of the scanner's optical system. The rate of increase of the beam's diameter on either side of the waist is a function of the beam's wavelength and the waist diameter.

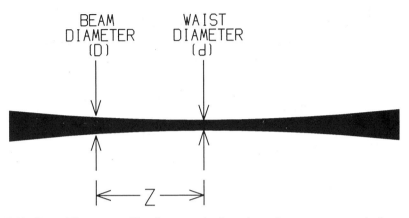

Figure 7-20: Beam Divergence. The diameter of a laser beam increases symmetrically on either side of the waist.

As shown in Figure 7-20, a laser beam's divergence is symmetrical on either side of the waist. The beam's diameter on either side of the waist is a function of the distance "Z" from the waist, the waist diameter "d," and the wavelength of the light. For a diffraction-limited beam, these parameters are related as follows:

$$D = \sqrt{d^2 + \left(\frac{4\lambda}{\pi d}\right)^2 Z^2}$$

where
D = diameter of beam at distance Z
d = waist diameter
λ = wavelength
Z = distance from waist

To use the above equation, the units of all dimensions must be the same. The following equation is for more conventionally used units:

$$D = \sqrt{d^2 + 0.0025\left(\frac{Z^2 \lambda^2}{d^2}\right)}$$

where
- D = diameter of beam (in mils) at distance Z
- d = waist diameter in mils
- λ = wavelength in nanometers
- Z = distance from waist in inches

The depth of field is that range of Z (on either side of the waist) that includes the area where D has not grown appreciably larger than X. Most scanning equipment can successfully decode a bar code symbol if the spot diameter D is no greater than $\sqrt{2}$ times the X dimension. Assuming that the waist diameter was initially set to $0.8X$, this implies a growth of $\sqrt{2}/0.8 = 1.77$ times. This factor allows us to substitute $D = 1.77d$ into the above equation to determine the depth of field for a given wavelength and X dimension. The relationship is:

$$\text{Depth of Field} = 58.3\frac{d^2}{\lambda}$$

where
depth of field is measured in inches
d is measured in mils
λ is measured in nanometers

Some scanners are able to operate successfully with a beam diameter of greater than $\sqrt{2}X$, therefore the above expression gives a conservative value of depth of field. Using those equations, depth of field will be calculated for a variety of X dimensions.

This analysis will assume a scanning wavelength of 633 nanometers. If the waist diameter is set equal to $0.8X$, the depth of field would be as shown in Table 7-1.

Table 7-1
Waist Diameter and Depth of Field

X (mils)	Waist Diameter (mils)	DOF (inches)
7.5	6.0	3.3
10.0	8.0	5.9
20.0	16.0	23.6
40.0	32.0	94.3

If a scanner has to accommodate a range of X dimensions, the waist diameter will have to remain fixed at a value consistent with the smallest value of X to be encountered.

Assuming that depth of field is the range of distances over which the beam diameter does not exceed $\sqrt{2}X$, the depth of field can be calculated for a given d, X, and λ from the following equation:

$$\text{Depth of Field} = \frac{40d^2}{\lambda}\sqrt{\frac{2\,X^2}{d^2}-1}$$

where
   depth of field is measured in inches
   X is measured in mils
   d is measured in mils
   λ is measured in nanometers

Assuming that the depth of field is defined as that range of distances extending out to the points where the beam diameter is equal to $\sqrt{2}X$, we can use the preceding equation to obtain the depth of field values shown in Table 7-2 for a wavelength of 633 nanometers

Table 7-2
Depth of Field Examples

X	DOF (inches) Waist Diameter		
(mils)	6 mils	10 mils	12 mils
7.5	3.3	2.2	– – –
10.0	4.9	6.3	5.7
12.0	6.0	8.7	9.1
16.0	8.3	12.8	14.6
20.0	10.5	16.7	19.4
40.0	21.3	35.2	41.9

CCD Depth of Field

The depth of field for a CCD scanner is calculated using similar approaches to traditional photography. In order to determine the total depth of field, it is necessary to know the magnification and numerical aperture of the lens system employed by the CCD camera, and the center-to-center spacing of the photodiodes in the CCD. Then,

$$\text{Depth of field} = 2NsM(M+1)$$

where
   N = the numerical aperture
   s = the photodiode center-to-center spacing
   M = the magnification of the camera's lens system

To determine the required magnification factor M, it is necessary to know the minimum X dimension of the symbols to be scanned, and a fill factor which we shall call "B." The fill factor is the ratio of the width of the image of the symbol's narrow elements on the image sensor to the photodiode center-to-center spacing.

Therefore,

$$M = X/(sB)$$

where
X = the width of the symbol's narrow elements
s = the photodiode center-to-center spacing
B = the fill factor

The fill factor B is often set to a value between 2 and 3. In most practical systems, M is typically greater than 50, therefore the DOF equation can be simplified as follows:

$$\text{Depth of field} = \frac{2NX^2}{(sB^2)}$$

In examining this last equation, it can be seen that the depth of field increases as the square of the X dimension. For a given value of X, the depth of field is a linear function of N. Therefore, one way of increasing the depth of field is to use a larger value of N (this corresponds to a smaller physical aperture diameter in the lens). Unfortunately, as N is increased, the symbol illumination requirements increase in a square relationship. This is why CCD scanners often use large numerical apertures in combination with very bright symbol illumination.

As discussed before, the effective depth of field for a CCD scanner can be increased by employing some type of autofocusing system.

7.2 Decoders

As described before, the decoder part of a bar code reading system analyzes the signal produced by the input device and deciphers the information encoded in the bar code symbol. The resulting data is either transmitted to an attached computer, stored locally for later transfer, or forwarded to an application program resident in the decoder itself.

The Decoding Process

All bar code reading systems contain a functional module that decodes the symbol's encoded information. In the typical contemporary reading system, this function is usually implemented in software running on a microprocessor, but it might also be realized by traditional hardwired logic. Whichever implementation is used, the following steps are included:

1. Determine whether the input device's spot is currently on a bar or a space. This determination is usually done by comparing the input device's output signal with a threshold value that is derived from recent scanning history. This is normally a function of the waveshaper.

2. Measure the width of each element as the input device's spot is scanned through the symbol. (In the case of symbologies that are best decoded by edge-to-similar-edge techniques, such as U.P.C., determine the T-distances.)

Except for the case of a CCD input device, actual physical measurements are not possible. Instead, the decoder measures the time taken for the input device's spot to traverse a given element of the symbol.

3. Quantize the symbol's element widths (or T-distances). For a two-width symbology, this means declaring element widths as either wide or narrow. For multiple width symbologies, the quantization may be down to four or more discrete levels (usually expressed in terms of a multiple of the X dimension or module width). A variety of algorithms (some are proprietary) have been employed to perform this quantization in the presence of nonuniform scanning velocity of the input device's spot, as might be produced by a manually scanned wand.

4. Decode the symbol's encoded data characters by comparing the quantized element widths (or T-distances) to a table of valid values for each character in the character set. To accommodate bi-directional scanning, the table of valid values has to include entries for symbols that have been scanned right to left as well as left to right.

5. If necessary, reverse the order of the decoded data characters to accommodate symbols that have been scanned right to left. The scanning direction is usually determined by examining the encoded pattern of the start and stop codes. The decoding algorithm will usually confirm that all characters have been scanned in the same direction. If a change of scanning direction is detected, the decoding is aborted.

6. Perform additional checks to confirm the validity of the scan. Such checks can include:

   • Confirmation of valid quiet zones

   • Correct check characters (if used)

   • Perceived scanning velocity is within predetermined limits

   • The perceived acceleration (character to character) is less than a predetermined maximum value which will reduce errors on contact scanners where the input device hangs up on a physical obstacle or bump

   • Secondary checks of message length, intercharacter gap, check characters, or other factors that can be used to enhance the overall data security

7. Transmit the decoded data to the next functional stage of the decoder. Note that additional row and symbol checking/assembly is required with Code 49, Code 16K, and PDF417.

Types of Decoders

Depending on their source of operating power and data communications scheme, decoders can be divided into three major categories: on-line, portable, and on-line portable:

On-Line Decoders: An on-line decoder is powered directly from the AC line. A hardwired connection transfers data between the decoder and the attached computer or data communications equipment.

On-line decoders are usually mounted in a fixed position (often bolted down) and require that the symbol be brought to the reader. Keyboards (either attached or integral), displays, and slot readers are often part of an on-line reader. Typical devices are shown in Figure 7-21.

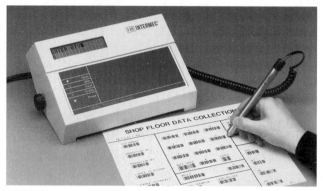

Courtesy of Intermec Corp.

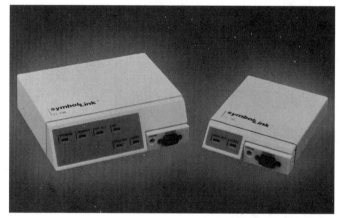

Courtesy of Symbol Technologies, Inc.

Figure 7-21: Typical On-Line Decoders. Several on-line decoders are shown here; they are connected directly to a data collection network for an application. They usually are powered by commercial AC power.

Portable Decoders: Portable decoders contain on-board data storage and are powered by batteries. Data is retained as it is collected and is then dumped to a host computer at a convenient time. A real-time radio link could also be used to transfer data from the portable to the computer. A portable reader is normally brought to the symbol, as in the case of an inventory control application when a physical inventory is performed. Typical devices are shown in Figure 7-22.

Courtesy of Intermec Corp.

Courtesy of Telxon Corp.

Courtesy of Datalogic Optic Electronics, Inc.

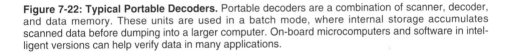

Figure 7-22: Typical Portable Decoders. Portable decoders are a combination of scanner, decoder, and data memory. These units are used in a batch mode, where internal storage accumulates scanned data before dumping into a larger computer. On-board microcomputers and software in intelligent versions can help verify data in many applications.

Early portable terminals used tape cassettes to store data, but all modern units now use semiconductor memory to retain data. CMOS memory chips require very little power to retain data and are ideally suited for use in portable terminals with battery power supplies.

There are two basic types of memory chips: RAM (random access memory) and ROM (read only memory). The data can be changed in a RAM chip. RAM memory is volatile, which means the data stored in it can be lost if power is disconnected. ROMs are nonvolatile which means that they retain data indefinitely. Most ROMs are preprogrammed by the manufacturer, and typically hold the software used to run the microcomputer in the portable terminal. This software provides the basic operations in a portable terminal: decoding, data transmission, display handling, etc. Data that is being collected is always stored in RAM. If this is not confusing enough, new memory devices starting to be introduced in the early 1990s combine some of the characteristics of RAM and ROM—so-called nonvolatile RAM technology will not lose data when power is removed.

Sometimes ROM can be programmed on a custom basis by the user, but special equipment is often required to write ROM patterns. Depending on the portable terminal's design, ROM or RAM can be used to retain any user application programs and reference databases required by the field application. In applications where a fixed reference database is needed for use in the field, portables with ROM technology fit well.

The amount of memory required is a function of the size of the user application program (if present), the amount of data to be collected in RAM, and the frequency that data will be dumped. RAM or ROM capacity is specified in bytes or kilobytes or megabytes. Typical portable units have somewhere between 64 kilobytes and 1 megabyte.

A byte can hold one alphanumeric or ASCII character. If only numeric data is used, it is possible to pack two digits into one byte. When this is done, a manufacturer will sometimes quote a numerical digit capacity that is twice the actual byte capacity. (These half bytes are sometimes called "nibbles" or "nybbles.")

When data is being extracted from a portable terminal as part of the dumping process, it is important that errors not be introduced. If large amounts of data are involved, the transmission time can be appreciable. It takes over nine minutes to transfer 64 kilobytes of data at 1200 baud on a serial line.

Most portable terminals can communicate with RS-232 compatible electrical signals, although in some cases an external interface device is required. RS-232 can be directly interfaced to most computer systems. If long distances are involved, modems are employed on either end of the link. A direct RS-232 connection can easily support communication rates of up to 19,200 baud or higher. The actual rates are limited by the hardware of the computer port to which the terminal is connected.

In order to guard against errors, the data is transmitted in a series of short blocks. Each block has additional error checking characters added that are algorithmically based on the data characters. One commonly used algorithm is called the "cyclic redundancy check" or CRC calculation. Only correctly transmitted data will result in the same calculated error-checking characters. The receiving computer examines these check characters and can request a retransmission of the block if discrepancies are detected. Using this acknowledge/negative acknowledge (ACK/NAK) protocol, reliable data can be transmitted through imperfect communication links, but additional time will be required.

Some portable terminals include built-in modems that can communicate at up to 2400 baud. These can be directly connected to the phone line and use the ACK/NAK protocol.

Many new portables incorporate one or more slots for PCMCIA (Personal Computer Memory Card International Association) devices. A variety of products have been developed for PCMCIA slots, including modems, faxes, LAN ports, wireless links, and memory devices. Three different mechanical slot widths are specified and are referred to as Type I, II, or III. It is even possible to have a small hard disk plug in to a PCMCIA slot! These cards were originally designed for handheld and lap top computers, but they have much utility in bar code data collection also. It is reasonable to assume that a PCMCIA card will ultimately be developed that incorporates a complete bar code scanner (except perhaps for the input device), allowing bar code scanning to be easily added to existing computers.

Acoustically coupled modems are available from some vendors and permit the use of any standard telephone handset to communicate with a remote computer.

Acoustic modems are usually limited to low data rates (300 baud or less). Some internal acoustic modems are one way: data cannot be sent from the computer to the terminal in order to support any error-checking protocol. To ensure data security, the complete contents of memory are transmitted two or more times; the receiving computer compares the multiple transmissions, and only accepts data that has been matched. This one-way acoustic transfer can involve significant time if large amounts of data are to be transferred.

All portable terminals use batteries to provide power. The two basic types are rechargeable (such as NiCad) and nonrechargeable (such as alkaline or lithium). Many portable terminals have two battery systems. A primary battery system runs the unit, and a backup battery (usually lithium) retains data in memory when the terminal is not turned on or while the main battery is being changed. Although NiCad batteries have been prevalent for many years, metal hydride technology is starting to be used to power portable data collection devices: this newer technology offers more battery capacity in a given size while eliminating the NiCad "memory effect." New rechargeable batteries are currently being developed that use more exotic chemistries. These will ultimately result in longer battery life and/or smaller size and lower weight.

The expected life of a set of batteries or a charge is dependent on the input device technology employed, the number of symbols to be scanned, and the use of any accessories or display lights.

Almost all portable terminals include some form of programmability. If equipped with an application program, a portable terminal becomes an extremely powerful device, incorporating databases, prompts, file manipulation, error messages and/or custom communication routines. Integral application programs allow transactions to be verified and/or edited at the time of data capture.

Programming languages for portables vary considerably between vendors. Some offer BASIC and/or C, while others offer languages specifically tailored to data collection, such as IRL or TCAL. Actual program development and/or debugging can be done on a personal computer or (in some units) on the actual portable terminal itself. Once tested, the application programs can be stored as a computer file, stored in a portable terminal's RAM, or programmed into a form of ROM called EPROM (for "erasable programmable ROM"). An EPROM will permanently retain the application program in a portable terminal even if the backup battery fails. For storing application programs, EPROM is rapidly being replaced by a more flexible nonvolatile technology referred to as "Flash Memory."

Newer "high end" portables are available that are designed to run general purpose computer operating systems such as MS-DOS. When so equipped, considerable flexibility is provided: a wide range of application software and developed tools are then available for ready use. One disadvantage is that memory requirements are likely to be higher for these more flexible, "open system units."

On-Line Portable Decoders: A recent development in portable data collection is the use of radio links between the portable terminal and the host computer. Rather than store collected data in the portable terminal's limited memory, it is transmitted directly to the computer. Prompts and error messages are transmitted from the computer to the portable terminal.

At the computer side of the link, a controller is used that can communicate with several different terminals on the same VHF or UHF frequency. Data transmission rates are in the 1200 to 4800 baud range if narrow band equipment is used, or over 100 kilobaud if a broadband (spread spectrum) system is used (see the separate chapter on RF networking).

Because of the transmitter and receiver power requirements, battery life is lower for an RF-linked portable terminal than for a traditional store-and-dump unit. RF terminals are often used on vehicles, where the vehicle's main battery is the power source. Representative radio-linked products are shown in Figure 7-23.

Courtesy of Intermec Corp.

Figure 7-23: Typical Radio-Linked Portable Reader Products. A portable decoder attached to a radio frequency transceiver becomes an on-line radio reader. This photo shows a vehicle-mounted terminal, a base station controller, and a portable RF terminal.

This type of decoder allows the reader to be brought to the symbol without sacrificing on-line interactivity. Although radio transmission is most commonly used for on-line portable decoders, other means of data communication such as optical links could also be used.

Operator Interface

Unless a fixed mount input device is used, an operator is associated with each bar code reading system. The particular application often requires that prompts or error messages be sent to the operator. This can take several forms:

1. Programmable beeps: the attached computer is able to cause the reading system to sound a series of controllable beeps. The number and tone of the beeps are usually programmable.

2. Status lights: The reading system can be controlled to selectively illuminate status lights that are located on the decoder; these lights have special significance in a given application and are labeled accordingly.

3. Displays: the decoder can include a display that is visible to the operator. This display may present numeric or alphanumeric messages to the operator in one or several lines, using LCD, LED, VF, CRT, Plasma, or other technologies.

Some applications require the use of a keyboard to enter exception data. This keyboard may consist of purely numeric keys, dedicated function keys, a full alphanumeric keyboard, or a combination. The error rate with keyboard use is expected to be far higher than when scanning bar code symbols. Some units have large displays and "touch screen" overlays. The actual keyboard boxes are shown on the display, and the operator touches the selection with a finger or pencil. If equipped with a high-resolution display and digitizer, some devices can actually capture signatures and other graphical information. In this respect, portable data collection terminals can have many similarities with the PDA's (Personal Digital Assistant) being developed in the computer industry.

Local Intelligence

Independent of other selection criteria, bar code reading systems can be divided into two generic categories: nonintelligent readers and intelligent readers. In a nonintelligent reader, data from the decoding process is passed in an unaltered format to either the host computer (on-line or wireless portable) or is stored (portable reader). In the case of an on-line reader, the host computer's application program is a part of every transaction. Figure 7-24 shows a block diagram of a nonintelligent reader.

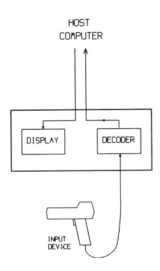

Figure 7-24: Nonintelligent Reader Concept. The simplest bar code reader is the nonintelligent device that simply decodes the bar code pattern and sends it to a host computer. Some form of visual and/or audio display is required to provide operator feedback from the host. In the reader itself, data are not checked or altered during passage to and from the host.

An intelligent reader is illustrated in Figure 7-25. Data from the decoding process interacts with an application program that is resident in the reader. This application program can perform local data editing on validation and can reformat the data. Prompts and error messages are generated locally, off-loading the host computer, and providing extremely short response time to the operator.

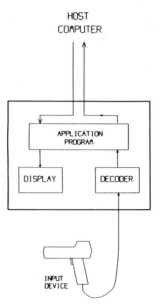

Figure 7-25: Intelligent Reader Concept. Intelligence for this kind of reader comes from an on-board microcomputer and its software. Local editing and data validation lower communications overhead and host computer processing requirements, resulting in more immediate response to the operator.

The local application program is typically retained in nonvolatile memory (i.e., it isn't lost if the reader loses power) and can be loaded into the reader via several different methods:

- Download from a host computer

- Transfer from another reader

- Enter via a locally attached CRT

- Enter via a connected or integral keyboard

- Enter via scanning a series of bar code symbols

- Plug in a pre-programmed chip or cartridge

The intelligent reader provides distributed intelligence to a data collection system, allowing for improved system response and off-loading the host computer. An intelligent reader can be operated in a store-and-forward mode, allowing data capture to continue at the reader level, even if the host computer is inoperative or unavailable. When the computer is back on-line, it can retrieve the transactional data that was stored in the intelligent reader's memory.

All communication to and from the host computer is handled by the application program; there is no direct connection between the data interface port and the reader's decoder, display, or keyboard (if present).

The actual application program is written in a high-level programming language. This high-level language is converted to machine code by an interpreter or compiler. Some equipment manufacturers require that this conversion be performed on a separate software development system; others allow this process to occur in the reader itself.

Autodiscrimination

As discussed in earlier chapters, there are many different symbologies that have been developed, several of which are in common use today. Most reading equipment includes the capability to decode several different symbologies. The user configures his reader to the desired choice by setting switches, scanning control labels, or sending commands from the host computer. The scanner's configuration is typically retained in some sort of nonvolatile configuration memory.

Readers are also available that can automatically recognize which symbology has been scanned, then use the appropriate decoding algorithm. The data is decoded independently of the symbology used. Called autodiscrimination, this feature is extremely useful when several different symbologies are encountered in a given application. The operator configures the reader with the list of symbologies that will be allowed, by setting switches or scanning control labels.

Limiting the list of allowed symbologies is advisable for a couple of reasons. It minimizes the probability that an inadvertent scan of a random bar code symbol will result in incorrect data being gathered. This, in turn, affects data security. Although the theoretical probability of a symbology recognition error is very low, there is a finite probability of a partial scan of one symbology's being recognized as a valid scan in another symbology. For many symbology combinations, this appears to be a small problem, but localized printing errors or extraneous markings on the substrate can combine with partial scans to create an operational concern. Limiting the list will also speed up the decoding process in most readers.

Opinions as to the magnitude of this effect in actual scanning applications differs. The probability of undetected errors entering a data capture system can be reduced through the use of bearer bars to eliminate partial scans and secondary data checking (perhaps in an intelligent reader's application program) of message length, data type, check characters, etc.

There is a problem in autodiscrimination of Interleaved 2 of 5 and Code 39. If Code 39 has been printed with a wide intercharacter gap (greater than 2X), certain partial scans of Code 39 can appear to be valid scans of an Interleaved 2 of 5 symbol. This can be eliminated by printing the Code 39 symbol with a nominal intercharacter gap width of 1X.

Certain partial scans of Interleaved 2 of 5 can appear to be valid scans of Code 39. This can be prevented by accepting only Code 39 messages that have more than N/2 characters, where N is the number of digits in all of the application's Interleaved 2 of 5 symbols. Both of these problems can also be avoided through the use of bearer bars.

With moving beam input devices, the incorporation of voting algorithms (the requirement that several scanning passes decode as the same message) can also reduce the potential for data errors induced by autodiscrimination characteristics.

Symbology Identifiers

With an autodiscriminating reader, the transmitted (or stored) data may have actually been encoded in one of several different symbologies. In some applications it is useful to know which symbology was just read. In order to identify the symbology associated with a particular message, AIM published a standard that described a scheme of inserting a prefix before the decoded message is transmitted or stored. The prefix is of the form:

]cm

where:

] = the symbol identifier flag

c = the code identification character

m = a modifier character giving additional information about the reader's mode or the symbology decoded.

The code identification characters are listed in Appendix L.

Manufacturer adoption of this particular symbology identification scheme is somewhat limited.

7.3 Interfacing Readers

Almost all applications involving bar code readers require that they be interfaced to a computer system. A variety of techniques and equipment are available to perform this function.

Keyboard Wedges

The term "wedge" is used to describe a class of bar code readers designed to be connected in series with the keyboard of a personal computer or CRT terminal

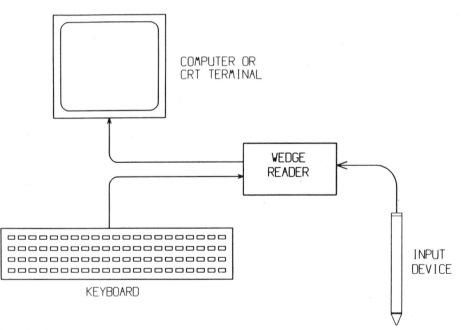

Figure 7-26: Keyboard Wedge Concept. The keyboard wedge emulates the operation of a detached keyboard for a terminal or personal computer. The keyboard plugs into the wedge, and the wedge in turn plugs into the original receptacle for the keyboard. The bar code scanner plugs into the wedge.

that is equipped with a detachable keyboard. The keyboard can still be used normally, but data resulting from the scanning of a bar code symbol will be treated by the PC or terminal as though it originated from the keyboard. Figure 7-26 illustrates the physical arrangement.

A keyboard wedge allows bar code reading capability to be rapidly added to an existing computer without requiring special programming. Wedges are sometimes equipped with auxiliary ports for transferring data from a portable terminal. It is possible to purchase replacement keyboards for some personal computers that incorporate a built in wand-type bar code reader.

ASCII Wedges

Most non-IBM mini-computers transfer data to and from attached terminals by means of asynchronous transmission of ASCII characters. Many bar code readers are provided with dual data connectors, allowing them to be connected in series with the terminal as shown in Figure 7-27. The actual data communication may employ RS-232, RS-422, or current loop levels.

Data from the host computer passes through the reader to the terminal's display.

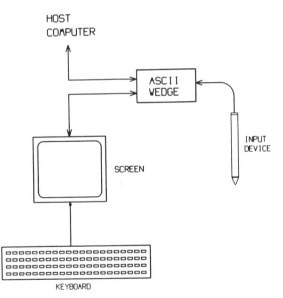

Figure 7-27: ASCII Wedge Concept. In the ASCII wedge connection, ordinary asynchronous RS-232C lines are used instead of the hardware dependent interconnections of the keyboard wedge. An ASCII wedge allows bar code data collection capability to be added easily to an existing asynchronous terminal, whether or not it has a detachable keyboard.

Data from the terminal's keyboard passes through the reader to the host computer. Data from the bar code reader is transmitted to the host computer as though it originated at the keyboard. No special software is required to interface the bar code reader.

Direct Connection

Bar code reading equipment is often interfaced to a host computer without being associated with a PC or terminal. A keyboard and/or display may be provided. The simplest interface is a direct, point-to-point connection, as shown in Figure 7-28.

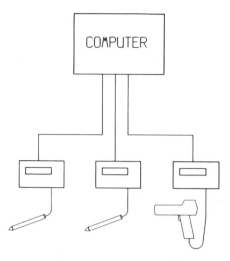

Figure 7-28: Point-to-Point Interface Concept. Devices are linked by dedicated connections in a point-to-point interface. Interconnection requires one I/O port for each bar code terminal.

The direct, point-to-point interface usually uses asynchronous ASCII data, and RS-232, RS-422, or current loop levels. Larger computers use terminal controllers to interface to attached peripherals.

If insufficient ports are available to support the required number of readers, a port concentrator can be used. A port concentrator communicates to the host via a single link but handles traffic to a quantity of bar code (or other) equipment via a series of point-to-point or multidrop lines, as shown in Figure 7-29. Further information on the network architecture and interfacing appears in Chapter 10.

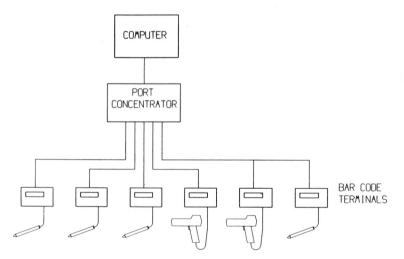

Figure 7-29: Port Concentrator Concept. A port concentrator is a specialized computer that interfaces multiple I/O ports for bar code and other peripherals. The port concentrator in turn talks to the host computer via a single port instead of many. This allows a network of connected devices to be controlled from a single port on the host.

8

Conveyor Bar Code Scanners

Automated material handling systems are becoming more and more prevalent. High-speed conveyors, diverters, packaging lines, transfer machines, and AS/RS (automated shipping/receiving systems) are being used to speed the flow of goods, reduce inventory levels, and increase industrial productivity. There are many applications where it is necessary to automatically scan bar code symbols affixed to objects as they are transported on a conveyor. Historically, these applications have been addressed with fixed mount, moving beam laser scanners; although vision-based systems (see Chapter 9) are starting to make inroads.

Some operating environments are quite controlled: symbols are in the same location on every object to be scanned, and the symbol orientation is fixed. Other scanning environments are more complicated: symbol position and orientation are unknown, or perhaps there is no control over the object surface that the symbol is located on. Scanner complexity is a function of the control with which symbols are placed and oriented.

High-performance conveyor laser scanners are often totally self-contained in a single physical unit, but they are sometimes split into two or more interconnected packages at the high end of the performance range. Unlike handheld scanners, it is uncommon to refer to the "input device" and "decoder" when describing fixed mount, moving beam laser scanners: the partitioning of the product architecture differs greatly between vendors.

8.1 Orientation-Dependent Laser Scanning

Many companies manufacture laser scanners that can be used when the symbol orientation is fixed in a given application. An internal scanning mechanism oper-

Courtesy of Microscan Systems, Inc.

Figure 8-1: Typical Fixed Mount, Moving Beam Scanner.

ates at high speed, usually in the range of 40 to 1000 scans per second producing a single scan line, allowing data to be captured from rapidly moving conveyor lines.

The scanning line may either be vertical or horizontal. As shown in Figure 8-2, these orientations are suitable for scanning ladder or picket fence bar code symbols.

PICKET FENCE ORIENTATION   LADDER ORIENTATION

Figure 8-2: Orientation. The two standard orientations for symbols on packages moving past scanners are referred to a "ladder" and "picket fence." Picket fence symbols have the bars running vertically. Ladder symbols have the bars running horizontally.

The scanning line length, scanning rate, bar height, symbol orientation, and conveyor speed should be such that the scanner has a minimum of four or five complete scanning opportunities as the symbol moves by. Often these units are equipped with raster scan adapters that move the scan line in a direction perpendicular to the scanning motion. This allows a larger area of the symbol to be examined, maximizing the probability of a good scan, even in the presence of marginal print quality or poor symbol placement.

In a system using a fixed mount, moving beam scanner, the relative orientation of the symbol and scanner should be arranged to maximize the chances of a successful read, even in the presence of a localized printing defect. A vertical scan line and ladder symbol orientation are ideally suited. The symbol's bar height contains redundant information, and by varying this dimension, it is possible to control the number of scanning opportunities for a given conveyor speed.

If the bar code symbol is arranged in a picket fence orientation, the fixed mount, moving beam scanner should have its scanning line tilted a few degrees off horizontal. As shown in Figure 8-3, this will allow more of the symbol's area to be scanned as the symbol moves by. Note that the maximum allowable tilt is a function of the symbol's bar height.

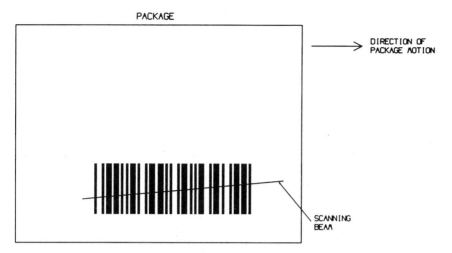

Figure 8-3: Scanning Picket Fence Symbols. The scanning line can be tilted slightly. The vertical redundancy built into the symbol's bar height allows fairly wide tolerance in the location and tilt of the scanning line.

Because of the high scanning speeds involved, fixed mount, moving beam scanners are usually restricted in the number of symbologies or message lengths that they can handle automatically. The decoding process is often accomplished with specialized electronic circuitry, rather than using software algorithms.

An external package sensor is usually mounted upstream of the scanner (see Figure 8-4). This photoelectric sensor turns on the scanning line when an object is detected. The scanning continues until either a successful decode occurs or an internal timer turns off the light source.

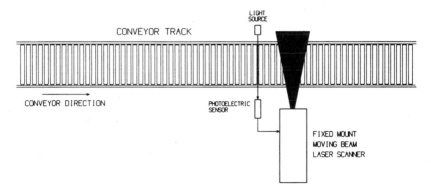

Figure 8-4: Placement of Package Sensor in an Automated Conveyor System. Real-time tracking of a bar coded object's position can be provided by a package sensor in an automated system. The scanner is activated just before the symbol moves into the reading area. Acquisition of the bar coded data identifies the particular object passing the scanner. A typical sensor is a photoelectric beam that is interrupted by passage of the object being tracked.

Fixed mount, moving beam scanners usually employ helium-neon lasers or solid-state laser diodes but they can also be designed with linear CCDs.

8.2 Omnidirectional Laser Scanning

Omnidirectional scanning is possible with specialized versions of fixed mount, moving beam scanners. A series of straight or curved scanning lines of varying directions, in the form of a "starburst" Lissajous pattern or other multi-angle arrangement, are projected at the symbol. One of more of them will be able to cross all of the symbol's bars and spaces, no matter what the orientation (assuming that the bars are tall enough). The scanners that are commonly seen built into counter tops at supermarkets fall into this category. Figure 8-5 illustrates an example of an omnidirectional scanner intended for industrial applications.

Courtesy of Accu-Sort Systems, Inc.

Figure 8-5. Omnidirectional Fixed Mount Scanner. Multiple scanning lines provide omnidirectional scanning of symbols that have sufficiently tall bars.

There is a strong relationship between the symbol's aspect ratio (ratio of bar height to symbol length) and the number of scanning lines required to provide complete omnidirectionality. Assume for a moment that the laser scanner projects a series of scan lines that are uniformly arranged at different angles. It is obvious that omnidirectional scanning can be accomplished using fewer scan lines if the aspect ratio is large, as illustrated in Figure 8-6.

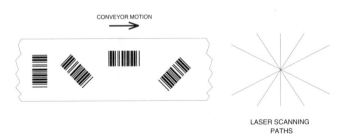

CONVEYOR MOTION

LASER SCANNING
PATHS

Figure 8-6: Omnidirectional Scanning. For omnidirectional scanners, fewer scan lines are required if the symbol aspect ratio is larger.

Various vendors have developed laser-based products for omnidirectional scanning using a wide range of scanning patterns. Some use starburst arrangements of laser lines, others use combinations of fixed lines with moving patterns. All are attempting to provide full omnidirectional scanning across the complete width of a conveyor while allowing the smallest possible aspect ratio. One way of simplifying the problem is to use a technique known as "scan stitching": special software is able to piece together adjacent partial scans of a linear symbol, eliminating the need for at least one scan line to pass through all the symbol's bars and spaces in a single path. Using scan stitching, it is possible to omnidirectionally scan linear symbologies down to an aspect ratio of approximately 0.25, whereas more conventional equipment has a practical lower aspect ratio limit of approximately 0.4. These scan stitching approaches often require lower conveyor speeds, and they can sometimes be "fooled" by the close proximity of other symbols.

9

Vision-Based Scanning

Noncontact scanning of linear bar code symbols has typically been performed using some form of laser scanner. A laser spot is repetitively scanned in a pattern, with the hope that at least one of the scanning paths will pass completely through a bar code symbol. Handheld laser scanners usually scan the laser spot in a straight line, and the operator is required to aim and orient the device so that the visible line passes through all of the bars and spaces of the symbol. Some handheld laser scanners use a rastering laser scan pattern in order to scan 2-D stacked symbologies that have controlled orientations.

The problem becomes somewhat more complicated if the application requires that bar code symbols on items be automatically read as the items move along on a conveyor line. If the location and orientation of the symbol can be carefully controlled, it is possible that an accurately pre-aligned fixed mount laser scanner projecting only a single scanning line can read the symbol. If the symbol orientation is known, but the location is not fixed, it is possible that a "rastering" laser scanner can help assure a high read rate. If neither the symbol's orientation nor its location are fixed, then a wide coverage omnidirectional laser scanner is required.

Omnidirectional laser scanners use multiple scan lines, sometimes in combination with "partial scan reconstruction" (or "scan stitching") in order to maximize the chance of actually decoding a symbol as it passes by the scanner. The various scan lines are projected at a variety of angles and positions. In order to be scanned omnidirectionally by a laser scanner, a symbol must have tall bars. Omnidirectional laser scanners typically require an aspect ratio of 0.4 or greater, although some slower equipment can tolerate smaller values.

The 2-D stacked symbologies are extremely difficult to read omnidirectionally with laser scanning technology. In practice, 2-D matrix or height modulated symbologies cannot be omnidirectionally scanned using laser-based equipment.

Vision-based scanning has the ability to overcome the above-described deficiencies that are associated with laser equipment. In either fixed mount or handheld form, a vision-based scanner can omnidirectionally scan 2-D stacked symbologies, 2-D matrix symbologies, height-modulated symbologies, and conventional linear symbologies with small aspect ratios. Recent developments in powerful digital signal processing (DSP) chips, high resolution imagers, and pattern recognition software have made this technology possible.

This is a specialized form of machine vision. No lasers are used. Basically, an electronic "picture" is taken that includes the symbol(s) to be read, and special-purpose software algorithms running on powerful DSP chips are used to find and decode the symbol(s).

There are three basic types of vision-based scanners that are available: handheld vision scanners, fixed mount vision scanners using 2-D imagers, and fixed mount vision scanners using 1-D imagers.

9.1 Handheld Vision Scanners

A handheld scanner based on vision technology incorporates some means of capturing a 2-D image of the area that is being examined. The electronic image is stored in the device's memory, and a DSP is used to find and decode any symbols that are present in the image. The scanner incorporates a means for illuminating the symbol. Figure 9-1 is a block diagram of a handheld vision scanner.

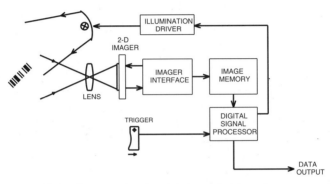

Figure 9-1: Handheld Vision Scanner. An electronic image is taken of a scene, and a DSP is used to find and decode the symbol(s).

Early handheld vision scanners required that physical contact be made with the symbol, but equipment is now available that allows scanning at a moderate distance. Initial units partitioned the block diagram shown in Figure 9-1 so that only the camera portion was held in the hand: a cable connected the camera to another package containing the bulk of the electronics. Units are now available that are totally self-contained, as is shown in Figure 9-2.

Scanners like that shown in Figure 9-2 incorporate a trigger. When the operator depresses the trigger, an illumination system (LED's or flash lamp) is momentarily activated, a "snapshot" of the field of view is taken, and the DSP begins processing the image. A repetitive mode could also be imagined, whereby multiple operations continue as long as the trigger is depressed until a symbol is successfully decoded.

The most convenient imaging component for a vision scanner is a 2-D CCD array. These components are commonly used in home camcorders, and resolution is typically 750 x 500 pixels. This finite resolution limits the size of the symbol that

Figure 9-2: Self-Contained, Noncontact Handheld Vision Scanner. This device is self-contained and directly produces decoded data.

can be read: the longest dimension of the symbol (in modules) must be less than one half the number of pixels in the shorter direction of the imager if full omnidirectional scanning is required. For example, if the scanner's 2-D imager has a 750 x 500 pixel resolution, the longest Code 128 symbol that can be omnidirectionally scanned is 22 characters total. Higher resolution 2-D imagers are available, but the cost is significantly higher. It is conceivable that multiple imagers (or one imager with a controllable beam-splitting means) could be used to achieve the same functionality as a single higher-resolution device at a price in design complexity.

Instead of using a 2-D CCD imager, a linear CCD array could be combined with an opto-mechanical scanner mechanism to capture a 2-D image. This technique adds complexity, but quite high resolution is achievable.

9.2 Fixed Mount Vision Scanners

The same approaches used in handheld vision scanners can obviously be applied in fixed mount equipment. Two different approaches are used: A 2-D imager can be used to take a "snapshot" of a scene, or a continuously strobed 1-D imager can be used in conjunction with a moving conveyor to examine a continuous image of objects moving by in front of it. Either approach can operate in an unattended manner, and all of the advantages of vision-based scanning are possible.

The hardware for a fixed mount scanner based on a 2-D imager can actually be put together with "off the shelf" components. A standard CCD camera (as might be used for video taping or security applications) can be connected to a "frame grabber" board in a personal computer. Assuming that appropriate lighting and optics are used, it will be possible to capture still images of the scene of interest. Specialized software is required in the personal computer to find and decode any machine readable symbols in the scene. The software can become quite complex (and slow) if it is required to find symbols in a cluttered background and decode them omnidirectionally. The performance of the system is limited both by the available computing power and by the limitations of the CCD camera and frame grabber. Most commonly-available cameras have somewhat limited resolution (typically 500 by 400 pixels), and the video bandwidth is limited by the applicable standard interfaces (NTSC or PAL). The net result of these shortcomings is that performance is limited if a system is put together using standard television components. However, perfectly adequate performance can be achievable if short mes-

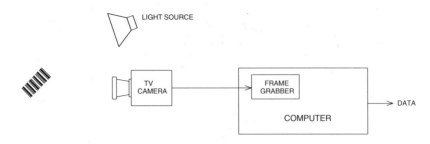

Figure 9-3: Fixed Mount Vision-Based Scanner. This type of scanner can be put together with readily available cameras, frame grabbers, and personal computers. Specialized software is required, and performance is often somewhat limited.

sages are used, especially if high efficiency 2-D matrix symbologies are used. Figure 9-3 shows a typical system.

Depending on the symbology chosen, and the system features desired, it might take a second or more for a personal computer to find a symbol in the field of view and decode it. If this equipment is required to scan symbols on items moving along a conveyor, the transport speeds must be quite low, and it may be necessary to trigger the scanner to only "take a picture" when it is known that there is a symbol in front of the camera. In order to eliminate blurring of the image due to transport motion in the frame grabber, it is possible to use a strobed illumination scheme or a high speed electronic shutter in the camera itself.

Under some situations normal room lighting (or sunlight) is sufficient for operation of the 2-D CCD camera, but most applications use dedicated lights to ensure appropriate illumination of the symbol.

Rather than using a commercial frame grabber, CCD camera, and personal computer, higher performance is possible if specially built hardware is used. This can eliminate the "bottleneck" that is often caused by the use of NTSC or PAL standards, thereby proving higher resolution and/or faster decoding. Rather than using the general purpose microprocessor typically present in a personal computer, this specialized equipment often contains dedicated DSP (Digital Signal Processor) chips that dramatically improve the image processing throughput.

A more complex approach is necessary to scan symbols on rapidly moving conveyor lines, especially if omnidirectional scanning, 2-D matrix symbologies, and/or large conveyor widths are used. This type of equipment is usually custom-built for the particular application, and almost always uses a high-resolution 1-D CCD imager oriented perpendicular to the direction of conveyor motion. The CCD writes successive lines of digitized image data into a video memory as the conveyor line moves, thereby building up a two-dimensional electronic image in memory. This is a continuous process: new lines of image data are being written into the memory as old ones are "falling off the end" of the memory. Powerful processing hardware is configured to find and decode symbols as they appear in the video memory. Figure 9-4 shows a representative piece of equipment.

Figure 9-4: High Speed Conveyor Belt Scanner. This type of scanner is typically mounted above a conveyor line, and it uses a 1-D CCD imager and powerful signal-processing hardware to omnidirectionally scan symbols as they move down the conveyor belt at high speed.

The rate at which data is read from the 1-D CCD is set such that the effective resolution of the electronic image in the video memory has equal resolution in the X and Y axes. As the conveyor speed varies, the imager strobe rate is adjusted to maintain appropriate resolution.

One of the limiting technical parameters with this equipment is the rate at which video data must be extracted from the linear CCD and processed. Although normal NTSC video bandwidths are less than 4.5 MHz, the bandwidth necessary for some scanning applications exceeds 20 MHz. In order to appreciate this parameter, we will calculate these requirements from basic application information.

Any CCD-based imaging system analyzes an image in terms of pixels of data. To resolve individual bar and space widths in order to be able to recognize and decode symbols, there must be a sufficient number of pixels with respect to the symbol's X dimension. A term called Beta is commonly used to describe the ratio of the symbol's X dimension to the pixel pitch. As expounded by Nyquist, the sampling theorem suggests that it might be possible to build equipment that can successfully decode linear width modulated symbols using a Beta approaching 1.0. In real world scanning situations, this is impractical, and most equipment employs a Beta of 2.0 or greater for width modulated symbologies. 2-D Matrix symbologies use even larger values of Beta.

Knowing the smallest X dimension to be encountered in an application, and knowing the Beta required by the software, it is possible to calculate the minimum number of pixels required in the 1-D CCD imager as a function of the width of the conveyor belt to be covered:

$$N = \frac{Beta *W}{X}$$

Where:
- N   is the number of pixels required
- Beta   is the desired ratio between X and the pixel pitch on the imager
- W   is the coverage width required for the conveyor
- X   is the smallest symbol X dimension to be encountered

In order to give the same apparent image resolution in both axes, the frequency that the imager will need to be strobed can be calculated as a function of conveyor speed as follows:

$$R = \frac{Beta * S}{X}$$

Where:

R   is the required strobe frequency (in Hz) for the imager
Beta is the desired ratio between X and the pixel pitch on the imager
S   is the linear speed of the conveyor
X   is the smallest symbol X dimension to be encountered

It should be apparent that the data rate from the imager into the scanner's video memory in Hz is simply equal to N times R. Therefore, combining the above equations and taking care of units of measure, we can show that the data rate is:

$$F = \frac{Beta^2 * S * W}{X^2}$$

Where

F   is the data rate from the imager (in MHz)
S   is the conveyor speed (in inches per second)
W   is the coverage width required for the conveyor (in inches)
Beta is the desired ratio between X and the pixel pitch on the imager
X   is the smallest symbol X dimension to be encountered (in mils)

As an example, if an application will be using symbols with a 15 mil X dimension on a conveyor that is 30 inches wide and moving at 50 inches per second (250 feet per minute), the data rate out of the imager will be almost 27 MHz if the system's Beta is 2.0. It can be seen that there is an inverse square relationship between the data rate and the X dimension, but only a linear relationship between the conveyor speed and the data rate. Therefore, it should be apparent that a given scanner can handle a maximum conveyor speed that is 4 times faster if the symbol X dimension is doubled.

So far, the discussion has assumed that symbols were being scanned directly on the surface of the conveyor. The situation changes if overhead scanning is required of varying height objects. See figure 9-5, which shows a cross section of a conveyor belt with an overhead camera.

In examining Figure 9-5, it is apparent that the scanner's optics will have to be set such that the entire width of the tallest object is covered. This implies that for shorter objects, an "overscan" situation will exist. This is not a problem, but it does mean that a dimension wider than the actual conveyor width will have to be used in calculating the system data rate, perhaps resulting in performance limitations in a given application. Obviously, the amount of overscan can be reduced by mounting the camera a long way from the conveyor belt (perhaps folding the optical path through the use of mirrors), but other limitations come into play.

Most overhead scanners include some type of autofocussing arrangement. The object height is measured just "up stream" of the camera, and the optical system is adjusted to ensure that the image is completely in focus. It would conceivably be pos-

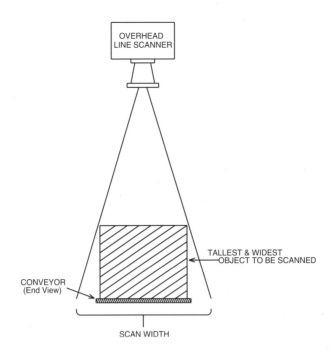

Figure 9-5: Geometry Of An Overhead Scanner. In order to ensure full coverage width of tall objects, it is necessary to "overscan" the conveyor belt.

sible to simultaneously adjust the magnification of a zoom lens using the same height information: this would potentially eliminate the need for any overscanning but would add significant complexity.

It can be seen that in some ways, vision-based scanning is more complex than traditional laser approaches, but there are many advantages:

- Omnidirectional scanning is possible of symbols with small aspect ratios, thereby reducing label cost.
- Any symbology type can be successfully scanned: linear, 2-D stacked, 2-D matrix, height modulated, circular, etc. Only software is affected by the choice of symbologies.
- It is often possible to exploit the powerful image-processing hardware to do spatial filtering of the image, thereby extracting as much information as possible from the symbol, even in the presence of interfering patterns or symbol damage.
- There are no moving parts associated with the scanning operation. Reliability can be extremely high.

10

Printing Bar Code Symbols

Bar code printing falls into two classifications: off-site printing and on-site printing.

Off-site printing refers to technologies that are used to generate bar code symbols for subsequent use. The production is usually done at a location different from where the symbols will be used; often the symbol generation is contracted out to an organization specializing in this technology. Off-site printing is usually used to create medium to large volumes of identical or sequenced symbols. Because of the time separation between symbol printing and use, this is described as a batch process.

On-site printing techniques are used to create bar code symbols at the time and place that they are to be used. The data encoded in each symbol can be different and is entered either via a local keyboard or controlled by an attached computer. On-site printers are often referred to as demand printers because of their ability to produce uniquely encoded bar code symbols on demand.

On-site printers can also be used to produce large quantities of identical or sequential symbols. With the availability of compact, high speed, computer-controlled printers, the distinction between on-site and off-site printing is narrowing.

Bar code symbols can be printed on a variety of substrates: labels, tags, pages, forms, conventional packages, or end items. The bar code is often printed in combination with other information, such as human-readable or graphic data.

A combination of printing techniques can be employed. Unchanging data can be preprinted with an off-site technique, and then an on-site printer can be used to add the variable data.

10.1 Off-Site Printing Techniques

Off-site printing techniques are classified as such either because they are incapable of printing variable data or because the size, cost, or complexity of the equipment would preclude use in a demand printer application.

A variety of techniques exist for off-site printing. The wet ink techniques include letterpress, offset lithography, flexography, rotogravure, and the inking wheel. Other techniques are photocomposition, hot stamping, and laser etching.

Wet Ink Techniques

Wet ink printing techniques include most of the so-called "traditional" printing methods. All of these methods selectively apply ink to a substrate material. The techniques differ primarily in the means of transferring the ink to the substrate. In almost all cases, a photographic positive or negative image of the bar code symbol is used to generate printing plates that are used in the printer. This photographic image is called a film master. The actual printed bars and spaces have a different width than the elements on the film master, depending on the particular printing process and depending on the characteristics of the substrate material and ink. This deviation, which manifests itself as a uniform gain or reduction in the width of all bars, is compensated for by adjusting the width of the film master's bars. This compensation is called bar width reduction (BWR), and the amount can be either positive or negative. Unfortunately, the bar width reduction varies between processes, substrates, and inks.

Letterpress: Letterpress is one of the oldest printing techniques. The raised areas of the printing plates retain ink. Plates are made from metal, photopolymer, or rubber, and the process uses a thick ink, which dries more slowly than ink used in some of the other techniques. A letterpress machine can be used to print on continuous webs or individual sheets. A series of rollers is used to apply the ink to the printing plate and impress the image onto the substrate material. Figure 10-1 shows one possible arrangement.

A specialized adaptation of letterpress, called a numbering wheel, can be used to print images containing sequentially varying data. The printing plate incorporates individual numbering wheels that have a series of raised characters on their circum-

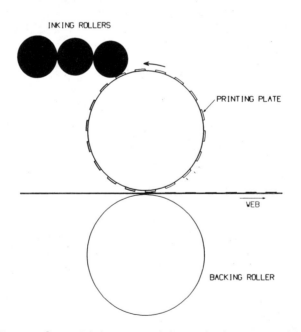

Figure 10-1: Letterpress Concept. In letterpress printing, a raised pattern containing the desired image is inked by rollers, then pressed into the moving paper (or other media) web, leaving the printed pattern. Letterpress is a mass printing technique, where the same image is printed over and over again.

ference. The wheels are indexed in a predetermined fashion during the printing process to create sequential data. Figure 10-2 shows typical arrangements of several numbering wheels in indexing mechanisms.

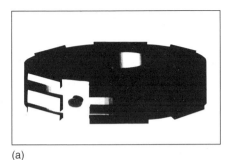

(a)

(b)   Courtesy of Leibinger, Inc.

Figure 10-2: Numbering Wheels. An adaptation called the numbering wheel allows variable bar code information to be combined with ordinary fixed letterpress printing plates. Each numbering wheel (a) contains multiple numeric digits and corresponding bar code patterns. Various assemblies of numbering wheels (b) with auto incrementing mechanisms allow long series of sequentially numbered bar code images to be printed with letterpress equipment.

The indexing mechanism, which is designed to be as thin as possible, fits into the spaces between adjacent wheels. Because of this space requirement, numbering wheels cannot be used to print continuous bar code symbologies.

Offset Lithography: Offset lithography is commonly referred to as "offset." It is a widely used printing technique and is capable of producing excellent print quality on a variety of substrates.

A printing plate is photochemically treated so that areas to be printed are made oil receptive and water repellent. The printing plate is fastened to the circumference of a roller and sequentially contacted with water and then ink. Since the ink is oil-based, it is only picked up by the image portion of the plate. The inked image is

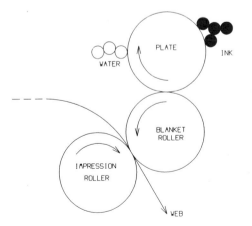

Figure 10-3: Offset Lithography Concept. In offset lithography, a master plate is made photographically and mounted on a cylinder. The photographically etched pattern of the plate passes inking rollers that selectively transfer ink to the plate. The inked portions of the master are then transferred to the intermediate blanket roller, and finally to the moving web of paper or other media. As with letterpress, offset lithography is a mass printing technique.

transferred to an intermediate roller, then impressed onto the substrate, as shown in Figure 10-3.

With proper techniques, offset can produce high-quality bar code symbols with X dimensions down to less than 10 mils. Commonly used inks allow images to be created that have adequate contrast in both the B633 and B900 wavelength bands.

Flexography: Flexography, commonly known as "flexo," is widely used to print on forms, labels, corrugated cartons, and other substrates. Figure 10-4 shows the operation of a flexo printing press.

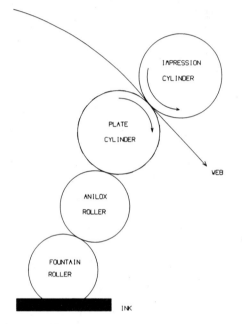

Figure 10-4: Flexography Concept. This technique uses a flexible printing plate wrapped around a cylinder. A series of rollers transfers ink from a reservoir up to the printing plate. The plate image is then transferred directly to the moving web. Flexography is also a mass printing technique.

The image to be printed is etched in reverse into a flexible rubber or photopolymer plate fastened to the circumference of a roller. Ink is transferred to the raised part of the plate by a roller. The substrate is pressed against the printing plate by a pressure roller.

Because of the flexible nature of the printing plate, distortions of the image can result, and special techniques must be used to ensure "in spec" bar codes. Flexo is usually used to print symbols with X dimensions of 20 mils or more, although much higher densities can be produced with care on quality substrates.

Rotogravure: Rotogravure employs a cylindrical printing plate in which the image to be printed is etched below the surface in the form of very small cells. Ink is applied to the surface, then scraped off the non-etched surface by a blade, as shown in Figure 10-5.

The substrate is pressed onto the surface of the plate, causing ink contained in the etched cells to be transferred. Because of the cellular pattern of the resulting

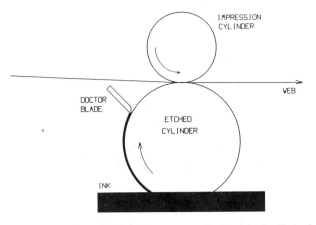

Figure 10-5: Rotogravure Concept. In rotogravure, a single etched cylinder is inked by passing it through a reservoir. Excess ink is removed by the doctor blade, after which the image is transferred directly to the moving web of paper or other medium. Rotogravure is a mass printing technique; every impression is identical.

image, the bar code quality produced by this technique is not high.

Inking Wheel: The inking wheel is an inexpensive technique for printing bar code or human-readable information onto a moving substrate. Also known as rotary encoding, this technique is illustrated in Figure 10-6.

A nondriven wheel possessing a raised image (like letterpress or flexo) is inked and then pressed into contact with a moving substrate. This method is commonly used to print information on corrugated cartons, but is restricted to large X dimensions (typically about 40 mils).

Figure 10-6: Inking Wheel. The inking wheel method is used to place fixed bar code images on media such as the corrugated containers shown in this photograph. The inking wheel's raised image is inked, then pressed onto the moving substrate. The inking wheel is a mass printing technique. Changing symbols requires changing wheels.

Other Off-Site Printing Techniques

Although wet ink processes are the most common off-site printing techniques, several others are also used.

Photocomposition: Specialized phototypesetting equipment can produce excellent quality bar code symbols on a variety of photosensitive substrates. Figure 10-7 illustrates a photocomposed label printed with a 3.3 mil X dimension.

Courtesy of Data Composition Inc.

Figure 10-7: A Photocomposed High-Density Label. Photocomposition makes very high resolution bar code images, as shown here. The image is formed electronically, transferred from an imaging device to a photosensitive graphic medium of the appropriate composition, then developed. Each image produced can have unique information. In the application shown here, individual bees are tagged with photocomposed labels.

A high-resolution image is computer-generated on a CRT and projected onto photosensitized material (either film or paper). After a developing and laminating process, the resulting symbols are sharp and accurate. This technique has been used to reliably produce high-quality symbols with X dimensions down to 3 mils, but the cost is somewhat higher than with other methods. Being computer-controlled, it is obviously possible to produce quantities of unique labels from a database.

Hot Stamping: In hot stamping, a heated metal printing plate presses a temperature-sensitive ribbon into the substrate material. Print quality is good, but the per-symbol expense is high.

Miscellaneous: As described below in 7.4, there are a number of special printing techniques including laser, and chemical forms of etching. Many of these techniques are best carried out off-site in batch mode.

Table 10-1 summarizes of the major off-site printing techniques that have been discussed here.

Table 10-1
OFF-SITE PRINTING TECHNIQUES

Technique	Smallest X Dimension That Can Be Reliably Printed	Advantages	Disadvantages	Comments
Letterpress	8 mils	Good quality		Numbering wheels can be used for sequential data with discrete symbologies
Offset	8 mils	Good quality		Oil-based inks
Flexography	10 mils	Can print on a variety of substrates		
Rotogravure	12 mils	Inexpensive	Mediocre quality	
Inking Wheel	40 mils	Inexpensive		Low equipment cost
Photocomposition	3 mils	Excellent quality	Higher cost	Data can be variable

10.2 On-Site Printing Techniques

Printing bar code labels or forms in advance of their need is often inconvenient or impossible. In these cases, an on-site printing capability is required.

Printing bar code symbols at the place of use is the quickest and easiest way to generate bar codes. A wide variety of printing technologies can be used to print bar code symbols on demand, encouraging the use of distributed printing. The technologies include dot matrix impact, drum, thermal, thermal transfer, ink jet, xerographic, magnetographic, and electrostatic.

Data to be printed is sent to the printer either by a built-in keyboard or, more typically, by a serial or parallel data link. The printers can be driven by an attached computer or a local CRT terminal.

Dot Matrix Impact Printers

Dot matrix printers were originally designed for printing pages of data as computer output devices, and depending on the model, quite high speeds can be obtained. When suitably programmed, these printers can generate bar code symbols. Dot matrix printers operate by driving a small round hammer (called a wire or needle) into an inked ribbon, which then contacts the paper. Figure 10-8 illustrates the arrangement.

Dot matrix impact printers can be designed to print on narrow webs (1 or 2 inches), but most are set up to work on full page width (8.5 inches or 11 inches). The two basic types of dot matrix mechanisms are referred to as serial printers and line printers.

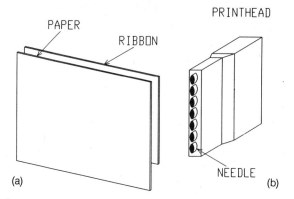

Figure 10-8: Dot Matrix Impact Printing Concept. The dot matrix impact printer transfers ink from a ribbon onto paper when a small hammer or needle hits the ribbon, forcing it against the paper. Diagram (a) is a side view showing how print head, paper, and ribbon are positioned; (b) is a top view showing how the print head moves back and forth to place characters serially on the paper substrate.

A serial printer uses a movable printhead with one or two vertical rows of adjacent or overlapping needles. The head traverses from side to side, printing one character at a time. Tall characters or graphics require multiple adjacent passes of the printhead, with intervening paper advances. Figure 10-9 shows the configuration. When printing bar code with the bars oriented parallel to the feed direction of the paper (the picket fence orientation), care must be taken that lines printed by subsequent passes of the printhead line up properly.

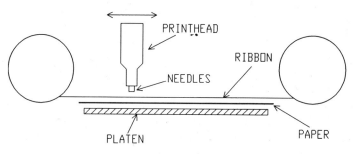

Figure 10-9: Serial Dot Matrix Printer Arrangement. A print head containing multiple needles moves back and forth to place characters serially on the paper substrate.

A dot matrix impact line printer is composed of many needles that are evenly spaced across a movable horizontal shuttle. The shuttle oscillates back and forth as the paper is advanced. Figure 10-10 shows the arrangement, and Figure 10-11 shows a typical printer that uses this technology.

In order to print bar codes, a dot matrix printer (whether impact, thermal, or laser technology) overlaps adjacent dots to produce approximations to straight-edged bars, as shown in Figure 10-12. As shown in the right half of Figure 10-12, inadequate dot overlap produces a poor approximation to crisp bars and spaces. A high-resolution scanner could easily misinterpret voids in the wide bars as addition-

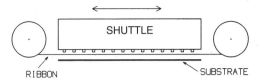

Figure 10-10: Dot Matrix Impact Line Printer Concept. With multiple impact pins, the oscillating shuttle does not need to move across the complete width of the paper. When its various pins are at the proper position, a hammer fires the pin through the ribbon making a mark on the paper.

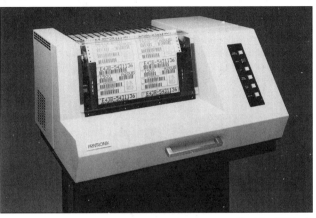

Figure 10-11: Typical Dot Matrix Impact Line Printer. There are many available varieties of dot matrix impact line printers, of which this is a typical example. Such printers, when used with bar code, often have special hardened print heads to minimize wear. Internal software for creating bar code images completes specialization of such printers for bar code applications.

al spaces or could miss a narrow bar, causing a low read rate and a high error rate.

Dot matrix impact printers almost always use a multiple pass ribbon. When the ribbon is new, the printed dots are significantly larger in diameter than the needles; as the ribbon is used, the printed dot diameter decreases, thereby reducing the dot overlap and reducing the effective bar widths. Careful control of ribbon type and replacement is essential to printing acceptable bar code symbols.

Most dot matrix impact printers generate an X dimension between 15 and 20 mils, producing a Code 39 density of about four characters per inch. A few printers are available with smaller needles, but great care is needed in selection of media (ribbon and paper) and in maintenance.

Drum Printers

Drum printers, often called formed font impact printers, were designed explicitly for printing bar code tags and labels. Figure 10-13 illustrates several typical drum printers.

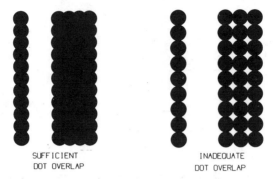

SUFFICIENT
DOT OVERLAP

INADEQUATE
DOT OVERLAP

Figure 10-12: Overlapping Dots Produce Solid Bars. Bars are formed by overlapping a series of dots as shown in this illustration. Dot matrix printers can produce good bar code images provided there is sufficient dot overlap (left). If the dots are just touching or completely isolated from one another, the image will be difficult if not impossible to read correctly. The dot overlap consideration is independent of the method used to form the image: ink and ribbon impact, thermal, laser/xerographic, mass printing, or other technology.

Courtesy of Intermec Corp.

Figure 10-13: Typical Drum Impact Printer. A continuously rotating drum has raised characters etched into its surface. When the drum is in the appropriate position, impact images are made by pressing the medium and ribbon onto the drum. Some of the characters available are graphic letters and other symbols.

A drum printer uses a continuously rotating drum that has bar code and human-readable characters etched into the outer surface. When a character to be printed rotates into the printing zone, a hammer drives the substrate material (paper, vinyl, or polyester) into a ribbon and then into the etched character on the drum. Both the substrate material and the ribbon are advanced by capstans.

The ribbon only runs through the printer once. Because it is not reused, ink smear does not vary and is compensated for in widths of the etched characters. Extremely good edge resolution and dimensional control are produced, enabling this type of printer to generate X dimensions of less than 5 mils. The resulting Code 39 density can be as high as 15 characters per inch.

Because of the etched print wheel, it is not possible to easily change symbologies or to rearrange the vertical format. The print wheels can be changed, but the vertical positions of bar code and human-readable lines must remain unchanged.

Because of their ability to accurately generate high-resolution symbols, drum printers are often used for labeling small items.

Thermal Printers

Thermal printing has been used for many years to generate hard copy for calculators and office machines, but it wasn't until 1981 that thermal printers were developed that could produce good quality bar code symbols. This coincided with the development of suitable thermally-sensitive media that would give aesthetically pleasing images with acceptable lifetimes.

All thermal printers use the same basic principle. A light-colored substrate (typically paper) is impregnated with a clear coating that changes to a dark color (usually black, sometimes blue) upon exposure to heat over a period of time. The image is not formed by burning but is created by a chemical reaction in the coating, brought on by the heat.

The image forms more rapidly at higher temperatures. If the temperature is below 140° F (60° C), the coating takes more than five years to darken. If the temperature is in the range of 400° F (200° C), the chemical reaction will occur within a few milliseconds.

A thermal printer selectively heats localized areas of the substrate material, thereby creating a dark image. The heating is performed by small electrical heaters that are part of a thermal printhead, which is in contact with the thermally sensitive substrate. Each of these heaters is controlled by logic in the printer. The heaters are in the form of rectangular dots or bars and, when activated, create an image in the substrate that closely matches the size and shape of the heating element. The same printer logic that controls the heating elements also controls the movement of paper past the printhead, thereby allowing a complete label or page to be imaged.

Because the printhead physically contacts the substrate, wear results as the substrate moves relative to the head. Printheads have a finite operational life and should be considered as a consumable item.

The three basic thermal printer configurations are the moving head, fixed head with formed heater bars, and the fixed head with linear array of heater dots.

In a moving head thermal printer, a small printhead with 7 to 24 dots is scanned laterally back and forth as thermal paper is advanced in a direction perpendicular to the head travel. This configuration is shown in Figure 10-14. Although this technique results in a low cost, it limits the printer's speed and causes high wear rates. Because of these disadvantages and problems associated with accurately lining up several passes of the printhead when printing bars, moving head thermal printers are seldom used for generating bar code symbols.

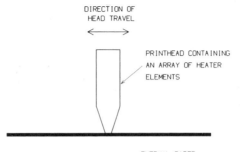

DIRECTION OF
HEAD TRAVEL

←──────→

PRINTHEAD CONTAINING
AN ARRAY OF HEATER
ELEMENTS

THERMAL PAPER
(MOVING OUT OF THIS PAGE)

Figure 10-14: Moving Head Thermal Printer Concept. Images are formed by elevating the temperature of selected spots on the printhead. The printhead is in contact with the special thermal paper. A dot matrix image results as corresponding spots on the paper are raised above a threshold temperature, where a permanent color change occurs. Either the printhead is scanned across the full width of advancing thermal paper, or the motion of the paper relative to a fixed printhead provides the scanning effect.

The fixed head printer with formed bars was the first type of thermal bar code printer to be commercially accepted. These devices are designed to print on tag or label stock, and Figure 10-15 illustrates a typical unit.

Courtesy of Intermec Corp.

Figure 10-15: Thermal Printer with Formed Bar. In this particular example, the printhead is stationary, and the paper moves past the formed bar printhead (see Figure 10-16).

In this type of printer, thermal stock is accurately moved past a fixed printhead and forced into contact with the heater elements by a flexible back-up roller. The printhead contains an array of heater dots that are used to print human-readable characters and a rectangular heater bar that is used to form individual elements of a bar code symbol. Wide bars are printed by overlapping several adjacent burns of the bar element as the thermal paper is advanced past the printhead. Figure 10-16 gives a close-up of one of these printheads.

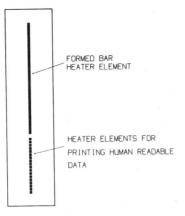

FORMED BAR
HEATER ELEMENT

HEATER ELEMENTS FOR
PRINTING HUMAN READABLE
DATA

Figure 10-16: Formed Bar Printhead Concept. The complete length of the bar is printed at one time. The dot matrix printing of associated human readable text is performed using the array of elements below the bar element in this diagram. This form of printhead is highly specialized to bar code applications.

More flexible than a drum printer, this type of printer is still rather restrictive in its printed format. Bar code symbols must always be printed in the picket fence orientation, and its vertical position is fixed.

The most common thermal printer configuration uses a fixed printhead with a linear array of heater dots. A representative printhead is illustrated in Figure 10-17. In this example, there are 320 rectangular dots, each of which is 0.01 inch (0.25 millimeter) square.

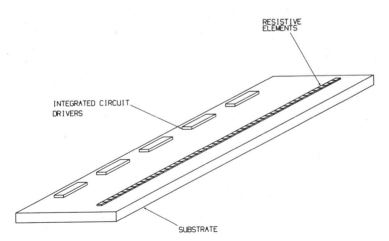

RESISTIVE
ELEMENTS

INTEGRATED CIRCUIT
DRIVERS

SUBSTRATE

Figure 10-17: Linear Array Thermal Printhead Concept. This form of thermal printhead can be used to form letters, bar codes, and other graphics without paying attention to actual position on the medium. It can print any pattern possible with an array of dots.

With this array, the printer can place printed dots anywhere on the medium as it moves by. This technology has been used for page printers as well as label printers. Several typical thermal label printers are shown in Figure 10-18.

Photos courtesy of Intermec Corp.

Figure 10-18: Typical Thermal Label Printers. Thermal label printers are a popular printing technique because of the format flexibility, image quality, speed, and cost. Many products are available; two representative examples are shown here.

Thermal printers are often rated in terms of the speed that the medium is advanced through the machine as printing is occurring. Typical speeds are in the range of 2.0 to 6.0 inches per second (50 to 150 millimeters per second), although some equipment is available that can operate at over twice this speed if the label format is optimized. High speeds sometimes require special thermal paper, and sometimes result in somewhat lower print quality than lower-speed printing. Many printers allow the user to select the machine's printing speed so that an optimum trade-off between speed and print quality can be made. Because of the simplicity of the thermal printing process, it is even possible to build portable, battery-powered thermal label printers, as shown in Figure 10-19.

Courtesy of Monarch Marking Systems, Inc.

Figure 10-19: Typical Battery Powered Thermal Label Printer. Since thermal printers are inherently lightweight and use little power, portable bar code label printers such as this model have become possible.

Thermal printing is a popular method of bar code generation because of the format flexibility, image quality, speed, and cost. The only drawback to thermal images is the requirement that the labels not be subjected to ambient temperatures in excess of 140° F (60° C) or to prolonged (two days') exposure to ultraviolet light (such as direct sunlight). For these reasons, thermal labels are usually restricted to indoor applications.

Thermal Transfer Printers

Thermal transfer printers have many similarities to direct thermal printers. A thermal printhead is used, but it is in contact with a special ribbon that releases its pigmenting materials above a certain threshold temperature. The ribbon is in physical contact with the substrate material (sometimes called the receiver paper), as shown in Figure 10-20.

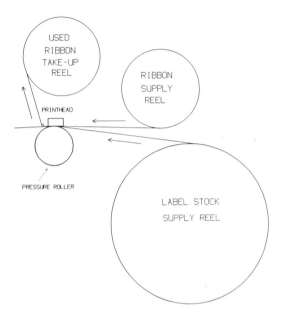

Figure 10-20: Thermal Transfer Printing Concept. Ink is thermally transferred from a ribbon onto plain paper. This eliminates the need for special thermal papers.

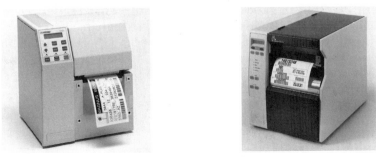

Photos courtesy of Zebra

Figure 10-21: Typical Thermal Transfer Label Printers. This type of printer produces stable images that are not affected by variations in the thermal environment after the image is formed. As a result a wide variety of products are available; a representative sample is shown here.

The resulting image is stable and unaffected by temperature or exposure to ultraviolet light. Several examples of thermal transfer label printers appear in Figure 10-21.

Thermal transfer printers are just as versatile as direct thermal printers, with the additional advantages that plain paper is used, the printed image is suitable for outside as well as inside applications, and printhead life is longer. The only disadvantage is the need for one more consumable product—the thermal ribbon.

Ribbon usage is usually identical to paper usage: the two media move through the printer in "lock step." Because the ribbon is so much thinner than most label media, a roll of ribbon holds many more linear inches than a roll of label stock, and therefore does not need to be changed as frequently. Some printers include a "head lift" mechanism, which allows the labels stock to be advanced over unprinted areas without dragging along (and wasting) the ribbon. Depending on the specific label design to be printed, this can reduce the operating cost for ribbons, but the complexity and cost of the printer is higher.

As of late 1994, several companies were developing thermal transfer printers that extend ribbon life by advancing the ribbon at a lower speed than the receiver paper. Again, this involves a trade-off between print quality and cost of consumables.

It is possible to use thermal transfer technology to produce colored images. A color thermal transfer label printer usually includes 4 print heads and 4 different colored ribbons. These devices tend to be more expensive, slower, and noisier than single-color machines.

Thermal and thermal transfer printers are available with printheads with dot densities of 100, 200, 300, and 400 dots per inch. These dot densities dictate the smallest X dimension that can be printed: the printer's software can always produce larger X dimensions by tiling multiple dots.

Both thermal and thermal transfer printers are usually equipped with convertible paper paths, which allow the equipment to operate in one or more of the following modes:

1. Straight Through—In this mode, the stock runs through the printer without any attempt to spool the result, or to separate adhesive labels from the backing.

2. Self Strip—In this mode, the printed media is wrapped around a small radius pin just after the printhead. Assuming the use of adhesive-backed labels, the backing is separated from the printed label at the pin, and the backing is spooled up on a roll for eventual disposal. The label is "presented" to the user to take away. Printing is inhibited until the previously-printed label has been removed.

3. Batch—In this mode, the printer spools up the media after printing. Large radius guides are used to prevent adhesive-backed labels separating from the backing material.

A new mode is becoming available for specially equipped thermal printers: linerless media. A special type of continuous media is used that has an adhesive on the back, and a release substance on the front surface. A cutter at the output of the printer slices the substrate up into individual adhesive labels after printing.

Xerographic Printers

The term "xerographic printing" is based on plain paper copier technology. It is widely available in contemporary laser printers. The xerographic process that formed the technological basis for the Xerox Corporation (originally called the Haloid Corporation) involves the use of a photosensitive semiconducting surface upon which an electrical charge has been deposited. This surface is exposed to an optical image, resulting in the discharge of selected areas, thereby creating an electrostatic image, which is then brought into contact with toner particles. The toner particles are selectively attracted to the latent electrostatic image. The resulting toner image is then transferred to plain paper and fixed in place by pressure and/or heat.

In a copier, the optical image is generated by the original to be copied. In a laser printer, the optical image is written onto the photosensitive surface (usually a drum configuration) by a controllable light source (scanned laser, LED array, or backlit liquid crystal display (LCD). Figure 10-22 illustrates the arrangement in a laser printer.

Referring to Figure 10-22, we can follow the process as the photosensitive print drum rotates. At the top of the figure, the photosensitive surface receives an electrostatic charge from a corona station. The drum then moves to an area where it is

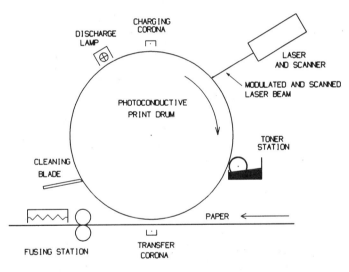

Figure 10-22: The Laser Printer (Xerographic Process) Concept. In the laser printer, an image is formed optically on an electrostatically charged, photo-conductive drum using a controlled laser beam. The charged areas of the drum attract toner particles that are then transferred to the paper medium by a corona discharge. The image is fused to the paper with a combination of heat and mechanical pressure. A cleaning blade removes any excess toner, which is recycled to the toner station's reservoir. This type of printer is also often called a laser printer.

selectively exposed to light from a modulated and scanned laser beam. The resulting electrostatic image then moves to a toner station, where toner particles are attracted to the charged areas of the drum. The latent toned image is transferred to the paper substrate at the transfer station, and the drum is discharged, cleaned, and returned to the charging area. As the paper leaves the transfer station, a combination of heat and pressure is used to fuse the toned image into the substrate, resulting in a permanent image.

Laser printers are almost always designed to print on pages. A representative device is shown in Figure 10-23. At the present time, laser printers are best suited for office environments, although some ruggedized industrial demand printers have recently been introduced.

Figure 10-23: Typical Laser Printer. Laser (xerographic) printers are widely used for office word processing output to plain paper. When customized with bar code software, high quality bar code images can be produced along with other graphics.

Laser printers contain a controller that coordinates the modulation and scanning of the laser beam with movement of the print drum and paper. The controller in effect controls the presence or absence of dots on the printed page. The dot resolution is typically either 300 or 600 dots per linear inch (12 or 24 dots/millimeter).

Laser printers are commonly used to produce bar code symbols when connected to a personal computer equipped with one of the many available software packages dedicated to this task. The software must compensate for the fact that the actual printed dot size is larger than would be suggested by looking purely at the printer's specified resolution (in dots per inch), and quite good print quality can result.

Electrostatic Printers

Like a laser printer, an electrostatic printer uses toner particles to form a contrasting image on a light-colored substrate material. There is no print drum in an electrostatic printer, however, and special paper (with a controlled dielectric constant and conductivity) must be used. Figure 10-24 illustrates the configuration used.

No optical system is used; an electrostatic printer directly deposits electrical charge onto the paper with an array of electrodes called the printhead. This electrical image then selectively picks up toner particles at the toning station, which can use either liquid or powdered toner. The final image is fused with heat and/or pressure.

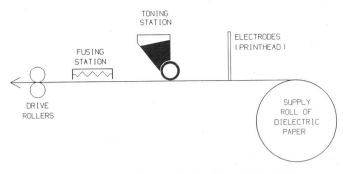

Figure 10-24: The Electrostatic Process Concept. In the electrostatic printing process, an electrical image consisting of a pattern of charges is placed directly onto special paper by electrodes of a print-head. The paper passes a toning station where the charged areas attract toner. The toner is then fused to the paper, making the image permanent.

Electrostatic printers operate with continuous webs of dielectric media. A subsequent cutter or conversion station is required to create individual labels. Alternatively, preconverted label stock (die cut adhesive labels on a release liner) can be used, but care must be taken that the adhesive used is compatible with the fusing process.

The resolution of the resulting image is a function of the number of electrodes in the printhead. Because of mechanical and electrical constraints, this number is currently limited to approximately 100 dots per inch. Figure 10-25 illustrates a printer using the electrostatic principle.

Courtesy of Markem Corporation

Figure 10-25: Typical Electrostatic Printer. This electrostatic printer is specialized to produce bar coded labels on demand. Text, graphics, and bar code information can be mixed in the images produced by this method.

Ion Deposition Printers

An ion deposition printer is a cross between an electrostatic and a xerographic printer. No optics are used, but the printer does have a print drum and uses plain paper. Figure 10-26 shows the arrangement.

The print drum is a hard, conducting cylinder, coated with an insulating layer.

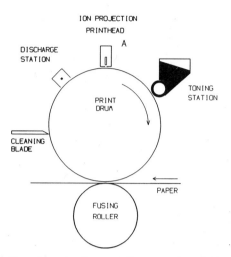

Figure 10-26: The Ion Deposition Process Concept. Ions are deposited on a hard, conducting cylinder with an insulated coating. Toner is attracted to the charge pattern created by the ions. As the print drum continues to rotate, the toner is then simultaneously transferred and fused to the paper by mechanical pressure of the fusing roller.

The printhead is a linear array of electrodes operating in a controlled electrical field. The controller causes the printhead to project controlled streams of ions onto the surface of the print drum, resulting in a charged image. This charged image selectively attracts toner particles at the toning station, and the toned image is transferred to plain paper by means of pressure. This pressure also fuses the image. Because of the pressures used in the transfer/fusing process, this technique is not compatible with many laminated label materials. Figure 10-27 shows a typical ion deposition printer. Image resolution is limited by the printhead. Current units can achieve 150 dots per inch.

Magnetographic Printers

A magnetographic printer is similar to an ion deposition printer, except that magnetic images are used instead of electrostatic images. This process is sometimes called magnetolithography. Figure 10-28 shows the physical arrangement.

The print drum is made of a material that can be easily magnetized. A printhead, consisting of a linear array of magnetic recording heads, writes a magnetic image onto the surface of the drum. This is analogous to the process of writing a magnetic image on recording tape for an audio cassette recorder.

The magnetic image then passes through a toning station, where magnetic toner particles are attracted to the magnetized areas on the print drum. The resulting image is then transferred to plain paper and fused. Image resolution, which is approximately 100 dots per inch, is limited by the physical space required to place multiple recording heads side by side.

Ink Jet Printers

The recent advent of drop-on-demand desktop printers with resolutions approaching that of laser printers has opened the viability of this technology to general-purpose bar code applications. Previously, ink jet bar code printers were low- res-

Courtesy of Dennison Manufacturing Co.

Figure 10-27: Typical Ion Deposition Printer. Ion deposition printers are used in high speed pro-duction applications to prepare bar coded labels. A printer such as this prints variable bar code and/or other graphic information on rolls of label stock.

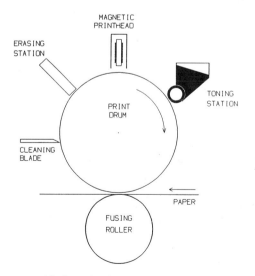

Figure 10-28: The Magnetographic Process Concept. This is the magnetic equivalent of the xero-graphic process. A magnetic print head writes a latent image on a rotating magnetic print drum. The drum rotates the image past a toning station, where magnetic toner particles are attracted to the latent image. The toner particles are then transferred and fused to the paper medium producing the permanent image on paper.

Printing Bar Code Symbols • **151**

olution devices intended for in-line printing applications directly on cartons.

The actual size of the printed dot is highly dependent on substrate properties. It is important that potential users of this technology carefully select materials to be used in order to ensure that the printed bar code symbols are printed within allowable specification. This process can be eased if larger values of X dimension are chosen.

In early 1995, color label printers were announced that used high-resolution ink jet technology. When using the appropriate substrate material, very good print quality can be produced.

10.3 Accessories for On-Site Printers

On-site printers are often integrated with accessory products to provide unique capabilities.

Power Take-Ups

Many printers have no provision for rewinding a web of medium as it is printed. If a series of labels are to be printed in a batch mode for later use, it is often convenient to use an external power take-up unit to rewind the printed labels. These devices are also called power rewinders. Power take-ups can be separate, stand-alone devices or can be built right into the printer, as illustrated in Figure 10-29.

Figure 10-29: Power Take-Up. The power take-up is a device for spooling of label stock from label printers.

Laminators

In some environments, additional protection is needed for the bar code label. A clear laminating material can be used to provide protection from abrasion or repeated contact scanning. Adhesive-backed laminating film can be manually placed onto labels, or an in-line laminator can be used with the printer. Figure 10-30 shows such a device packaged with a drum printer.

Applicators

To be useful, bar code labels need to be attached to the object that is to be identified. The back side of the label normally has an adhesive layer for this purpose. Labels can be applied manually, but high-volume production environments create a

Figure 10-30: Drum Printer With Laminator. When bar coded labels are used in applications that require repeated scanning with contact scanners, abrasion will eventually degrade unprotected labels to the point of unreadability. To provide protection for such cases and other harsh environments, printers such as this are available where labels are laminated with a thin plastic film.

demand for automatic application. A variety of automatic applicators are available that use mechanical arms or air blasts to place adhesive-backed labels onto objects as they move by on a conveyor system. An example is shown in Figure 10-31.

Cutters

Some printers (especially thermal and thermal transfer) are equipped with a cutter assembly which cuts the media into individual labels immediately after it is printed. This allows continuous rolls of media to be used, and is ideal for the generation of tags.

Verifiers

Printers are available with built-in electro-optical devices that confirm the quality of the printed image directly after it is created. These printers are typically referred to as "verifying printers." The verifiers usually consist of a bar code laser scanner that is configured to read symbols on labels as they exit from the printer. Feedback to the printer is provided to ensure that a printing problem (such as a defective print head dot) does not produce quantities of unscannable labels. It is usually necessary to configure the label's format so that the direction of the bar code symbol's bars is parallel to the direction of paper motion. Because current verifiers are actually reading the symbols based on a scan that is perpendicular to the label motion, this technology is not yet capable of verifying 2-D matrix symbologies.

10.4 Special Printing Techniques

A number of specialized techniques can be used for generating bar code symbols.

Figure 10-31: Label Applicator. In production line situations, label applicators such as this can automatically apply preprinted labels from reels.

Laser Etching

A high-powered laser equipped with a positioning and modulation system can be used to create bar codes on certain substrates by selectively burning away a surface coating. Either a white coating is placed over a dark colored substrate, or a dark coating is put onto a light background. The top coating is then selectively burned away by a laser, creating a bar code symbol.

An alternative technique has been used on high-gloss substrates such as those used in thin film hybrid circuit manufacturing. A laser is used to selectively and partially etch the surface, causing a diffuse (rough) area. When the substrate is scanned at an angle other than 90 degrees, the etched areas reflect light back to the scanner, whereas the specular properties of the nonetched areas will appear to be black to the scanner. Because of the rough surface that normally results from the laser etching process, noncontact scanning is usually preferred.

Silk Screening

A high resolution silk screening process can be used to produce fixed content low-density bar code symbols. Either dark-colored ink can be screened onto a light-colored background, or a light-colored ink can be screened onto a dark background. In either case, inks need to be selected that match the spectral and reflectivity requirements of the scanning equipment.

Because of the screen resolution and variable spreading properties of the process, X dimensions should be kept large to ensure that the resulting symbol meets specifications. With care, values down to 25 mils are achievable.

If screened and cured onto a hard surface, the image may be physically bumpy; noncontact scanning methods are therefore preferable.

Painting

Through the use of a stencil or a machine-controlled, high-resolution spray gun, low density bar code symbols can be painted onto a substrate. The line widths generated by this technique usually have very poor tolerances, so X dimensions must be quite large (greater than 40 mils).

Figure 10-32: Typical Photochemically Generated Metal Label. In applications requiring rugged permanent labels, bar code images and other graphics can be photochemically etched onto metal. The equipment required to do this is highly specialized. This form of label tends to be produced by label vendors at a higher unit cost than paper stock labels.

Chemical/Photochemical Methods

Bar code symbols can be imaged onto specially prepared metal tags through chemical or photochemical processing. The resulting image is durable and permanent, but the specular properties of the substrate can cause reading difficulties at certain angles. Metal tags are commonly used to identify physical assets that have a long expected life. Figure 10-32 illustrates a typical photochemically generated metal label.

Hot Stamping

A hot stamping press is somewhat similar to a thermal transfer printer, except for the fact that it produces constant data. A heated metal printing plate is forced into a thermally sensitive ribbon, which then makes contact with the substrate. This process can print on a variety of different materials, but should be restricted to producing symbols with large X dimensions.

Molding/Casting/Embossing

It is possible to create a "3-D symbol" by embossing a flat substrate with bars or spaces. Similarly, a bar code symbol can be created in relief by a molding or casting process. The difficulty lies in the scanning process, because the reflectivity is nominally the same for the bars and the spaces! Specialized lighting arrangements can be used to cast shadows from the elements, but this arrangement is only suited for scanning under carefully controlled conditions where the position and alignment of the symbol and scanner are fixed.

As of the end of 1994, at least one manufacturer offered a special purpose hand-held scanner intended specifically for scanning this type of symbol. A conventional moving beam laser scanner mechanism is used to illuminate the symbol, but the reflected light is collected by a 2-D CCD array located off the primary axis. This

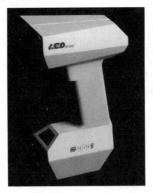

Figure 10-33: Handheld Scanner For Embossed Symbols. The geometric arrangement allows the scanner to detect the different "height" of a linear symbol's bars and spaces.

arrangement uses geometric methods to actually detect the difference in distance between the bars and spaces and the scanner. Figure 10-33 shows such a device.

10.5 Media

Media refers not only to substrate materials (labels, tags, pages), but also to ribbons used in the printing process. The quality of the final printed image is highly dependent on using a medium with properties that are appropriate for the printing process and specific equipment used.

Face Material

Face material refers to the substrate material in its unconverted form (before it has been cut to size, laminated with adhesive and release liner, etc.). The many measurable properties of face material can affect the printed image. Some of these properties are thickness, density, moisture content, surface roughness, porosity, compressibility, overcoat, resistivity, and dielectric properties.

Face material that is to be used in a thermal printer must be coated with a special thermally sensitive layer; several formulations are used, depending on the desired sensitivity and spectral characteristics. The face material does not necessarily need to be paper. Some printing techniques can also work successfully with polyester or vinyl materials. Nonpaper substrates are suited to harsher environments.

The Conversion Process

Face material needs to be converted to a usable form. Often this simply involves cutting the material into pages, forms, or tags. The process is more involved if labels are to be produced.

A label consists of die-cut face material that has been coated with adhesive and laminated onto a release liner. The liner (or backing) has a low-stick surface that allows the label to be removed easily.

The die-cutting operation defines individual labels in the face material without cutting the release liner. Butt-cut and ladder-stripped are the two most common die-cutting configurations. They are illustrated in Figure 10-34.

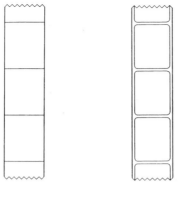

BUTT-CUT   LADDER-STRIPPED

Figure 10-34: Label Configurations. Reeled paper stock adhesive labels come in two basic configurations. Butt-cut labels have a simple linear die cut separating successive labels. Ladder-stripped
labels have a more complex die-cut pattern surrounding the active label area. In either case, the
labels are removed from the carrier strip at the time of application to an object.

Even with on-site printing methods, labels are sometimes preprinted with fixed
data or graphics. This is usually done with a wet ink process that is configured in
line with the converting press.

Converted labels are available with special tamper resistant properties. A special
face material and aggressive adhesive result in a label that becomes unreadable if an
attempt is made to remove it after it has been initially applied to a target surface.

Thermal Sensitivity

Thermal ribbons and thermal stock are available in different thermal sensitivities.
This is analogous to the ASA rating used in photographic film. More sensitive
material can result in higher printing speeds. Thermal and thermal transfer printers
have a number of controls that can be used to optimize print quality and overall
performance. If thermal materials with different sensitivities are used, it is necessary to change the "exposure" parameters of the printer in order to ensure that
printed symbols are of high quality. A mistake that many users make is to set the
exposure control too high: this results in a very dark label which has bars which are
too wide and spaces which are too narrow.

11

Printing Specifications and Symbol Quality

Every symbology has an associated set of specifications that must be adhered to during the printing process. Failure to comply with the published printing tolerances will result in the creation of symbols that give a low first read rate and a high substitution error rate. Printing specifications include limits on dimensional tolerances, spots, voids, edge roughness, and reflectivity and contrast.

Up until 1990, the acceptance of a symbol was determined by laboriously measuring each parameter individually: the assumption was that if each was within allowable limits, then the reading performance would be satisfactory using readily available scanning equipment. In 1990, publication of ANSI's "Guideline For Bar Code Print Quality" introduced an approach that attempted to mimic the operation of a bar code reader, and allowed the development of automatic devices for categorizing the print quality of bar code symbols.

Before we describe the methodology used in the ANSI approach, we will review the "traditional" way of measuring and checking symbols.

11.1 Dimensional Tolerances

Tolerances on printed element widths and/or placements for several different width modulated linear symbologies are outlined in Table 11-1.

Note that all tolerances shown in Table 11-1 are stated as a function of X. Definitions of the three tolerances are as follows:

1. Bar or space tolerance: the deviation (positive or negative) from the nominal width of any element. These are illustrated as "b" and "s" in Figure 11-1.

2. Edge-to-similar-edge tolerance: for continuous symbologies, deviations from the nominal dimension between similar edges of adjacent elements within a character; this is illustrated as tolerance "e" in Figure 11-1.

3. Pitch tolerance: for continuous symbologies, deviations from the nominal dimension between the leading edge of adjacent characters; this is illustrated as tolerance "P" in Figure 11-1.

Table 11-1
PRINTING TOLERANCES

Symbology	Bar or Space Tolerance	Edge-To-Similar-Edge Tolerance	Pitch Tolerance
Code 39	$\pm\dfrac{4}{27}(N-\dfrac{2}{3})X$	– – – – –	– – – – –
Interleaved 2 of 5	$\pm(\dfrac{18N-21}{80})X$	– – – – –	– – – – –
Code 11	$\pm(\dfrac{18N-21}{88})X$	– – – – –	– – – – –
Traditional Codabar	±1.5 mils at 10 CPI	– – – – –	– – – – –
Rationalized Codabar	$\pm\dfrac{(5N-8)}{20}X$	– – – – –	– – – – –
UPC/EAN	$\pm(X-0.009)$ if $X<0.013$ $\pm(0.47X-0.00216)$ if $X>0.013$	$\pm0.14692X$	$\pm0.29X$
Code 93 (std. tol.)	$\pm(0.45X-0.001)$	$\pm0.20X$	$\pm0.20X$
Code 93 (alt. tol.)	$\pm(0.45X-0.001)$	$\pm0.15X$	$\pm0.30X$
Code 128	$\pm(0.45X-0.001)$	$\pm0.20X$	$\pm0.20X$
Code 49	$\pm(0.40X-0.0005)$	$\pm0.20X$	$\pm0.20X$
Code 16K	$\pm(0.40X-0.0005)$	$\pm0.20X$	$\pm0.20X$
PDF417	$\pm(0.40X-0.0005)$	$\pm0.20X$	$\pm0.20X$

Figure 11-1: Tolerances. There are three fundamental dimensions to a bar code symbol's image of a character, each with its own tolerances. The symbols b and s refer to the deviations of the bar and space widths respectively from their nominal dimensions; p is the deviation from nominal of the overall character width; e is the deviation of edge-to-similar-edge dimensions from their nominal values.

The printing tolerances for a given symbology were based on the assumption of a specific width-determining algorithm in the reader. Appendix O describes how the tolerances were derived for Code 39.

It must be emphasized that the published tolerances are for the printing process. Approximately half of the available tolerance budget has been reserved for the bar code reader. If a symbol is printed with dimensions that are at the extremes of the published printing tolerances, there will still be adequate margin for the reader to do an effective decoding job. If symbols are printed with dimensions that are beyond the published printing tolerances, it might still be possible to read the symbol, but the first read rate and substitution error rate will suffer. Just because a symbol is readable, it is not necessarily within dimensional tolerances ("in spec").

Several commercially available instruments can be used to automatically determine if a symbol's dimensions are in compliance with published printing specifications. These devices are called verifiers and use some scanning means (either manual or automatic) to quickly measure the width of each bar and space. Verifiers typically have an overall accuracy of better than 1 mil. Representative equipment is shown in Figure 11-2.

Courtesy of RJS, Inc.

Courtesy of RJS, Inc.

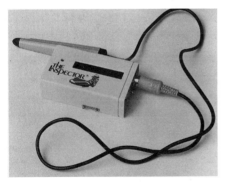

Courtesy of RJS, Inc.

Courtesy of Symbol Technologies, Inc.

Figure 11-2: Typical Verifiers. Verifiers can be used to check the dimensions of a bar code symbol. The varieties of verifiers available range from totally automatic machines that automatically perform an evaluation scan pattern (see Figure 5-2) to simple units with handheld contact scanners.

If a verifier uses a circular aperture to do the measuring, edge roughness can result in different perceived element widths for different scanning paths. This can be minimized by using a rectangular aperture, which tends to measure the average edge position.

A rectangular aperture is the preferred geometry for finding the average element widths, but it does not simulate the effect of a bar code reader's circular aperture.

It is possible to manually measure a symbol's element widths by using an optical comparator with 50X magnification. Results are affected by the operator's attempt to line the graticule up with the average edge, but studies have shown that inter-operator repeatability is better than 0.5 mils when measuring symbols with well-defined edges.

Determining exact edge location with any type of aperture or equipment is a challenging problem. The accepted definition of edge location today is as follows: use a device that measures reflectivity over a defined aperture size (a reflectome-ter); the aperture should be circular, with a diameter of 0.8 times the nominal X; move the aperture through the edge to be measured; the starting and ending positions should be well beyond the edge; the edge position is defined to be at the center of the aperture when the reflectivity is at the midpoint of the reflectivities observed on either side of the edge. See Figure 11-3.

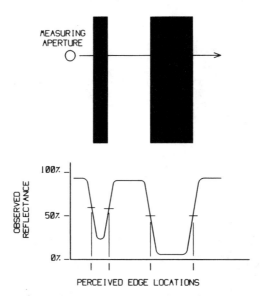

Figure 11-3: Edge Location. Given X, the minimum element width of a bar code symbol, slide a 0.8X measuring aperture across a given edge. The edge position is defined to be the center of the 0.8X measuring aperture when the observed reflectance through the aperture is at the halfway point between the extremes of reflectance observed when the aperture is in the adjacent bar or space.

11.2 Spots, Voids, and Edge Roughness

A symbol whose average dimensions are within specification can still prove to be unreadable if there are excessive edge roughness, spots, or voids. This problem is aggravated by the use of an input device that has a spot size much smaller than the value of X used. Figure 11-4 illustrates such a problem.

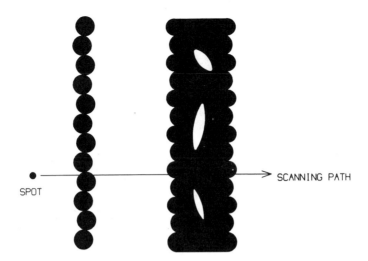

SPOT

SCANNING PATH

Figure 11-4: Excessive Resolution. This illustrates a case of excessive resolution. Suppose that the X dimension of the symbol is the width of the wide bar at the right. Suppose that dirt or printing errors produce the bar feature at the left and the voids in the real bar at right. These noise features are wider than the spot size shown. When the spot scans across the object at the left or one of the voids in the real bar at right, an erroneous feature will be perceived. Decreasing the spot resolution by increasing its size closer to the X dimension filters out this form of noise.

As the spot in Figure 11-4 is scanned through the elements, the unwanted spots and voids are large enough that additional erroneous bars and spaces will be perceived by the reader. This will result in a poor (or zero) first read rate, and potentially a high substitution error rate.

Obviously, extraneous spots and voids that are much smaller than the input device's spot size will not have an adverse effect. Several attempts have been made over the years to quantify "allowable" printing defects. A number of bar code standards employ an approach that was originally developed as part of the ANSI MH10.8M-1983 specification. This standard allows any number of spots and voids, so long as a single printing defect:

1. Will cover no more than 25 percent of the area of a circle whose diameter is 0.8X.

2. Will not completely cover a circle whose diameter is 0.4X.

In Figure 11-5, defect 1 is allowable, according to this standard, whereas defect 2 is not.

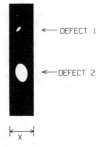

Figure 11-5: Allowable Printing Defects. ANSI Specification MH10.8M-1983 relates allowable defects in printing to the minimum element width, X, of a bar code symbol. Defect 1 in this illustration is allowable because its area covers no more than 25 percent of the area of a circle whose diameter is 0.8X, and it does not completely cover a circle of 0.4X diameter. Defect 2 is not allowable because by the same standard it is too large. This illustration shows voids in bars. The same standard applies to spots located in the spaces between bars.

There is no commercially available equipment that can automatically determine whether a symbol's spots and voids are in spec according to the criteria outlined in MH10.8M-1983.

In 1985, the AIM series of USS (Uniform Symbol Specification) publications outlined a new method of characterizing allowable printing defects. This involved the use of a circular 0.8X measuring aperture that is scanned through the complete symbol, keeping track of the observed reflectivity. The resultant scan reflectance profile is then examined (either manually or automatically) to find the darkest space and the lightest bar. The difference in reflectivity between these two elements is defined as the minimum reflectance difference (MRD), as shown in Figure 11-6.

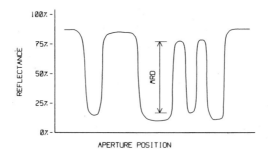

Figure 11-6: Minimum Reflectance Difference. Minimum reflectance difference (MRD) is the difference in reflectivity between the darkest space and the lightest bar of an entire symbol.

An allowable spot or void is any printing defect that causes less than a 0.25 MRD perturbation in the observed reflectivity pattern. Figure 11-7 shows an example of both an allowable and an unallowable void. Using ANSI's "Guideline for Bar Code Print Quality," the level of defects is measured by comparing the maximum observed reflectance non-uniformity to the SC value. The resulting factor is used in determining the overall symbol grade.

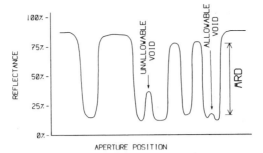

Figure 11-7: Void Classification. Printing defects may be classified based on their reflectance perturbation. If the perturbation caused by the defect is greater than 25 percent of the minimum reflectance difference for a symbol, then it is unallowable. This illustration shows two examples of reflectance perturbations for comparison.

Edge roughness is a measure of the departure of an element's edge from a perfectly crisp, straight transition. It is perceived as differences in an element's width along its length. Bar code standards do not usually put specific limits directly on edge roughness. Limits on edge roughness are indirectly specified through the definition of edge location.

Recall from Section 8.1 that an edge is defined in terms of the position of a 0.8X circular aperture when the observed reflectivity is midway between that of the adjacent bar and space. An implicit limit on edge roughness results from the requirement that all possible scanning paths through a symbol encounter only elements whose perceived widths are in spec, per the tolerance formulas listed in Table 11-1. Figure 11-8 illustrates examples of both allowable and out-of-spec edge roughness.

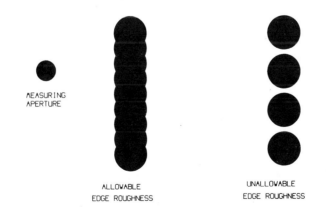

Figure 11-8: Edge Roughness. Edge roughness causes perceived differences in element widths for different scanning paths. In the illustration at left, the edge roughness is a minor perturbation of the width of the bar as viewed by the measuring aperture shown. In the illustration at right, edge roughness is shown at an unallowable extreme where the dots of the pattern do not overlap at all.

11.3 Reflectivity and Contrast

Bar code is an optical technology. The printed image must possess certain minimum optical properties in order for reading equipment to function. All measurements must, of course, be made at the wavelength specified.

Bar code scanners respond to the difference in reflectivity between a symbol's bars and spaces. Let's consider for a moment a theoretical symbol that has bars with zero reflectivity and spaces with 100 percent reflectivity. This theoretical symbol will also have no spots, voids, or edge roughness. If a reflectometer were used to measure the reflectivity at all points along a scanning path through the symbol, and if the measuring aperture were a circle whose diameter was much less than X, a scan reflectance profile similar to A in Figure 11-9 would be observed.

A bar code scanner, however, ideally uses an aperture diameter (or spot size) of 0.8X. If a plot is made of the reflectivity observed through a 0.8X diameter aperture as it is scanned through the theoretical symbol, plot B in Figure 11-9 would be observed.

(a)   (b)

Figure 11-9: Theoretical Reflectance Plots. The theoretical reflectivity plot at left (a) corresponds to an infinitesimal aperture. A theoretical reflectivity plot (b) for a 0.8X aperture crossing some bar code pattern is shown at right. The 0.8X aperture is a good match to a symbol's element widths.

Real-world bar code symbols have optical properties that result in scan reflectance profiles (using a 0.8X circular aperture) that are quite different from those shown in Figure 11-9. A typical plot is shown in Figure 11-10.

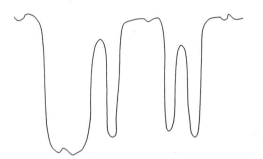

Figure 11-10: Real-World Reflectance Plot. In the real world of real symbols seen by real scanners, the plot of reflectivity versus distance through the scan is less precise. This illustration is a more typical, but definitely readable, plot of perceived reflectivity.

A bar code reading system requires a minimum difference in the reflectivity of adjacent bars and spaces in order to function. The minimum necessary difference varies between equipment, but manufacturers usually ensure that a safety margin exists beyond the minimum difference specified in the bar code standard.

Most symbols are specified with two parameters: background reflectance and print contrast signal (PCS). Background reflectance is a measure of the reflectivity in the symbol's spaces, and PCS indirectly specifies the ratio of reflectivity between the bars and spaces.

PCS is defined as:

$$\frac{R_L - R_D}{R_L} \times 100\%$$

where
R_L = reflectivity of the light elements
R_D = reflectivity of the dark elements

A common specification for symbols with X dimensions less than 40 mils is:

minimum background reflectivity: 50 percent.
minimum print contrast signal: 75 percent.

The 75 percent print contrast signal requirement is equivalent to requiring that the reflectivity of the bars be no more than one-quarter of the reflectivity of the spaces. Using this often-quoted set of optical specifications, we can see that the resulting minimum difference in reflectivity between bars and spaces is 37.5 percent. In order to function with symbols printed in accordance with this specification, bar code reading systems must be able to operate correctly with a 37.5 percent difference in bar and space reflectivity.

The only disadvantage of using the print contrast signal approach to specifying reflectivity is that it precludes the use of symbols with high background reflectivity but marginal PCS. Consider an example symbol which has a bar reflectance of 25 percent and a space reflectance of 75 percent.

The print contrast signal of this example symbol is 67 percent, which is clearly less than the common requirement of 75 percent. The reflectivity difference, however, is 50 percent, which is much better (from a scanning standpoint) than the 37.5 percent minimum that the reading equipment must be designed to handle.

In order to avoid this limitation with print contrast signal, AIM introduced the minimum reflectance difference (MRD) approach in 1985. (This was also mentioned in section 8.2.) MRD is the difference in reflectivity between the lightest bar and the darkest space, as measured using a 0.8X circular aperture. Figure 11-11 shows an example of determining the minimum reflectance difference.

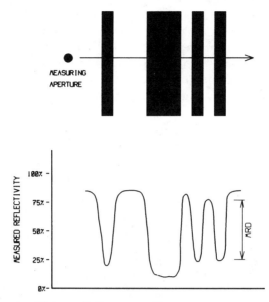

Figure 11-11: Measuring Minimum Reflectance Difference (MRD). A symbol has a single value of minimum reflectance difference, determined from the measured plot of reflectance versus distance through the scan.

AIM defines the minimum reflectance difference requirements of a symbol as follows:

- For symbols with X less than 40 mils, minimum MRD is 37.5 percent.

- For symbols with X greater than or equal to 40 mils, minimum MRD is 20 percent.

No matter whether minimum reflectance difference or point contrast signal is used, it is necessary to define the measuring geometry and reflectivity standard in order to get reproducible results. The standard geometry used in measuring bar code symbols is shown in Figure 11-12.

The symbol under test is illuminated by a source whose axis is at 45 degrees to the symbol's surface. The viewing system has its axis perpendicular to the symbol's surface and subtends 15 degrees.

Either the light source or the receiver restricts the sample field to a circular aperture whose diameter is 0.8X. The other optical path has a field of view on the sample large enough to include a circle whose diameter is at least ten times as large as that given above. The two alternatives represent either flood illumination with sample area viewing defined at the receiver or illuminant sampling of the area. The ANSI procedure requires flood illumination. Note that these are diffuse reflectance measurements. Specular (shiny) surfaces should not be specified or measured in this manner. The diffuse reflectance of a surface is defined as the ratio of the diffusely reflected radiation from the surface to that reflected from a specially prepared magnesium oxide or barium sulfate standard that is measured under the same illuminating and viewing conditions.

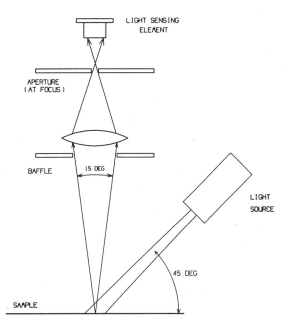

Figure 11-12: Measuring Geometry. This is the optical layout used when measuring bar code symbols for conformance with most existing bar code standards.

11.4 The ANSI Guideline for Bar Code Print Quality

Starting in 1985, members from two existing ANSI subcommittees (MH10.8 and X3A1.3) investigated factors affecting the readability of bar code symbols and methods that could be used for quantitative evaluation. This resulted in the 1990 publication of ANSI's "Guideline For Bar Code Print Quality." This document is not specific to a particular symbology and is designed to be used in conjunction with an appropriate symbology and/or application standard.

The approach is to make a series of 10 scan reflectance profiles using the standard measurement geometry and a specified aperture diameter at a particular wavelength. The scans should be approximately equally spaced over the area of the label, as shown in Figure 5-2. The wavelength(s) used should correspond to the requirements from the application standard. The measuring aperture may be specified in the application standard, or, if none is stated, the size may be selected from Table 5-1.

If the intended value of X is unknown, the actually achieved average width of the narrow element widths (called Z) is used instead.

For each scan, the largest value of reflectance (corresponding to the lightest space) is called R_{max}, and the smallest value (corresponding to the darkest bar) is called R_{min}. The determination of bars and spaces is made by drawing a horizontal line through the scan reflectance profile at the mid point between R_{max} and R_{min}. This line is called the global threshold, and is shown in Figure 11-13. The largest value of reflectance in each region above the global threshold is R_s, the space reflectance. The smallest value of reflectance measured in the region below the threshold is R_b, the bar reflectance.

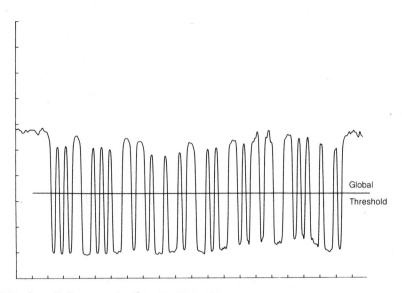

Figure 11-13: Scan Reflectance Profile with Global Threshold. Bars and spaces are identified by the value of the local reflectance relative to the global threshold.

If the R_{min} value for a particular scan is greater than one half of R_{max}, that particular scan is assigned a grade of F. The edges between bars and spaces are defined for a particular scan by the locations where the scan reflectance crosses a value that is halfway between the associated R_s and R_b values. Using the perceived edge locations, an attempt is made to decode the scan using the reference decode algorithm applicable to the symbology. If the scan cannot be decoded, that particular scan will be declared to have an F grade. All scans that are able to be decoded are then subjected to evaluation on the basis of symbol contrast (SC), edge contrast, modulation (MOD), defects, and decodability.

The complete symbol evaluation process has several steps and is illustrated by a flow diagram in Figure 11-14.

Symbol Contrast (SC)

Calculate SC for a particular scan by subtracting R_{min} from R_{max}, then assign a grade based on the resulting value:

SC	Grade
≥70%	A
≥55%	B
≥40%	C
≥20%	D
<20%	F

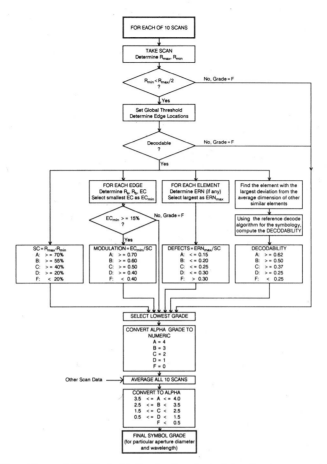

Figure 11-14: Flow Chart of ANSI's Guideline for Bar Code Print Quality Procedure.

Edge Contrast (EC)

For each element edge of a given scan, the edge contrast is equal to the difference between R_s and R_b for adjoining elements, including quiet zones. If the minimum value of EC for a particular scan is less than 15 percent, that scan is assigned a grade of F.

Modulation (MOD)

Calculate MOD for a particular scan by dividing the minimum value of EC by SC. Assign a MOD grade based on the resulting value:

MOD	Grade
≥0.70	A
≥0.60	B
≥0.50	C
≥0.40	D
< 0.40	F

Defects

Printing defects are evaluated according to their effect on the observed local reflectance of the evaluation scans. Unwanted dips or spikes in reflectivity have an associated element reflectance nonuniformity (ERN) as illustrated in Figure 11-15.

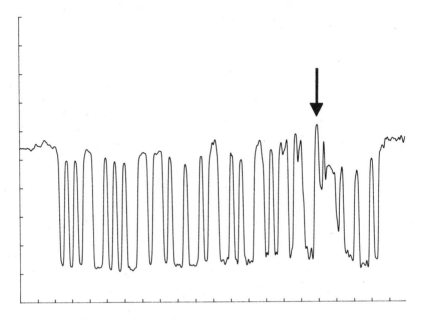

Figure 11-15: Effect of Defects on a Scan Reflectance Profile.

The largest observed value of ERN for a particular scan is referred to as ERN_{max}, and it is divided by SC to determine the defects factor. A grade is assigned based on the value of this factor:

Defects	Grade
≤0.15	A
≤0.20	B
≤0.25	C
≤0.30	D
>0.30	F

Decodability

Rather than put absolute limits on the symbol's printed dimensions, a factor called decodability is determined. Decodability is a measure of how clearly distinguishable the different element sizes are in a symbol. This is the most complicated part of the ANSI methodology to understand, but is certainly one of the more important contributions made by this particular standardization effort.

The determination of decodability is symbology dependent. Each symbology has a preferred decoding method, referred to as the "reference decode algorithm." The appendices include these algorithms for the symbologies described. In the case of

Code 39, the reference decode algorithm describes how wide elements are differentiated from narrow elements by comparing the measured width with a reference value based on the character width. As an element departs from its intended width, it can approach this threshold width value, and may potentially be misinterpreted. As described in the next chapter, it is for this reason that safety margin is built into the dimensional tolerances stated in printing specifications.

As used in this ANSI document, decodability refers to the portion of the safety margin that is left when examining the element that has the largest deviation from its intended value.

This is best explained with a simple example. Consider a Code 39 symbol printed with a 10 mil X dimension and a 3:1 wide-to-narrow ratio. Each character width is therefore 150 mils. The reference decode algorithm distinguishes wide from narrow elements by comparing them to a threshold of one-eighth of the character width, or 18.75 mils in this example. Suppose that every element in this example symbol is printed exactly at the nominal value except for one narrow bar on the end which is printed as 15 mils wide instead of 10 mils. The character width would now be 155 mils, and the new threshold would be 155/8 = 19.38 mils. It is evident that a narrow element could grow all the way up to (but just short of) 19.38 mils before it is misinterpreted as wide, therefore our one misprinted bar has only consumed (15-10)/(19.38-10), or 53 percent of the available margin. The remaining margin is 47 percent. Obviously, larger values of remaining margin correspond with more exact printing and therefore should be assigned better grades. The grade assignment for decodability is based on the remaining margin expressed as a fraction:

Decodability	Grade
≥0.62	A
≥0.50	B
≥0.37	C
≥0.25	D
< 0.25	F

Different formulas apply to different symbologies, but the approach is always the same. The element with the largest deviation is identified, and then the remaining margin is calculated based on the reference decode algorithm.

Final Grade Determination

For each of the ten evaluation scans, the grade is determined for each of the above described criteria, and the entire scan is assigned a grade equal to the worst individual grade observed. This alpha grade is converted to a numerical value between 0 and 4. The numerical average of all 10 grades is then calculated, and this average score is converted to an alpha grade for the entire symbol.

The final grade is stated as a letter followed by the aperture number and wavelength used. As an example, B/20/630 indicates a B grade symbol that was evaluated with a 20 mil diameter aperture at 630nm. The same symbol can have several different grades, depending on the aperture and wavelength used for the evaluation.

This procedure is obviously very time consuming. The use of computers or totally automatic equipment is almost mandatory if a quantity of symbols is to be evaluated. Equipment is available that can automate the entire procedure.

11.5 Print Quality of 2-Dimensional Symbologies

All of the above methodology was initially developed for conventional linear width modulated symbologies. The advent of 2-dimensional symbologies has complicated the issue further.

The first two 2-D stacked symbologies (Code 49 and Code 16K) have relatively tall bars (8X is the minimum height), fixed length, a moderate number of rows, and no error correction characters. It is possible to use either the ANSI or traditional approaches to measure the print quality of these symbologies.

PDF417

PDF417 allows for shorter bars, can have many rows, and includes error correction capability. These factors have resulted in a different method for print quality determination. A two-pronged approach is used:

1. The start and stop patterns are evaluated in accordance with the ANSI Guidelines to determine the parameters "decode" and "decodability" using an appropriate aperture. A grade is assigned to this evaluation.

2. The entire symbol is scanned with an appropriate aperture using the reference decode algorithm, then the percentage of unused error correction is determined. A grade is assigned based on this percentage:

Percentage of Unused Error Correction	Grade
$\geq 62\%$	A
$\geq 50\%$	B
$\geq 37\%$	C
$\geq 35\%$	D
$< 25\%$	F

The overall symbol grade is then defined as the lesser of the two grades determined from the above two steps.

CODE ONE

The accepted method for determining a print grade for Code One symbols involves making measurements of the recognition pattern and then actually decoding the symbol to examine how much of the error correction capability was used as part of this process. The symbol grade is defined as the lesser of the two grades determined from the following two steps:

1. The recognition pattern is evaluated in accordance with the ANSI Guidelines to determine the parameters "decode" and "decodability" using an appropriate aperture. A grade is assigned to this evaluation.

2. The entire symbol is scanned with an appropriate aperture using the reference decode algorithm, then the percentage of unused error correction is determined. A grade is assigned based on this percentage:

Percentage of Unused Error Correction	Grade
$\geq 62\%$	A
$\geq 50\%$	B
$\geq 37\%$	C
$\geq 25\%$	D
$< 25\%$	F

ArrayTag

The developers of the ArrayTag symbology have proposed a novel approach for determining the print quality of their symbology. We will look at their approach in some detail since these techniques could be applied to other symbology forms.

The quality grade of an ArrayTag symbol is determined from measurements made on the symbol or an image of the symbol taken under specified conditions. The overall quality grade is the lowest of a contrast grade, a hexagonal contour grade, a geometry grade, and a readability grade. These four grades are defined as follows.

Contrast Grade

Using a specified optical arrangement, an electronic image is taken of the symbol, and a histogram is made of the pixel intensity values. The intensity values are proportional to localized reflectivity values.

A threshold T is chosen that differentiates between the black and white intensity groupings based on the method of the Otsu algorithm ["A Threshold Selection Method From Gray-Level Histograms," N. Otsu, IEEE Transactions on Systems, Man, and Cybernetics, vol. SMC-9, January 1979]. Figure 11-16 shows a typical intensity histogram and threshold.

The mean μ_{black} and standard deviation, σ_{black} of the black intensities, and the mean μ_{white} and standard deviation σ_{white} of the white intensities are then calculated. From these four parameters and N, the number of intensity levels, two contrast grades, G_{c1} and G_{c2} are generated based on the following categories:

$(\mu_{white} - \mu_{black}) / N$	G_{C1}	$(\sigma_{black} + \sigma_{white}) / N$	G_{C2}
≥ 0.85	A	≤ 0.10	A
≥ 0.65	B	≤ 0.30	B
≥ 0.45	C	≤ 0.50	C
≥ 0.25	D	≤ 0.70	D
< 0.25	F	> 0.70	F

The contrast grade G_c is the lowest of grade G_{c1} and G_{C2}.

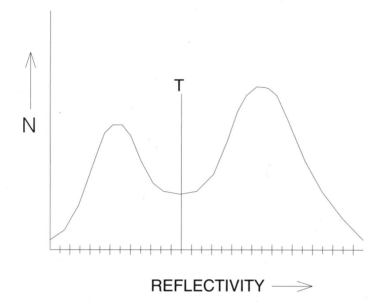

REFLECTIVITY $\longrightarrow$

Figure 11-16: Intensity Histogram. This histogram shows the distribution of localized reflectivity in the symbol. The threshold T differentiates between black and white elements.

Contour Grade

The contour grade G_n is determined by the average width, w, of the hexagonal contour formed by the contrasting border cells relative to the cell diameter d. Looking at Figure 11-17, the width of a segment is defined as the distance between two parallel lines L_1 and L_2 that are parallel to the line between the hexagonal vertices P_1 and P_2 for the segment. L_1 is located so that all pixels, with the exception of holes, above L_1 and within cells C_1 and C_2, are within 0.5σ of the mean intensity of their cell. L_2 is located so that all pixels, with the exception of holes, below L_2, and within cells C_3 and C_4, are within 0.5σ of the mean intensity of their cell.

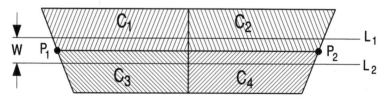

Figure 11-17: Contour Grade. This parameter is a measure of the "sharpness" of the interface between black and white border cells.

The contour grade G_n is defined as follows:

w / d	G_n
≤ 0.1	A
≤ 0.25	B
≤ 0.50	C
≤ 0.75	D
> 0.75	F

Geometry Grade

The geometry grade G_g is determined from the coordinates x_i, y_i $i = 1$ to 6, of the six vertices of the contrasting hexagonal contour. From the six coordinates, calculate the length deviation L_d, and the angle deviation A_d, as defined below:

L_d = (length of longest side—length of shortest side) / average side length

A_d = largest angle between two adjacent sides—smallest angle between two adjacent sides

The geometry grade G_g is defined as:

	G_g
$L_d \leq 0.05$ and $A_d \leq 2^\circ$	A
$L_d \leq 0.05$ and $A_d > 2^\circ$	B
$L_d > 0.05$ and $A_d \leq 2^\circ$	C
$L_d > 0.05$ and $A_d > 2^\circ$	D
> 0.1 or $A_d > 5^\circ$	F

Readability Grade

The reference decode algorithm is used to decode the symbol, and the number of errors that were detected and corrected by the Reed Solomon algorithm is recorded. The readability grade G_r is based on this number as follows:

Errors Detected	G_r
0	A
1	B
≥ 2	F

Other 2-D Matrix Symbologies

As of early 1995, symbol print quality procedures had not yet been officially adopted for other 2-D Matrix symbologies. It is expected that, when published, they will use a somewhat similar approach to those described above.

12

Data Security

A successful data collection system will allow data to be collected rapidly, economically, and accurately. The use of machine readable symbols such as bar code to transfer information from one place and time to another is analogous to the use of a conventional wired or wireless data transmission system: similar concerns exist and similar parameters are relevant. Taking some liberties, the following table illustrates this point:

Data Transmission Parameter	Wired or Wireless Term	Bar Code Term
Reliability	Up Time	First Read Rate
Error Rate	Error Rate	Substitution Error Rate
Channel Capacity	Bandwidth	Area Efficiency
Channel Quality	Signal To Noise Ratio	Print Quality

As in conventional data transmission systems, a bar code system is designed to reliably transfer as much information as possible within the constraints of symbol area and symbol print quality (as perceived by the scanner). Even if perfect symbols and sophisticated scanning equipment is used, there is a high likelihood that a number of the symbols will be scanned under less than ideal conditions: with excessive tilt or skew, or at the very far extreme of scanning range. This will result in the scanner being presented with a less than optimum signal, thereby increasing the probability of a non-read or a data error. Needless to say, system designers strive to reduce the error rate to acceptable levels wherever possible.

The basic error rate of a bar code system can be very small if a secure symbology is used, print quality is high, and properly designed reading equipment is employed. The overall system error rate can be reduced to arbitrarily low levels if sufficient redundancy and checking characters are used in the data messages.

12.1 Linear Symbology Data Security

For a given level of print quality and scanning environment (scanner acceleration, optical distortion, propensity for partial scans, etc.), different linear symbologies will result in different error rates.

All symbologies are basically secure. This means that errorless data can be transferred if the symbol is carefully printed with all dimensions exactly at nominal, and if the decoding process directly measures the element widths. Errors are introduced by a combination of the following factors:

1. Symbol element widths that deviate from nominal.

2. Excessive bar reflectance or inadequate space reflectance that lead to a marginal optical signal to the scanner.

3. The presence of unwanted spots and voids in the printed symbol.

4. Reading systems based on moving beams or hand-actuated wands do not directly measure the widths of the printed elements. Instead, the time for a scanning spot to traverse an element is measured. Because of acceleration (especially with hand-scanning), the perceived element widths are warped. Even vision-based scanners can be affected by optical distortion produced when scanning symbols that are not normal to the scanner.

5. For reading systems based on moving beams, scanning paths should ideally move completely through a symbol, beginning and ending with a quiet zone. Partial scans often occur, sometimes resulting in erroneous information's being decoded.

All symbologies are subject to the introduction of errors through a combination of the above factors. The degree of resistance to one or several of these effects varies between symbologies.

Several attempts have been made to calculate the theoretical resistance of different linear symbologies to the above effects. Due to the unpredictable nature of errors, this is a difficult and often inconclusive task. One of the easiest analyses to understand is made by calculating a linear symbology's safety factor with respect to three types of printing errors:

1. Two element widths within a character deviating from their nominal widths in a worst case fashion (one character element widening, one narrowing).

2. A single element width deviating from its nominal value.

3. All bars within a symbol uniformly shrinking or widening.

The safety factor indicates, under uniform scanning velocity conditions, the percentage of the total breakdown tolerance (where errors may occur) that remains after the published printing tolerance has been allocated. As an example, a symbology with a 65 percent safety factor has consumed 35 percent of the total breakdown tolerance in its printing specifications. This is analogous to stating that 65 percent of the tolerance budget has been reserved for the reading system. This safety factor is necessary to compensate for the following reading system considerations:

- Scanner acceleration effects or optical distortion
- Scanner resolution mismatches
- Quantization errors
- Digitization errors

The following sections calculate the safety factor for eight different linear symbologies.

Code 39

One of USS-39's appendices discloses the decoding algorithm assumed for deriving Code 39's tolerances. It is commonly called the Factor R algorithm. A derivation of Code 39's printing tolerances is provided in Appendix O.

Two error cases need to be considered. Case A represents a narrow element being misinterpreted as wide, and Case B illustrates a wide element being misinterpreted as narrow.

For the case of narrow elements inadvertently being decoded as wide (Case A, the worst case), the algorithm is shown to break down when the bar or space width tolerance exceeds a value of:

$$E = \pm\left(\frac{N}{3} - \frac{2}{9}\right)X$$

where
E = the bar or space width error
N = the wide-to-narrow ratio
X = the width of a nominal narrow module

This tolerance derivation assumes the traditional value of 1/8 for the factor R and assumes that one element grows in width an amount E while the overall character width shrinks by an equal amount.

The published printing tolerance for Code 39 is 4/9 of the tolerance at which breakdown will occur. The 5/9 safety factor is reserved for errors in the reading process such as scanner resolution, substrate scattering, scanner acceleration, signal conditioning, thresholding, and quantization.

Applying the safety factor yields the published tolerance formula for Code 39:

$$t = \pm\frac{4}{27}\left(N - \frac{2}{3}\right)X$$

Note that this truly is a worst case scenario, requiring two independent and opposite printing errors.

Another case to examine is that of a single element's growing or shrinking by an amount E. Here, Case A is the worst case, resulting in breakdown when

$$E = \pm\left(\frac{3N - 2}{8}\right)X$$

Comparing this value of breakdown to the published Code 39 printing tolerance formula yields a safety factor of 0.605.

Another interesting case is that of uniform growth or shrinkage of all elements. Case A is again the worst case, resulting in breakdown when the uniform growth reaches a value of

$$\left(\frac{3N-2}{7}\right)X$$

The corresponding safety factor is 0.654.

Interleaved 2 of 5

Similar to Code 39, the Factor R breakdown tolerance for Interleaved 2 of 5, assuming two worst case errors is:

$$E = \pm\left(\frac{36N-42}{71}\right)X$$

Again, reserving approximately 5/9 (actual value used is 0.55625) of the tolerance budget for the reader yields the published printing tolerance of

$$t = \pm\left(\frac{18N-21}{80}\right)X$$

Looking at the effect of a single element error, breakdown occurs when the width error exceeds

$$E = \pm\left(\frac{18N-21}{32}\right)X$$
(Case B)

Comparing this to the published printing tolerance, it is apparent that 60 percent of the total tolerance budget has been allocated to the reader.

Examining the uniform bar width growth, breakdown occurs when the uniform width error exceeds

$$\left(\frac{36N-42}{57}\right)X$$
(Case B)

Comparing this to the published printing tolerance, 64 percent of the total tolerance budget is reserved for the reader.

Code 11

Using the Factor R decode algorithm with R set equal to 7/32, the breakdown tolerance of Code 11 in the presence of two errors is:

$$E = \pm\left(\frac{18N - 21}{39}\right)X$$

Reserving approximately 5/9 (actual value used is 0.55682) of the tolerance budget for the reader yields the published printing tolerance of:

$$t = \pm\left(\frac{18N - 21}{88}\right)X$$

Looking at a single edge error, breakdown occurs when

$$E = \left(\frac{18N - 21}{32}\right)X \qquad \text{(Case B)}$$

Comparing this to the published printing tolerance, 64 percent of the total budget has been allocated to the reader.

In examining uniform ink spread, breakdown occurs when the uniform growth exceeds

$$\frac{(18N - 21)}{25}X$$

where
    N is less than 2.5

Comparing this to the published printing tolerance indicates that 72 percent of the tolerance budget has been allocated to the reader.

Codabar

Codabar (both Traditional and Rationalized) is often decoded using the largest bar/largest space algorithm. In this algorithm, separate thresholds for bars and spaces are defined as 5/8 times the width of the largest bar and space (respectively) encountered in a given character.

When printed at a density of ten characters per inch, the published printing tolerance for Traditional Codabar is 1.5 mils. In examining actual nominal dimensions for space widths in the character ":" (the value of E), the breakdown width tolerance can be determined. Consider the two 9.3 mil spaces. If one space width increases by E and the other shrinks by E, breakdown will occur when

$$9.3 - E = \frac{5}{8}(9.3 + E)$$

or where E = 2.146 mils.

The safety factor that was applied in the publication of the 1.5 mil printing tolerance can now be calculated as

$$\frac{1.5}{2.146} = 0.699$$

This is analogous to saying that 30.1 percent of the total error budget has been reserved for the Codabar reader in this case. If only one space shrinks in the previous example, the safety factor is 0.43, implying that 57 percent of the total error budget has been reserved for the reader.

USS-Codabar describes a Rationalized Codabar having a published bar and space tolerance of

$$t = \pm\left(\frac{5N - 8}{20}\right)X$$

Using a threshold value of 5/8 times a character's wide element, this tolerance formula reserves 35 percent of the total tolerance budget for the reader. When only a single element is allowed to vary, the published tolerance formula reserves 60 percent of the tolerance budget for the reader. And, in the case of uniform ink spread, 85 percent of the total tolerance budget is reserved for the reader.

U.P.C.

U.P.C. is decoded using edge-to-similar-edge algorithms. The total character width P is measured, and the two T-distances are quantized into modular widths, based on the assumption that P is 7 modules wide.

Three tolerances are defined:

    e = edge-to-similar-edge tolerance
    p = pitch tolerance (character width)
    b = bar or space width tolerance

The published values for e and p are:

    e = 0.14692X
    p = 0.29X.

Consider the case where a T-distance is intended to be five modules, but is measured short by an amount e, and where the character length (or pitch) is measured long by an amount p. The perceived modular T-distance will be

$$7\left(\frac{5 - e}{7 + p}\right) \quad \text{or} \quad 7\left(\frac{5 - 0.14692}{7 + 0.29}\right)$$

or 4.66 modules. This error of 0.34 modules (5.00–4.66) represents 68 percent of the allowable error before decode breakdown will occur.

For most characters, decoding of U.P.C. may be performed by edge-to-similar-edge techniques, and there is theoretically no need to closely specify actual bar or space width tolerance. Because of scanner resolution, U.P.C. bar and space width is toleranced so that the minimum allowable bar or space width is 8.2 mils. When decoding the U.P.C. characters 1, 7, 2, and 8, comparing actual bar widths is necessary. To maximize the differentiation between these characters, U.P.C. limits bar and space width tolerances as follows:

$(X - 0.009)$ for $X < 0.013$
$(0.47X - 0.00216)$ for $X > 0.013$

These formulas are based on the assumption that no allowable feature will be smaller than 9 mils when U.P.C. is printed at highest density ($X = 10.4$ mils, $M = 0.8$). Because of the 1, 7, 2, 8 ambiguity problem, however, some bars are printed at 12/13 of a module width. This means that the smallest feature size with U.P.C. could be as small as 8.2 mils.

Note that the above analysis was based on the published formulae for e and p (e $= 0.14692X$, p $= 0.29X$). Many printer mechanisms (such as dot matrix printers) can hold equal tolerances on e and p.

If e is set equal to p, determining the permissible tolerance at breakdown is possible. Again consider the case of a five module T distance being misinterpreted as four modules wide.

$$\text{set } 4.5 = 7\left(\frac{5-e}{7+e}\right)$$

solving, e $= 0.30434$ modules

If one were to assign 50 percent of the tolerance budget to the reader (more conservative than Traditional U.P.C.), then the printing tolerance for e and p would become

$$e = p = \pm 0.152 \text{ modules}$$

Code 93

Code 93 is designed to be decoded using edge-to-similar-edge algorithms. Depending on the type of printing equipment used, one of two sets of tolerance formulae may be used to determine the tolerance of e and p.

The standard Code 93 tolerances are based on the assumption that the printing equipment can control all dimensions equally well. This is a valid assumption for matrix or thermal printers. The standard tolerances are:

$e = 0.20X$
$p = 0.20X$

If a printing technique is used that can maintain tight tolerances within a character but that less accurately controls character-to-character pitch (such as a drum printer), the following alternate tolerances may be used:

$$e = 0.15X$$
$$p = 0.30X$$

In order to examine safety margins, let us use the standard tolerances and examine the case where a five module T-distance is perceived as short by an amount e and the character width is perceived wide by an amount p. The perceived modular T-distance will be:

$$9\left(\frac{5-e}{9+p}\right) = 9\left(\frac{5-0.20}{9+0.20}\right) = 4.696 \text{ modules}$$

This error of 0.304 modules (5.0 - 4.696) represents 60.8 percent of the allowable error before decode breakdown will occur.

Using the same example, let us now use the alternate tolerance set. The perceived modular T-distance will be:

$$9\left(\frac{5-e}{9+p}\right) = 9\left(\frac{5-0.15}{9+0.3}\right) = 4.694 \text{ modules}$$

This error of 0.306 modules (5.0– 4.694) represents 61.2 percent of the allowable error before decode breakdown occurs.

Because of the use of edge-to-similar-edge decoding techniques, there is theoretically no need to closely constrain individual bar or space width. However, practical considerations of resolution, modulation transfer function (MTF), spots, and voids suggest that this aspect does need to be controlled.

The Code 93 bar and space width tolerance is specified as:

$$(0.45X - 0.001)$$

This results in a minimum allowable feature size of 5.125 mils when X = 7.5 mils. If a single element is examined, breakdown will occur when:

$$E = 0.5X$$

This implies that the published formula has a

$$\left(1-\frac{0.2}{0.5}\right)100\% = 60\%$$

safety factor for the standard tolerances, and 70 percent for the alternate.

USS-128

Code 128 has similarities with both U.P.C. and Code 93. Edge-to-similar-edge decoding algorithms are used, and the maximum T-distance is seven modules. The tolerances for e and p are:

$$e = 0.20X$$
$$p = 0.20X$$

Consider the case that a seven-module T-distance is perceived as short by an amount e at the same time that character width is perceived as wide by an amount p. The perceived modular T-distance will be:

$$11\left(\frac{7-e}{11+p}\right) = 11\left(\frac{7-0.2}{11+0.2}\right) = 6.679 \text{ modules}$$

This error of 0.323 modules (7.0 - 6.679) represents 64.67 percent of the allowable error before decode breakdown will occur. The bar and space tolerance is the same as that for Code 93.

Note that Code 16K will have similar characteristics.

Code 49

Edge-to-similar-edge decoding algorithms are used, and the maximum T-distance is 10 modules. The tolerances for e and p are:

$$e = 0.2X$$
$$p = 0.2X$$

Consider the case that a 10-module T-distance is perceived as short by an amount e at the same time that character width is perceived as wide by an amount p. The perceived modular T-distance will be:

$$16\left(\frac{10-e}{16+p}\right) = 16\left(\frac{10-0.2}{16+0.2}\right) = 9.679 \text{ modules}$$

This error of 0.321 modules (10.0-9.679) represents 64 percent of the allowable error before decode breakdown will occur.

A summary of these safety factors is presented in Table 12-1.

	Bar or Space Tolerance	Edge-To-Similar-Edge Tolerance	Pitch Tolerance	Percentage of Total Tolerance Budget Allocated to the Reader		
				Single Element	Worse Case	Uniform Ink Spread
Code 39	$\pm\dfrac{4}{27}\ (N-\dfrac{2}{3})X$	- - - -	- - - -	61%	55%	65%
Interleaved 2 of 5	$\pm\left(\dfrac{18N-21}{80}\right)X$	- - - -	- - - -	60%	56%	64%
Code 11	$\pm\left(\dfrac{18N-21}{88}\right)X$	- - - -	- - - -	64%	56%	72%
Codabar	± 1.5 mils at 10 CPI	- - - -	- - - -	57%	30%	n.a.
Rationalized Codabar	$\pm\dfrac{(5N-8)}{20}\ X$	- - - -	- - - -	60%	35%	85%
UPC-A	$\pm(X-0.009)$ if $X<0.013$ $\pm(0.47X-0.00216)$ if $X>0.013$	±0.14692X	±0.29X	71%		
Code 93 (std. tol.)	±(0.45X−0.001)	±0.20X	±0.20X	60%	39%	100%
Code 93 (alt. tol.)	±(0.45X−0.001)	±0.15X	±0.30X	70%	39%	100%
Code 128, Code 16K	(0.45X−0.001)	±0.20X	±0.20X	60%	32%	100%
Code 49		±0.20X	±0.20X	60%	36%	100%

The safety factors referred to above should not be solely used for evaluating the relative security of different symbologies; other factors such as encodation and redundancy also have a major effect.

12.2 Symbology Performance Tests

AIM sponsored a performance test of seven different symbologies between 1986 and 1987. The test was conducted by the State University of New York (SUNY) at Stony Brook. A variety of printing technologies and vendors were used to generate a large quantity of variable data symbols containing a system check character. Eight different readers were used for the test, all interfaced to a computer that examined the system check character. Approximately three million characters were scanned in each of the following symbologies:

- Code 39
- I2/5 (fixed length)
- U.P.C.-A
- U.P.C.-E
- Codabar
- Code 128
- Code 93

All symbols were 12 characters long, except for U.P.C.-E, which contained six digits. Because of the nature of the test, short reads of Interleaved 2 of 5, or autodiscrimination errors with Code 39, were precluded. All readers were set to autodiscriminate as many of the symbologies as possible. Optional check characters were not used for Code 39, Interleaved 2 of 5, or Codabar. The other four symbologies included their mandatory check characters.

The test indicated that the U.P.C.-E and Codabar symbologies had an appreciably higher error rate than the other codes, and that Code 128 and Code 93 demonstrated the highest data security.

Several autodiscrimination errors were observed. In each case, a symbology was misinterpreted by the reader as a valid U.P.C.-E or short (one or two-character) Codabar symbol. The scanning equipment differed widely in their susceptibility to this type of error.

Based on a post-test examination of the errors observed, it was determined that if Code 39, Interleaved 2 of 5, and Codabar had used a check character (which the reader examined), their security would have been much higher.

In 1990, the Ohio University undertook the construction of a symbology testing facility. This facility is jointly sponsored by AIM and the Health Industry Business Communications Council (HIBCC), and was initially designed to specifically examine the performance that can be expected from potential Code 49 and Code 16K bar code applications in health care environments. The test apparatus consisted of commercially available handheld moving beam scanners which were positioned by robotic arms and interfaced to specialized data acquisition boards installed in microcomputers. Standard reference decode algorithms (such as those disclosed in the appendices of this book) were implemented. For the initial testing, a large quantity of "carriers" were labeled with a variety of bar code symbols. The carriers were formed to simulate the size and shape of typical packages used in the health care industry.

The statistical objective of the test was to determine if Code 49 and/or Code 16K could be expected with a 95 percent confidence factor to exhibit a substitution error rate of less than one error in a million characters. Code 39, Code 128, and U.P.C.-A were also included. A total of almost 70 million characters were scanned, and there were no errors with either Code 49 or Code 16K. Code 39 and Code 128 each exhibited one error, and U.P.C.-A produced 21 errors.

Based on the 1991 test at Ohio University, it can be approximated with 95 percent confidence that the error rates for both Code 49 and Code 16K are somewhere between 1 in 5 million and 1 in 300 million characters.

Ohio University also used the testing facility to perform a test of PDF417, DataMatrix, and Code 39. After scanning over 94 million characters, it can be approximated with a 95 percent confidence factor that the error rate for both PDF417 and DataMatrix are somewhere between 1 in 10 million and 1 in 600 million, and the rate for Code 39 is between 1 in 1.7 million and 1 in 4.5 million.

12.3 Effect of Print Quality

The performance of a bar code system is highly dependent upon the quality of the printed symbols. Consider for a moment the outcome of a single scanning attempt of a linear symbology (such as making one scan of a symbol with a wand). There are three possible outcomes:

1. The reader beeps, and the correct information is decoded.

2. The reader does not beep and no data is decoded.

3. The reader beeps but the information is different from that encoded in the symbol (a character substitution error).

The probability that outcome (1) occurs is the first read rate (FRR). When good quality symbols are used by trained operators, the first read rate should exceed 90 percent. Poorer quality symbols will result in lower first read rates. For a given reader, first read rate can be used as a rough measure of symbol quality.

Although there is a strong relationship between first read rate and substitution error rate, the particular decoding algorithm implemented in the reading system can affect the values obtained. It is possible to imagine a reader that would have an extremely aggressive algorithm, which would extract information (meaningful or otherwise) from any arrangement of light and dark areas. Such a reader would have a 100 percent first read rate (it would beep at anything), but would have a very poor substitution error rate. Conversely, a reader could be designed that insisted that the perceived element widths be very close to the nominal values. This reader would beep very infrequently, but would also have a very low substitution error rate. Reading equipment manufacturers must strike a compromise that will ensure a good first read rate when scanning in spec symbols, while minimizing substitution error rate across a wide range of print quality.

The probability of a substitution error [outcome (3)] is highly dependent on symbol quality and hence first read rate. For Code 39 without a check character, this dependence has been calculated theoretically and confirmed experimentally to follow the relationship illustrated in Figure 12-1.

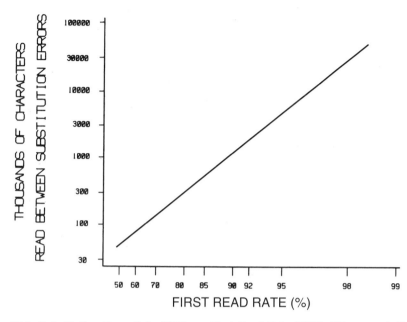

Figure 12-1: Substitution Error Rate (SER) vs. First Read Rate (FRR). Differences in first read rate because of print quality have a large effect on the probability of substitution errors.

Note that Figure 12-1 represents the relationship for Code 39 symbol lengths of 20 characters. The relationship between substitution error rate and first read rate for Code 39 is derived in Appendix P.

Figure 12-1 indicates that there is an extremely strong relationship between first read rate and substitution error rate. Halving the first read rate results in the error rate increasing by several orders of magnitude! It is important to keep the first read rate high by printing symbols in spec. Figure 12-1 illustrates the relationship for Code 39. Other symbologies will show a similar relationship, although the absolute numbers will be different.

12.4 Use of Check Characters

As in any data transmission scheme, the error rate of a bar code system can be drastically reduced through the use of check characters. A check character is an additional character included in the encoded message that is mathematically based on the other characters in the message. The bar code reader confirms that the observed check character is consistent with the rest of the observed data characters before accepting the data.

To illustrate how check characters can be used, we will examine Code 39's optional modulo 43 check character that can be included as the last character of a message. The procedure for calculating this character is as follows:

1. Referring to Table 12-2 below, determine the character value for each data character in the original message.

2. Sum all of the character values.

3. Divide the sum from step (2) by 43. The check character is the character corresponding to the value of the remainder.

4. Add the check character to the end of the data message.

Table 12-2
CODE 39 Character Values for Check Digit Computation

Character	Character Value	Character	Character Value
0	0	M	22
1	1	N	23
2	2	O	24
3	3	P	25
4	4	Q	26
5	5	R	27
6	6	S	28
7	7	T	29
8	8	U	30
9	9	V	31
A	10	W	32
B	11	X	33
C	12	Y	34
D	13	Z	35
E	14	–	36
F	15	.	37
G	16	space	38
H	17	$	39
I	18	/	40
J	19	+	41
K	20	%	42
L	21		

As an example, consider the message "CODE 39." The sum of the character values would be $12 + 24 + 13 + 14 + 38 + 3 + 9 = 113$. After dividing by 43, the quotient is 2, and the remainder is 27. The character whose value is 27 is "R." The complete message, including the check character would therefore be "CODE 39R."

Interleaved 2 of 5 uses a weighted check digit for its optional check character. It is calculated as follows:

1. Identify even- and odd-positioned digits in the message with the right-handed message digit always defined as an even-positioned digit.

2. Sum the numeric values of the odd-positioned digits.

3. Sum the numeric values of the even-positioned digits and multiply the total by three.

4. Sum the odd and even totals from (2) and (3).

5. Determine the smallest number that, when added to the sum in (4), will result in a multiple of 10. This number is the value of the check digit.

6. Determine whether the total number of digits (message plus check digits) is odd or even. If odd, add a leading, nonsignificant zero to the message to produce an even number of total digits as required for a valid Interleaved 2 of 5 symbol.

The improvement in data security when check characters are used is significant. In the case of Code 39, it is reasonable to assume that the error rate will be reduced by a factor of 43. The actual improvement is considerably better than this, however. In order for a check character not to prevent a data error, the symbol must contain two or more offsetting errors such that the observed check character still appears to be correct. This is an unlikely event.

As an example, consider a 15-character Code 39 symbol printed with poor quality, such that the substitution error rate is 1 in 100,000, or 10^{-5}. The probability that the symbol will be decoded with an error is

$$P_S = 1 - (P_C)^N$$

where

P_S = probability of the symbol containing an error
P_C = character substitution error rate
N = number of characters in the symbol
In this case, $P_S = 1.5 \times 10^{-4}$.

The probability of an undetected error in a Code 39 symbol containing a mod 43 check character is

$$P_S = \frac{1}{42} \frac{N(N-1)}{2} (P_C)^2 (1 - P_C)^{N-2}$$

If a check character is used in this example, the symbol error rate would be

$$P_S = \frac{1}{42} \frac{15 \times 14}{2} (10^{-5})^2 (1 - 10^{-5})^{13} = 2.5 \times 10^{-10}$$

In this example, the use of a check character reduced the probability of an undetected error in the symbol by over 1 million times! More than one check character (using different weighting sequences) can be used to reduce symbol error rates even further.

Note that Code 93, Code 128, Code 49, and Code 16K incorporate check characters into the symbology. The error rates for these symbologies have proven to be extremely small.

12.5 Error Correction Characters

Error correcting characters are additional characters that are added to a data message before it is transmitted that allow the original message to be recovered even if corruption has occurred in the transmission channel. This technique is commonly used in data communications and rotating disk computer storage systems.

Error correcting characters are an integral part of most 2-D matrix symbologies because the small symmetric (usually square) data cells have no vertical redundancy (as in linear symbologies), and there is a high probability that one or more cells will be in error due to minor localized printing defects or symbol damage. Without the use of error correcting characters, modern 2-D matrix symbologies would not be viable in many applications.

One 2-D stacked symbology, PDF417, has the provision for optional error correcting characters. Since this symbology is specified to allow bar heights as small as 3X, the use of error correcting characters is important in successful system design.

Several different schemes for error correction have been developed over the years, but the two most common methods use either Reed Solomon codes or Convolution codes. Most symbologies use the Reed Solomon technique.

The Reed Solomon correction character values are determined from the remainder after dividing the data character values in the symbol by a specific polynomial expression. The mathematics is based on the algebra of finite fields (called "Galois Fields") and is quite complicated, but it is well within the processing power of modern scanning equipment. Two types of errors can be corrected: "erasures," which are undecodable characters, and "errors", which are misdecoded symbol characters. The maximum number of correctable characters is generally defined by the following expression:

$$e + 2t \leq d$$

where:

e = number of erasures
t = number of errors
d = number of error correction characters

13

Data Communications

A key part of any automatic identification system is the data communications subsystem, which links the labeling and reading equipment with the data processing resource.

A data communications system can be as simple as a cable between a reader and the serial port of a dedicated personal computer, or it can involve large numbers of local and remote devices communicating with a large mainframe computer through the use of communication controllers, local area networks, and preprocessors. No matter what the extent of the data communications system, five issues must be addressed:

1. Accuracy: the accuracy of the acquired data must not be compromised by the data communications system.

2. Speed: how fast is data transferred between the bar code peripherals and the computing resource (and vice versa)?

3. Compatibility: ensuring that the bar code products and the computing resource can interchange compatible and understandable data.

4. Flexibility: the ability to reconfigure the system as operational needs change.

5. Growth: the ease of expanding the current system and integrating it with new systems.

13.1 ISO Model

The International Standards Organization (ISO) has developed a model to describe data communications. The key concept in this model is describing communications in terms of autonomous layers. Figure 13-1 depicts the model called the open systems interconnection (OSI) model, which has seven layers. The physical layer, for example, describes the cable, connectors, signal levels, and basic signaling. Specifications for this layer can be developed without reference to the content of the messages being transmitted. The designers at each end of the communications link can address the network control aspects of the communications without worrying about the physical media being used, i.e., coaxial cable, twisted pairs, radio waves, etc. It is this concept of dividing the description of the communications process into layers that has facilitated the rapid development of standards for those layers. The OSI model is a powerful tool for understanding communications

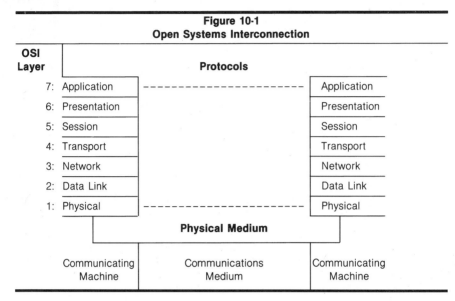

Figure 10-1
Open Systems Interconnection

OSI Layer	Protocols		
7: Application	----------------------		Application
6: Presentation			Presentation
5: Session			Session
4: Transport			Transport
3: Network			Network
2: Data Link			Data Link
1: Physical	----------------------		Physical

Physical Medium

Communicating Machine	Communications Medium	Communicating Machine

Figure 13-1: The Reference Model for Open Systems Interconnection (OSI). The Open Systems Interconnection model is based on the assumption of peer-to-peer communication. Each layer of one communicating machine communicates with the same layer of the second communicating machine.

and for describing compatible systems.

Two systems on a communication channel are not compatible unless they are compatible on all levels of the OSI model. A device that has an RS-232C interface does not make it compatible with another RS-232C device unless all of the layers of protocol have been addressed. The RS-232C specification only addresses the physical layer.

As powerful as this model is, it is limited by the assumption of completely autonomous layers. Any layer is strongly influenced by the adjacent layers, and care must be taken in defining the interface between layers. Also, overall parameters like throughput require consideration of many if not all of the layers.

13.2 Signaling

Point-to-Point Communication

The majority of existing systems use point-to-point communication, whereby two devices communicate with each other over a single channel. These systems are radially connected. Each remote device has an independent channel back to the system controller. Telephone calls are organized this way with the switched network establishing a channel between the end points. Even conference calls involve a central point with separate channels to each of the callers.

Hand-Carried Data

The simplest point-to-point channel is hand-carried data, often in the form of a floppy disk. This scheme is applicable to systems that are loosely connected and only pass files periodically, such as in shop floor data collection where batch files are output at the end of each shift. The bandwidth of this system is substantial. If it takes five minutes (300 seconds) to hand carry a disk between systems, and a 3 1/2-inch disk has approximately 1.4 megabytes on it, the data rate of this "sneaker-net" is over 37,000 bits per second. This is faster than a 19,200 baud communications channel.

RS-232C

The most common physical interface for communications is the RS-232C interface published by the Electronic Industries Association (EIA) in 1969. RS-232C defines an interface between a piece of data terminal equipment (DTE) and a piece of data communication equipment (DCE) for example the interconnection between a computer terminal (DTE) and a modem (DCE). The expectation is that both pieces of equipment are in the same area because the specification limits the line length to 50 feet. The standard specifies the signaling voltage levels and the function of the signals on a 25-pin connector (see Figure 13-2). The connector is not specified but the 25 pin subminiature D connector is usually used.

(a)

Pin Number	Description
1	Protective Ground
2	Transmitted Data
3	Received Data
4	Request to Send
5	Clear to Send
6	Data Set Ready
7	Signal Ground (Common Return)
8	Received Line Signal Detector
9	(Reserved for Data Set Testing)
10	(Reserved for Data Set Testing)
11	Unassigned
12	Secondary Received Line Signal Detector
13	Secondary Clear to Send
14	Secondary Transmitted Data
15	Transmission Signal Element Timing (DCE Source)
16	Secondary Received Data
17	Receiver Signal Element Timing (DCE Source)
18	Unassigned
19	Secondary Request to Send
20	Data Terminal Ready
21	Signal Quality Detector
22	Ring Indicator
23	Data Signal Rate Selector (DTE/DCE Source)
24	Transmit Signal Element Timing (DTE Source)
25	Unassigned

(b)

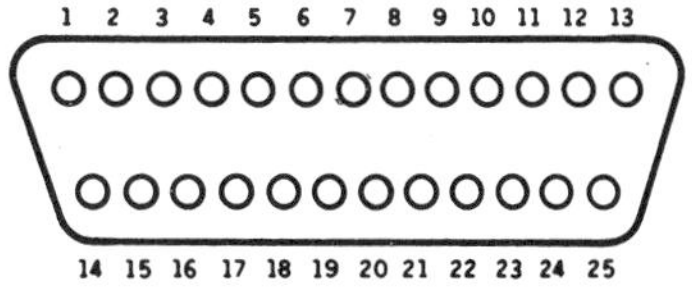

Figure 13-2: ANSI RS-232C Assignments. RS-232C is the most common physical interface between communicating machines. The standard defines electrical levels for binary signaling and assigns logical meaning to 25 connector pins (a). The de facto physical connectors used in computer industry practice are the DB-25P/DB-25S with pin layout shown (b). Since only a subset of the 25 pins are used for most peripherals, some vendors use smaller connectors with different pin numbering arrangements.

The data directions are defined in terms of the DTE: transmitted data is data from the terminal, received data is data to the terminal. A complete set of control signals are defined for controlling a modem. The intent of the standard is to specify the interconnection to a modem. A complete data channel consists of two pieces of data terminal equipment interconnected by two modems (see Figure 13-3). The standard does not address the communications between the modems.

RS-232C is commonly used to connect two devices directly, without modems.

Figure 13-3: Modem Interconnect. Modems are used when RS-232 communication distances exceed a nominal 50-foot distance, or where the communication needs to use the telephone network.

This nonstandard application of the standard causes problems because the use of the control signals is undefined in that case: the only signals that can be used are transmit data and received data. The use of RS-232C over distances exceeding 50 feet is undesirable because both ends share a common ground level, and electrical noise can easily be introduced.

Modems are used to isolate systems and communicate over long distances. The name comes from MOdulator-DEModulator. A modem takes the binary information and modulates a carrier (phase, frequency, amplitude modulation, or a combination of schemes). At the receive end, the modem extracts the binary data from the modulated carrier. Modems can be full duplex, having a communications channel open in both directions at all times, or half duplex, with the channel open in one direction at a time. In the half duplex case, the data rate can be higher because the entire bandwidth of the channel is used, but time is lost in turning around the channel to transmit in the opposite direction. In some half duplex cases, a narrowband reverse channel is kept open for supervisory communications.

Once the data is modulated on the carrier, the modem provides the drivers for the physical link. Isolation to the physical link is provided by transformers and/or optocouplers. Some modems provide lightning protection and isolate the terminal equipment from line faults. The physical media can be the switched telephone network or a variety of dedicated media such as leased lines, twisted pairs, fiber optics, microwave links, RF links, etc.

In most cases the modems are directly connected to the link. For portable applications, it is possible to acoustically couple the modem to a standard telephone handset. The modem generates tones that drive a speaker placed over the mouthpiece. A microphone placed over the earpiece receives the tones from the other end of the link.

In RS-232C environments with modems, the flow of data is controlled at the lowest levels by the modem control signals, Request To Send (RTS) and Clear To Send (CTS). When a terminal is ready to transmit, it asserts Request To Send, and when the channel is ready for data, it asserts Clear To Send. Upon receiving Clear To Send, the terminal transmits its data.

In full duplex situations where modems are not used, data is controlled by using flow control. In this scheme, two ASCII characters are used to control the flow of data. When the receiving system's buffer is close to full, it sends an XOFF (ASCII DC3) to the transmitting system. The transmitting system stops sending, but the extra buffer in the receiving system continues to receive characters during the communication and processing delays. When the receiving system's buffer is empty (or nearly so), it transmits an XON (ASCII DC1) that signals the transmitting system to resume communications. The transmitting system must keep track of the status of the channel, i.e., whether the last control character was an XON or an XOFF.

RS-422

The EIA's RS-422 standard specifies the voltage and impedance levels for data transmission on balanced lines. The data is transmitted on twisted pairs. The two wires in the pair are labeled A and B. One state is defined as wire A positive with respect to wire B, and the other is wire B positive with respect to wire A.

The receiver looks at the difference in potential between the wires and not the potential with respect to ground. This feature allows the grounds at each end of the link to be isolated from each other, eliminating ground currents and their associated noise. The RS-422 standard specifies a maximum distance of 4000 feet for data rates up to 100 kilobits/second with conservative noise margins.

RS-422 is different from RS-232C in that it addresses only signaling and does not address the function of the signals. It is applied to the direct connection between systems (see Figure 13-4). The EIA has published a companion standard to RS-422 that addresses the functionality of the signals, RS-449. This standard is meant to supersede RS-232C but has found little acceptance because of the large installed base of RS-232C equipment. The main application of RS-422 is direct connection of equipment rather than the RS-449 application of interfacing through modems.

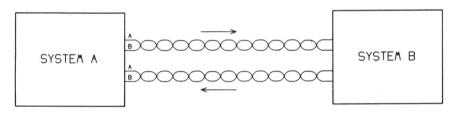

Figure 13-4: RS-422. RS-422 is a successor to RS-232 intended for longer direct connection distances. Balanced lines provide good noise immunity.

Multidrop

In the preceding discussions two systems were communicating over a single channel. Now we turn to data communications schemes where a number of systems are interconnected using a common medium. Such schemes are called multidrop.

The EIA standard RS-485 specifies a scheme for interconnecting a number of systems on a common balanced line (see Figure 13-5). The signaling is very similar to RS-422. All of the systems listen with their transmitters off. When one system is addressed, it turns on its drivers and then transmits a response. The RS-485 standard specifies the leakage currents and common mode voltages (voltages between the twisted pair and the local ground) that are required for multidrop operation. The standard allows 32 devices to share a common cable. The grounds are isolated from each other by virtue of the differential receivers.

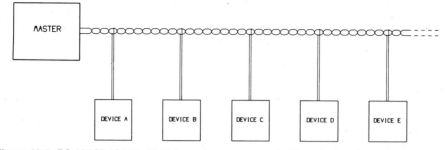

Figure 13-5: RS-485 Multidrop. Multiple devices are connected to a single balanced pair in a party-line configuration. A software protocol is required to sort out specific destinations for communications to or from the master.

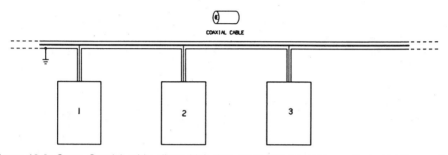

Figure 13-6: Coax. Coaxial cable allows high data rates and provides excellent shielding against noise. Coaxial cable communication buses are used for many local area networks of personal computers as well as such combined hardware/software standards as the Manufacturing Automation Protocol (MAP).

The alternate medium is coaxial cable (see Figure 13-6). The scheme is similar to the balanced line case except that standard coaxial cable is used. Isolation must be provided by other means, most commonly transformers. There are no standards similar to RS-485 for coaxial cable communications (although some standards are imbedded in communications protocols like Ethernet). Because the signals are transformer coupled, a signaling scheme that has little or no DC component (such as biphase) is used.

In biphase modulation the signal is one polarity for the first half of a bit time and the other polarity for the second half. In each bit time the average value is zero, eliminating the need to restore the DC level after AC coupling. A "1" is encoded by having the first half positive and a "0" by having the first half negative.

In some systems, modems provide the multidrop switching. In this case the modems only transmit when the connected system has been addressed. The control is provided by the connected device (DTE) using the RS-232C control lines.

Another medium for multidrop communications is the "ether," i.e., using radio communications. A number of devices share one (half duplex) or two frequencies (full duplex) for communications. Alohanet, developed by the University of Hawaii, used this medium and was the precursor of Ethernet. A protocol is used to ensure that one device is transmitting while all others are receiving.

This scheme is used in radio frequency portable terminals. In factory applications of this technology, the site must be surveyed to find the appropriate locations for the base stations and antennas to assure coverage of the operating area. Standing waves and shielding by internal structures can create dark spots where communications are impossible. The portable terminal either must be moved to complete the transaction or must store the transaction for future transmission. The advantage of radio communications is real-time feedback in a portable environment. Each installation must be licensed, and the bandwidth available is limited by regulations. This limits the scheme to narrow bandwidths and modest data rates (typically 1200 or 4800 baud, although more complex modulation schemes can increase this rate). Recently a broad band RF technology that does not require site licensing has been approved. See Section 14.3 for further details.

Multidrop Protocol: Once the multidrop media is chosen, a protocol is required to control access to the medium. Since only one device can transmit at a time, a scheme to manage who is going to talk next is required. The protocols are either masterless, where the control is passed from device to device, or have a master that manages all communications. Masterless systems have the advantage that the system can continue to operate even if a subsystem fails. Systems with masters usually have simpler protocols and lower connect costs.

One masterless system uses contention to allocate that common resource. In its simplest form a device that wants to transmit first listens on the medium and then, if no one is transmitting, begins to transmit. Messages are protected with strong error detection. A receiver knows when two or more messages have collided, because the error detection algorithm will detect this event. The transmitter then waits a random length of time and tries again.

In more recent implementations, the transmitter monitors the medium during transmission to detect a collision. When a collision occurs the transmitter immediately stops and waits a random length of time and retries. Such a system is called carrier sense multiple access/collision detection (CSMA/CD). Ethernet uses this protocol, which is specified in IEEE standard 802.3.

An alternate method of controlling access to the medium is called token passing. In this case, a short message, called a token, is passed from station to station. When a station has the token, it can complete one transaction before passing the token to the next station. The transaction is limited in length to ensure that the maximum time for a token to be passed to all of the stations is limited. This maximum time is N x T, where N is the number of stations and T is the maximum length of a transaction including acknowledgment and retries.

In the case of a token bus, the token is passed in a logical sequence that is not necessarily related to the physical layout of the network. Such a scheme is described in IEEE Standard 802.4 (Token-Passing Bus). If the network is arranged in a ring, the sequence of passing the token can take advantage of the topology. In this case the token is passed from station to station around the ring in physical sequence. This scheme is described in IEEE Standard 802.5 (Token Ring).

In the masterless cases, CSMA/CD has the advantage that at low loading of the channel there is no delay in transmitting. The token-passing schemes require that a station wait until the token comes back to the station. At high channel loading, contention schemes use increasing amounts of the channel capacity to resolve collisions, and thus have less overall channel capacity than the token-passing schemes.

The most common systems with a master use a poll-select protocol. When the master wants to transmit information to a station, it sends a select character to the station. The station responds that it is ready to receive data, then the master sends the data. Otherwise the master polls the stations one by one to see if they have data for the master. This scheme is usually the simplest to implement at the stations and thus has the lowest connect cost. In the simple implementation, all data must go through the master. Data goes from station A to the master and then from the master to station B, requiring two transmissions on the medium.

13.3 Synchronous Communication

In the early days of data communication, each character was sent asynchronously. The encoding of the characters was preceded by a start bit and followed by a stop bit. These start and stop bits synchronized the mechanisms at each end for each character sent. When communications moved from mechanical mechanisms to electronic systems, designers realized that better use of the available channel bandwidth could be achieved by grouping blocks of data and eliminating the start and stop bits. Also, more efficient modulation could be used if the bits were sent synchronously with the carrier.

One of the most popular synchronous protocols is IBM's SDLC (Synchronous Data Link Control). In this protocol, the message is bracketed by flag characters (01111110). All control information is identified by its location relative to the flag characters (see Figure 13-7). This is a bit-oriented protocol, and the information can be any number of bits long (it does not have to be an integral number of bytes, although most implementations use byte-oriented data). To prevent a string of 01111110 in the data from being interpreted as a flag character, a technique of bit stuffing is used. Whenever the transmitter sees five 1s in a row in the data, it inserts a 0 after the fifth 1. The receiver looks at the incoming bit stream and whenever it sees five 1s, it looks at the next bit. If the next bit is a 1, then this is a flag character; if the next bit is a 0, then it is deleted from the data. The insertion and deleting of 0s makes the protocol completely transparent to the data.

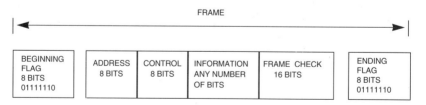

Figure 13-7: SDLC. SDLC is an IBM communication protocol specifying information packets called frames. Data in the frames are bracketed by an overhead of flag patterns, address information, control information, and frame check sum information.

13.4 Error Protection

All data transmissions are subject to interference that can change the data. Examples of sources are lightning, ground currents, electrical discharge, welding, electrical equipment, radio transmitters, crosstalk, etc.

To minimize data errors caused by interference, some form of redundancy must be built into the data. Figure 13-8 shows a serial message arranged in bytes. The bits are transmitted in the order shown in the boxes. One form of redundancy is to use every eighth bit as a parity bit (transverse parity). For odd parity, the number of 1s in the eight bits is odd (e.g., 01010100). The receiver checks the parity, and if any eight-bit character fails the test, the message is rejected. This technique will detect any single-bit errors. If a noise spike changes the state of two adjacent bits, the parity check will not detect the error.

CK 9	CK1				25	17	9	1
CK10	CK2				26	18	10	2
CK11	CK3				27	19	11	3
CK12	CK4				28	20	12	4
CK13	CK5				29	21	13	5
CK14	CK6				30	22	14	6
CK15	CK7				31	23	15	7
CK16	CK8				32	24	16	8

Figure 13-8: Error Detection. Messages transmitted through communication lines can have error detection information as part of the protocol used. Extensive checking of the data bits in a serial stream can be provided through longitudinal redundancy checks (LRCs) operating on blocks of data. In this simplified schematic of such a fixed length block, bits are numbered in the order sent, ending with 16 LRC bits CK1 to CK16. If the calculated LRC code at the receiving end differs from the LRC data sent with the block, the communications protocol would provide for a retransmission of the block.

For greater security, a longitudinal redundancy check (LRC) pattern is used. In most modern systems this is the last 16 bits of the message. The LRC pattern is calculated longitudinally and thus detects bursts of noise that are not detected by the transverse parity. In protocols like SDLC, an LRC is used but transverse parity is not (in order to preserve data transparency).

When an error is detected in a block of data, the receiving station sends a negative acknowledgment to the transmitting station. The transmitting station then retransmits the block. After a preset number of retries, the transmitting station abandons the effort and generates an appropriate system error message. In multidrop systems, a station cannot tell if it was addressed when it receives a message with errors. In that case the transmitting station gets no acknowledgment and tries again.

13.5 Installation

Whenever data is transmitted via cables that leave a building, special care must be taken for lightning protection. If modems are used and the data is transmitted over telephone lines, the telephone company will take responsibility for the lightning protection. Otherwise a low impedance path to ground (ground rods or the building ground grid) must be provided where the lines enter the building. The building itself should be inspected to ensure that the structure is solidly grounded. This care is required both to protect the equipment and for personnel safety. The installation must comply with applicable building codes.

All equipment cases should be grounded locally for personnel safety. If two pieces of equipment share a common ground through the data communications path but are separately grounded to local grounds, a ground loop is formed. A difference in potential between the two grounds causes a current to flow in the common ground connection. This can introduce noise in the signal leads, as shown in Figure 13-9. The solution is to provide isolation between the two systems through transformers or optical couplers.

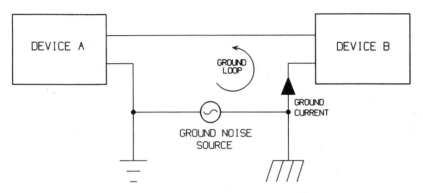

Figure 13-9: Ground Loops. Localized differences in ground voltages can cause noise currents to flow through data cables.

If a shielded cable is used, there are advantages to grounding the shield at both ends. The ground currents in the shield generate magnetic flux around the cable; this flux induces equal voltages in the signal leads (see Figure 13-10). This induced voltage minimizes the voltage seen by the line isolation.

If the equipment is in a shielded enclosure and there is a short direct path to ground, the equipment will not be susceptible to electrostatic discharge (ESD). ESD is usually generated by personnel walking on an insulated floor in a dry atmosphere. When they touch a piece of equipment, a discharge that can upset the operation of the equipment occurs. With a shielded, grounded enclosure, the discharge is harmlessly dissipated into the ground. In any installation, consideration must be given to the path for ESD.

13.6 Local Area Networks

A model for local area networks in automatic identification systems is shown in Figure 13-11. This model divides the networks into two regions, the automatic identification network and the plant network. These two regions are divided by the cell controller.

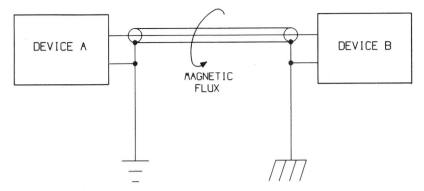

Figure 13-10: Magnetic Flux And Grounding. Shielded cable should be used for communications lines. This helps prevent inductive coupling from one cable to another or from external noise sources into the cable. To be effective, the cable shields are grounded at both ends.

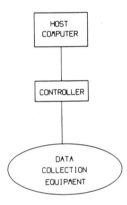

Figure 13-11: Typical Local Area Network Concept for Bar Code. A host computer typically talks to one or more local area network controller(s). Each controller in turn manages network traffic for multiple peripheral subsystems including video terminals, data collection equipment, and printers.

The automatic identification network interconnects the readers and printers that are at workstations throughout an area. This network is characterized by short messages (less than 80 characters) and fast response times (typically under 0.3 seconds). Often it is installed in hostile environments (welding, electrical machinery, etc.).

The plant networks exchange files between subsystems. They are characterized by block-oriented data and modest response times. The simplest form has a host computer that communicates with each of the subsystems. The next higher system distributes the processing among the cell controllers, but keeps the database centralized at the host. The most sophisticated systems eliminate the host and distribute the database as well as the processing. In this case the database is located in the machine that needs the most access to it. The last version provides the quickest response time and the greatest flexibility. Such systems are a recent development.

One plant network that is emerging as the standard for industrial applications is the manufacturing automation protocol (MAP). MAP was pioneered by General Motors Corporation and now is supported by the major computer manufacturers, and manufacturers of automation equipment. The MAP Users Group is sponsored by the Society of Manufacturing Engineers (SME). The intention is to specify protocols for all levels of the OSI model (see Figure 13-1). This effort has been unique in demonstrating a high level of compatibility.

13.7 Trends

Automatic identification systems began by emulating existing peripheral equipment. For example, if bar code readers emulate interactive terminals to a mainframe computer, then they can be installed with a minimum of modification to the existing mainframe software. This approach has the advantage of ease of installation, but it has limitations because a reader is not a terminal.

The next stage is for the controllers to process the data for a local area (for example, shop floor data collection in a work center). This distributes the processing. The next level of sophistication is to distribute the database also. For example, the badge file can be transferred to the time-and-attendance controller. This puts the data where it is most used. This requires either sophisticated networking of the database or multiple copies of files. Multiple copies run the risk of diverging from each other as transactions are processed, resulting in confusion if not error.

The trend is toward cell controllers where a controller manages all the functions in an area. Here a controller manages the data collection as well as the movement of material, etc. These controllers are interconnected by a network such as MAP. These systems have shared databases and standardization at high levels. Such systems are in the future, but demonstration systems are already operational.

14

Wireless Data Networks

A data collection network does not necessarily have to be interconnected with hard wiring. Portable devices needing to have immediate access to remote data require some type of wireless medium to accomplish this. Even fixed mount devices are commonly being linked with wireless networks because of the flexibility and reasonable cost that such an approach offers over wired alternatives. Information can be transmitted in a wireless fashion via several different techniques: optics, sonics, magnetics, radio, etc. Radio frequency (RF) has proven to be the most practical and versatile.

14.1 Introduction to Radio Frequency Communication

Radio waves are electromagnetic waves, as is light, but in a different part of the electromagnetic spectrum. See Figure 14-1.

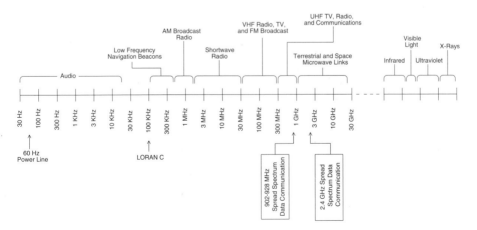

Figure 14-1: Radio Communication Frequencies within The Electromagnetic Spectrum. Radio waves are just one form of electromagnetic radiation. Specific locations in the spectrum can be identified by either the frequency or the wavelength.

In free space, electromagnetic waves travel at the speed of light, or about 300,000 kilometers per second. Waves that have a higher frequency (which means that they oscillate more frequently in a given period of time) will therefore have a shorter wavelength. As an example, an AM broadcast station operating at 1000 kilohertz (1000 KHz) will be transmitting radio waves with a 300-meter wavelength, while an FM broadcast station operating at 100 megahertz (100 MHz) will be transmitting on a 3-meter wavelength.

All radio waves travel in straight lines. Radio waves with frequencies higher than about 30 MHz typically propagate in "line of sight" paths, without reflecting or refracting in the earth's atmosphere. Higher frequencies will however diffract at corners, sharp edges, and openings. Radio waves can travel into or out of conductively surrounded areas such as metal buildings if there are openings (such as windows) with dimensions of over about a quarter wavelength. Radio waves with frequencies less than about 30 MHz are subject to being reflected off of certain ionization layers which are hundreds of miles above the earth: this is how ham radio operators and short wave broadcasters are able to send their signals thousands of miles around the world. The maximum frequency that can be reflected off of the ionisphere varies as a function of the time of day and the 11 year sunspot cycle. This reflection phenomenon is not a consideration for wireless data communication networks used in bar code systems because frequencies of over 150 MHz are used, and these are typically restricted to "line of sight" transmission paths.

An RF signal by itself conveys no information other than its presence or absence. Early radio communications were conducted using Morse code, which basically turned the RF signal on and off in specific patterns representing the characters to be sent. In order to carry voice or other programming material, the RF signal must be caused to vary in some predetermined way as a function of the information to be sent. This is called modulating the RF signal. The unmodulated RF signal is typically called the "carrier."

The three most common ways of modulating an RF signal are either by varying its amplitude (called amplitude modulation, or AM), by varying its frequency (frequency modulation, or FM), or by varying its phase (called phase modulation, or PM). Note that phase modulation and frequency modulation are closely related. Some advanced high speed modulation schemes actually combine elements of amplitude and phase modulation.

Most private voice-based business radio systems such as taxi dispatching, walkie-talkies, etc., operate on frequencies of higher than 150 MHz and use frequency modulation. Being voice, the information consists of an analog signal with a maximum bandwidth of about 3 KHz. The North American cellular phone system, which operates in the 850 MHz range, was originally built using FM to carry the voice channels, but is just now being expanded in many areas using digital technology to encode sampled voice signals. European cellular phones, which operate in the 900 MHz range, are already making use of digital technology using a system known as GSM.

14.2 RF Data Transmission

Because radio systems were originally intended primarily for the transmission of voice and/or music information, the frequency assignments and regulations have been developed around systems transmitting analog information having a maximum frequency content of about 3 KHz (for voice), or 10 KHz (for music). In order to transmit digital data, a modem is commonly used, which allows transmission of digital data through an analog transmission channel. Obviously, a modem is necessary on both ends of an RF communication channel. The modem can modulate the carrier with AM, FM, or PM. For so-called "narrowband systems," government regulations restrict the data rate such that the amount of RF spectrum occupied by the system will be no greater than that of a voice system. Depending on the type of modem employed, this implies a maximum data rate of 2400, 4800, or 9600 baud. Narrowband radio systems are licensed in a similar fashion to the two-way radios commonly used in taxis and other commercial applications.

In 1989, the Federal Communications Commission (FCC) created a new frequency band allocation for low power digital radio communication using digital spread spectrum technology. The frequency range from 902 MHz to 928 MHz was allocated to this application in the U.S. The FCC also allocated bands at 2.4 GHz (2,400 MHz) and 5.7 GHz (5,700 MHz). Although restricted to low transmitter power (and hence short range), no user license is required. A few other countries also implemented similar regulations.

After several years of standard development, a pan-European organization known as ETSI (European Telecommunications Standards Institute) published a standard for spread spectrum data communication that is being adopted by most of the countries in Europe. In a similar fashion to the FCC, the ETSI standard allows unlicensed operation of low-power spread spectrum systems in bands at 2.4 GHz and 5.7 GHz.

As of early 1995, there is no such thing as a single radio system that is completely transferable from one country to another with assurances of regulatory compliance. No worldwide standard exists for a common frequency band, although there are many similarities in the region of 2.4 GHz. Equipment will need to be configured to the country of intended use. It is entirely feasible from a technical standpoint to build a spread spectrum data transceiver in the 2.4 GHz range that could be easily configured to operate in more than one continent; sooner or later these products will become available.

14.3 Spread Spectrum

Most radio links in use today are so-called "narrowband systems." An attempt is made to reduce the amount of RF spectrum consumed by a given RF channel so that a large number of simultaneous RF transmissions can occur in a given range of frequencies. RF spectrum is a scarce commodity, and every effort is usually made to reduce the amount required for a given application. Spread spectrum technology takes a different approach to spectrum conservation. Rather than avoiding interference with other users by spacing out different narrowband transmissions at different frequencies, spread spectrum theoretically allows multiple broad band transmissions to occur in the same portion of spectrum.

Spread spectrum techniques were originally developed for military applications because of the anti-jamming capability provided. Spread spectrum communication spreads the RF energy over a wide range of frequencies so that only a small amount of energy is concentrated in one place, thereby making detection and jamming difficult. In a data collection application, this means that a spread spectrum transmission can co-exist with narrowband transmissions with minimal interference.

There are several different methods of spread spectrum modulation. The two currently standardized on by the FCC and ETSI are referred to as "direct sequence" and "frequency hopping." Both methods actually modulate the signal with the data to be transmitted by varying the instantaneous phase of the radio frequency carrier. The two methods differ in how the signal is spread out to occupy a wide bandwidth.

In a direct sequence system, the actual instantaneous phase of the carrier signal is rapidly switched back and forth through a controlled angle via a pseudo-random digital signal that has had its pattern selectively inverted by the actual data to be transmitted. The pseudo-random digital signal is generated by a read-only memory or a device known as a maximal length multiple feedback shift register, which generates a pseudo-random sequence of alternating ones and zeros that repeats on a regular basis. Because the sequence of bits is generated at high speed, the resulting modulated signal occupies a substantial block of RF spectrum (indeed, it may occupy the entire allocated frequency band). The receiving equipment includes circuitry that can recognize and lock onto the sequence and then recover the modulated information. If different pseudo-random patterns are used, multiple spread spectrum transmissions can simultaneously use the same portion of RF spectrum. If one were to tune in a radio to a channel occupied by a direct sequence signal, it would not be possible to discern anything other than a slightly higher background noise level. This is because even though the total transmitted power can be several hundred milliwatts, the amount of power in a given segment of bandwidth is very low. Rather than spread the signal over the entire frequency band, manufacturers usually set up the transmitters so that the occupied spectrum only occupies a few megahertz: this divides the regulated frequency band into a series of "channels." With the availability of multiple channels and multiple spreading codes, many users may simultaneously use the available spectrum.

A frequency hopping system is more similar to a narrowband system in that the data to be transmitted is directly modulated onto the carrier signal, usually using a form of frequency shift keying. The frequency of the carrier is however caused to jump about between a number of specific values in the allowable frequency band in a pre-determined pseudo-random fashion. Once the receiving equipment is synchronized to the sequence, it can follow the transmit frequency as it hops about. If one of the frequencies that is used is subject to interference, the system will detect that data is being corrupted while on that frequency, and the data will be re-transmitted on another frequency in the sequence. The full allowed transmit power is used at each frequency, but any given frequency is only used for a small portion of time.

There are proponents of both direct sequence and frequency hopping approaches, but in the end result the performance differences are not large, and can vary from application to application. Figure 14-2 illustrates graphically the difference between direct sequence and frequency hopping.

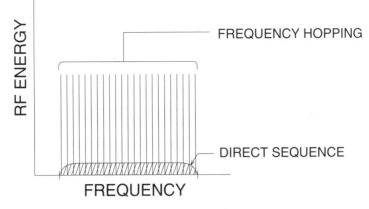

Figure 14-2: Spread Spectrum Approaches. In a frequency hopping system a full power narrow-band carrier is caused to jump between a number of predetermined values. In a direct sequence system the entire transmitter power is uniformly spread across the frequency range. This chart shows the RF energy as a function of frequency for the two systems.

Different specifications apply to direct sequence and frequency hopper systems:

902–928 MHz (U.S. only)

	Direct Sequence	Frequency Hopper
Maximum Carrier Power	1 Watt	1 Watt
Power Spectral Density	+ 8 dBm max. in any 3 KHz	n.a.
Time On A Given frequency	n.a.	0.4 sec max.
Number Of Frequencies	n.a.	50 min.

2400 MHz (ETSI)

	Direct Sequence	Frequency Hopper
Maximum Output Power	100 mW EIRP	100 mW EIRP
Power Spectral Density	+ 10 dBm per MHz max.	+ 20 dBm max. in any 100KHz
Time On A Given Frequency	n.a.	0.4 sec max.
Number Of Frequencies	n.a.	20 min.

When compared to a traditional narrowband modulation method such as FM, spread spectrum offers a number of advantages for the transmission of digital data in a data collection network:

1. Data transmission rates can be very high, often in excess of 100 kilobits per second.

2. The system can be highly immune to narrowband interference.

3. No individual site license is required in the U.S. to install a spread spectrum system operating in accordance with the FCC rules.

4. Unauthorized interception of the transmitted data is highly unlikely.

The primary disadvantage of spread spectrum is the shorter ranges achieved. Restricted by regulation to low transmitter power and low gain antennas, ranges are typically 1500 feet outdoors, and 500 feet indoors for 900 MHz systems, and about one half of this at 2.4 GHz. To extend the operating area, multiple repeaters can be used. Sometimes these receive on one spreading code or frequency range and re-transmit on a different spreading code or frequency range. A cellular network can be developed using this concept, and the repeater-to-repeater hand-offs can be made totally transparent to the user.

The RF spread spectrum circuitry and its associated controller can be built into the bar code reader's package, or it may be a separate cable-connected unit. There are some PCMCIA cards that contain everything (including the antenna) in one package, allowing existing products to quickly be interfaced to RF data collection systems.

Spread spectrum systems are best applied within a well-defined area. If it is necessary to have coverage over a complete metropolitan area, a higher power narrowband system may be more appropriate, even though the data rates will be significantly less. Actual ranges will vary considerably from site to site, and are affected by the performance specifications of particular equipment, reflective and absorptive materials in the user environment, local interference, and antenna location. It is essential that an RF survey be conducted that matches the characteristics of the proposed manufacturer's equipment.

As of early 1995, every spread spectrum manufacturer's system is proprietary. There are no industry-wide standards that would allow a user to intermix equipment from different vendors. Differences exist in frequency, modulation, data rate, encoding, and protocol. An IEEE standardization activity known as 802.11 is attempting to develop and publish standards that could ultimately lead to the possibility that compatibility may exists between vendors of RF spread spectrum equipment. All major suppliers of RF data collection equipment are participating in this standardization effort.

14.4 Application to Data Collection

An RF-based data collection network has many advantages over a wired architecture. Data throughput can often be higher than wired systems, and installation time is low. Portable terminals, whether handheld or vehicle-mounted, can be on-line to a host computer system without compromising their portability.

RF networks are not necessarily limited to portable applications. If fixed mount scanning or printing equipment is to be added in a facility where it is impractical or excessively expensive to run additional data cables, RF modems can offer an inexpensive and easy solution.

Typically, an RF network employs a base station that controls all communication with remote units. The base station can communicate with any of the remote devices on one or several frequencies or (if spread spectrum is used) spreading codes. Sometimes communication with remote devices is through intermediate repeater stations. The base station incorporates a controller that can look like a conventional wired network controller as far as the host computer is concerned.

Many different types of control protocols are used by multiple station RF networks. One common approach is to use a polling method, whereby each remote unit is sequentially interrogated by the base station. Another is the CSMA/CD (Carrier Sense Multiple Access/Collision Detection) technique, whereby a device wishing to send will wait for the common frequency to become idle, then will transmit the desired message while simultaneously listening to determine if a "collision" occurs with another station's transmission. If a collision is detected, the device aborts the transmission, waits for a random period of time, checks that the channel is clear, then retries.

The base station may use multiple antennas in order to get appropriate area coverage. Sometimes multiple base stations are also driven by a single network controller.

15

Systems Design

The term "systems design" is often used to cover all the phases leading up to actual implementation of a bar code system. Actually, systems design is only one of the four distinct phases in any bar code development project. The four phases in a bar code project are definition, system analysis, system design, and implementation.

A key ingredient to the success of any bar code system is the early and continuous involvement of a team leader, often referred to as the bar code champion.

15.1 Definition Phase

During the definition phase, the flows of material and information are examined and modeled. Grid flow, data flow, and/or work flow diagrams are useful tools in modeling the proposed system. The actual users of the proposed system must take an active role in this phase.

When modeling the system, planners must take care not to overemphasize data input rather than data output! The system is presumably being used to provide useful outputs (reports, summaries, etc.), not to "gobble up data."

The flow of information can be categorized as follows:

1. Action information: usually real time in nature, this data is used to cause some action, e.g., such as diverting a flow or configuring a test fixture.

2. Archival information: this data is not acted on immediately but is stored for traceability requirements.

3. Report Information: this data may not be acted on immediately, but is used in a report that is used for decision making; examples would be inventory levels, labor hours, or cost summaries.

15.2 Analysis and Design Phases

The charts and flow diagrams developed during the definition phase are an important input to the analysis and design phases. Structured modeling techniques and network simulation models (examining material and information flow relationships) can be effective tools during these phases.

Three types of system architecture can be used: a stand-alone system; a fully integrated, on-line system; and a hybrid system. A stand-alone system uses a separate, dedicated computing resource to manage the data collection activity. Data is transferred between the data collection computer and the corporate processor in a batch mode at regular intervals. In a fully integrated, on-line system, the bar code peripherals, be they printers or readers, are connected directly to the existing corporate data processing system. A hybrid system provides computing capabilities at the bar code reader but is still basically a fully integrated, on-line system.

Stand-Alone System

The data collection computer (DCC) is the heart of the stand-alone system. It can be as simple as a desk-top microcomputer, or it can be a fully loaded minicomputer. Its job is to handle data coming from all of the connected terminals, check for specific formats, update local databases, and respond with prompts or error messages. The DCC runs a specific, application-dependent program. Figure 15-1 illustrates a typical stand-alone system architecture.

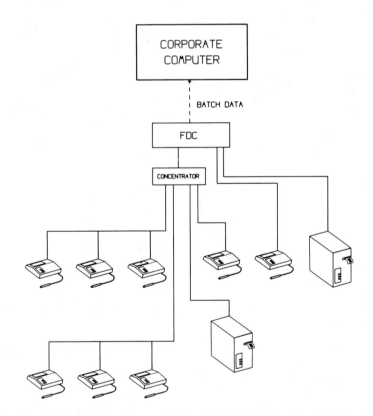

Figure 15-1: Stand-Alone System Concept. The data collection computer (DCC) is self-contained and operates without real-time communication with the corporate computer. Batch communication with the corporate computer is done in batch mode using telecommunications, disk, or tape.

Data is transferred between the factory data collection computer and the corporate computer via batch mode. This can occur either through the transfer of a physical medium (such as a disk) or through a wired connection.

In order to allow a large number of terminals to be connected, port concentrators can be employed to expand the DCC's input/output capability, or a multidrop topology can be used.

A stand-alone system has several advantages:

1. By its very nature, a stand-alone system is independent of the corporate data processing system, and can continue to operate when the "big system" goes down for maintenance or problems.

2. Depending on the factory data collection computer's computing power and the number of attached terminals, a stand-alone system can offer fast system response time.

3. Because it is self-contained, it is easy to make hardware or software changes to a stand-alone system without fear of unduly perturbing the corporate computer.

4. Costs are steadily declining for microcomputers and minicomputers. Stand-alone systems are potentially quite inexpensive.

5. Many existing manual systems are batch oriented, and implementing a stand-alone system is usually easy.

6. Typically the end user is heavily involved in the purchase, implementation, and maintenance of the stand-alone system. This is often not the case for the on-line, fully integrated or hybrid system approaches.

7. A stand-alone system will not place an additional computing burden on the corporate computer.

The disadvantages of stand-alone systems are all a by-product of one of the listed advantages: independence between the two computing systems.

1. Any required database that exists in the corporate computer must be duplicated in the factory data collection computer, raising the potential for errors and increased overhead.

2. Because of the batch mode of intercomputer communication, changes in one database do not immediately flow through to the other database, causing possible confusion and errors.

3. Without real-time access to the corporate computer's central database, the factory data collection computer cannot perform exhaustive checking of transactions.

4. The stand-alone system is often implemented and maintained to a high degree by the user group. This state of affairs may cause anxiety on the part of the corporate data processing (MIS) department, which is chartered to manage all corporate computer resources.

Fully Integrated, On-Line System

A fully integrated, on-line system incorporates bar code peripherals as part of the corporate computing system. The system can have many forms, depending on the type of computing hardware. Typically, most systems will use cluster controllers or the equivalent to interface with the actual terminals.

The bar code terminals can be connected directly to a cluster controller if they are designed to emulate a computer terminal. If a protocol converter instead of a cluster controller is used, generic ASCII bar code readers may be employed. Figure 15-2 shows a typical system. Some bar code equipment has optional interface capability to connect directly to many corporate computer networks without requiring external converters or emulators. Some higher end bar code terminals include card slots that comply with industry standards, allowing a variety of third-party interface cards to easily be integrated.

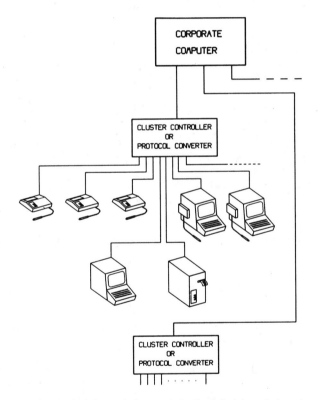

Figure 15-2: Fully Integrated System Concept. In the fully integrated system, the corporate computer is a part of every transaction. Real-time responses occur without the inherent time delay of a batch mode of operation. One or more cluster controllers handle message traffic between the corporate computer and the individual terminals of the system design.

When a bar code symbol is scanned, data from the reader flows all the way up to the mainframe to interact with an application program. Conversely, prompts or error messages flow from the mainframe all the way down to the individual reader. The user must recognize that the host computer is part of every transaction.

Advantages to the fully integrated system are:

1. A primary advantage of the fully integrated, on-line system is the capability of updating central databases in real time.

2. Because of the availability of the current database, extensive validation or reasonableness checking of each transaction is possible.

3. With minimal changes, bar code data collection can be added to existing system hardware and software through the use of appropriate bar code products.

4. The fully integrated, on-line system is generally managed by the data processing department. The DP department is often in the best position to fully appreciate the scope of any computer-related capital investment. This group may also be the best vehicle for providing on-going support.

Disadvantages of the fully integrated approach include:

1. System response time can easily become an operational problem. Because the central computer is involved in every transaction, it is easy for the entire system to slow down to a snail's pace during high activity periods. Slow responses frustrate not only the application users but also all of the other original users of the corporate computer.

2. Because of the scarcity and complexity of support software for implementing a fully integrated, on-line system, implementation is often a prolonged experience.

3. A major commitment of hardware and software resources must be made to successfully implement a fully integrated system.

Hybrid System

A hybrid or front-end pre-processing system offers the real-time database updates of a fully integrated system with the fast response and easier implementation of a stand-alone system. This is achieved by offloading a significant portion of communication and processing overhead from the main computer. This may be accomplished either by using a front-end data collection computer that interacts with the corporate computer in real time or by using bar code terminals that possess local intelligence. The first approach is shown in Figure 15-3.

In Figure 15-3, nonintelligent terminals are under the control of a front-end minicomputer or microcomputer. Prompts and error messages are generated by the minicomputer, which also performs data checking. Any necessary data files are downloaded from the host to the minicomputer. Interaction occurs in real time. Completely assembled and checked transactions or groups of transactions are transferred on-line to the host computer. An example of a hybrid system using intelligent terminals is shown in Figure 15-4.

Here, local editing, checking, and prompt generation is performed by the intelligent terminals. These terminals run their own application programs that are either stored locally in nonvolatile memory or downloaded from the host computer.

A complete transaction, which may be the result of several different scanning

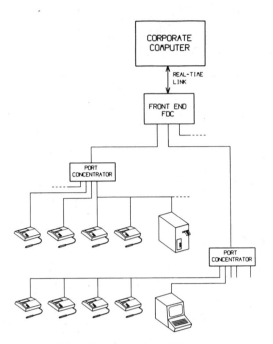

Figure 15-3: Hybrid System Using Preprocessing. A front end computer assembles and checks transactions before forwarding data to the host. An added layer of computing is used to improve responses.

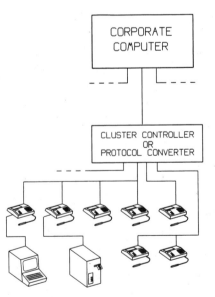

Figure 15-4: Hybrid System Using Intelligent Terminals. Application software in the terminals is used for data verification, editing, and transaction assembly. The application is thus split up between numerous local processors residing in the local terminals.

events, is built up by the local intelligent terminal. Data checking is performed, and all user prompts and messages are generated locally. When completed, the transaction is transmitted to the host for acceptance.

Advantages of hybrid systems are:

1. A hybrid system offers very good response times. Each individual scan of a bar code does not need to wait while that particular message winds its way up to the host computer for entry, verification, and acknowledgment.

2. Because checking and transaction building occurs outside of the corporate mainframe, a minimum of host software development is necessary.

3. Data that does get to the host computer has already been subjected to validity checks, minimizing the potential for database contamination.

Some of the disadvantages of the hybrid approach are:

1. A hybrid system is somewhat more complicated than either a stand-alone or fully integrated system, but the system is easily modularized, allowing implementation activities to occur in parallel.

2. At certain times, database files will simultaneously exist in more than one location. This can raise data security concerns.

3. The hybrid system requires more processing power to be distributed away from the host computer than does a fully integrated system. The net effect is that the hybrid system often requires more initial expense but gives higher performance than the other two alternate systems.

4. The front end pre-processing system may mean some loss of control over the data collection for the central DP group in that these systems are often implemented by third parties. Normally the loss of control is not quite as severe as is often the case with the stand-alone system.

Equipment Selection and Installation

Once the appropriate system architecture has been selected, specific requirements for the bar code equipment can be determined. In selecting appropriate bar code reading equipment, many choices and considerations arise:

1. Is an operator going to be involved in the scanning operation or will fixed mount scanners be used?

2. Will fixed readers or portables be used? If portable readers are to be used in a batch mode, consideration must be given to the number and location of stations where data may be dumped.

3. Will wireless devices be used? If so, what range is required? Will coverage be required in several different buildings or areas that may not be transparent to RF? What data rates are necessary? Should narrowband or spread spectrum be used? An RF survey should be conducted before finalizing decisions regarding specific equipment, antennas, and repeaters.

4. Based on the application, which is the most appropriate scanning device: wands, lasers, 1-D CCDs, or 2-D CCDs? This choice is highly influenced by the type of symbology to be used.

5. Should the readers have local intelligence? If so, how much, and how will the programs be loaded? Will proprietary or industry standard languages be used?

6. Is a display required? If so, is alphanumeric capability needed? How many characters are required? How many lines? Is graphics required? Is a touch screen appropriate?

7. Will a keyboard be used for entering exception data?

8. Will any of the equipment be subjected to extremes of temperature or humidity? In some applications, the data collection equipment will have to survive being washed down. Will it be mounted or used outdoors?

9. Will extremes of lighting (either dark or bright) dictate the type of display and/or scanner to be used?

10. Will the symbols being scanned have contrast in the infrared as well as the visible spectrum? The choice of input device needs to consider this fact.

11. What is the range of symbol X dimensions that must be accommodated?

12. Among which symbologies will the equipment be required to autodiscriminate?

13. Is this an open or a closed system? (See 15.4 below.)

There are also many considerations associated with printing bar code symbols:

1. Will the system use only the pre-existing symbols on products arriving at the facility, or will symbols be added as part of the operation?

2. Will variable, sequenced, or fixed data be required on the symbols? Is off-site or on-site printing appropriate?

3. If labels are used, will they be applied automatically or by hand?

4. If in-line labeling is used, what speed and latency requirements are there?

5. What printing technology is appropriate?

6. Will a protective laminate be required?

7. How often will the supplies have to be replenished in the printing equipment?

8. Will the printing equipment be required to operate at extremes of temperature or humidity?

15.3 Implementation

If possible, incorporate the implementation phase in logical stages. If an existing manual system is being replaced by the bar code system, run them both in parallel until the new system is fully debugged, tested, and trusted.

Education and training are essential parts of any successful bar code implementation. It is important that everyone who will use or be affected by the system be fully aware of the system's objectives and operation. All operators should have an opportunity to train on the equipment in a nonthreatening environment.

When the system has been operating in a production environment for some months, its success (or lack thereof) should be evaluated. Lessons learned from initial systems can prove extremely valuable in fine-tuning follow-up bar code system implementations.

15.4 Open vs. Closed Systems

Depending on the perspective and application, a bar code system can be classified as either open or closed. The industry trend is definitely toward open systems, that is, systems that are designed around standards that let them be expanded in many directions. Proprietary systems limit growth potential, and the applications being considered cover many technologies that require a variety of approaches. An open system, for example, allows a robotics system from one vendor to share a database with an automatic identification system from another vendor. Systems based on widely accepted standards allow the user to draw on the experience of a broad base of users.

An open system requires the adoption of both a symbology and an application standard by all affected parties. An open system means that the person or organization that is labeling objects with bar code symbols has no knowledge of how or where (or whether) the symbols will be read. An example of an open system is the labeling of food products that will be sold through retail stores. The U.P.C./EAN system that is employed is successful because there is industry-wide agreement on:

- coding structure
- symbology
- range of X dimensions
- wavelength of scanning
- symbol placement

Because of the acceptance of the U.P.C./EAN standards, there is high confidence that symbols printed by any manufacturer can be successfully scanned and interpreted by any scanning-equipped retail store. Because of the tight specification of optical properties and range of X dimensions, scanner design is "steered" to a compatible form.

A closed system is one whereby a single user, manufacturer, or institution has total control of the bar code system, including all printing and reading locations. Because industry-wide compatibility is not required, the system coordinator is free to choose:

- coding structure
- symbology
- range of X dimensions
- wavelengths of scanning
- symbol placement

In an effort to reduce symbol size, an implementor of a closed system might elect to use X dimensions smaller than 7.5 mils or might even consider developing a unique symbology.

There may be good reasons to use a nonstandard symbology, wavelength, or X dimension. But if there aren't, sticking to industry-accepted standards is a good idea. This will allow the use of commonly available equipment and will allow the system to be easily converted to an open one at a later time, if desired.

16

Applications

Bar code can be effectively used in a wide variety of applications. A book such as this can only scratch the surface in documenting the myriad of ways that bar code has been (or can be) used. Ongoing trade publications such as *ID Systems* magazine provide much information about ways that bar code techniques are applied.

This section provides a brief overview of the applicability of bar code to several different industries and applications.

16.1 Library Applications

The basic library application goes beyond just the tracking of books; similar product and information flows are experienced in manufacturing tool rooms, hospital radiology departments, and insurance company claim folder tracking. Items are stored in a central location, then loaned to borrowers, who agree to return the items within a predetermined time period.

Effective library systems require that each book be labeled with a bar code. In order to ensure adequate symbol life, the label can be placed inside the front cover, or protected by a laminate if placed on the outer cover. Each book has a unique code: the ISBN number can be used or a sequential license plate can be generated. A database management program links the bar code to the publication's name, author, and other catalog data.

Each authorized borrower is issued a card that includes a bar code symbol. This borrower number can be a Social Security number or a sequentially assigned code. An appropriate flag character may be included in at least one of the two symbol types to avoid mistaking borrower numbers for book numbers.

At each check-out/check-in desk, two transaction symbols are permanently and conveniently placed on the work surface. A bar code reader (probably equipped with a handheld, moving beam laser) is interfaced to the system's microcomputer or minicomputer. One transaction symbol contains data that will be recognized by the computer as indicating that a book has been borrowed, while the other symbol is used when a book is returned.

When borrowing books, the patron takes them to the desk and presents the borrower card. The attendant then:

1. Scans the borrower's card.

2. Scans each book's symbol.

3. Scans the borrow transaction symbol.

The complete transaction sequence is prompted either via a program running in the reader itself or by the attached computer. Error indications are given if the data is entered out of sequence.

The computer's database has now linked the book's code with the borrower's code and a date. After the allowable loan period has expired, the computer can automatically generate suitable reminder letters to the delinquent borrower.

When books are returned, they are automatically removed from the database's OUT file as they are scanned in conjunction with the RETURN transaction symbol. If the book is overdue, an indication of this fact (and the associated fine) can be made automatically.

Inventory checks can easily be conducted using a portable bar code reader. This process is accelerated if the book identification symbols are on the outer cover. If the shelves are also bar coded with location codes, an inventorying operation can also confirm that the books are filed in the correct area.

16.2 Inventory Control

The use of bar code can significantly reduce the effort required to do a physical inventory, while simultaneously increasing the accuracy level.

Portable readers are used to scan inventory items and/or boxes that have been marked with bar coded part numbers. If appropriate, bar coded shelf identification labels are also scanned as part of the transaction sequence.

Objects that are too small to mark individually are precounted and kept in labeled bags containing two bar code symbols: the part number and the quantity. Symbols encoding quantity information use flag characters or other schemes to avoid being misinterpreted as part numbers.

During the actual inventory-taking process, a simple application program in the portable reader prompts the operator through the sequence and checks for the entry of duplicate part numbers. The operator is asked first to enter the part number and then to enter the quantity. Quantity data is entered either by scanning the quantity symbol on a sealed package or by counting the items and entering the data via a keyboard or barboard. Field checks in the portable's application program ensure that valid data is being entered.

During the physical inventory process, the portable's application program is building a data file in its memory, containing a list of part numbers and quantities. Optionally, the file may also include location and/or time information.

When the inventorying operation is complete, or at other regular intervals, the contents of the portable reader are uploaded to the host computer system either via modem or direct connection. If a radio-linked device is being used, the uploading can occur while the operator is performing the inventory operation.

The process is somewhat different for a cycle count. At the start of the operation, a data file is downloaded from the host computer into the portable reader. This file lists the part numbers to be checked as well as the current estimate of the inventory level. The file may also have location data, and may have been processed so that the operator takes an orderly route through the stockroom or warehouse.

When the cycle count file has been downloaded, the portable reader's display prompts the operator as to which part number or location to check. The operator is then asked to scan the symbol on the object to be counted. The application program confirms that the object has the correct part number and then prompts the operator to enter the quantity counted. If the quantity counted does not match the quantity expected (based on the downloaded file), the application program makes an entry into the exception file. The operator is then prompted to move to the next item to check.

When the operator has completed the list of items, the portable terminal is connected to the host computer so that the inventory level file can be updated.

16.3 Work-in-Process Tracking

A manufacturing company's inventory has three components: raw material, work in process (WIP), and finished goods. Of these, WIP is the hardest type of inventory for many companies to control. WIP includes components and assemblies that are currently being worked on as well as semifinished products and assemblies that are waiting between work centers.

It is natural to want to have high WIP buffers between manufacturing operations in order to minimize the possibility of shortages. The disadvantages of this approach are:

1. More capital is tied up in WIP, thereby incurring excessive interest costs.

2. Higher occupancy costs (rent, insurance, heat, light, taxes, etc.).

3. Larger quantity of product to rework if problems are found or design changes occur.

4. Poor visibility of quality problems.

5. Poor responsiveness to changes in the production schedule.

6. Greater exposure to obsolete inventory costs.

The annual cost of WIP inventory can be as high as thirty percent, providing ample incentive for reducing the WIP levels. Taken to the extreme, WIP can be reduced all the way to just in time (JIT) levels with a single unit batch size.

As WIP and batch sizes are reduced, accurately tracking the flow of materials, assemblies, and products becomes increasingly important. Bar code has successfully been used to track WIP in a variety of industries.

A bar code WIP tracking system can have many forms. In its simplest configuration, a computer (microcomputer, minicomputer, or mainframe) is connected to a series of on-line readers and at least one printer. Each work center has a reader that an operator uses to log products or assemblies as they pass through. Assuming that the products themselves are not individually bar code serialized (in many cases they are), a paper work order follows the actual product flow.

The work order has a bar coded work order number and lists all of the operations that are to be performed. Each operation description has a bar code next to it that uniquely identifies the operation number.

As an operator completes an operation, the bar code reader is used to enter the serial number or work order number, the operation code, the employee ID, and the quantity completed. If exceptions are required to the normal routing, this can also be indicated through the scanning of appropriate preprinted labels.

The data collection network time-stamps each transaction and updates a database. The collected data can be used as feedback to a material requirements planning system, and can also provide reports on:

- Work order status

- WIP levels

- Bottlenecks

- Productivity

- Yield

16.4 MRP and MRP II Applications

MRP II stands for "manufacturing resource planning," which is rapidly overtaking traditional material requirements planning (MRP) as an effective computer-based tool in manufacturing operations. MRP II has the ability to significantly decrease production costs and increase quality.

MRP II is more than just a software program; it is a way of conducting business. It has been traditional to grade the effectiveness and commitment to MRP II on a three-level scale: Class A, Class B, and Class C. For MRP II to be truly effective, a company must reach and maintain a Class A rating.

Class A has associated with it a number of procedural and accuracy requirements. Bar code can effectively be used to achieve the following Class A minimum accuracy requirements:

Inventory Accuracy	95 percent
Bill of Materials Accuracy	98 percent
Routing Accuracy	95 percent

An ongoing program of cycle counting using bar code (described in Section 16.2) is a cost-effective way of achieving the Class A inventory accuracy goal. Bar code can contribute to the attainment of the other accuracy goals as well.

MRP II software is available from many vendors and can be run on a variety of computers.

With accurate data files in place, the main driving function of an operating MRP II system is the master production schedule, which determines what products will be built in which time period. The master production schedule is arrived at iteratively, based on inputs from business planning and capacity planning, as shown in Figure 16-1.

The MRP II system needs to be made aware of any failures to follow the actual plan on the factory floor (due to yields, scrap, shortages, etc.). When discrepancies occur, the production schedule may need to be modified to reflect the consequences of the deviation. Early and accurate visibility of problems can be provided by a bar code WIP (work in-process tracking system, as described in Section 16.3). Like all computer-based systems, MRP II relies on accurate and timely data. Bar code is ideally suited to fill this information need.

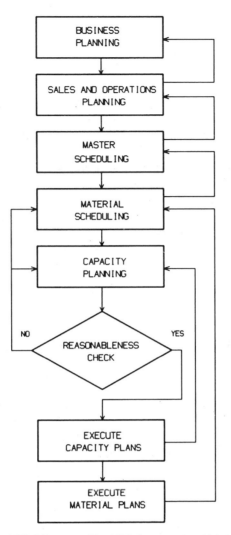

Figure 16-1: The Iterative MRP II Process. The MRP II process is a high-level planning method. Bar code systems enter the process as a means of tracking real-world operations resulting from such designs. Business planning and capacity planning are conducted on a continuous basis.

16.5 Receiving Applications

The receiving dock at most corporations can be a hectic place. Material often arrives in spurts, and there is no uniform package size or labeling format. Expediters are rummaging through the area, disrupting the receiving staff as they search for the "hot" items that are needed to pay off their shortage list. Each packaging slip needs to be reconciled with the outstanding purchase order field, either with manual paperwork or via a computer terminal. During peak periods, significant backlog can develop in the receiving area.

If packages that are received have been pre-marked with bar code by the vendor, transaction time can be significantly reduced. If the vendor is fully integrated into a mutually agreeable electronic data interchange (EDI) system, your computer already knows what packages to expect at the receiving dock. If your vendor marks the packages with unique bar coded serial numbers, a simple scanning operation at the receiving area can update the computer as products are received.

If EDI is not being used, bar code can still speed the data entry process if the following fields are encoded onto an exterior label: purchase order number, item line number, and quantity.

The vendor could use a local demand type printer to create the labels (see Section 16.6 below) or could apply labels provided with the initial purchase order. Even if the product being received is not bar coded, this technology can be used to track items through Receiving Inspection, on their way to Stores.

If unmarked packages are being received, the following scenario describes one possible implementation of a bar code tracking system.

1. Packages are received manually. The clerk takes the packing list to an on-line computer terminal and manually enters the purchase order number, then selects the line item that has been received.

2. At this point, the computer's database is now aware that the item has arrived on the premises. If this part is required to fill a critical shortage, a message can be presented to the clerk to provide special handling or routing.

3. The computer then assigns a unique serial number to the package. This will be used to track the package until it arrives in Stores. An on-line demand printer (probably a thermal label printer operating in self-strip mode) prints a label containing a human-readable description, priority code (if any), and bar-coded serial number incorporating appropriate flag characters. The clerk applies the label to the package.

4. The clerk then places the package on a cart. Each cart used in the receiving area is assigned a number, which is encoded on a prominent bar code symbol. As the clerk places the package on the cart, the computer's database is given the cart number by scanning the cart label with an on-line reader.

5. This receiving operation continues until a cart is filled, at which point it is transferred from the receiving department to the receiving inspection department. This movement is recorded by the use of an on-line reader located near the physical door. This reader is used to scan the cart label and transaction label. Because all of the individual package identities are linked to the cart number, the computer's database now knows the location of each item.

6. In the receiving inspection department, each inspection station is provided with an on-line reader. As an inspector completes the inspection, the reader is used to scan the package label; then a bar code menu is used to indicate how many items have been accepted at the disposition. Because the reader is on-line to the computer, any items that are currently required on the production line can be identified by an exception message on the reader's display. The exception message can cause the item to be routed directly to the area where it is needed, bypassing the normal trip through Stores.

7. The cart label is scanned as the cart of inspected items is moved into the stockroom. As items are removed from the cart, scanning the package label can remove that item from the cart's inventory and assign it to the stockroom.

The use of this bar code tracking system can give real-time visibility of the location and status of all items that have been received but are not yet in the stockroom and available for picking.

16.6 Shipping Applications

Bar code can be used very effectively in several ways in a shipping department. A primary use is in meeting customer labeling requirements. To satisfy the labeling requirements of certain end customers, a bar code label may have to be included on the shipping package. Industries where this may be a requirement include automotive, retail, health care, and defense. Refer to the applicable industry standard (referenced in Chapter 5) for details on the particular labeling requirements.

If the bar code marking standard requires that the same, constant data be encoded on each package, the bar code symbols can either be preprinted on the shipping carton or off-site techniques can be used to produce batches of identical adhesive labels.

If variable data is required, an on-site printer can be used to produce shipping labels. The exact label format can be stored in the printer's controller or in an attached computer. The appropriate variable data can be automatically sent to the printer based upon the entry (via bar code) of a work order number or preassigned serial number.

A second use of bar code in the shipping department is in establishing an accurate shipping log. If a manufacturer or distributor ships standard but individually serialized products to a wide variety of end users, bar code can be used to create an accurate serial number log at the point of shipping.

Assume, for example, that the Finished Goods Inventory area has a stock of 100 units of each of four standard product types: A, B, C, and D. Each of the products is in a package and has been marked with a bar code product description (A, B, C, or D) and serial number.

As a shipping request is received by the Shipping Department, the clerk uses a reader that is on-line to the company's host computer to verify the transaction and capture additional data. The shipping request form has a bar code symbol that acts as a license plate, pointing to the customer name, address, and ordered items. When this symbol is scanned, the application program will first check the database to verify that there is no credit hold, and then specify to the operator the product type and quantity to be shipped.

As the clerk moves packaged products to the shipping dock, both bar code symbols on the packages are scanned. The application software (in the host computer or the reader) confirms that the correct products and quantities are being staged, and it automatically updates the computer's serial number file. This file, which associates every serial number with an end customer and ship date, is used for warranty validation, recalls, or updates. The computer drives a local printer to generate shipping labels and packing lists, and data is sent to the invoicing software indicating exact serial numbers and product types shipped.

A third use of bar code occurs when a company ships from a central distribution warehouse to one of many standard shipping locations. Individual shipping labels are often not used if the product is being transferred by a company truck. Assuming that no intermediate stops are made, the important issue is to have an accurate inventory of what is placed on the truck. This can be done by scanning symbols on the products or cartons as they are moved onto the truck. This data capture results in the generation of an accurate manifest which can be reconciled when the truck is unloaded.

A variety of other bar code applications pertinent to a shipping operation are possible. This brief list may stir the imagination as to other opportunities.

16.7 Route Accounting

Many retail outlets are serviced on a regular basis by sales/delivery people who drive a pre-determined route on a repetitive basis. They stop at each of their customer's, check inventory levels on the shelves, and re-stock if necessary. As a final step, they provide the customer with a delivery receipt, and create a transaction record, which will ultimately result in an invoice being sent. This operation can beneficially employ bar code technology.

A driver might start his route in the morning by picking up a portable reader that has had the day's route downloaded to it. Together with a list of stores to visit might be notes regarding accounts receivable status, order history, etc. The driver takes the portable reader into the store as he examines the merchandise level on the shelves. Any time he determines that additional product should be brought in, he scans the U.P.C./EAN symbol on one of the existing items, then enters a quantity. This process is repeated for other items in the store, then he goes out to the van and gets the portable reader to generate a list of items and quantities to be replenished. The driver selects these items, takes them in to the store, and places them on the shelf. If an attached printer is available, he can print a delivery receipt which can be signed by the store manager, indicating receipt of the material. Alternately, if the portable reader has a signature capture capability, the receipt acknowledgment can be captured and stored electronically.

The driver then goes on to the next location on his route for the day, and the process is repeated. At the end of the day, the driver returns to his depot and uploads the day's transactions from the portable, allowing the corporate computer to update records, start the invoicing process, and rationalize van inventory levels.

16.8 Electronic Data Interchange

Electronic data interchange (EDI) is a business communications concept that offers substantial cost benefits. Simply stated, EDI describes the direct communication of specified data between the computers of two companies or institutions involved in a business transaction. For example, a manufacturer's computer may (as the result of an MRP run) realize the need to order a quantity of a particular component from a supplier. In the traditional way of doing business, an exception report would go to the Purchasing Department, where a buyer would manually place an order with the supplier.

With EDI, the manufacturer's computer automatically establishes communication with the designated vendor's computer and places an electronic order. The vendor's computer responds with a confirmed shipping date. No paperwork changes hands. The adoption of industry-wide EDI standards simplifies these interchanges for customers who have multiple vendors and vendors who have multiple customers.

Bar code helps close the loop in an EDI transaction by tracking the actual physical product. Consider the following scenario:

1. The manufacturer's computer places an electronic order with the vendor's computer. A confirmed shipping date is established.

2. If the manufacturer's computer does not receive an electronic shipping notice by the shipping date, an exception message is generated that requires manual intervention.

3. When the product is about to be shipped by the vendor, this fact is established through EDI. The customer's computer then gives the vendor's computer a series of serial numbers to be encoded into bar code and placed on each master carton or pallet to be shipped. Alternatively, the vendor may preassign serial numbers, and use EDI to advise the customer's computer of this information.

4. At the vendor's shipping dock, an on-line bar code label printer is used to label the packages.

5. When the physical items are received at the customer's receiving dock, the clerk scans the symbol on each package. The computer matches the unique serial numbers, thereby closing the loop on the transaction. If all packages associated with the shipment have not been received within a specified period of time from the confirmed shipping date, an exception message is generated.

EDI is a powerful concept that is used to reduce costs and save time in business transactions. It can be an effective ingredient in a JIT system. It must be emphasized that EDI is the transfer of data: bar code is a complementary technology that tracks the flow of actual physical products.

16.9 Retail Applications

The use of bar code is already well established and highly visible in retail sales institutions. Virtually all multilane supermarkets use counter-mounted bar code scanners (usually called slot scanners) in combination with electronic POS terminals. These slot scanners are reading the U.P.C. or EAN symbols that appear on almost all prepackaged food and convenience products.

General merchandise and convenience stores are also moving toward bar code scanning as part of the checkout process. Because of the wide variety of product shapes and sizes, handheld laser scanners, CCD scanners, or wands are often used instead of slot scanners.

The scanner is interfaced to a small computer located in the store. When an item is scanned, the data from its U.P.C. symbol is used as a license plate and the in-store computer sends the price and description information back to the POS terminal. Because of the on-line nature of this system, inventory levels can be automatically decremented, and real-time information can be provided as to the effectiveness of local promotions.

In most supermarkets, bar code shelf labels are also used. These often use a modified Plessey symbology rather than U.P.C. and are used as part of the reordering or restocking process.

In a store's back room, bar code can be used to simplify the receiving and unboxing process. In this instance, the Interleaved 2 of 5 Shipping Container Symbol is often present on cases of products shipped to stores.

In order to ensure freshness, reduce obsolescence, decrease excess inventory, and respond to quickly changing buying habits, a program known as "Quick Response" is used by many retail chains and suppliers. This program uses bar code to track individually serialized shipping cartons directly to the retailer's receiving dock by means of a UCC-128 symbol.

16.10 Tester Configuration

Sophisticated automatic test equipment is being used more and more often in manufacturing plants and service centers. This equipment invariably has to be set up uniquely for the specific version or revision of the product or component to be tested. Many testers allow a bar code scanner to be interfaced and used for configuring the tests to be run.

Two approaches to labeling can be used:

1. A bar code symbol can be used that uniquely identifies the type of item that is labeled. This is used as a license plate to access a database of stored configurations in the tester's memory.

2. The item to be tested can include a bar code that encodes the actual tester configuration and limits. This eliminates the need for a database in the tester but usually requires that more information be encoded.

In a manufacturing application, bar code can also be used in conjunction with automatic test equipment in a paperless rework concept. For example, consider the testing of circuit board assemblies. During the manufacturing process, each assembly is labeled with a unique bar coded serial number. An automatic tester is used that places the circuit assembly on a special fixture and runs a series of preprogrammed tests. The tester incorporates a fixed-mount, moving beam scanner and records the assembly's serial number before testing begins. If the assembly fails one of the tests, the actual results and possible cause are recorded in the tester's database.

The assembly is placed in a defective pile, to await analysis by a technician. When the technician receives a defective assembly, he uses a bar code scanner at the workstation to read the assembly's serial number. This reader is on-line to the tester's database so the test results and possible cause list can be sent to a computer terminal at the technician's workstation. The technician now has specific information to aid in troubleshooting the assembly. When the rework has been completed, the assembly is again sent to the automatic tester. Furthermore, the tester's (or an attached computer's) software can be programmed to identify assemblies that have been through the rework cycle more than a specific number of times. This will allow the lemons to be identified and scrapped.

16.11 Warehousing

Public and private warehousing applications offer several opportunities for effective bar code use. One possible example follows:

1. As products are received, the description and other pertinent information is manually entered into the local computer's database. The computer then drives an on-line bar code label printer in the receiving area to produce a unique bar code serial number label. A label is applied to each warehoused unit.

2. The items to be stored are placed in a holding area, waiting for a forklift operator to take them. The operator has a portable bar code reader and scans the item that is to be stored. He then places the item in the next available storage location and scans the bar code affixed to it. These two bar code fields have now been linked in the reader's memory. Several times a day, the portable's data is uploaded to the host computer. If a portable radio reader had been used, this step could be eliminated.

3. When items are to be picked, the host computer downloads a pick list into an operator's portable terminal. The portable's display prompts the operator to go to a specific storage location. The operator then scans the symbol on the stored item, the portable confirms that this is the correct item, and the operator is then prompted to proceed to the next location. If it is not the correct item, an error message is given.

16.12 Health Care Applications

The health care industry has three main constituents: manufacturers, distributors, and providers. A provider can be a hospital, doctor's office, nursing home, or clinic. Increasing competition as well as cost containment pressure from the government and insurers has increased attention on bar code applications. Product recalls and liability suits have also fueled the adoption of bar code in the health care industry.

Manufacturers and Distributors

Manufacturers and distributors of health care products (drugs, devices, instruments, etc.) have problems similar to those of companies dealing with nonhealth products. Bar code can be used for the usual applications, including inventory control, time and attendance, WIP tracking, shipping, receiving, document tracking, asset management, security, and labor tracking.

In some product categories, extensive batch tracking and traceability verification is required. Bar code can effectively be used to aid with this requirement. Also, if expiration dates are bar coded on packages, it is easy to use a preprogrammed portable bar code reader to identify out-of-date products.

Blood Banking

The blood banking industry has been using bar code since 1977 to ensure that expiration dates are not exceeded and to drastically reduce blood grouping and transfusion errors. With the increased frequency of blood-carried diseases, bar code is being effectively used to ensure traceability back to individual donors. Individual donors in American Red Cross blood donation drives in recent years have selected one of two bar coded labels to confidentially answer a critical question regarding their self-assessed AIDS risk.

Health Care Providers

Hospitals provide a multitude of potential bar code applications. There is increasing pressure to run these institutions like businesses, and bar code data collection is ideally capable of providing real-time, accurate data to the management information systems. A sampling of applications includes:

- Receiving and central storeroom activities
- Patient identification
- Exchange cart replenishment
- Patient billing
- Patient charting
- X-ray library
- Medical device library
- Asset management
- Pharmacy
- Bedside medication verification
- Time and attendance

16.13 Postal Applications

Bar code is ideally suited to the tracking and sortation of all forms of mail: letters, flats, and parcels. The United States Postal Service (USPS) has been one of the leaders in applying bar code technology to postal applications: as the nation's largest employer, it is hoping that this drive will result in reduced operating costs and higher levels of service.

The USPS has been successful in getting a significant portion of U.S. mailers to include the height-modulated Postnet symbology on letter and flat mail. An example of this is shown in Figure 16-2.

Mailers who use the Postnet symbol are given discounted postal rates. The USPS sortation machines are equipped with high-speed scanners that can read the Postnet symbols at linear speeds of up to 750 feet per minute: automatic diverters channel the letter or flat mail into specific output bins based on the encoded information. Mail that does not include the Postnet symbol has one sprayed on with ink jet printers based on data recovered either by in-line OCR scanners or manual key-

The Economist

SUBSCRIPTION DEPARTMENT
PO BOX 58510
BOULDER CO 80322-8510

‖‖‖‖‖‖‖‖‖‖‖‖‖‖‖‖‖‖‖‖‖‖‖‖‖‖‖‖‖

Figure 16-2: Postnet Symbol On Letter Mail. A large portion of U.S. letter and flat mail is marked with the Postnet symbology by mailers. The symbol encodes the Zip Code plus additional sequencing information.

ing. Figure 16-3 is a flow diagram for letter mail as it moves through the USPS system.

Scanning bar code symbols on flats becomes more difficult, because the orientation of the address block cannot be controlled effectively. OCR equipment is not usable with randomly oriented address blocks, so the solution is to use an omnidirectional bar code scanner: the USPS has over 2,000 of these devices deployed on flats sorting machines.

Canada has also used bar code in postal applications for several years. One of the earliest uses was in the tracking of priority mail using Code 39. Much of the prepaid business reply mail in Canada includes a Code 93 symbol, as shown in Figure 16-4. For conventional letter mail, a system has been used that consists of a 27 bar symbol printed with fluorescent ink. This is expected to be replaced in the future with a 4-State height-modulated symbol using error-correction encoding.

The U.K. has for many years used an automatic identification system on mail that prints phosphorescent markings on the front surface of envelopes. More recently, scanning equipment is being installed that can read fluorescent, phosphorescent, or black inks. Customers are being encouraged to print 4-State symbols that encode the destination postal code directly on envelopes.

Two additional codemarks based on the 4-State symbology may be printed on a piece of letter mail as it is processed by Royal Mail: a routing codemark, and a tag codemark that can uniquely identify each piece.

Parcels, bundles, and small packages can also be handled effectively by using bar

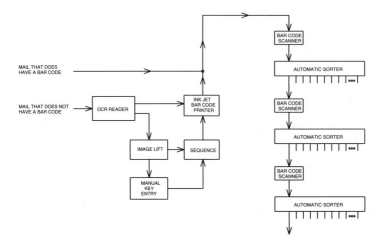

Figure 16-3: Letter Mail Flow Diagram. All sortation of letter mail at the USPS is based on data encoded in the Postnet bar code symbol.

Figure 16-4: Business Reply Card. Much of the Canadian pre-paid business reply mail includes a Code 93 symbol.

code in combination with automatic sortation equipment. In this case, a bar code symbol is placed on top of the parcel, and it is omnidirectionally scanned as it moves along on a conventional conveyor. Two approaches can be used:

1. Use a bar code symbol that encodes postal code or actual delivery point information. It would be preferable that the originator of the parcel print the bar code, but it is also possible to have a postal operator generate and apply a bar code based on a manually keyed address. Sortation can be performed directly on the basis of the bar code data without access to a computer database.

2. At the time that the parcel enters the mail system, apply a sequentially printed bar code symbol that will function as a "license plate." An operator manually keys the address into the computer, and the data is associated with the bar code number. For subsequent sortation purposes, automatic scanners will read the bar code data and access the database to generate diverting instructions.

16.14 Package Delivery

The majority of packages are not carried by government-associated postal entities, but are instead moved by private companies. There has been phenomenal growth in "overnight" express services offered by independent companies using their own fleets of trucks and aircraft, or buying cargo space on passenger flights. Bar code has been used in a variety of applications involving tracking, sortation, and delivery confirmation.

Companies offering guaranteed overnight delivery by a fixed time the next morning are constantly searching for ways to speed their processing; this allows them to pick up items later in the day and still be assured of sufficient time to meet their delivery deadlines. Bar code can be used to help this process, thereby giving a competitive advantage.

Many of the major shipping companies give their larger customers printers and/or pre-printed labels for labeling items prior to being picked up. In this case, the data format, data content, X dimension, and symbology will be fixed within a system, and the shipping company can optimize their scanning and data processing system based on this knowledge.

Again, these are just a few of the possible applications for bar code and are presented to stimulate the bar code implementor's imagination. As described at the beginning of this book, bar code is applicable wherever there is a need for accurate, real-time data associating people, physical items, or transactions with computer databases.

16.15 Airline Applications

Airlines have used bar code technology for many years to track spare parts, tools, fixtures, test equipment, and baggage containers. More recently, bar code has been used to track luggage, or even to allow for its automatic sortation. Luggage is a problematic product category to scan symbols on, because there is a wide variety of sizes, shapes, and materials. It is hard to determine which side is "up" on some luggage items, and in some cases an attached label will not be visible to scanning equipment at all.

In order to maximize the performance of luggage scanning systems, tags often have several redundant bar code symbols, and usually employ tall bars. Banks of laser scanners or area scanners are used to examine all accessible surfaces of the luggage as it moves along a conveyor. Some systems place individual luggage items in carrier baskets or totes. This eliminates much of the scanning difficulty that would otherwise be caused by the variability in size and shape of the luggage.

Bar code can also be used as a deterrent to certain terrorist activity by ensuring a complete reconciliation of baggage to boarded passengers. As a passenger checks in, he receives a bar coded boarding pass. Each piece of checked luggage is marked with a bar code tag that contains two symbols: one indicates the destination, and the other provides a link (either directly or via an intermediate database) to the passenger. As luggage is loaded onto the aircraft, the symbols are scanned, thereby creating a list of all baggage, and the associated passenger. As passengers board the aircraft their boarding passes are scanned to create another data file. It is then possible for a computer to compare the data files and ensure that no baggage is on board that does not have an associated passenger in a seat. If someone is determined to have checked baggage but not boarded, it will be possible to remove the suspicious bags before clearing the flight for departure.

17

Legal Aspects

A few years ago there would have been no need to devote a section of a text book such as this to legal aspects associated with bar code technology. Unfortunately however, several trends require that we at least mention the topic. In recent years the patent offices seem prone to grant patents for "inventions" which are overly broad, not truly novel, or perhaps obvious in nature. Perhaps fueled by this realization, there has been a trend in recent years for companies in the automatic identification field to attempt to gain competitive advantage by "patenting everything in sight," irrespective of the merits of their claims. Both of these trends ultimately result in higher costs to end users, and inhibit technical progress in many areas.

One prolific U.S. inventor has exploited weaknesses in the U.S. patent system to use the so-called "continuation process" to extend the effective life of a series of patents originally issued in the 1950s on automated inspection equipment; he claims that these patents now cover many manufacturing applications using bar code. Despite the fragility of these claims, this individual has managed to get multi-million dollar settlements out of several large manufacturers who are using bar code in their production process. Armed with a large war chest, we can expect to see more counter-productive disruptions from this inventor.

The patent files are also becoming cluttered with numerous bar code application patents. This seems completely contrary to the spirit of using bar code wherever accurate, real-time data is required. Many patents have been issued on applications which seem intuitively obvious once the basic concept of bar code is understood. In order to speculate on how bizarre the situation has become, consider the following fictional scenario:

> Assume that a U.S. patent has just been issued on the incandescent light bulb. After 17 years this basic patent will expire, but now a cagey inventor gets a patent on the use of a light bulb mounted in a bathroom so that it is possible to shave before the sun comes up in the morning. He then gets other application patents that cover a variety of applications which would otherwise make use of candles or lanterns. Even though the use of a light bulb in these different ways seems obvious once the basic concept of the light bulb is understood, the current U.S. patent system is perfectly capable of granting patents in this fictional scenario. This is clearly ludicrous!

In the '70s and '80s, most successful and popular symbologies were developed by manufacturers of bar code equipment, who then placed them in the public domain. This meant that anyone was free to develop printing and scanning equipment for these symbologies, and/or to use them without any financial encumbrance or licensing. These early developers even went so far as to assist their competitors in developing products to work with the new symbologies: it was recognized that in the long term, everyone would benefit through a spirit of open cooperation and support. In more recent years, however, symbology developers have attempted to surround their creations with walls of patents that prevent others from developing supporting equipment (or even from using the symbology at all) unless royalties are paid. Usually this type of proprietary symbology would languish by the wayside, but in recent times intense marketing efforts and ambiguous policy statements have been combined to try to create demand for these proprietary symbologies, and hence result in a flow of royalty revenues. In mid-1994 some progress was made by more enlightened industry principals toward an open approach to full symbology availability, but this area deserves close scrutiny.

Appendix U contains a summary of just some of the patents that have been issued in the bar code field to give the reader a feel for what has been going on.

Basically, there are three types of patents likely to be encountered in the bar code field: symbology patents, hardware patents, and application patents. A potential user of bar code technology presumably does not need to be concerned with hardware patents related to equipment that he buys for his system: presumably the supplier of the equipment will have paid royalties to any pertinent patent holders (and passed on the costs via higher equipment prices). Users do, however, need to look out for the other two patent types. If a system is built using a proprietary symbology, there may very well be some financial obligation to the patent holder of that symbology. Similarly, if a user implements a bar code system that practices an application described in an issued application patent, royalties may be due.

The author regrets having to end the main section of this text on such a sour note, but these developments are truly cause for alarm, and potential equipment manufacturers or users need to be extremely careful and vigilant as they step through this legal minefield!

APPENDICES

The remainder of this book consists of additional technical and reference materials about the technology of bar code.

Appendices A through N add additional details for the specification of several bar codes: Interleaved 2 of 5, Rationalized Codabar, Code 39, Code 128, Code 93, Code 49, Code 16K, PDF417, Code One, DataMatrix, MaxiCode, Array Tag, Postnet, and 4-State. Material collected in these appendices fills out the information on formal specifications of the various bar codes mentioned in the text. To avoid duplicating illustrations, several references are made to figures and tables contained in earlier chapters.

Appendix O provides details of the printing tolerance derivation for the Code 39 symbology. Similar analysis can be done for every other bar code symbology. Appendix P gives a similarly thorough explanation of reader error rate derivation, using Code 39 as an example of one of the more widely used symbologies.

Appendix Q summarizes the FACT Data Identifiers, Appendix R describes the AIM Symbology Identifiers, and Appendix S lists the EAN Prefix Identifiers.

Appendix T provides the names and addresses of the standards organizations relevant to various bar code symbologies and application areas. Appendix U is a summary of many patents that are relevant to bar code symbologies, equipment, and/or applications. Appendix V is a glossary of selected bar code terms.

The bibliography contains references to selected original materials on the subject of bar code symbologies, equipment, and applications. The book concludes with an index of the key terms found in the text, appendices, and figure captions.

Interleaved 2 of 5 Specification

Interleaved 2 of 5 (I 2/5) is a continuous, self-checking numeric symbology using two element widths. Each character has five bars and five spaces, two wide and three narrow in each case. Each character encodes two digits. Every symbol starts and ends with a unique start/stop pattern. A summary of Interleaved 2 of 5's main characteristics is as follows:

Character Set	:	Numeric
Symbol Length	:	Must be an even number of digits; normally used in fixed-length applications
Check Digits	:	Optional
Overhead Characters	:	Approximate equivalent of 1.1 digits per symbol or 0.55 characters per symbol
Density	:	Maximum of 18 digits per inch when printed using a 7.5 mil X dimension

Interleaved 2 of 5 Symbol Description
Each Interleaved 2 of 5 symbol consists of:

1. Leading quiet zone
2. Start pattern
3. Data characters
4. Stop pattern
5. Trailing quiet zone

Figure 4-17 illustrates a typical Interleaved 2 of 5 symbol encoding the data "1991".

Interleaved 2 of 5 Encodation
Each data character has five bars and five spaces, and encodes two digits. Bars and spaces may be either wide or narrow. One digit is encoded in the width of the bars in a 2 of 5 relationship, and another digit is encoded in the spaces using a similar arrangement. The encodation of the 10 numeric digits are shown in Figure 4-11. Figure 4-12 shows a typical 2-digit interleaved 2 of 5 pattern for the digits "38".

Note that an Interleaved 2 of 5 symbol can only encode messages containing an even number of digits. If necessary, a leading "0" may be added so that the resulting message contains an even number of digits. The start and stop patterns used with Interleaved 2 of 5 symbols are illustrated in Figure A-1.

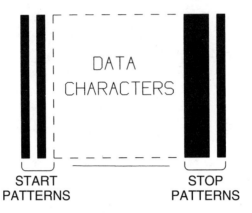

START PATTERNS   **STOP PATTERNS**

Figure A-1: Interleaved 2 of 5 Code. The I 2/5 uses these start and stop patterns to frame the data characters in a complete symbol. The direction of scan is unambiguously determined by the first two bars scanned: if the first two bars were narrow, the scan was from left to right; if the first two bars were narrow then wide, separated by a narrow space, the scan was from right to left.

Interleaved 2 of 5 Dimensions

The minimum value of X is 7.5 mils for symbols used in open systems. X shall be constant throughout a symbol.

The ratio of the nominal wide element width to the nominal narrow element width is designated as N and must remain constant throughout a symbol. The allowable range of N is 2.0 to 3.0, but N must exceed 2.2 if X is less than 20 mils.

For open systems the minimum bar height is 15 percent of the symbol length or 0.25 inches, whichever is greater.

The minimum quiet zone width is 10X. For optimum hand scanning, it is recommended that the quiet zone width be at least 0.25 inches.

The overall length of an Interleaved 2 of 5 symbol is a function of X, N, and the number of digits to be encoded:

$$L = (D(2N+3)+6+N)X$$

where
L = length of symbol, excluding quiet zones
D = number of data digits
X = X dimension
N = wide to narrow ratio

Interleaved 2 of 5 Dimensional Tolerances

The allowable printing width tolerances are given by the expression:

$$t = \pm\left(\frac{18N - 21}{80}\right)X$$

where
   t   = the allowable width deviation about the nominal
         dimension of a given element
   X = X dimension
   N = wide-to-narrow ratio

The tolerance t applies to the printed width of all elements, both wide and narrow. These tolerances should not accumulate within a character. The overall character width shall not deviate from nominal by more than 2t.

For measuring purposes, the edge of a bar/space transition is defined as the center of a circular sampling aperture of diameter no greater than 0.8X when the apparent reflectance of the sample viewed through the aperture is halfway between the maximum and minimum reflectances obtained by that aperture on the adjacent bar and space.

Interleaved 2 of 5 Optical Properties

Reflectivity measurements are made at a wavelength of 633 nanometers with illuminating and viewing axes separated by 45 degrees, with one of the axes positioned perpendicular to the sample surface. The aperture of each of the two optical systems should subtend an angle of no more than 15 degrees. The measured diffuse reflectance is defined as the ratio of the light reflected from the sample to that reflected from a specially prepared magnesium oxide or barium sulfate standard measured under the same conditions. One of the optical paths must restrict the sample field to an area equal to that of a circle of 0.8X, and the other path's sample field must have an area greater than that of a circle of 8X.

The maximum bar reflectance is 30 percent. The minimum space reflectance is 25 percent. The minimum reflectance difference (MRD) is equal to the reflectivity difference between the darkest space and the lightest bar. The minimum value of MRD is 37.5 percent if X is less than 40 mils and 20 percent if X is equal to or greater than 40 mils.

Interleaved 2 of 5 Check Digit

A check digit is sometimes used to enhance the data security of Interleaved 2 of 5. The check digit is appended to the data digits before they are encoded, and its value is calculated as follows:

1. Starting with the least significant data digit, assign an alternate 3,1,3,1,..., weighting to the digits to its left.
2. Sum the products of the digits with their associated weights.
3. The check digit is the digit which, when added to the sum from step 2, produces a sum that is a multiple of 10.

As an example, if the data is "47365", the check digit would be calculated as follows:

1.
Data	4	7	3	6	5
Weights	3	1	3	1	3

2. Sum = (4x3) + (7x1) + (3x3) + (6x1) + (5x3) = 49
3. The check digit is therefore 1, and the complete message to be encoded is 473651.

Interleaved 2 of 5 Short Scans

A partial scan of an Interleaved 2 of 5 symbol can often appear to be a valid scan of a shorter symbol. This is due to the simple patterns used for start and stop codes. In order to prevent this problem, applications using Interleaved 2 of 5 should require that all symbols be the same length (shorter symbols can be padded with leading zeros) and that all reading equipment be programmed to accept only that fixed message length. Bearer bars would also minimize this problem. (See Figure 4-18).

Interleaved 2 of 5 Dimensional Verification

The following procedure should be used to determine if an Interleaved 2 of 5 symbol meets the specified dimensional tolerances:

1. Measure and record the perceived width for every element in the symbol and the two quiet zones.
2. Decode the symbol, confirming that there are valid start, stop, and data characters.
3. As determined by decoding, sort the widths of all the characters' elements (excluding quiet zones) into four groups: narrow bars, narrow spaces, wide bars, and wide spaces.
4. If it is desired to evaluate symbol quality against values of X and N specified in an application standard, those values can be used directly in step 9, skipping steps 5 through 8.
5. Compute the average width in each group:
   ANB = average narrow bar
   ANS = average narrow space
   AWB = average wide bar
   AWS = average wide space
6. Compute X as follows:

$$X = \frac{ANB + ANS}{2}$$

7. Compute N as follows:

$$N = \frac{AWB + AWS}{2X}$$

8. Confirm that X and N are within allowed ranges:
   a. Check that X is greater than or equal to 0.0075"; if not, declare X = 0.0075".
   b. Check that N is greater than or equal to 2.0; if not, declare N = 2.0.
   c. If X is less than or equal to 0.020", then check that N is greater than or equal to 2.2; if not, declare either X = 0.020 or N = 2.2.
   d. Check that N is less than or equal to 3.0; if not, declare N = 3.0.
9. Compute the printing tolerance:

$$t = \frac{18N - 21}{80} X$$

10. Confirm that all measured widths fall within allowed limits, otherwise the symbol is not in conformance:
    a. Check that all narrow elements fall within X - t to X + t.
    b. Check that all wide elements fall within NX - t to NX + t.

If X or N were changed in step 8c, it might be necessary to use the opposite assumption in order to meet the requirement that all the measured widths fall within the allowed limits.

11. Confirm that the sum of the widths of any number of adjacent elements within any character does not deviate from nominal (using X and N as measured or assumed above) by more than 2t, otherwise the symbol is not in conformance.
12. Confirm that each quiet zone is at least 10X wide, otherwise the symbol is not in conformance.

Note: In step 8a, the 7.5 mil limit is consistent with present practice for open systems. In closed applications, a lower limit may be used.

Rationalized Codabar Specification

Rationalized Codabar is fully compatible with traditional Codabar in all applications. It is a discrete, self-checking numeric symbology including six other characters and four unique start/stop characters. Two-element widths are employed. Each character has four bars and three spaces. A summary of Rationalized Codabar's main characteristics is as follows:

Character Set	:	10 digits
		6 special characters
Symbol Length	:	Variable
Overhead Characters	:	2 per symbol
Other Features	:	Concatenation ability
Density	:	Maximum of 12.8 characters per inch when printed using a 7.5 mil X dimension

Rationalized Codabar Symbol Description
Each Rationalized Codabar symbol consists of:

1. Leading quiet zone
2. Start character
3. Data characters
4. Stop character
5. Trailing quiet zone

Figure 4-23 illustrates an example of a Rationalized Codabar symbol encoding the data "$12345". Note that the "A" and "B" characters are the start and stop characters.

Rationalized Codabar Encodation
Each Rationalized Codabar symbol has four bars and three spaces. A bar or space may be wide or narrow. Figure 4-25 defines the bar and space patterns for each rationalized codabar character code.

Any one of the four start/stop characters (A, B, C, or D) can be used as the start or stop character; their significance is usually application dependent.

Rationalized Codabar Dimensions

The minimum value of X is 7.5 mils for symbols used in open systems. X shall be constant throughout a symbol. The ratio of the nominal wide element width to the nominal narrow element width is designated as N and must remain constant throughout a symbol. The allowable range of N is 2.0 to 3.0, but N must exceed 2.2 if X is less than 20 mils. The minimum width of the intercharacter gap is (X - t), where t is the applicable printing tolerance and the maximum is:

- 5.3X for values of X less than 10 mils
- 3X or 53 mils (whichever is greater) for values of X equal to or greater than 10 mils

For open systems, the minimum bar height is 15 percent of the symbol length or 0.25 inches, whichever is greater. The minimum quiet zone width is 10X. For optimum hand scanning, the quiet zone width should be at least 0.25 inches.

The overall length of a Rationalized Codabar symbol is a function of X, N, the intercharacter gap width, and the number and type of data characters, as given by:

$$L = [C(2N+5)+(W+2)(3N+4)]X+(C+N+1)I$$

where

L = length of symbol, excluding quiet zones
C = number of data digits and the characters -,$
W = number of : / . and + characters
X = X dimension
N = wide-to-narrow ratio
I = intercharacter gap width

Many printers generate symbols with an intercharacter gap width of X. In this case, the expression for symbol length can be simplified to:

$$L = [C(2N+6)+(W+2)(3N+5)-1] X$$

Rationalized Codabar Dimensional Tolerances

The allowable printing width tolerances are given by the expression:

$$t = \pm \frac{(5N-8)}{20} X$$

where

t = the allowable width deviation about the nominal dimension of a given element
X = X dimension
N = wide-to-narrow ratio

The tolerance t applies to the printed width of all elements, both wide and narrow. These tolerances should not accumulate within a character. The overall character width shall not deviate from nominal by more than 2t.

For measuring purposes, the edge of a bar/space transition is defined as the center of a circular sampling aperture of diameter no greater than 0.8X when the apparent reflectance of the sample viewed through the aperture is halfway between the maximum and minimum reflectances obtained by that aperture on the adjacent bar and space.

Rationalized Codabar Optical Properties

Reflectivity measurements are made at a wavelength of 633 nanometers with illuminating and viewing axes separated by 45 degrees, with one of the axes positioned perpendicular to the sample surface. The aperture of each of the two optical systems should subtend an angle of no more than 15 degrees. The measured diffuse reflectance is defined as the ratio of the light reflected from the sample to that reflected from a specially prepared magnesium oxide or barium sulfate standard measured under the same conditions. One of the optical paths must restrict the sample field to an area equal to that of a circle of 0.8X, and the other path's sample field must have an area greater than that of a circle of 8X.

The maximum bar reflectance is 30 percent. The minimum space reflectance is 25 percent.

The minimum reflectance difference (MRD) is equal to the reflectivity difference between the darkest space and the lightest bar. The minimum value of MRD is 37.5 percent if X is less than 40 mils, and 20 percent if X is equal to or greater than 40 mils.

Rationalized Codabar Symbol Concatenation

The American Blood Commission (ABC) has adopted a convention for label concatenation whereby some decoders, often designated as reading "ABC Codabar," will respond to symbols ending with the "D" stop character by waiting and looking for an adjacent symbol within 0.75 inch (19 millimeters) with a "D" start character. If the second symbol is found, the two data messages are concatenated into one with the "D" characters omitted. This procedure works bidirectionally and can concatenate any number of labels in a row up to the maximum message length allowed by the decoder.

Rationalized Codabar Dimensional Verification

The following procedure should be used to determine if a Rationalized Codabar symbol meets the specified dimensional tolerances:

1. Measure and record the perceived width for every element, the intercharacter gaps, and the two quiet zones.
2. Decode the symbol, confirming that there are valid start, stop, and data characters.
3. As determined by decoding, sort the widths of all the characters' elements (excluding intercharacter gaps and quiet zones) into four groups: narrow bars, narrow spaces, wide bars, and wide spaces.

4. If it is desired to evaluate symbol quality against values of X and N specified in an application standard, those values can be used directly in step 9, skipping steps 5 through 8.
5. Compute the average width in each group:
   ANB = average narrow bar
   ANS = average narrow space
   AWB = average wide bar
   AWS = average wide space
6. Compute X as follows:

$$X = \frac{ANB + ANS}{2}$$

7. Compute N as follows:

$$N = \frac{AWB + AWS}{2X}$$

8. Confirm that X and N are within allowed ranges:
   a. Check that X is greater than or equal to 0.0075"; if not, declare X = 0.0075".
   b. Check that N is greater than or equal to 2.0; if not, declare N = 2.0.
   c. If X is less than 0.020", then check that N is greater than or equal to 2.2; if not, declare either X = 0.020" or N = 2.2.
   d. Check that N is less than or equal to 3.0; if not, declare N = 3.0.
9. Compute the printing tolerance:

$$t = \frac{5N - 8}{20}X$$

10. Confirm that all measured widths fall within allowed limits, otherwise the symbol is not in conformance:
    a. Check that all narrow elements fall within X - t to X + t.
    b. Check that all wide elements fall within NX - t to NX + t.

If X or N were changed in step 8c, it might be necessary to use the opposite assumption in order to meet the requirement that all the measured widths fall within the allowed limits.

11. Confirm that the sum of the widths of any number of adjacent elements within any character does not deviate from nominal (using X and N as measured or assumed above) by more than 2t, otherwise the symbol is not in conformance.
12. Confirm that all intercharacter gap widths (from step 1) are equal to or greater than X - t, otherwise the symbol is not in conformance.

13. If X is less than 10 mils, confirm that all intercharacter gaps are less than 5.3X, otherwise the symbol is not in conformance. If X is greater than or equal to 10 mils, confirm that all intercharacter gaps are less than 0.053" or 3X, whichever is greater, otherwise the symbol is not in conformance.

14. Confirm that each quiet zone is at least 10X wide, otherwise the symbol is not in conformance.

Note: In step 8a, the 7.5 mil limit is consistent with present practice for open systems. In closed applications, a lower limit may be used.

APPENDIX C

Code 39 Specification

Code 39 is a discrete, variable length, self-checking, alphanumeric symbology employing two-element widths. Every character has five bars and four spaces; three of the elements in any given character are wide, and six are narrow. Every symbol starts and ends with a unique start/stop character. A summary of Code 39's main characteristics is as follows:

Character Set	:	26 uppercase letters
		10 digits
		7 special characters
		Extendable to full 128 ASCII character set using a two-character precedence code scheme.
Symbol Length	:	Variable
Check Characters	:	Optional
Overhead Characters	:	2 per symbol
Other Features	:	Concatenation ability
Density	:	Maximum of 9.8 characters per inch when printed using a 7.5 mil X dimension

Code 39 Symbol Description
Each Code 39 symbol consists of:

1. Leading quiet zone
2. Start character
3. Data characters
4. Stop character
5. Trailing quiet zone

Figure 4-26 illustrates a typical Code 39 symbol

Code 39 Encodation
Each Code 39 character consists of five bars and the four intervening spaces; three of the nine elements are wide and six are narrow. Each character has either two or zero wide bars. Figure 4-25 shows the encodation of bar and space patterns for each character code. The asterisk character is exclusively used as a start/stop code.

Code 39 Dimensions

The minimum value of X is 7.5 mils for symbols used in open systems. X shall be constant throughout a symbol.

The ratio of the nominal-wide element width to the nominal narrow-element width is designated as N and must remain constant throughout a symbol. The allowable range of N is 2.0 to 3.0, but N must exceed 2.2 if X is less than 20 mils.

The minimum width of the intercharacter gap is (X minus t), where t is the applicable printing tolerance and the maximum is:

- 5.3X for values of X less than 10 mils
- 3X or 53 mils (whichever is greater) for values of X equal to or greater than 10 mils

For open systems, the minimum bar height is 15 percent of the symbol length or 0.25 inches, whichever is greater. The minimum quiet zone width is 10X. For optimum hand scanning, the quiet zone width should be at least 0.25 inches. The overall length of a Code 39 symbol is a function of X, N, the intercharacter gap width, and the number of data characters, as given by:

$$L = (C+2)(3N+6)X+(C+1)I$$

where

L = length of symbol, excluding quiet zones
C = number of data characters
X = X dimension
N = wide-to-narrow ratio
I = intercharacter gap width

Many printers generate symbols with an intercharacter gap width of X. In this case, the expression for symbol length can be simplified to

$$L - [(C+2)(3N+7)-1] X$$

Code 39 Dimensional Tolerances

The allowable printing width tolerances are given by the expression

$$t = \pm\frac{4}{27}\left(N-\frac{2}{3}\right)X$$

where

t = the allowable width deviation about the nominal dimension of a given element
X = X dimension
N = wide to narrow ratio

The tolerance t applies to the printed width of all elements, both wide and narrow. These tolerances should not accumulate within a single character. The overall character width shall not deviate from nominal by more than 2t.

For measuring purposes, the edge of a bar/space transition is defined as the center of a circular sampling aperture of diameter no greater than 0.8X when the apparent reflectance of the sample viewed through the aperture is halfway between the maximum and minimum reflectances obtained by that aperture on the adjacent bar and space.

Code 39 Optical Properties

Reflectivity measurements are made at a wavelength of 633 nanometers with illuminating and viewing axes separated by 45 degrees, with one of the axes positioned perpendicular to the sample surface. The aperture of each of the two optical systems should subtend an angle of no more than 15 degrees. The measured diffuse reflectance is defined as the ratio of the light reflected from the sample to that reflected from a specially prepared magnesium oxide or barium sulfate standard measured under the same conditions. One of the optical paths must restrict the sample field to an area equal to that of a circle of 0.8X, and the other path's sample field must have an area greater than that of a circle of 8X.

The maximum bar reflectance is 30 percent. The minimum space reflectance is 25 percent.

The minimum reflectance difference (MRD) is equal to the reflectivity difference between the darkest space and the lightest bar. The minimum value of MRD is 37.5 percent if X is less than 40 mils, and 20 percent if X is equal to or greater than 40 mils.

Code 39 Full ASCII Mode

If suitably programmed, a Code 39 reader can decode the 128 ASCII character set by using paired character sequences made up of the character $. % or / followed by one of the 26 letters, as shown in Table 4-4.

Code 39 Check Character

An optional check character is defined for Code 39 applications requiring higher levels of data security. When used, the check character is positioned between the final data character and the stop character. The check character is determined as follows:

1. Using Table C-1, determine the numerical value of each of the data characters.
2. Sum the values of all the data characters.
3. Find the modulo 43 remainder of the sum from step 2.
4. The check character is that character whose value from Table C-1 is equal to the remainder from step 3.

As an example, if the data characters are "TEST", the values would be summed as 29 + 14 + 28 + 29 = 100. 43 goes into 100 twice, with a remainder of 14. The letter "E" has a value of 14 and is therefore the check character.

Table C-1
CODE CHARACTER VALUES

Character	Value	Character	Value
0	0	M	22
1	1	N	23
2	2	O	24
3	3	P	25
4	4	Q	26
5	5	R	27
6	6	S	28
7	7	T	29
8	8	U	30
9	9	V	31
A	10	W	32
B	11	X	33
C	12	Y	34
D	13	Z	35
E	14	—	36
F	15	.	37
G	16	Space	38
H	17	$	39
I	18	/	40
J	19	+	41
K	20	%	42
L	21		

Code 39 Symbol Concatenation

It is sometimes advantageous to break up long messages into multiple, shorter symbols. If the first data character of a Code 39 symbol is a space, the reader may be programmed to append the information contained in the remainder of the symbol to a storage buffer (data not transmitted). This operation continues for all successive symbols with a leading space, with messages being added to the end of previously stored messages. When a message is read which does not contain a leading space, the contents are appended to the buffer, the entire buffer is transmitted, and the buffer is cleared.

Code 39 Dimensional Verification

The following procedure should be used to determine if a Code 39 symbol meets the specified dimensional tolerances:

1. Measure and record the perceived width for every element, the intercharacter gaps, and the two quiet zones.
2. Decode the symbol, confirming that there are valid start, stop, and data characters.
3. As determined by decoding, sort the widths of all the characters' elements (excluding intercharacter gaps and quiet zones) into four groups: narrow bars, narrow spaces, wide bars, and wide spaces.
4. If it is desired to evaluate symbol quality against values of X and N specified

in an application standard, those values can be used directly in step 9, skipping steps 5 through 8.

5. Compute the average width in each group:

$$\begin{aligned} ANB &= \text{average narrow bar} \\ ANS &= \text{average narrow space} \\ AWB &= \text{average wide bar} \\ AWS &= \text{average wide space} \end{aligned}$$

6. Compute X as follows:

$$X = \frac{ANB + ANS}{2}$$

7. Compute N as follows:

$$N = \frac{AWB + AWS}{2X}$$

8. Confirm that X and N are within allowed ranges:
   a. Check that X is greater than or equal to 0.0075"; if not, declare X = 0.0075".
   b. Check that N is greater than or equal to 2.0; if not, declare N = 2.0.
   c. If X is less than 0.020", then check that N is greater than or equal to 2.2; if not, declare either X = 0.020" or N = 2.2.
   d. Check that N is less than or equal to 3.0; if not, declare N = 3.0.

9. Compute the printing tolerance:

$$t = \frac{4}{27}\left(N - \frac{2}{3}\right)X$$

10. Confirm that all measured widths fall within allowed limits, otherwise the symbol is not in conformance:
    a. Check that all narrow elements fall within X - t to X + t.
    b. Check that all wide elements fall within NX - t to NX + t.

If X or N were changed in step 8c, it might be necessary to use the opposite assumption in order to meet the requirement that all the measured widths fall within the allowed limits.

11. Confirm that the sum of the widths of any number of adjacent elements within any character does not deviate from nominal (using X and N as measured or assumed above) by more than 2t, otherwise the symbol is not in conformance.

12. Confirm that all intercharacter gap widths (from step 1) are equal to or greater than X - t, otherwise the symbol is not in conformance.
13. If X is less than 10 mils, confirm that all intercharacter gaps are less than 5.3X, otherwise the symbol is not in conformance. If X is greater than or equal to 10 mils, confirm that all intercharacter gaps are less than 0.053" or 3X, whichever is greater, otherwise the symbol is not in conformance.
14. Confirm that each quiet zone is at least 10X wide, otherwise the symbol is not in conformance.

Note: In step 8a, the 7.5 mil limit is consistent with present practice for open systems. In closed applications, a lower limit may be used.

Code 128 Specification

Code 128 is a continuous, variable length alphanumeric symbology encoding the full ASCII 128 character set. Every character is made up of 11 modules containing three bars and three spaces. Bar and space width is one, two, three, or four modules. Three different start characters are used to select one of three character sets, including a high-density numeric arrangement that can encode two numeric digits in each character. A summary of Code 128's main characteristics is as follows:

Character Set : 107 unique characters, including:
    4 function characters
    4 code set selection characters
    3 start characters

Symbol Length : Variable

Check Character : 1

Overhead Characters : 3 per symbol

Other Features : Concatenation ability
    Ability to encode all 128 characters

Density : Maximum of 12.1 alphanumeric characters per inch or 24.2 numeric digits per inch when printed using a 7.5 mil X dimension

Code 128 Symbol Description
Each Code 128 symbol consists of:

1. Leading quiet zone
2. Start character
3. Data characters
4. Check character
5. Stop character
6. Trailing quiet zone

Figure 4-29 and 4-30 illustrate typical Code 128 symbols.

Code 128 Encodation
Each Code 128 character has three bars and three spaces comprising a total of 11 modules. Each bar or space can be one, two, three, or four modules wide. The total

number of modules representing bars in a character is an even number, and the number of modules representing spaces in a character is odd.

A particular bar/space pattern can have three different meanings, depending on whether character subset A, B, or C is being used. The choice of start character defines the character subset at the beginning of a symbol, but shift characters allow the subset to be changed in the symbol. Figure 4-28 defines the bar and space patterns for each character.

Referring to Figure 4-28, note that Code A, B, or C characters change the symbol code subset from the previous value. The change is in effect until the end of the symbol or until another change character is encountered. The shift character changes the subset for the next character only from subset A to B or B to A. The function characters FNC1, FNC3, and FNC4 are used for reader-specific definition. FNC2 is used for concatenation. If an FNC1 character is used immediately following the starting symbol character, the subsequent data should be interpreted in a manner defined by the Uniform Code Council and the European Article Numbering Association.

Code 128 Dimensions

The minimum value of X is 7.5 mils for symbols used in open systems. X shall be constant throughout a symbol. For open systems, the minimum bar height is 15 percent of the symbol length or 0.25 inches, whichever is greater. The minimum quiet zone width is 10X. For optimum hand scanning, the quiet zone width should be at least 0.25 inches.

The overall length of a Code 128 symbol is a function of X and the number and type of data characters, as given by:

$$L = (11C + 35) X$$

where
L = length of symbol, excluding quiet zones
C = number of data characters, including function characters and shift characters. Note that one data character
     can encode two numeric digits if character subset C is used
X = X dimension

Code 128 Check Character

The check character is positioned after the data characters and immediately before the stop character. The check character is the character whose value is equal to the modulo 103 sum of the value of the start character and the weighted values of the following characters. The weighting values follow the progression 1, 2, 3, 4, ..., beginning with the first data character following the start character. For example, the check character for a symbol encoding the message "C128" is calculated as follows:

Encoded Characters	StartA	C	1	2	8
Weighting		1	2	3	4

The sum of the product of the character values and the weighting sequence is:

$$103 + (1x35) + (2x17) + (3x18) + (4x24) = 322$$

Divide 322 by 103 to get 3, with a remainder of 13. The check character is therefore "-", which has a value of 13 in the A character set column of Figure 4-28.

Code 128 Dimensional Tolerances

Three tolerances apply to a Code 128 symbol (see Figure D-1):

1. b: deviation of individual bar or space width from the nominal dimension
2. e: deviations from the nominal width between an edge of one bar and the similar edge of an adjacent bar
3. p: deviations from nominal of the overall character width

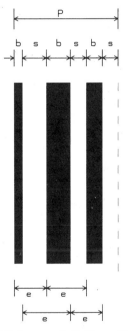

Figure D-1: Code 128 Dimensional Tolerance Definitions. Three tolerances are defined: b is the deviation from nominal of any bar or space width; e is the deviation from nominal of any edge-to-similar-edge width; and p is the deviation from nominal of the overall character width.

The Code 128 printing tolerances are as follows:

b = (±0.40X - 0.0005) inch
e = ±0.20X
p = ±0.20X

For measuring purposes, the edge of a bar/space transition is defined as the center of a circular sampling aperture of diameter no greater than 0.8X when the apparent reflectance of the sample viewed through the aperture is halfway between the maximum and minimum reflectances obtained by that aperture on the adjacent bar and space.

Code 128 Optical Properties

Reflectivity measurements are made at a wavelength of 633 nanometers with illuminating and viewing axes separated by 45 degrees, with one of the axes positioned perpendicular to the sample surface. The aperture of each of the two optical systems should subtend an angle of no more than 15 degrees. The measured diffuse reflectance is defined as the ratio of the light reflected from the sample to that reflected from a specially prepared magnesium oxide or barium sulfate standard measured under the same conditions. One of the optical paths must restrict the sample field to an area equal to that of a circle of 0.8X, and the other path's sample field must have an area greater than that of a circle of 8X.

The maximum bar reflectance is 30 percent. The minimum space reflectance is 25 percent.

The minimum reflectance difference (MRD) is equal to the reflectivity difference between the darkest space and the lightest bar. The minimum value of MRD is 37.5 percent if X is less than 40 mils, and 20 percent if X is equal to or greater than 40 mils.

Code 128 Symbol Concatenation

It is sometimes advantageous to break up long messages into multiple, shorter symbols. If a Code 128 symbol contains an FNC2 character, the reader appends the information to a storage buffer (data not transmitted). The operation continues for all successive symbols that contain an FNC2 character, with messages being added to the end of previously stored messages. When a symbol is read that does not contain an FNC2 character, the contents are appended to the buffer, the entire buffer is transmitted, and the buffer is cleared.

Code 128 Dimensional Verification

The following procedure should be used to determine if a Code 128 symbol meets the specified dimensional tolerances:

1. Measure and record the perceived width of every element. Record the width of the two quiet zones.
2. Decode the symbol, confirming that there are valid start, stop, and data characters.
3. Confirm that the number of elements E is 6n + 1, where n is an integer with a value of 3 or greater.
4. If it is desired to evaluate symbol quality against a value of X specified by an application standard, that value of X should be used starting in step 7 and skipping steps 5 and 6.
5. Compute L, the sum of the element widths, including all elements in the symbol except the last bar.
6. Compute X as follows:

$$X = \frac{6L}{(E-1)11}$$

Check that X is greater than or equal to 0.0075"; if not, declare X = 0.0075".

7. Compute the printing tolerances:
   b = (0.40X-0.0005) inch
   e = 0.20X
   p = 0.20X
8. Confirm that every element falls within one of four categories:
   a. 1X ±b
   b. 2X ±b
   c. 3X ±b
   d. 4X ±b
9. Confirm that all sums of adjacent bar and space pairs, or space and bar pairs fall within one of six categories:
   a. 2X ±e
   b. 3X ±e
   c. 5X ±e
   d. 6X ±e
   e. 7X ±e
10. Confirm that the width of each character is equal to 11X ±p.
11. Confirm that each quiet zone is at least 10X wide.

Note: In step 6, the 7.5 mil limit is consistent with present practice for open systems. In closed applications, a lower limit may be used.

Code 93 Specification

Code 93 is an alphanumeric, variable length symbology employing four different bar widths. Each symbol includes two check characters. The main characteristics of Code 93 are as follows:

Character Set	:	26 letters
		10 digits
		7 special characters
		Extendable to full 128 ASCII character set using 4 special precedence characters
Symbol Length	:	Variable
Check Characters	:	2 per symbol
Overhead Characters	:	4 per symbol
Other Features	:	Concatenation ability
Density	:	Maximum of 14.8 characters per inch when printed using a 7.5 mil X dimension

Code 93 Symbol Description

Each Code 93 symbol consists of:
1. Leading quiet zone
2. Start character
3. Data characters
4. First check character "C"
5. Second check character "K"
6. Stop character
7. Termination bar
8. Trailing quiet zone

Figure 4-33 illustrates a Code 93 symbol encoding the data "CODE 93" with the check digits "E0".

Code 93 Encodation

Each Code 93 character is divided into nine modules and has three bars and three spaces. The bars and spaces may be one, two, three, or four modules wide.

Figure 4-32 defines all of the Code 93 character patterns. Note that the special characters ⑤, ⑳, ⊘, and ⊕, are used as precedence characters for the full ASCII mode.

The start/stop character is represented as "☐". When used as a stop character, an additional 1 module bar is added to close off the final space.

Code 93 Check Characters

Every Code 93 symbol contains two check characters (referred to as "C" and "K") that immediately precede the stop character.

Check character "C" is the modulo 47 sum of the data character values (see Table E-1) and a weighting sequence, where the weights from right to left are in the sequence 1,2,3....19,20,1,2,3,....19,20,1,2,....

Check character "K" is the modulo 47 sum of the data character values (see Table E-1) and a weighting sequence, where the weights from right to left, beginning with the check character "C" are in the sequence 1,2,3,....14,15,1,2,3,....14,15,1,2,....

Check character generation is illustrated by the following example, which has the data message "CODE 93".

Data	C	O	D	E	sp	9	3	"C" "K"
Data Values	12	24	13	14	38	9	3	
C Weights	7	6	5	4	3	2	1	
K Weights	8	7	6	5	4	3	2	1

To obtain "C", calculate the sum of the products:

$$(1x3) + (2x9) + (3x28) + (4x14) + (5x13) + (6x24) + (7x12) = 484$$

Divide 484 by 47 to get 10 with a remainder of 14. The value of "C" is therefore 14, which corresponds to the character "E".

To obtain "K", calculate the sum of the products:

$$(1x14) + (2x3) + (3x9) + (4x38) + (5x14) + (6x13) + (7x24) + (8x12) = 611$$

Divide 611 by 47 to get 13, with a remainder of 0. The value of "K" is therefore zero, which corresponds to the character "0."

Note that the Code 93 reader uses "C" and "K" for checking the decoded message but does not transmit them.

Code 93 Dimensions

The minimum value of X is 7.5 mils for symbols used in open systems. X shall be constant throughout a symbol. For open systems, the minimum bar height is 15 percent of the symbol length or 0.25 inches, whichever is greater. The minimum quiet zone width is 10X. For optimum hand-scanning, the quiet zone width should be at least 0.25 inches.

The overall length of a Code 93 symbol is a function of X and the number of data characters, as given by:

$$L = [(C + 4) + 1] X$$

where
   L = length of symbol, excluding quiet zones
   C = number of data characters
   X = X dimension

Code 93 Dimensional Tolerances

For measuring purposes, the edge of a bar/space transition is defined as the center of a circular sampling aperture of diameter no greater than 0.8X when the apparent reflectance of the sample viewed through the aperture is halfway between the maximum and minimum reflectances obtained by that aperture on the adjacent bar and space.

When printing Code 93, three different tolerances need to be considered (see Figure E-1):

1. b: the bar and space width tolerance
2. e: the tolerance between similar edges of adjacent bars within a character
3. p: the tolerance between the leading edge of the first bar of one character and the leading edge of the first bar of an adjacent character

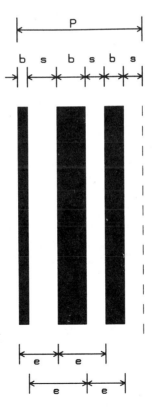

Figure E-1: Code 93 Dimensional Tolerance Definitions. Three tolerances are defined: b is the deviation from nominal of any bar or space width; e is the deviation from nominal of any edge-to-similar-edge width; and p is the deviation from nominal of the overall character width.

The tolerance b is:

b = ±(0.45X–0.001) inches for X dimensions of 7.5 mils or more
b = ±0.30X for X dimensions less than 7.5 mils

The tolerances e and p are interrelated, and two different tolerance formulas are used depending on the characteristics of the printer used:

Standard	Alternate
e = ±0.20X	e = ±0.15X
p = ±0.20X	p = ±0.30X

The distance between the trailing edge of the last bar in one character and the leading edge in the first bar of the next character must be no less than (X - b).

Note that the choice of either the standard or alternate tolerance formulas is made based on the type of printing equipment used and must remain fixed throughout an entire symbol.

Code 93 Optical Properties

Reflectivity measurements are made at a wavelength of 633 nanometers with illuminating and viewing axes separated by 45 degrees, with one of the axes positioned perpendicular to the sample surface. The aperture of each of the two optical systems should subtend an angle of no more than 15 degrees. The measured diffuse reflectance is defined as the ratio of the light reflected from the sample to that reflected from a specially prepared magnesium oxide or barium sulfate standard measured under the same conditions. One of the optical paths must restrict the sample field to an area equal to that of a circle of 0.8X, and the other path's sample field must have an area greater than that of a circle of 8X.

The maximum bar reflectance is 30 percent. The minimum space reflectance is 25 percent.

The minimum reflectance difference (MRD) is equal to the reflectivity difference between the darkest space and the lightest bar. The minimum value of MRD is 37.5 percent if X is less than 40 mils, and 20 percent if X is equal to or greater than 40 mils.

Code 93 Full ASCII Mode

Code 93 can represent any of the 128 ASCII characters by using paired character sequences made up of the character ⑤, ⑳, ⊘, and ⊕, followed by one of the 26 letters, as shown in Table E-1.

Code 93 Symbol Concatenation

It is sometimes advantageous to break up long bar code messages into two or more shorter symbols. If the first data character of a Code 93 symbol is a space, the bar code reader appends the information contained within the message (excluding the leading space) to its buffer. This operation continues for all Code 93 messages that contain a leading space.

When a Code 93 message that does not contain a leading space is read, the message is added to the reader's buffer, the entire buffer is transmitted, and the buffer is cleared.

Table E-1
FULL ASCII CHARACTER ENCODATION

ASCII	CODE 93	ASCII	CODE 93	ASCII	CODE 93	ASCII	CODE 93
NUL	(%)U	SP	Space	@	(%)V	`	(%)W
SOH	($)A	!	(/)A	A	A	a	(+)A
STX	($)B	"	(/)B	B	B	b	(+)B
ETX	($)C	#	(/)C	C	C	c	(+)C
EOT	($)D	$	$	D	D	d	(+)D
ENQ	($)E	%	%	E	E	e	(+)E
ACK	($)F	&	(/)F	F	F	f	(+)F
BEL	($)G	'	(/)G	G	G	g	(+)G
BS	($)H	(	(/)H	H	H	h	(+)H
HT	($)I	)	(/)I	I	I	i	(+)I
LF	($)J	*	(/)J	J	J	j	(+)J
VT	($)K	+	+	K	K	k	(+)K
FF	($)L	,	(/)L	L	L	l	(+)L
CR	($)M	−	−	M	M	m	(+)M
SO	($)N	.	.	N	N	n	(+)N
SI	($)O	/	/	O	O	o	(+)O
DLE	($)P	0	0	P	P	p	(+)P
DC1	($)Q	1	1	Q	Q	q	(+)Q
DC2	($)R	2	2	R	R	r	(+)R
DC3	($)S	3	3	S	S	s	(+)S
DC4	($)T	4	4	T	T	t	(+)T
NAK	($)U	5	5	U	U	u	(+)U
SYN	($)V	6	6	V	V	v	(+)V
ETB	($)W	7	7	W	W	w	(+)W
CAN	($)X	8	8	X	X	x	(+)X
EM	($)Y	9	9	Y	Y	y	(+)Y
SUB	($)Z	:	(/)Z	Z	Z	z	(+)Z
ESC	(%)A	;	(%)F	[	(%)K	{	(%)P
FS	(%)B	<	(%)G	\	(%)L	|	(%)Q
GS	(%)C	=	(%)H	]	(%)M	}	(%)R
RS	(%)D	>	(%)I	^	(%)N	~	(%)S
US	(%)E	?	(%)J	_	(%)O	DEL	(%)T

Note: The complete set (/) A through (/) Z decodes as the character shown in the adjacent column above. For example, (/) Y will decode as digit 9. The character pairs (%) X, (%) Y and (%) Z decode as DEL.

Code 93 Dimensional Verification

The following procedure should be used to determine if a Code 93 symbol meets the specified dimensional tolerances:

1. Measure and record the perceived width for every element. Record the width of the two quiet zones.

2. Decode the symbol, confirming that there are valid start, stop, and data characters.

3. Confirm that the number of elements E is 6n + 1, where n is greater than or equal to 4.

4. If it is desired to evaluate symbol quality against a value of X specified by an application standard, that value of X should be used starting in step 7, and skipping steps 5 and 6.

5. Measure and record the length L_s of the symbol, including all elements except the last bar.

6. Compute X as follows:

$$X = \frac{L_s}{9}\left(\frac{6}{E-1}\right)$$

Check that X is greater than or equal to 0.0075"; if not, declare X = 0.0075".

7. Calculate the bar and space width tolerance:
   b = 0.45X - 0.001 inches
8. Confirm that the width of every element falls within one of the following four ranges:
   a. 1X ±b
   b. 2X ±b
   c. 3X ±b
   d. 4X ±b
9. Calculate the standard and alternate tolerances for character pitch (p) and edge-to-similar-edge (e) as follows:

Standard		Alternate	
e_S =	0.20X	e_a =	0.15X
p_S =	0.20X	p_a =	0.30X

10. Confirm that the following criteria are met using either the standard (e_S, p_S) or the alternate (e_a, p_a) tolerances:
   a. The width of every character is equal to 9X + p.
   b. The width of each adjacent bar/space of space/bar pair within a character falls within one of the following four ranges:
   (I)   2X ±e
   (ii)   3X ±e
   (iii)   4X ±e
   (iv)   5X ±e
11. Confirm that each quiet zone is at least 10X wide.

Note: In step 6, the 7.5 mil limit is consistent with present practice for open systems. In closed applications, a lower limit may be used.

APPENDIX F

Code 49 Specification

Code 49 is a multirow, continuous, variable length symbology encoding the full ASCII 128 character set. Each row is composed of 18 bars and 17 spaces. There are between two and eight adjacent rows, each divided by a separator bar. Each row contains a row number, and the last row contains information indicating how many rows there are in the symbol. A summary of Code 49's main characteristics is as follows:

Character Set	:	All 128 ASCII characters
		3 function characters
		3 shift characters
Symbol Length	:	70 modules, excluding quiet zone
Symbol Height	:	2 to 8 rows
Maximum Message Length	:	49 alphanumeric characters or 81 digits
Check Characters	:	1 per row, plus 4 or 6 per symbol
Other Features	:	Concatenation ability
		Rows may be scanned in any order
Net Data Density	:	Maximum of 93.3 alphanumeric characters per inch or 154.3 numeric digits per inch when printed using a 7.5 mil X dimension

Code 49 Symbol Description

Each Code 49 symbol consists of two to eight rows. Each row consists of:

1. Leading quiet zone
2. Start pattern
3. Four data words encoding eight characters; the last character is a row check character
4. Stop pattern
5. Trailing quiet zone

Each row is separated by a one-module separator bar. Figure 4-40 shows Code 49 symbols of various lengths.

Code 49 Encodation

Each row contains four words structured in a (16,4) format. Figure 4-41 illustrates a typical row, including the start and stop patterns.

Each word encodes two characters from the character set described in Table 4-8. Each character is assigned a corresponding value.

Based on the characters encoded, each word can have a value from 0 to 2400. The word value is equal to the value of the character in the right half of the word plus 49 times the value in the left half of the word.

Each word value can be encoded in either odd or even parity. The exact bar/space patterns form a very long table of binary data which is part of the Code 49 symbology's definition. Table F-1 shows a representative sample extracted from the full definition of this table. In the table, a 1 represents a black module, and a 0 represents a white module.

Table F-1 is a representative extract from the full listing of the Code 49 word set, to give a flavor of the definition. AIM's Technical Symbology Committee has created the USS-49 standard for this symbology; readers interested in the full definition should contact AIM (see Appendix T).

The individual rows are uniquely identified by the parity of words within the row, as illustrated in Table F-2.

Table F-2
Map of Code 49 Record Parity

	Word 1	Word 2	Word 3	Word 4
Row 1	odd	even	even	odd
Row 2	even	odd	even	odd
Row 3	odd	odd	even	even
Row 4	even	even	odd	odd
Row 5	odd	even	odd	even
Row 6	even	odd	odd	even
Row 7	odd	odd	odd	odd
Last Row	even	even	even	even

Note that the words in the last row are always encoded with even parity, irrespective of the total number of rows in the symbol. The last character in every row is equal to the MOD 49 sum of the other seven characters in the row.

The characters encoded in a Code 49 symbol can be described in matrix notation as follows:

$$
\begin{array}{ll}
\text{Row 1} & C_{11} \; C_{12} \; C_{13} \; C_{14} \; C_{15} \; C_{16} \; C_{17} \; C_{18} \\
\text{Row 2} & \quad\quad C_{21} \; C_{22} \; C_{23} \; C_{24} \; C_{25} \; C_{26} \; C_{27} \; C_{28} \\
\bullet & \\
\bullet & \\
\bullet & \\
\text{Row r} & C_{r1} \; C_{r2} \; C_{r3} \; C_{r4} \; C_{r5} \; C_{r6} \; C_{r7} \; C_{r8}
\end{array}
$$

Note that r has a value between 2 and 8.

VALUE	ODD PARITY	EVEN PARITY	VALUE	ODD PARITY	EVEN PARITY	VALUE	ODD PARITY	EVEN PARITY
0000	1100100101000000	1011111001011100	0066	1110000111011010	1100100110111000	0132	1000110111010000	1000110001001100
0001	1111001001010000	1100000101101110	0067	1100011110110100	1111001001101110	0133	1110001101110100	1011110011011100
0002	1110110010100000	1000011011011100	0068	1001111101101000	1011001101110000	0134	1100110110101000	1100110000100110
0003	1111101001101000	1100000100100110	0069	1110011111011010	1100100100011000	0135	1111001110111010	1011110001001100
0004	1100101101000000	1001001011001100	0070	1101111110110100	1111001000100110	0136	1011110111010000	1000010111011100
0005	1111100101101000	1001111011011100	0071	1101000101000000	1011000100101000	0137	1110111101110100	1000110011001100
0006	1101101101000000	1100011100100110	0072	1111010001010000	1110110001001100	0138	1100000100010100	1001110111011100
0007	1111101101010100	1001111001010100	0073	1111110001010100	1001011101111000	0139	1000011000101000	1000010001000100
0008	1111110110110100	1101111100100110	0074	1111010011010000	1100010111011100	0140	1110000110001010	1001110110011100
0009	1100010010100000	1000000101001100	0075	1111101001101000	1001001100110000	0141	1100011100010100	1100010110001010
0010	1110100010100000	1000000100001000	0076	1101011101000000	1110010011001100	0142	1001110001010000	1001110001010100
0011	1001100101000000	1000111011001100	0077	1111010111010000	1001000100000100	0143	1110011110001010	1101111001000100
0012	1110011001010000	1100011100100010	0078	1111110101110100	1110010001000100	0144	1000001001101000	1100001011100110
0013	1111011010010100	1100001101100100	0079	1100100010100000	1101100001001000	0145	1000110110110100	1000110111011100
0014	1101111100010100	1011111101100100	0080	1111001000000010	1111011001000010	0146	1000111100110100	1100000100110010
0015	1110011100101000	1100111100010010	0081	1011000101000000	1100101110011000	0147	1100000110011010	1000110011001100
0016	1010110111001010	1011111100010100	0082	1110110001100010	1111001011011010	0148	1000111100110100	1011110111011100
0017	1000101101000000			1000010010100010	1011011100110000	0149	1011111001101000	1100111001100010
0018	1110001011			1000000	1100100110001000	0150	1110111110011010	1011110011000100
0019	110011			0	1111100100110010	0151	1100000101110100	1000010111100010
0020	111				111001100010000	0152	1000011011110110	1000110111011100
0021	1	1000111100110	2259	1101	110011000100	0153	1100000110111010	1001110111000100
0022	00	1001100011110110	2260	11010001	1100010000	0154	1100000101110100	1011110111011000
002	00110	1000101111110110	2261	11010000100	1000100	0155	1001110111011100	1000001000101110
0	0011100	1000100111110010	2262	10101111000111	001000	0156	1100011110111010	1000111000101110
	100001100	1011101111110010	2263	1010011100000110	0010	0157	1101111101110100	1000011001101110
	0100000100	1011100111110010	2264	1010001100000100 1	0	0158	1000001100010100	1000011000010100
	111000011000	1101010011000000	2265	1011000010111110	100	0159	1100001110001010	1001110001101110
	0101110001000	1010111100100010	2266	1001000110111110	1110	0160	1000111100010100	1001110000100010
	10011000001000	1111110101001010	2267	1001000010011110	110001	61	1000000110110100	1000010111011100
	1110100110000010	1110101000100000	2268	1011001110111110	100111101		1100000110011010	1000001001100110
	1100100010111110	1100101100011110	2269	1011000110011110	11100111101		00111100110100	1000110111011100
04	1011000101100110	1101101011100000	2270	1011000010001110	1101111101011		110011010	1000010001000
.205	1001001101111100	1111011010111000	2271	1001011101111110	1000001010001000		1001110	100011110
2206	1000001001111100	1111110101011110	2272	1001011101111110	1100000101101000	2		
2207	1101100010011110	1100010101101100	2273	1001000110011110	1000110110001000	2339		
2208	1100101110111110	1111001010011000	2274	1001000010000110	1110011101101000	2340	1000110	10
2209	1010111011111100	1010110010001000	2275	1011011110001110	1000111101000100	2341	1011110100000111	1011100101110000
2210	1100100110011100	1110110100110000	2276	1011011110001110	1011111100100000	2342	1000010100000110	1110111001011100
2211	1010001100111100	1111110101001100	2277	1011000110001110	1110111110100010	2343	1001110100000110	1100010110111000
2212	1100100010011110	1001110000000000	2278	1011000010001110	1100000110101110	2344	1000110100000110	1111000101101110
2213	1011000010001110	1110010100110000	2279	1001011110001110	1000011101011000	2345	1011110100000010	1001101101110000
2214	1001011100111100	1111110010100100	2280	1001001110001110	1000011101011100	2346	1110100010111110	1000010010011000
2215	1001001100011100	1111100010000000	2281	1001000110001110	1001111011011110	2347	1101011011111100	1111000100100110
2216	1001000100000100	1111011010100000	2282	1010000110111110	1011111110111110	2348	1101010010011110	1001100100110010
2217	1101100010000110	1111110110100010	2283	1010000010011110	1000001110011000	2349	1010110011111000	1110011001001100
2218	1000010101111110	1100110101011000	2284	1010011110111110	1000001101001000	2350	1101011001111110	1101111001001010
2219	1011011100011100	1110011010111000	2285	1010001110011110	1000110110001100	2351	1010001000111110	1110110110011010
2220	1100100110000110	1011101011110000	2286	1010000110001110	1100111110100010	2352	1110100000011110	1000101100110000
2221	1001001100010110	1101011010111000	2287	1010000010000110	1011111101100100	2353	1101011000111100	1110000101001100
2222	1100100010000010	1111110110101110	2288	1010111100111110	1000000010001000	2354	1101000100000110	1000010010001000
2223	1011000100000100	1100010100100000	2289	1001100110001110	1000000110100010	2355	1010101000011000	1110001001100100
2224	1010111100010110	1111000101001100	2290	1001000110001110	1000011110001000	2356	1011011100001110	1011110100010100
2225	1001001100000100	1001110100110000	2291	1010000110000110	1000011110100010	2357	1010001000000110	1110011001000100
2226	1101100100000010	1110010110011000	2292	1101010011111000	1001111110001010	2358	1110100100000110	1111001100100010
2227	1000011011111110	1101110000000110	2293	1111110010011110	1011111111011010	2359	1101011000000100	1011110010000100
2228	1000010011011110	1101110100101000	2294	1010100011110000	1110100010111000	2360	1101010000000100	1011110011000100
2229	1000100010011110	1111101110100100	2295	1110101000111100	1111101001011100	2361	1001100101111100	1100010110001000
2230	1011110100011110	1100000101001000	2296	1010101000111100	1010101101110000	2362	1101111011111100	1111000101100010
2231	1011100100011110	1110000101001000	2297	1111010100001110	1111010101110110	2363	1100010110111110	1001101100000100
2232	1001101110011110	1100110100100000	2298	1010100000110000	1111110101101110	2364	1011011011111100	1110011011000100
2233	1001101110011110	1111001101001000	2299	1110101000000100	1010010001100000	2365	1001100100111110	1011111011000000
2234	1001100010011110	1110110001101000	2300	1010101000000110	1111010001100010	2366	1011001001111100	1111011101100010
2235	1000101110011110	1101110110001000	2301	1111110100000010	1111110100100110	2367	1001011001111100	1000010010111000
2236	1000100010001110	1111101110001000	2302	1101110111111100	1010101001000000	2368	1001100010111100	1110000100110110
2237	1011101110011110	1100011101011000	2303	1010101110111110	1110110101001000	2369	1010110100011110	1100011000101110
2238	1000100010000110	1111000110101110	2304	1011010111111000	1111010101001100	2370	1100101100001110	1001110010111000
2239	1000100010001110	1101101110001000	2305	1111011010011110	1010100010100000	2371	1011011100011100	1110011100101000
2240	1011110001100010	1110011101011000	2306	1010101000011110	1101010000100000	2372	1100010000011110	1101111000001010
2241	1001101100011110	1101111010111000	2307	1110010100111110	1111101001000100	2373	1011001000001100	1100000101101100
2242	1001100100000110	1111110111010110	2308	1101101000011100	1101011000100100	2374	1001011000011100	1000110110111000
2243	1001100100000010	1100000101100110	2309	1100101000001100	1111010110001100	2375	1001001000001100	1100000101001100

C_{r7} indicates the number of rows in the symbol, and the starting mode of the symbol. C_{r7} is calculated as follows:

$$C_{r7} = 7(r - 2) + M$$

where

r = the number of rows
M = the starting mode:

0 Regular alphanumeric mode
1 Concatenate alphanumeric mode
2 Regular numeric mode
3 Group mode (see Appendix B)
4 Regular alphanumeric mode, shift 1
5 Regular alphanumeric mode, shift 2
6 Reserved

In alphanumeric mode, data is interpreted as alphanumeric characters until an ns (numeric shift) character is encountered. In numeric mode, the symbol begins with an implied "ns" character. Modes 4 or 5 begin with an implied "shift 1" or "shift 2" character. Modes 1 and 3 allow data from multiple Code 49 symbols to be concatenated by the reader.

Again using a matrix notation, the symbol's words can be referenced in the following manner:

$$
\begin{array}{cccc}
W_{11} & W_{12} & W_{13} & W_{14} \\
W_{21} & W_{22} & W_{23} & W_{24} \\
\bullet & & & \\
\bullet & & & \\
\bullet & & & \\
W_{r1} & W_{r2} & W_{r3} & W_{r4}
\end{array}
$$

Symbols with six or less rows have two overall check words, referred to as X and Y. Symbols with seven or eight rows have an additional check character, referred to as Z. The values of these check words is determined as follows:

$$X = 49\,C_{r5} + C_{r6} = W_{r3}$$
$$Y = 49\,C_{r3} + C_{r4} = W_{r2}$$
$$Z = 49\,C_{r1} + C_{r2} = W_{r1} \text{ (if r is 7 or 8)}$$

Check words X, Y, and Z are weighted check sums, calculated as follows:

$$Z = \left(Z_{00}\ C_{r7} + \sum_{i=1}^{r-1} \sum_{j=1}^{4} Z_{ij}\ W_{ij} \right) \text{MOD } 2401$$

$$Y = \left(Y_{00}\ C_{r7} + \sum_{i=1}^{r-1} \sum_{j=1}^{4} Y_{ij}\ W_{ij} + Y_{r1}W_{r1} \right) \text{MOD } 2401$$

$$X = \left(X_{00}\ C_{r7} + \sum_{i=1}^{r-1} \sum_{j=1}^{4} X_{ij}\ W_{ij} + X_{r1}W_{r1} + X_{r2}W_{r2} \right) \text{MOD } 2401$$

where

X_{ij}, Y_{ij}, and Z_{ij} are weighting factors from the following sequence as shown in Table F-3.

The steps involved in encoding the data "EXAMPLE 2" are as follows:

1. Determine the character values for the first row.

$$
\begin{array}{lll}
E & = & 14 \quad C_{11} \\
X & = & 33 \quad C_{12} \\
A & = & 10 \quad C_{13} \\
M & = & 22 \quad C_{14} \\
P & = & 25 \quad C_{15} \\
L & = & 21 \quad C_{16} \\
E & = & \underline{14} \quad C_{17} \\
  &   & 139
\end{array}
$$

2. Determine the check character for Row 1:

$$C_{18} = 139 \text{ MOD } 49 = 41$$

3. In this example, only two rows are required to encode the message. The data character values for the second row are:

$$
\begin{array}{lll}
sp & = 39 & = \quad C_{21} \\
2 & = 2 & = \quad C_{22}
\end{array}
$$

4. This is a regular, alphanumeric two-row symbol, therefore:

$$C_{r7} + 7(2\text{-}2) + 0 = 0$$

5. Calculate symbol check characters:

$$Y = [(16 \times 0) + (9 \times 719) + (31 \times 512) + (26 \times 1246) + (2 \times 727)$$
$$+ (12 \times 1864)] \text{ MOD } 2401 = 1729.$$
$$X = [(20 \times 0) + (1 \times 719) + (9 \times 512) + (31 \times 1246) + (26 \times 727) + (2 \times 1864)$$
$$+ (12 \times 1729)] \text{ MOD } 2401 = 895.$$

6. Check words Y and X are broken into their components:

$$Y = 1729 = (49 \times 35) + 14$$
$$X = 895 = (49 \times 18) + 13$$

7. Calculate the check character for the second row:

$$C_{28} = (38 + 2 + 35 + 14 + 18 + 13 + 0)\text{ MOD } 49 = 22$$

8. Arrange in a matrix of characters:

14	33	10	22	25	21	14	41
38	2	35	14	18	13	0	22

9. Convert into a matrix of words:

719	512	1246	727
1864	1729	895	22

10. Table F-1 is then used to determine the actual bar and space patterns, which are printed in a complete Code 49 symbol. The example in Figure 4-31 has a data message fitting exactly into a two-row symbol. If the message does not fill all of the available character positions, it is padded out using trailing ns characters.

Code 49 Numeric Mode

Long sequences of numeric digits can be compressed through the use of the numeric mode. Whenever the ns (numeric shift) character is encountered, numeric mode is entered (or exited). The ns character "toggles" between numeric mode and regular mode.

In numeric mode, five digits are represented as three characters, each of which can assume any value 0 through 47. If C_1, C_2, and C_3 represent the three characters, the value in numeric mode is equal to $(48)^2 C_1 + 48C_2 + C_3$.

Whenever the number of digits to be encoded is a multiple of 5 plus 1, the last digit is represented by a single numeric character. Whenever the number of digits to be encoded is a multiple of 5 plus 3, the last three digits are represented by two characters where the three-digit number is equal to $48C_1 + C_2$.

Whenever the total number of digits to be encoded is a multiple of 5 plus 4, the last four digits are represented by three characters, where the weighted value of the three characters is 100,000 plus the four-digit number represented.

Whenever the total number of digits to be encoded is a multiple of 5 plus 2, the last seven digits are considered to be 4 followed by 3, and are represented by three and two characters respectively. Examples:

1.	12345	transforms to 5	H	9			
2.	123456	transforms to 5	H	9	6		
3.	12345678	transforms to 5	H	9	E	6	
4.	123456789	transforms to 5	H	9	F2	G	
5.	1234567	transforms to ↑	F1	2	B	$	

Table F-3
Factors for Code 49

Row i	Col j	X i,j	Y i,j	Z i,j
0	0	20	16	38
1	1	1	9	31
1	2	9	31	26
1	3	31	26	2
1	4	26	2	12
2	1	2	12	17
2	2	12	17	23
2	3	17	23	37
2	4	23	37	18
3	1	37	18	22
3	2	18	22	6
3	3	22	6	27
3	4	6	27	44
4	1	27	44	15
4	2	44	15	43
4	3	15	43	39
4	4	43	39	11
5	1	39	11	13
5	2	11	13	5
5	3	13	5	41
5	4	5	41	33
6	1	41	33	36
6	2	33	36	8
6	3	36	8	4
6	4	8	4	32
7	1	4	32	3
7	2	32	3	19
7	3	3	19	40
7	4	19	40	25
8	1	40	25	29
8	2	25	29	10
8	3	29	10	24
8	4	10	24	30

Code 49 Concatenation

If a Code 49 symbol starts in Mode 1, the reader appends the information to a storage buffer (data not transmitted). The operation continues for all successive symbols starting in Mode 1, with messages being added to the end of previously stored messages. When a symbol is read that is not in Mode 1, or when the concatenation event is separately concluded by a reader command, the contents are appended to the buffer, the entire buffer is transmitted, and the buffer is cleared.

Symbols that start in Mode 3 provide a more strongly controlled form of concatenation as described in the following Group Mode section.

Code 49 Group Mode

Group Mode (Mode 3) allows multiple symbols to be concatenated into a single record, retaining data in the correct order, irrespective of scanning sequence.

Each symbol is printed in Mode 3, and the first data character indicates how many symbols are in the group and its sequential number according to Table F-4.

For example, if the first character of a Mode 3 symbol is P (value 25), then it is the fifth symbol in a group of seven. The character values in the above table can be calculated from value $= i-1 + 0.5j(j-1)$ for the ith symbol in a group of j.

The maximum number of symbols in a group is 9.

The following example illustrates Group Mode:

Consider the text "CODE 49 IS A MULTI-ROW, CONTINUOUS, VARIABLE LENGTH SYMBOLOGY ENCODING THE FULL ASCII 128-CHARACTER SET. EACH ROW CONTAINS 18 BARS."

Encoding this text in Group Mode produces three Code 49 symbols with data characters arranged as follows:

```
Mode = 3   3  C O D E    4        Mode = 3   4  G T H     S Y
           9    I S    A                        M B  O L  O G Y
           M U L T I  -  R                        E N  C  O D I
           O W ,      C O N                     N G      T H E
           T I N U O U  S                       F U L L    A S
           ,      V A R I  A                    C I  I      1  2 8
           B L E    L E   N                     -  C H  A R A C

                        Mode = 3   5  T E R    S E
                                   T  .        E A C
                                   H     R O W    C
                                   O N T A I N  S
                                       1  8    B A R
                                   S  .
```

The above symbols could be scanned in any order. If all three symbols decode properly, the reader will output the data in proper sequence. If the middle symbol were damaged, however, the reader would require an Enter or equivalent to close out the group reading activity.

Table F-4
Code 49 Mode 3 Symbol/Group Codes

Symbol Number	Group Size	First Character Value	First Character Character
1	2	1	1
2	2	2	2
1	3	3	3
2	3	4	4
3	3	5	5
1	4	6	6
2	4	7	7
3	4	8	8
4	4	9	9
1	5	10	A
2	5	11	B
3	5	12	C
4	5	13	D
5	5	14	E
1	6	15	F
2	6	16	G
3	6	17	H
4	6	18	I
5	6	19	J
6	6	20	K
1	7	21	L
2	7	22	M
3	7	23	N
4	7	24	O
5	7	25	P
6	7	26	Q
7	7	27	R
1	8	28	S
2	8	29	T
3	8	30	U
4	8	31	V
5	8	32	W
6	8	33	X
7	8	34	Y
8	8	35	Z
1	9	36	–
2	9	37	.
3	9	38	space
4	9	39	$
5	9	40	/
6	9	41	+
7	9	42	%
8	9	43	shift 1
9	9	44	shift 2

This Enter could come from a keyboard, a Code 39 start/stop symbol (**), or an empty Code 49 symbol (2 rows of ns). In this case, the reader would output a message such as:

CODE 49 IS A MULTI-ROW, CONTINUOUS, VARIABLE LEN {DATA MISSING} ER SET. EACH ROW CONTAINS 18 BARS.

Code 49 Function Codes

Code 49's character set includes three function characters: F1, F2, and F3. Special meaning has been assigned to the use of F1 or F2 in a symbol.

F1 is used to indicate that the next character or characters are a data system identifier.

F2 is used to indicate the end of a field. This allows a single Code 49 symbol to contain several different variable-length data fields.

F3 is reserved for future use.

Code 49 Full ASCII Character Set

ASCII characters beyond the basic Code 49 character set are encoded as a character pair where the first character of the pair is either a Shift 1 or a Shift 2 character. Table 4-9 describes the pairings for all 128 ASCII characters.

Code 49 Dimensions

The minimum value of X is 7.5 mils for symbols used in open systems. For closed systems, X must be greater than or equal to 3.0 mils. X shall be constant throughout a symbol.

The minimum quiet zone is one module on the right side of the symbol, and 10 modules on the left side.

The minimum bar height is 8X, but may be increased for symbols with less than 8 rows.

The overall length of a symbol is equal to 70X, excluding quiet zones.

The overall height of a symbol is a function of X, the bar height, and the number of rows, as follows:

$$H = [(h + 1)R + 1]X$$

where
    H = height of the symbol
    h = height of the individual bars, in multiples of X
    R = number of rows (2 to 8)

The number of rows in a Code 49 symbol is a function of the number and type of characters to be encoded. For regular mode symbols encoding alphanumeric data from the basic character set, the number of characters that can be contained in a Code 49 symbol is equal to:

$$C = 7R - 5 \text{ for } 2 \leq R < 7$$
$$7R - 7 \text{ for } 7 \leq R \leq 8$$

Code 49 Dimensional Tolerances

Three tolerances apply to a Code 49 symbol:

1. b: deviation of individual bar or space width from the nominal dimension
2. e: deviations from the nominal width between an edge of one bar and the similar edge of another bar
3. p: deviations from the nominal overall word width

Figure F-1 illustrates the definition of these tolerances.

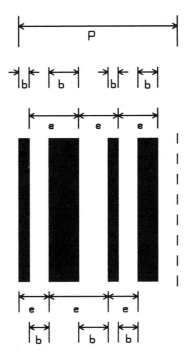

Figure F-1: Code 49 Dimensional Tolerance Definitions. Three tolerances are defined: b is the deviation from nominal of any bar or space width, e is the deviation from nominal of any edge-to-similar-edge width, and p is the deviation from nominal of the overall character width.

In open systems where X is equal to or greater than 7.5 mils, b must be controlled such that all elements (both bars and spaces) are larger than the greater of (5.6 mils or 0.65X). If X is greater than 20 mils, all elements must be larger than the greater of (13 mils or 0.55X). For closed systems with X less than 7.5 mils, all elements must be larger than the greater of (2.7 mils or 0.75X).

$$e = 0.2X$$
$$p = 0.2X$$

For measuring purposes, the edge of a bar/space transition is defined as the center of a circular sampling aperture of diameter no greater than 0.8X when the apparent reflectance of the sample viewed through the aperture is halfway between the maximum and minimum reflectances obtained by that aperture on the adjacent bar and space.

Code 49 Optical Properties

Reflectivity measurements are made at a wavelength of 633 nanometers with illuminating and viewing axes separated by 45 degrees, with one of the axes positioned perpendicular to the sample surface. The aperture of each of the two optical systems should subtend an angle of no more than 15 degrees. The measured diffuse reflectance is defined as the ratio of the light reflected from the sample to that reflected from a specially prepared magnesium oxide or barium sulfate standard measured under the same conditions. One of the optical paths must restrict the sample field to an area equal to that of a circle of 0.8X, and the other path's sample field must have an area greater than that of a circle of 8X.

The maximum bar reflectance is 30 percent. The minimum space reflectance is 25 percent.

The minimum reflectance difference (MRD) is equal to the reflectivity difference between the darkest space and the lightest bar. The minimum value of MRD is 37.5 percent if X is less than 40 mils, and 20 percent if X is equal to or greater than 40 mils.

Code 49 Dimensional Verification

The following procedure should be used to determine if a Code 49 symbol meets the specified dimensional tolerances:

A) For each row

1. Confirm that the bar count is equal to 18.
2. Confirm the presence of leading and trailing quiet zones.
3. Confirm the presence of a valid start and stop pattern.
4. Code 49 is designed to be decoded using "edge-to-similar-edge" measurements. The bar code reader makes seven width measurements of every word that is being decoded. These measurements are called S t_1, t_2, t_3, t_4, t_5, and t_6, as defined in Figure F-2.
5. Convert the six measurements $t_1...t_6$ into corresponding normalized values T_1, $T_2...T_6$, in terms of integral multiples of a module width, as follows:

$$t_i < \frac{2.5S}{16} \text{ , then } T_i \text{ is declared as two modules, otherwise}$$

.
.
.

$$\text{If } \frac{8.5S}{16} < t_i < \frac{9.5S}{16} \text{ , then } T_i \text{ is declared as nine modules.}$$

Otherwise T_i is declared as 10 modules.

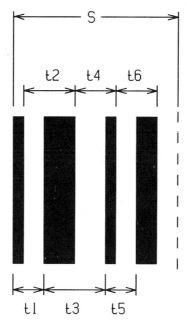

Figure F-2: Code 49 t-distances. Code 49 is designed to be decoded using edge to similar edge measurements.

6. The six values T_1, T_2, ... T_6 now uniquely determine a single USS-49 word that can be identified by the table look up techniques.

7. Decode all four words using the approach outlined in steps 5 and 6, assuming a constant scanning direction.

8. Identify the row number by checking the word parity patterns.

9. Convert the word values into character values.

10. Confirm that the row check character is correct.

B) Identify the last row (the one that has four words with even parity), and examine the second to last character. Confirm that the expected number of rows is equal to the number actually observed.

C) Verify that the symbol check characters are correct.

D) Perform such other checks as beam acceleration, absolute timing dimensions, etc., as are deemed prudent and appropriate considering the specific reading device and intended application environment.

Code 16K Specification

Code 16K is a multirow variable-length symbology encoding the full ASCII 128 character set. There are between two and 16 adjacent rows, each divided by a separator bar. Existing U.P.C. and Code 128 character patterns are employed. Rows are identified by the use of unique start/stop patterns. A summary of Code 16K's main characteristics is as follows:

Character Set	:	All 128 ASCII characters
		4 Function characters
		3 Code set change characters
		7 Shift characters
		1 Pad/Message separator character
Symbol Length	:	70 modules, excluding quiet zones
Symbol Height	:	2 to 16 rows
Maximum Message Length	:	77 ASCII characters, or 154 digits
Other Features	:	Concatenation ability
		Rows may be scanned in any order
Net Data Density	:	Maximum of 146.7 ASCII characters or 293.3 digits per inch when printing 16 rows with a 7.5 mil X dimension.

Code 16K Symbol Description

Each Code 16K symbol consists of 2 to 16 rows. Each row consists of:

1. Leading quiet zone
2. A start character
3. A 1X guard bar
4. Five symbol characters
5. A stop character
6. Trailing quiet zone

Rows are separated from each other by 1X thick separator bars. The top and bottom of the symbol have separator bars that extend to the end of the quiet zones.

The far left character in the top row is the mode character. The two far right characters in the bottom row are symbol check characters. Figure G-1 illustrates a Code 16K symbol.

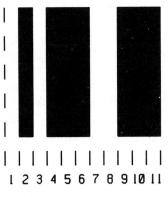

Figure G-1: Code 16K example.

Code 16K Encodation

There are 107 different Code 16K characters, each consisting of 11 modules. Each character has three spaces interleaved with three bars, starting with a space. Each element may be 1, 2, 3, or 4 modules wide.

The sum of all the bar module widths in a given character must be an odd number. Figure G-2 illustrates the character "A".

Figure G-2: The Character "A" encoded as a Code 16K character. Code 16K uses the "reverse video" of Code 128 encodation (spaces and bars are interchanged).

Code 16K has three character sets, as shown in Figure G-3. The code set is initially defined by the starting symbol character and may be changed within the symbol by the characters "Code A," Code B," or "Code C." Shift characters may be used to temporarily change the code set for the next one, two, or three symbol characters.

Special characters provide information to the reading equipment and are not transmitted as data.

Starting Symbol Character

The starting symbol character S defines the starting mode m the number of rows r. The starting mode specifies the initial code set, and may also represent an implied leading FNC 1 character or implied leading shift character as shown in Table G-2.

Figure G-3: Code 16K Encodation. Code 16K has three character sets.

Table G-1
CODE 16K STARTING MODE

Starting Mode	Initial Code Set	Implied Leading Shift Character
0	A	None
1	B	None
2	C	None
3	B	FNC 1
4	C	FNC 1
5	C	Shift B
6	C	Double Shift B

The value of the starting character is calculated as:

$$S = 7(r - 2) + m$$

where

s = the value of the starting character
r = is the number of rows
m = is the starting mode

Starting symbol character value 105 is used for an optional Code 16K feature that allows an extended message length by stacking and concatenating several symbols.

Function Characters

If an FNC 1 character is used immediately following the starting symbol character, or if it is implied by the mode, the subsequent data will be interpreted in a manner defined by the Uniform Code Council and International Article Numbering Association.

When an FNC 2 character immediately follows a starting symbol character, the reader will temporarily store the remaining data in the symbol and append it as a prefix to the next data read from a Code 16K symbol. If multiple append symbols are read consecutively, their data will be combined in the order scanned with the last nonappend mode symbol.

When an FNC 2 character is the third symbol character following the starting symbol character, the data following the FNC 2 will be concatenated with other symbols in a prescribed order. The value of the second symbol character will be used to define the order of concatenation and the total number of symbols to be concatenated:

value/10 = order of concatenation,
modulo 10 (value) = total number of symbols.

For example, if the value of the second symbol character is 37, then this symbol is the third symbol of seven to be concatenated.

If the reader decodes a Code 16K symbol without the concatenate mode, or a non-Code 16K symbol, it will discard the previously acquired data for concatenation.

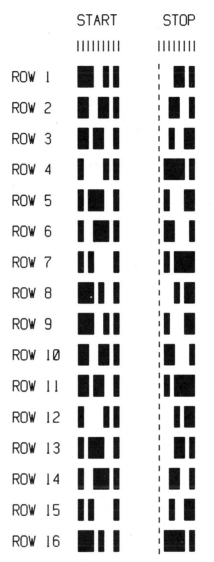

Figure G-4: Code 16K Start and Stop Patterns. Each row (up to a maximum of 16) has its own unique arrangement of start and stop character patterns.

An FNC 3 character indicates that the subsequent data is to be used for reader initialization.

Pad Character

When a pad character appears at the end of the symbol characters, just before the check characters, it represents no data. This is used to fill the last row or rows whenever the number of data characters do not require the number of symbol characters in the symbol.

Whenever this character is inserted within the symbol characters encoding data, it functions as a data separator. This allows a single Code 16K symbol to contain

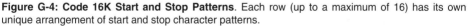

several different variable length data fields. The reader will treat the data encoded before and after this character as if they came from separate symbols, i.e., any data suffix and data prefix characters should be inserted between the data fields when they are stored or transmitted.

Start and Stop Characters

Eight different start and stop patterns are used to identify the individual rows of a Code 16K symbol. Figure G-4 illustrates the particular arrangements.

Check Characters

The far right character in the last row is called the C2 check character. The character immediately to the left of C2 is called the C1 check character.

C1 is calculated by taking the modulo 107 sum of the preceding character values and an ascending weighting series beginning with 2 for the starting symbol character. The summation ends with the character immediately to the left of C1.

C2 is calculated by taking the modulo 107 sum of the preceding character values and an ascending weighting series beginning with 1 for the starting symbol character. The summation ends with the C1 character.

Code 16K Dimensions

Three tolerances apply to every character of the Code 16K symbol:

b: deviation of individual bar or space width from the nominal dimension!
e: deviation from the nominal distance from the edge of one bar and the similar edge of another bar.
p: deviation from the nominal character width.

Only the bar measurement applies to the guard bar.
The maximum allowable tolerances are a function of the symbol's X dimension, as outlined below:

$$b = (0.4\,X - 0.0005)\ \text{inch}$$
$$e = 0.2\,X$$
$$p = 0.2\,X$$

PDF417 Specification

PDF417 is a multirow, continuous, variable length symbology which has high data capacity. Every symbol has between 3 and 90 rows. Each row contains a start pattern, a left row indicator, from 1 to 30 data characters, a right row indicator, and a stop pattern. Both the number of rows and their length are selectable, allowing the aspect ratio to be adjusted to particular labeling applications. There are no separator bars between rows.

Each symbol character consists of 4 bars and 4 spaces in a 17 module structure. There are three mutually exclusive sets of symbol patterns, or "clusters." Each cluster has 929 distinct patterns. Adjacent rows use different clusters, so it is possible for the decoder to tell if the scanning path is crossing row boundaries without the use of separator bars.

Every symbol includes at least two error-correction codewords. An option permits up to 510 additional error-correction codewords to be added to the symbol.

There are three different data compaction modes that define the mapping between codeword values and decoded data. The modes are: Text Compaction, Numeric Compaction, and Byte Compaction. In addition, the final interpretation of decoded data is subject to translation through the use of a Global Label Identifier (GLI).

A summary of PDF417's main characteristics is as follows:

Character Set	:	All 128 ASCII Characters
		All 128 Extended ASCII Characters
		8-Bit Binary Data
		Up to 811,800 Different Interpretations
Symbol Height	:	3 to 90 Rows
		Minimum row height is 3X
Symbol Width	:	90X to 583X
Error Correction Characters	:	2 to 512
Maximum Data Capacity	:	1850 text characters
(at error correction level 0)		2710 digits
		1108 bytes
Other Features:		Designed so that cross-row scans can be successfully used.
		Selectable levels of error correction.

Options : Concatenation (Macro PDF417)
Global label Identifiers (GLI)
Truncated PDF417

PDF417 Symbol Description

Each PDF417 symbol consists of 3 to 90 stacked rows surrounded by a quiet zone on all four sides. Each row consists of:

1. Leading quiet zone
2. Start pattern
3. Left row indicator character
4. One to thirty data characters
5. Right row indicator character
6. Stop pattern
7. Trailing quiet zone

Each character has four bars and four spaces in a 17 module (n,k) structure, and is assigned a value between 0 and 928. For this symbology, it is common to refer to these character values as "codewords."

The number of characters in a row and the number of rows can be adjusted to vary the overall symbol's aspect ratio in order to best fit into the available space. Figure H-1 shows the structure of an example PDF417 symbol.

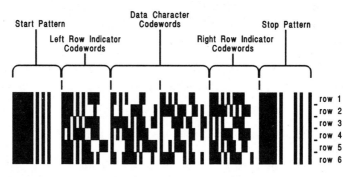

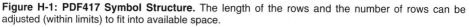

Figure H-1: PDF417 Symbol Structure. The length of the rows and the number of rows can be adjusted (within limits) to fit into available space.

Each row has a left and right row indicator. Between these row indicators is the data region. The left-most character in the top row of the data region defines the total number of characters in the data region, excluding the error correction characters. The characters in the data region are designed to be read from left to right starting on the top row, immediately after the length-defining character. The maximum number of PDF417 characters in the data region is 928.

Character Encoding

Each PDF417 character is 17 modules in length, and consists of 4 bars and 4 spaces. Each bar or space can be from 1 to 6 modules long. Three different character sets (called "clusters") are defined. Within each cluster, each character has a unique bar/space pattern, and is assigned a value (called the "codeword") between 0 and 928. An excerpt from the table of unique PDF417 character patterns is shown in Figure H-2.

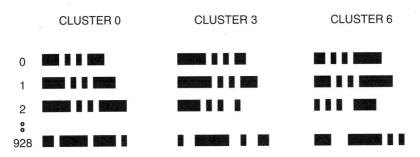

Figure H-2: Excerpt From The PDF417 Character Pattern Table. Three different character sets (or "clusters") are defined. Each character is assigned a value (called the "codeword") from 0 to 928.

An example PDF417 character is shown in Figure H-3. Using the nomenclature from this figure, the cluster number may be calculated as: cluster number = $(b_1 - b_2 + b_3 - b_4 + 9)$ mod 9. Only cluster numbers 0, 3, and 6 are valid for PDF417.

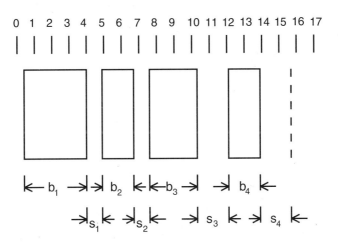

Figure H-3: Example PDF417 Character. The values b and s are the widths of the bars and spaces respectively, measured in modules.

Row Encoding

Each row uses character patterns from a single cluster. Adjacent rows use different clusters in the sequence 0, 3, 6, 0, 3, 6, ... The cluster number is equal to ((row number-1) mod 3) * 3. Because no two adjacent rows will use the same cluster number, it is possible for the reading equipment to detect if a scan has crossed from one row into another.

Every row starts with a left row indicator and ends with a right row indicator.

These row indicators are characters whose value is based on the particular row number, the total number of rows (3 to 90), the number of columns (1 to 30), and the error correction level (0 to 8). The values for the row indicators are given as follows:

Left Row Indicator	Right Row Indicator	
$30 x_i + y$	$30 x_i + v$	if $c_i = 0$
$30 x_i + z$	$30 x_i + y$	if $c_i = 0$
$30 x_i + v$	$30 x_i + z$	if $c_i = 0$

Where

x_i = (row number–1) div 3 for i = 1 to 90
y = (number of rows–1) div 3
z = (error correction level) * 3 + (number of rows - 1) mod 3
v = number of columns in the data region–1
c_i = cluster number of row i

> Note: Div is the integer division operator, rounding down.
> Mod is the remainder after division

Character Modes

Actual data to be represented in a PDF417 symbol is encoded using one of three data compaction modes. Mode latch and shift characters allow modes to be intermixed in a symbol in such a fashion as to minimize the overall size. The three modes are: Text Compaction (TC), Byte Compaction (BC), and Numeric Compaction (NC).

For each of the three clusters, each unique character is assigned a character value (codeword) between 0 and 928 as shown in Figure H-2. These are assigned as follows:

VALUE	USE
0–899	Data encodation according to the current compaction mode and GLI interpretation
900	Latch in TC mode
901	Latch in BC mode (where the number of bytes to be encoded is not a multiple of 6)
902	Latch in NC mode
913	Shift to BC mode for the next codeword
924	Latch in BC mode (where the number of bytes to be encoded is a multiple of 6)
925, 926, 927	Used for GLI interpretation (see later section)
922, 923, 928	Used for Macro PDF417 (see later section)
921	Reader initialization
903–912 and 914–920	Reserved for future use

A mode latch codeword causes a shift to the new mode which stays in effect until another mode switch is specifically performed, whereas a mode switch codeword only switches the mode for the next codeword.

Text Compaction Mode (TC)

Within the Text Compaction mode there are four sub-modes: Alpha, Lowercase, Mixed, and Punctuation. Within each TC sub-mode there are 30 defined characters with assigned values of 0 to 29 as shown in Figure H-4.

VALUE	ALPHA Character	LOWER Character	MIXED Character	PUNCTUATION Character
0	A	a	0	;
1	B	b	1	<
2	C	c	2	>
3	D	d	3	@
4	E	e	4	[
5	F	f	5	\
6	G	g	6	]
7	H	h	7	_
8	I	I	8	'
9	J	j	9	~
10	K	k	&	!
11	L	l	cr	cr
12	M	m	ht	ht
13	N	n	,	,
14	O	o	:	:
15	P	p	#	lf
16	Q	q	-	-
17	R	r	.	.
18	S	s	$	$
19	T	t	/	/
20	U	u	+	"
21	V	v	%		
22	W	w	*	*
23	X	x	=	(
24	Y	y	^	)
25	Z	z	pl	?
26	sp	sp	sp	{
27	ll	as	ll	}
28	ml	ml	al	`
29	ps	ps	ps	al

Note:

cr	=	carriage return
ht	=	horizontal tab
lf	=	line feed
sp	=	space
ll	=	latch to lowercase sub-mode
ps	=	shift to punctuation sub-mode
ml	=	latch to mixed sub-mode
as	=	shift to alpha sub-mode
al	=	latch to alpha sub-mode
pl	=	latch to punctuation sub-mode
ps	=	pad character

Figure H-4: Text Compaction Sub-Modes. Two text characters can be encoded into a single PDF417 data character. Sub-modes of the Text Compaction mode are provided to move between available text character sets. Shift and latch characters are used to change between sub-modes.

Two text characters can be encoded in a single PDF417 character. The PDF417 symbol character value is equal to $((30 * H) + L)$, where H is the value corresponding to the leading character, and L is the value corresponding to the second text character.

Note that a latch from any mode to the Text Compaction mode is assumed to start out in the Alpha sub-mode.

Byte Compaction Mode (BC)

A sequence of bytes can be encoded into a sequence of PDF417 codewords by using Byte Compaction mode. This is done by using a base 256 to base 900 conversion.

If the number of bytes to be encoded is a multiple of 6, then mode latch 924 is used to precede the encoded data: 6 bytes are encoded into 5 codewords by using a 256 to 900 base conversion from left to right, starting at the most significant byte. As an example, the hex sequence (00H, 01H, 10H, 02H, A0H, 12H) is encoded into codeword sequence (924, 0, 6, 233, 896, 2). The first codeword (value 924) indicates that the sequence to follow is a multiple of 6 bytes, and the other values reflect the base conversion as follows:

$$0*256^5 + 1*256^4 + 16*256^3 + 2*256^2 + 10*256^1 + 18 = 4,563,536,402$$
$$\text{and}$$
$$0*900^4 + 6*900^3 + 233*900^2 + 896*900^1 + 2 = 4,563,536,402$$

If the number of bytes to encode is not a multiple of 6, the leading codeword of the sequence is 901. If the number of bytes to encode is 7 or more, the method of base 256 to 900 conversion (described above) is used to encode as many groups of 6 bytes as possible, then the remaining bytes (5 or less) are encoded directly using 1 codeword for each byte.

Numeric Compaction Mode (NC)

Using a base 10 to base 900 conversion process, the Numeric Compaction mode can pack just under 3 decimal digits into a single PDF417 character. It is not recommended to use the Numeric Compaction mode if the string of digits to be encoded has a length of less than 13.

Strings of digits are encoded using the following algorithm:

1. Partition the string of digits into groups of 44 digits. The last group may have less than 44 digits.
2. For each of the groups, place a digit "1" in front of it, then perform a base 10 to base 900 conversion.

As an example, consider the string of digits "000213298174002". Since there are only 15 digits, there is only one group in this example. Add a leading 1 and perform the base 10 to 900 conversion as follows:

$$1,000,213,298,174,002 = 1*900^5 + 624*900^4 + 434*900^3 + 632*900^2 + 282*900^1 + 202$$

The PDF417 codeword sequence is therefore $(1, 624, 434, 632, 282, 2)$.

Encoding

Using different mode and shift sequences, it is possible to represent a given string of data characters by several different codeword sequences. If the symbol is not completely filled up by the available data, codeword 900 should be used as a pad character(s) (this must be done before the optional Macro PDF417 Control Block and the error correction codewords).

Global Label Identifier (GLI)

Specific interpretation of the meaning of the encoded bytes can be provided by a special codeword sequence known as a Global Label Identifier (GLI). The character definitions provided above all assume that GLI 0 is in effect (the default). Using codewords 925, 926, and 927 with following modifiers, it is possible to switch to one of 811,800 possible GLI's.

Start And Stop Patterns

Specific bar/space arrangements are defined for PDF417 start and stop patterns. These are clearly shown in Figure H-1.

Quiet Zones

A minimum quiet zone of 2X is required on all four sides of the PDF417 symbol.

Error Detection And Correction

Each PDF417 symbol contains at least 2 error correction codewords. The error correction level for a symbol is selectable between one of 9 levels at the time of printing. The actual number of error correction codewords is defined as follows:

Error Correction Level	Number Of Error Correction Codewords
0	2
1	4
2	8
3	16
4	32
5	64
6	128
7	256
8	512

The error correction codewords can be used to correct two types of problems: erasures (where a character is undecodable), and actual errors (where the position and value of a character are unknown). The capacity of the PDF417 error correction characters is related to the type and number of defects. The sum of the number of erasures and twice the number of errors must be less than the number of error correction characters minus 2 if all data is to be recovered successfully.

The actual error correction codewords are calculated using Reed Solomon techniques. This process is non-trivial, and it is suggested that interested parties contact AIM (see Appendix T) to request a copy of USS-PDF417 if detailed information is required.

As more data is encoded in a PDF417 symbol, it is recommended that higher error correction levels be used, as outlined below:

Number Of Data Codewords	Error Correction Level
1–40	2
41–160	3
161–320	4
321–863	5

Transmitted Data

The data transmitted by a PDF417 reader consists of a series of 8-bit bytes reflecting the symbol's codewords translated according to the data compaction modes in effect. Start and stop characters, length descriptor, row indicators, mode switch characters, and error correction characters are not transmitted.

There are certain special codewords with values greater than 902 which are not mode identifier codewords. These are transmitted as an escape character followed by three decimal digits representing the character's value. The default escape character is the backslash.

Truncated PDF417

In certain environments where label damage is unlikely, the right row indicators can be eliminated, and the stop pattern can be reduced to a single module bar. This variant is called Truncated PDF417, which results in a smaller symbol with somewhat less readability.

Macro PDF417

Large data files can be encoded into a series of linked PDF417 symbols using a standard methodology referred to as Macro PDF417. Additional control information is contained in a Macro PDF417 Control Block which defines the file ID, the concatenation sequence, and other information. The reader then uses the Control Block information to reconstruct the original file independent of the scanning order.

The Control Block follows a symbol's data characters, and is placed immediately before the error correction characters. It begins with a marker codeword of value 928, then contains at least two mandatory fields: the segment index, and the file ID. It may also contain other optional fields. Using Numeric Compaction mode, the segment index is 2 codewords in length, and consists of a value between 0 and k-1 representing the relative position of the data, where k is the number of symbols. The segment index is padded to five digits with leading zeros before Numeric Compaction is used. Maximum value of k is 99,999.

For each Macro PDF417 symbol in a sequence, the file ID contains the same value. The file ID is a variable length field which begins with the codeword following the segment index and ends at the start of the optional fields or the end of the Control Block. The file ID value is between 0 and 899. Optional Control Block fields can be used to include file name, time stamp, file size, sender, and/or addressee.

The Control Block in the symbol representing the last segment of a Macro PDF417 file ends with a codeword with the value of 922.

Code One Specification

Code One is a two-dimensional matrix symbology consisting of an array of light and dark data modules and fixed reference patterns. A large number of the symbol characters are allocated to error detection and correction. This symbology is designed to be read using two-dimensional imaging techniques, and as such is considered as being omnidirectional.

There are 10 different versions and 14 sizes of the Code One symbol. Most applications use versions A, B, C, D, E, F, G, and H, which have a variety of different data capacities. The capacity approximately doubles between adjacent versions. It is usual to use the smallest version that has sufficient capacity for the application. Versions S and T have a fixed height that is suited to printing with 8 or 16 nozzle ink jet printers.

Code One has six different data character sets. The default is the ASCII code set, whereby one ASCII data character is encoded per symbol character, numeric data is packed as two digits per character, and extended ASCII uses the Function 4 character as a shift or latch. The C40 code set encodes three alphanumeric data characters into two symbol characters. The Text code set similarly packs three low-ercase alphanumeric characters into two symbol characters. The EDI code set includes the common Electronic Data Interchange data characters as well as field and record delimiters. The Decimal Code set is useful for long digit sequences, packing 12 digits into five symbol characters. The Byte code set is used to encode a mix of ASCII and extended ASCII data or binary data.

A summary of Code One's characteristics is as follows:

Character Set :	All 128 ASCII Characters
	All 128 Extended ASCII Characters
	1 Pad/Message Separator Character
	8-bit Binary Data
Symbol Size :	From 9 modules by 13 modules to 134 modules by 148 modules
Orientation :	Omnidirectional
Error Correction Characters :	4 to 560
Maximum Data Capacity :	2218 text characters (per symbol) 3550 digits 1478 bytes

Symbol Description

A Code One symbol consists of square modules in a data region and fixed patterns for recognition and reference. Figure I-1 shows an example of a Code One Symbol.

Figure I-1: Example Code One Symbol. Square data modules are used to encode the data, and fixed patterns are used for recognition and referencing.

There are ten different symbol versions that are suited to different message lengths. These versions are labeled from smallest to largest as S, T, A, B, C, D, E, F, G, and H. Versions S and T have a different structure form the others, and are available in three sizes each. Characteristics of each are given below:

Version	Width (modules)	Height (modules)	Number Of Symbol Characters	Alphanumeric Capacity	Numeric Capacity	Full ASCII Capacity
S-10	13	9	8*	-	6	-
S-20	23	9	16*	-	12	-
S-30	33	9	24*	-	18	-
T-16	19	17	20	13	22	10
T-32	35	17	40	34	56	24
T-48	51	17	60	55	90	38
A	18	16	20	13	22	10
B	22	22	35	27	44	19
C	32	28	70	64	104	44
D	42	40	135	135	217	91
E	54	52	252	271	435	182
F	76	70	510	553	886	370
G	98	104	1012	1096	1755	732
H	134	148	2040	2218	3550	1480

* these are 5-bit characters. All the others are 8-bit.

Note that the dimensions are given in terms of modules, which are equivalent to X dimensions. Each version has its own unique recognition pattern and array of reference marks. Figure I-2 illustrates the arrangement for versions A, B, and C, and Figure I-3 shows the S versions. Figure I-4 shows the T version arrangements.

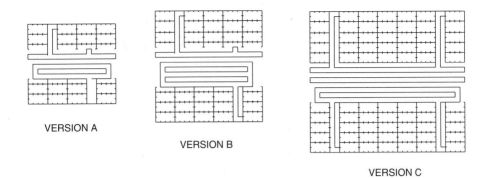

VERSION A

VERSION B

VERSION C

Figure I-2. Code One versions A, B, and C. Each Code One version has its own unique arrangement of data cells, recognition pattern, and reference pattern.

VERSION S-10   VERSION S-20   VERSION S-30

Figure I-3. Code One S versions. The S versions are designed to be printed with an eight nozzle ink jet (or other) printer.

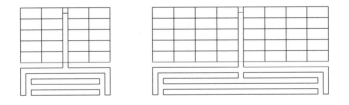

VERSION T-16   VERSION T-32

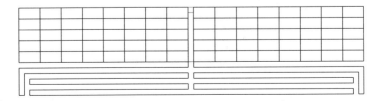

VERSION T-48

Figure I-4. Code One T versions. The T versions are designed to be printed with a 16 nozzle ink jet (or other) printer.

In the data region, each module represents one bit of data. Zero is represented by a white module, and one is black. Arrays of two rows of four modules each encode byte patterns, which have a value of 0 to 255. The most significant bit is in the upper left corner, and the least significant bit of the byte pattern is in the lower right corner. In some versions a few of the byte patterns are split by the recognition or reference patterns. The symbol patterns are ordered left to right and top to bottom.

Six different code sets are used to encode the data, and special character values or bit strings are used to switch between the sets. The six sets are:

SET	CAPABILITY
ASCII	full ASCII data
C40	mostly uppercase alphanumeric data
Decimal	numeric data
Text	mostly lowercase text data
EDI	Electronic Data Interchange (EDI) data set
Byte	Binary data

ASCII Code Set

The default code set is the ASCII code set, which encodes ASCII data using character values 1 to 128 (the character value is equal to one more than the ASCII value). This code set also encodes double density numeric data by encoding digit pairs 00 through 99 with character values 130-129 (numeric value plus 130). The ASCII code set also includes other special characters as shown below:

Character Value	Data or Function
1–128	ASCII data (1 plus the ASCII value)
129	Pad character
130–229	2-digit numeric data (130 plus the numeric value)
230	Change to C40 code set
231	Change to Byte code set
232	FNC1
233	FNC2
234	FNC3
235	FNC4
236	Same as FNC1 with a change to the Decimal code set
238	Change to EDI code set
239	Change to Text code set
240–255	Change to Decimal code set (the low order 4 bits are to be treated as the first bits of the first 10-bit code)

C40 Code Set

Three alphanumeric characters are packed into two Code One symbol characters. Uppercase alphabetic characters, numbers, and the space character can be encoded as a single C40 value. All other ASCII characters and special characters require two C40 values starting with one of the three shift characters. Note that a shift character only affects the C40 value that immediately follows. The C40 code set values are assigned as follows:

C40 Value	Data Character	ASCII Values
0	Shift 1	–
1	Shift 2	–
2	Shift 3	–
3	space	32
4–13	0–9	48–57
14–39	A–Z	65–90

Three C40 values (V1, V2, and V3) to be encoded are combined to form a value between 1 and 64,000 as follows:

$$(1600 * V1) + (40 * V2) + V3 + 1$$

This value is then represented in two Code One symbol characters, where the two characters are taken together as representing a 16 bit binary word with value between 0 and 65,535.

If a symbol character of value 255 immediately follows a pair of characters encoding a C40 code set value, then the mode switches back to the ASCII code set.

The C40 code set remains in effect through to the end of the data, except where a single symbol character is "left over" at the end of the data area, in which case this is encoded as a single ASCII character in the ASCII code set.

One of the C40 shift characters can be used as a pad if two characters are to be encoded as the last two data symbol characters.

The C40 Shift 1 code set encodes the ASCII control characters. These are formed by a Shift 1 character followed by a second C40 value of between 0 and 31 which represents the ASCII value to be encoded.

The C40 Shift 2 code set encodes punctuation and some special non-ASCII characters. These characters are encoded by using a Shift 2 character followed by a second C40 character whose value is as follows:

C40 Value	Encoded Data	ASCII Values
0–14	!–/	33–47
15–21	:–@	58–64
22–26	[–_	91–95
27	FNC1	–
28	FNC2	–
29	FNC3	–
30	FNC4	–
21	pad	–

The C40 Shift 3 code set encodes lowercase alphabetic characters and the remaining punctuation characters. These characters are formed by using a C40 Shift 3 character followed by a second C40 character whose value is equal to 96 plus the ASCII value.

The entire encodable character set using the C40 mode can be outlined as follows:

Data Character	C40 Value(s)	Data Character	C40 Value(s)	Data Character	C40 Value(s)	Data Character	C40 Value(s)
NUL	0,0	"	1,1	D	17	f	2,6
SOH	0,1	#	1,2	E	18	g	2,7
STX	0,2	$	1,3	F	19	h	2,8
ETX	0,3	%	1,4	G	20	I	2,9
EOT	0,4	&	1,5	H	21	j	2,10
ENQ	0,5	'	1,6	I	22	k	2,11
ACK	0,6	(	1,7	J	23	l	2,12
BEL	0,7	)	1,8	K	24	m	2,13
BS	0,8	*	1,9	L	25	n	2,14
HT	0,9	+	1,10	M	26	o	2,15
LF	0,10	,	1,11	N	27	p	2,16
VT	0,11	-	1,12	O	28	q	2,17
FF	0,12	.	1,13	P	29	r	2,18
CR	0,13	/	1,14	Q	30	s	2,19
SO	0,14	0	4	R	31	t	2,20
SI	0,15	1	5	S	32	u	2,21
DLE	0,16	2	6	T	33	v	2,22
DC1	0,17	3	7	U	34	w	2,23
DC2	0,18	4	8	V	35	x	2,24
DC3	0,19	5	9	W	36	y	2,25
DC4	0,20	6	10	X	37	z	2,26
NAK	0,21	7	11	Y	38	{	2,27
SYN	0,22	8	12	Z	39	I	2,28
ETB	0,23	9	13	[	1,22	}	2,29
CAN	0,24	:	1,15	\	1,23	~	2,30
EM	0,25	;	1,16	]	1,24	DEL	2,31
SUB	0,26	<	1,17	^	1,25	FNC1	1,27
ESC	0,27	=	1,18	_	1,26	FNC2	1,28
FS	0,28	>	1,19	`	2,0	FNC3	1,29
GS	0,29	?	1,20	a	2,1	FNC4	1,30
RS	0,30	@	1,21	b	2,2	PAD	1,31
US	0,31	A	14	c	2,3	Shift1	0
SP	3	B	15	d	2,4	Shift2	1
!	1,0	C	16	e	2,5	Shift3	2

Decimal Code Set

In the Decimal code set, three digits of decimal data are encoded into a 10-bit binary string representing one more than the value. The "switch to Decimal mode" character uses only the four most significant bits of a Code One character byte to effect the switch, so the four least significant bits are treated as the beginning of a 10-bit binary string. Strings of 10 binary bits follow each other without regard for character byte boundaries.

If six consecutive ones occur at the beginning of a 10 bit string, the mode switches back to the ASCII code set to encode any remaining digits. If after the six ones there are four or six bits left before the next Code One character byte boundary, then the first four bits may encode an additional digit where 0001 represents 0 and

1010 represents 9. A 1111 four-bit field indicates that no additional digit is encoded. When only two bits are left, a 01 string is used to pad to the next character byte boundary.

The same encodation applies if four or six bits remain in the last symbol character that can encode data. If 8 bits remain at the end, the symbol character is encoded in ASCII mode.

Text Code Set

Normal printed text mostly uses lowercase characters, and Code One's Text code set is designed to encode this sort of data efficiently. This is identical to the C40 code set except that the encodation of uppercase and lowercase letters are reversed. A symbol character of value 255 immediately following a pair of symbol characters in Text mode switches back to the ASCII mode. The Text code set encodation is as follows:

Data Character	Text Value(s)	Data Character	Text Value(s)	Data Character	Text Value(s)	Data Character	Text Value(s)
NUL	0,0	"	1,1	D	2,4	f	19
SOH	0,1	#	1,2	E	2,5	g	20
STX	0,2	$	1,3	F	2,6	h	21
ETX	0,3	%	1,4	G	2,7	i	22
EOT	0,4	&	1,5	H	2,8	j	23
ENQ	0,5	'	1,6	I	2,9	k	24
ACK	0,6	(	1,7	J	2,10	l	25
BEL	0,7	)	1,8	K	2,11	m	26
BS	0,8	*	1,9	L	2,12	n	27
HT	0,9	+	1,10	M	2,13	o	28
LF	0,10	,	1,11	N	2,14	p	29
VT	0,11	-	1,12	O	2,15	q	30
FF	0,12	.	1,13	P	2,16	r	31
CR	0,13	/	1,14	Q	2,17	s	32
SO	0,14	0	4	R	2,18	t	33
SI	0,15	1	5	S	2,19	u	34
DLE	0,16	2	6	T	2,20	v	35
DC1	0,17	3	7	U	2,21	w	36
DC2	0,18	4	8	V	2,22	x	37
DC3	0,19	5	9	W	2,23	y	38
DC4	0,20	6	10	X	2,24	z	39
NAK	0,21	7	11	Y	2,25	{	2,27
SYN	0,22	8	12	Z	2,26	|	2,28
ETB	0,23	9	13	[	1,22	}	2,29
CAN	0,24	:	1,15	\	1,23	~	2,30
EM	0,25	;	1,16	]	1,24	DEL	2,31
SUB	0,26	<	1,17	^	1,25	FNC1	1,27
ESC	0,27	=	1,18	_	1,26	FNC2	1,28
FS	0,28	>	1,19	`	2,0	FNC3	1,29
GS	0,29	?	1,20	a	14	FNC4	1,30
RS	0,30	@	1,21	b	15	PAD	1,31
US	0,31	A	2,1	c	16	Shift1	0
SP	3	B	2,2	d	17	Shift2	1
!	1,0	C	2,3	e	18	Shift3	2

EDI Code Set

EDI (Electronic Data Interchange) alphanumeric and separator data is encoded in the EDI code set using the C40 code set's method of packing three data characters in two symbol characters. It encodes uppercase alphabetic characters, numbers, space, and the three standard EDI terminator and separator characters using the following values:

Value	Data
0	EDI segment terminator
1	EDI segment separator
2	EDI sub-segment separator
3	space
4–13	the digits 0 through 9
14–39	the letters A through Z

Byte Code Set

Binary data can be encoded directly into a Code One symbol 8 bits at a time using the Byte code set. The length of the code set data field in bytes is defined by one or two symbol characters following the "switch to Byte code set" characters. If a single character with all zeros follows the switch character, it means that all remaining data characters in the symbol should be interpreted as Byte mode data. If the length of the binary data is between 1 and 249 bytes, the first character following the switch character defines the length directly. The length of longer strings of bytes are defined by two characters C1 and C2, where the length is equal to $((C1 - 249)*250) + C2$. C1 can have a value between 250 and 255, and C2 can be between 0 and 249.

FNC1

If an FNC1 character is present in the first data position, the Code One symbol is assumed to comply with a specific industry standard. An FNC1 character in any other symbol position is used as a field delimiter, and is transmitted as a GS character (ASCII value of 29).

FNC2

If the first character in a Code One symbol is FNC2, the reader temporarily stores the decoded data, and adds it as a prefix to the next symbol read. This process continues until a symbol is read that does not have an FNC2 character in the first position, in which case all of the temporarily stored data is added as a prefix to the latest data and transmitted.

If an FNC2 character is present in the second character position, up to 15 Code One symbols may be concatenated in a specific order using group mode. The value of the first character (preceding the FNC2) indicates both the total number of symbols in the group, and the particular sequence number of that symbol using the following approach:

$$\text{sequence number} = (\text{div } 15(\text{value})) + 1$$
$$\text{total number of symbols} = (\text{modulo } 15(\text{value})) + 1$$

where div represents integer division rounding down, and modulo is the remainder after division.

FNC4

Extended ASCII data (values 128–255) is encoded with FNC4. When shifted by FNC4, data encoded in ASCII, C40, and Text code sets have their values increased by 128 from their normal ASCII values. A single FNC4 character affects only the following character, whereas two FNC4 characters in sequence toggle into (and out of) the extended ASCII mode.

Error Correction

Every Code One symbol includes error correction characters based on Reed Solomon techniques. The number of error correction characters is specified for each Code One version as follows:

Code One Version	Data Characters	Error Correction Characters
A	10	10
B	19	16
C	44	26
D	91	44
E	182	70
F	370	140
G	732	280
H	1480	560

The actual calculation of the error correction characters is a mathematically complex, non-trivial task. Specific details can be obtained from the published AIM specification for Code One.

Versions S and T

Versions S and T were designed specifically for high speed printing using printing techniques with 8 or 16 rows of nozzles, hammers, or the like. Three sizes of each version are defined by a suffix indicating how many vertical columns are contained. As shown in Figures I-3 and I-4, these symbols have unique reference patterns.

The S version characters contain only 5 modules. Version S-10 contains four 5-bit characters, making up one 20-bit value representing 6 digits of data. Version S-20 encodes twelve digits in one 40-bit value, and version S-30 encodes 18 digits in one 60-bit value.

Quiet Zones

Code One versions A through H do not require quiet zones on any sides of the symbol. Versions S and T require a minimum of a 1X quiet zone on each side and the bottom.

Other Details

Many other details regarding Code One are described in the applicable AIM Uniform Symbology Specification.

DataMatrix Specification

DataMatrix is a variable size 2-D matrix symbology capable of encoding a number of different character sets, including all 128 ASCII characters. The symbology consists of an array of data cells within a distinct perimeter pattern. User-selectable error correction capabilities are included. DataMatrix is designed to be read using vision-based scanning equipment, and is inherently omnidirectional.

The developers have submitted a specification for DataMatrix to AIM's Technical Symbology Committee for possible generation of a USS. The following material is based on information provided to the author by International DataMatrix Inc. in late 1994.

The main characteristics of DataMatrix are:

Encodable Character Set	:	All ASCII Characters
		All ISO Characters
		All EBCDIC Characters
Code Type	:	Two-Dimensional Matrix
Symbol Size	:	Data dependent
Data Capacity	:	1 to 2000 Characters
Symbol Error Detection	:	16-Bit or 32-Bit Cyclic Redundancy Check
Symbol Error Correction	:	Convolutional Code Algorithms

Symbol Description

Each DataMatrix symbol consists of:

1. Perimeter quiet zone.
2. Border composed of two solid edges and two dashed edges.
3. Data "cells" inside the border which are dark or light.

The border's two solid sides combined with the two alternating light and dark sides are used for symbol identification, orientation, and cell location. A perimeter quiet zone of 10percent is required on all four sides of the symbol. Figure J-1 illustrates an example DataMatrix symbol.

Figure J-1: Example DataMatrix Symbol. The perimeter pattern consists of two solid lines and two dashed edges.

A DataMatrix symbol can contain from 1 to 2000 characters of information. After all information characters are entered, the resulting binary information bits are compressed and combined with other required system information bits. Once the total number of bits are assembled, the required number of rows and columns in the symbol can be determined.

Data Encodation

Data can be encoded with six different encodation methods. These methods are numeric, uppercase alphabetic, uppercase alphanumeric, uppercase alphanumeric with punctuation, ASCII 7-bit, and ISO 8-bit. The encodation method used is based on the characters to be encoded.

Numeric Encodation

In numeric encodation, each binary segment of 4 to 21 bits represents one to six digits. The compression scheme looks at each digit of the decimal data to be encoded and adds one to it. The resulting string of numbers are referred to as C_1 through C_6, and they are converted to a bit stream by performing a base conversion as follows:

Number of Data Characters	Encodation Equation	Bit Length
1	C_1	4
2	$(11*C_2)+C_1$	7
3	$(121*C_3)+(11*C_2)+C_1$	11
4	$(1{,}331*C_4)+(121*C_3)+(11*C_2)+C_1$	14
5	$(14{,}641*C_5)+(1{,}331*C_4)+(121*C_3)+(11*C_2)+C_1$	18
6	$(161{,}051*C_6)+(14{,}641*C_5)+(1{,}331*C_4)+(121*C_3)+(11*C_2)+C_1$	21

For encoding numeric information strings of more than six data characters, repeat the use of equation C_6 until six or fewer data characters remain to be encoded; then use equation C_1 through C_6, as appropriate, depending on the number of characters remaining. A space character can also be encoded, its value is set to 1.

Uppercase Alphabetic Encodation

In uppercase alphabetic encodation, each binary segment represents one to five data characters. Each data character is assigned a decimal character code, as shown below for the ASCII character set:

Character Code (decimal)	Data Character	Character Code (decimal)	Data Character
0	SPACE	13	M
1	A	14	N
2	B	15	O
3	C	16	P
4	D	17	Q
5	E	18	R
6	F	19	S
7	G	20	T
8	H	21	U
9	I	22	V
10	J	23	W
11	K	24	X
12	L	25	Y
		26	Z

Sequences of data characters are compressed through the use of the uppercase alphabetic encodation method. When using the uppercase alphabetic encodation method, from one to five data characters are represented as a single binary segment. This binary segment is from five to 24 bits long. In this table, C_1, C_2, C_3, C_4, and C_5 represent from one to five consecutive data character code values. This table also lists the bit length of the resulting binary segment.

Number of Data Characters	Encodation Equation	Bit Length
1	C_1	5
2	$(27 * C_2) + C_1$	10
3	$(729 * C_3) + (27 * C_2) + C_1$	15
4	$(19{,}683 * C_4) + (729 * C_3) + (27 * C_2) + C_1$	20
5	$(531{,}441 * C_5) + (19{,}683 * C_4) + (729 * C_3) + (27 * C_2) + C_1$	24

For encoding uppercase alphabetic information strings of more than five data characters, repeat the use of equation C_5 until five or fewer data characters remain to be encoded; then use equation C_1 through C_5, as appropriate, depending on the number of characters remaining.

Uppercase Alphanumeric Encodation Method

In uppercase alphanumeric encodation, each binary segment represents one to four data characters. These data characters are the exact data to be encoded into the symbol. The encodation is as follows:

Character Code (decimal)	Data Character	Character Code (decimal)	Data Character
0	SPACE	18	R
1	A	19	S
2	B	20	T
3	C	21	U
4	D	22	V
5	E	23	W
6	F	24	X
7	G	25	Y
8	H	26	V
9	I	27	0
10	J	28	1
11	K	29	2
12	L	30	3
13	M	31	4
14	N	32	5
15	O	33	6
16	P	34	7
17	Q	35	8
1		36	9

Sequences of data characters are compressed through the use of the uppercase alphanumeric encodation method. When using this encodation method, from one to four data characters are represented as a single binary segment. This binary segment is from six to 21 bits long. The following table details the four equations for computing the binary segment. In this table, C_1, C_2, C_3, and C_4 represent from one to four consecutive data character code values. This table also lists the bit length of the resulting binary segment.

Number of Data Characters	Encodation Equation	Bit Length
1	C_1	6
2	$(37 * C_2) + C_1$	11
3	$(1{,}369 * C_3) + (37 * C_2) + C_1$	16
4	$(50{,}653 * C_4) + (1{,}369 * C_3) + (37 * C_2) + C_1$	21

For encoding uppercase alphanumeric information strings of more than four data characters, repeat the use of equation C_4 until four or fewer data characters remain to be encoded; then use equation C_1 through C_4, as appropriate, depending on the number of characters remaining.

Other Encodation

Compressed encodation schemes are also provided for the following character sets:

- Uppercase alphanumeric with punctuation
- 7-bit ASCII
- ISO 8-bit

Similar approaches are used to the three already described. In each case a different set of compression equations is used.

Error Detection

Each symbol contains one error detection binary segment using a Cyclic Redundancy Check (CRC). There are two different algorithms which may be used for calculating the binary segment, a 16-bit method and a 32-bit method. If more than 500 characters are to be encoded, the 32 bit method should be used.

There are two steps in calculating the CRC for a symbol. First, the encodation method reference number is converted into a string 16 bits long. The following table details the value of each encodation method string. The encodation method string precedes the string of binary segments to form the data string for CRC calculation.

Encodation Method	CRC Size	Encodation Method String (Hex)
Numeric	16-Bit	01 00
Numeric	32-Bit	0B 00
Uppercase Alphabetic	16-Bit	02 00
Uppercase Alphabetic	32-Bit	0C 00
Uppercase Alphanumeric	16-Bit	04 00
Uppercase Alphanumeric	32-Bit	0E 00
Uppercase Alphanumeric with punctuation	16-Bit	03 00
Uppercase Alphanumeric with punctuation	32-Bit	0D 00
ASCII 7-Bit	16-Bit	05 00
ASCII 7-Bit	32-Bit	0F 00
ISO 8-Bit	16-Bit	06 00
ISO 8-Bit	32-Bit	10 00

The 16-bit CRC calculation treats the data as a string of bits with the low-order bit of the first character first and the high-order bit of the last character last. The 16-bit CRC is the remainder after dividing the CRC data string by the CCITT polynomial $X^{16} + X^{12} + X^5 + 1$, in which the value of X is 2, making the value of the polynomial equal to 10001000000100001_2.

The 32-bit CRC is the remainder after dividing the CRC data string by the polynomial $X^{32} + X^{26} + X^{23} + X^{22} + X^{16} + X^{12} + X^{11} + X^{10} + X^8 + X^7 + X^5 + X^4 + X^2 + X^1 + 1$, in which the value of X is 2, making the value of the polynomial equal to $100000100110000010001110110110111_2$.

Putting A Symbol Bit Stream Together

The length of the data string is encoded into a binary segment. The following table details the maximum number of characters which may be encoded as well as the length of the data length binary segment. The data length binary segment is generated by taking the length number starting at the least significant bit for nine or 14 bits per the following table. This binary segment is either nine or 14 bits long and is merged into the user data bit stream.

The encodation method binary segment is of variable length and encodes the key for the method of encodation used in the compressed data binary segments. The following table also details the value of each binary segment. The final seven or nine bit encodation method binary segment is merged into the user data bit stream.

Encodation Method	CRC Size	Max Data Characters	Data Length Binary Segment Length	Binary Segment Values (binary)
Numeric	16-Bit	500	9	00000
Numeric	32-Bit	2000	14	010000001
Uppercase Alphabetic	16-Bit	500	9	10000
Uppercase Alphabetic	32-Bit	2000	14	110000001
Uppercase Alphanumeric	16-Bit	500	9	01000
Uppercase Alphanumeric	32-Bit	2000	14	001000001
Uppercase Alphanumeric/punctuation	16-Bit	500	9	11000
Uppercase Alphanumeric/punctuation	32-Bit	2000	14	101000001
ASCII 7-Bit	16-Bit	500	9	00100
ASCII 7-Bit	32-Bit	2000	14	011000001
ISO 8-Bit	16-Bit	500	9	10100
ISO 8-Bit	32-Bit	2000	14	111000001

The encodation method binary segment of variable length, the error detection binary segment of 16-bits or 32-bits long, the data length binary segment of 9 or 14 bits long, and the compressed data binary segments of mixed lengths long are concatenated into a single user data bit stream. The user data bit stream is generated by first adding the encodation method binary segment from least to most significant bit, the error detection binary segment from least to most significant bit, then the data length binary segment from least to most significant bit, and then the compressed data binary segments in order from least to most significant bits. This user data bit stream is used as input to generate the encoded bit stream.

The error correction binary segment is of variable length and encodes the key for the method of error correction used in the remainder of the matrix. The value of each binary segment based upon the error correction coding technique selected by the user.

The encoded bit stream is created by presenting the bit stream generated so far to the appropriate error correction state machine. This output is then prepended with the error correction binary segment. The DataMatrix bit stream is then built by concatenating the error correction technique binary segment and the encoded bit stream. The DataMatrix bit stream is XORed with a master black/white bit stream which contains a pseudo-random distribution of 1s and 0s.

The density of the DataMatrix is chosen by finding the smallest square grid that can contain the number of bits in the DataMatrix bit stream. Any extra grid positions are filled with zeros. Borders are then added to the grid to complete the symbol.

MaxiCode Specification

MaxiCode is a fixed-size 2-D matrix symbology which is made up of offset rows of hexagonal elements arranged around a unique circular finder pattern. Hexagonal elements allows dense packing, and provides fixed center-to-center spacing of all elements. The central finder pattern and fixed symbol size allow for easy scanning on high speed conveyors.

ASCII data is encoded in six-bit symbol characters. There are five different code sets. A single MaxiCode symbol can encode up to 93 characters of data.

At the time of publication, the MaxiCode specification was being reviewed by AIM's Technical Symbology Committee with a view to making it a USS. The following data is based on information provided to the author by United Parcel Service of America Inc., and it should be considered as preliminary and subject to change before final approval of a USS for this symbology.

A summary of MaxiCode's characteristics is as follows:

Character Set	:	All 256 ASCII Characters
Symbol Size	:	1.11 inch x 1.054 inch nominal (including Quiet zone)
Nominal Element Size	:	0.035 inch x 0.041 inch hexagon
Maximum Data Capacity	:	93 characters
Check Characters	:	Two selectable levels of Reed Solomon error correction
Other Features	:	Omnidirectionally scannable. Concatenation capability

MaxiCode Symbol Description

The symbol is a fixed geometry, and consists of a central finder pattern surrounded by a square array of hexagonal elements. There are 33 rows in the symbol, which are alternately 30 and 29 elements wide. There is a minimum of one element of quiet zone on all sides. Figure K-1 illustrates the arrangement.

Figure K-1: MaxiCode Symbol. A central finder pattern is surrounded by a square array of interlocking hexagons.

The finder pattern consists of four concentric dark circles on a light background. As shown in Figure K-2, there are six fixed patterns that are used for orientation information. The four elements labelled M1 through M4 are used to denote the mode of the symbol.

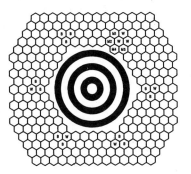

Figure K-2: Orientation And Mode Elements. A fixed pattern is used to determine symbol orientation, and four elements are used to define the symbol's mode.

After accounting for the finder pattern and orientation elements, a MaxiCode symbol has 866 elements for data encodation and error correction.

Symbol Characters

For character-based encodation, the elements are arranged into 144 6-bit symbol characters which are used for data encodation, error correction, and reader control. The symbol characters each contain six elements, and they are nominally arranged into three rows of two each, ordered from lower left to upper right. Because of the presence of the finder pattern and the orientation patterns, there are eight symbol characters near the center and nine characters on the right side of the symbol that are noncontiguous.

Binary Encodation

Long strings of numeric data are encoded in binary strings of up to 30 bits, starting with the most significant bit. If the string to be encoded is less than 30 bits long, leading zeros are used to bring the length up to 30 bits. The Numeric Shift (NS) character must immediately precede each binary string.

Message Structure

A MaxiCode symbol is divided into five messages, each of which contains data and error correction bits. Data strings can occupy more than one message.

Message 1 is called the Primary Message, and it is composed of 120 bits located in symbol characters 1 through 28. Nine characters of data are encoded in 54 bits, 4 bits are used as Mode Indicators, and 60 bits are used for error correction. The Primary Message uses Enhanced Error Correction (see later description). A special application symbol called the Structured Carrier Message contains a 56-bit binary string instead of the nine characters in the primary message.

Messages 2 through 5 contain a total of 744 bits and may be configured for two different levels of error correction. With Standard Error Correction (the default), a maximum of 84 symbol characters can be encoded. With Enhanced Error Correction, a maximum of 68 symbol characters can be encoded. The messages are located as follows:

Message	Symbol Characters
2	122 to 155
3	91 to 121
4	60 to 90
5	29 to 59

Data Encodation

MaxiCode has 64 6-bit symbol character patterns. Five different Code Sets are used to encode all 256 ASCII characters. Code Set A is intended to provide for the majority of data encodation needs. Table K-1 shows the specific patterns used.

Table K-1
MaxiCode Symbol Character Patterns

Codeword Value		Code Set A		Code Set B		Code Set C		Code Set D		Code Set E	
Dec	Binary	Char	Dec	Char	Dec	Char	Dec	Char	Dec	Char	Dec
0	000000	CR	13	`	96	À	192	à	224	NUL	0
1	000001	A	65	a	97	Á	193	á	225	SOH	1
2	000010	B	66	b	98	Â	194	â	226	STX	2
3	000011	C	67	c	99	Ã	195	ã	227	ETX	3
4	000100	D	68	d	100	Ä	196	ä	228	EOT	4
5	000101	E	69	e	101	Å	197	å	229	ENQ	5
6	000110	F	70	f	102	Æ	198	æ	230	ACK	6
7	000111	G	71	g	103	Ç	199	ç	231	BEL	7
8	001000	H	72	h	104	È	200	è	232	BS	8
9	001001	I	73	i	105	É	201	é	233	HT	9
10	001010	J	74	j	106	Ê	202	ê	234	LF	10
11	001011	K	75	k	107	Ë	203	ë	235	VT	11
12	001100	L	76	l	108	Ì	204	ì	236	FF	12
13	001101	M	77	m	109	Í	205	í	237	CR	13
14	001110	N	78	n	110	Î	206	î	238	SO	14
15	001111	O	79	o	111	Ï	207	ï	239	SI	15
16	010000	P	80	p	112	_	208	∂	240	DLE	16
17	010001	Q	81	q	113	Ñ	209	ñ	241	DC1	17
18	010010	R	82	r	114	Ò	210	ò	242	DC2	18
19	010011	S	83	s	115	Ó	211	ó	243	DC3	19
20	010100	T	84	t	116	Ô	212	ô	244	DC4	20
21	010101	U	85	u	117	Õ	213	õ	245	NAK	21
22	010110	V	86	v	118	Ö	214	ö	246	SYN	22
23	010111	W	87	w	119	´	215	,	247	ETB	23
24	011000	X	88	x	120	Ø	216	ø	248	CAN	24
25	011001	Y	89	y	121	Ù	217	ù	249	EM	25
26	011010	Z	90	z	122	Ú	218	ú	250	SUB	26
27	011011	[Code Page]		[Code Page]		Reserved		Reserved		Reserved	
28	011100	FS	28	FS	28	Reserved		Reserved		Reserved	
29	011101	GS (FNC1=GS)	29	GS (FNC1=GS)	29	Reserved		Reserved		Reserved	
30	011110	RS	30	RS	30	Reserved		Reserved		Reserved	
31	011111	[NS]		[NS]		Reserved		Reserved		Reserved	
32	100000	space	32	{	123	Û	219	û	251	ESC	27
33	100001	!	33	|	124	Ü	220	ü	252	FS	28
26	011010	Z	90	z	122	Ú	218	ú	250	SUB	26
34	100010	"	34	}	125	Ý	221	y	253	GS	29
35	100011	#	35	~	126	_	222	_	254	RS	30
36	100100	$	36	DEL	127	ß	223	ÿ	255	US	31
37	100101	%	37	;	59	ª	170	¡	161	NBSP	160
38	100110	&	38	<	60	Ø	172	¨	168	¢	162
39	100111	'	39	=	61	±	177	«	171	£	163
40	101000	(	40	>	62	2	178	-	175	¤	164
41	101001	)	41	?	63	3	179	°	176	¥	165
42	101010	*	42	[	91	m	181	´	180	3	166
43	101011	+	43	\	92	1	185	x	183	§	167
44	101100	,	44	]	93	º	186	,	184	©	169
45	101101	-	45	^	94	_	188	»	187	SHY	173
46	101110	.	46	_	95	_	189	¿	191	®	174
47	101111	/	47	space	32	_	190	{C138}		¶	182
48	110000	0	48	,	44	{C128}		{C139}		{C149}	

322 • *The Bar Code Book*

Codeword Value		Code Set A		Code Set B		Code Set C		Code Set D		Code Set E	
Dec	Binary	Char	Dec	Char	Dec	Char	Dec	Char	Dec	Char	Dec
49	110001	1	49	.	46	{C129}		{C140}		{C150}	
50	110010	2	50	/	47	{C130}		{C141}		{C151}	
51	110011	3	51	:	58	{C131}		{C142}		{C152}	
52	110100	4	52	@	64	{C132}		{C143}		{C153}	
53	110101	5	53	Reserved		{C133}		{C144}		{C154}	
54	110110	6	54	Reserved		{C134}		{C145}		{C155}	
55	110111	7	55	Reserved		{C135}		{C146}		{C156}	
56	111000	8	56	[2 Shift A]		{C136}		{C147}		{C157}	
57	111001	9	57	[3 Shift A]		{C137}		{C148}		{C158}	
58	111010	:	58	[2 Shift D]		Reserved		Reserved		{C159}	
59	111011	[Shift B]		[Shift A]		Reserved		Reserved		Reserved	
60	111100	[Shift C]		[Shift C]		Reserved		Reserved		Reserved	
61	111101	[Shift D]		[Shift D]		Reserved		Reserved		Reserved	
62	111110	[Shift E]		[Shift E]		Reserved		Reserved		Reserved	
63	111111	[Latch B]		[Latch A]		Reserved		Reserved		Reserved	

Notes: 1. The relationship between the ASCII decimal value and the code set/codeword value remains constant whatever Code Page is in use. It is only the interpreted data character which changes.

2. Although ASCII characters 128 to 159 have no interpretation in the default Code Page interpretation *(ISO 8859 Part 1)*, provision is included for them to enable different code page interpretations. These characters are identified as {C128} in the table.

Four bits (57-60) in the Primary Message are used as Mode Indicators. These indicate whether the Secondary message uses Standard (SEC) or Enhanced (EEC) Error Correction, the structure of the Primary message, and an alternate default ISO Code Page, as follows:

Mode	Description	Mode Bits
0	Structured Carrier Message	0000
1	Standard Symbol, SEC	0001
2	Full EEC Symbol	0010
3	Alternate Code Page, SEC	0011
4	Alternate Code Page, full EEC	0100

Symbology Control Characters

MaxiCode has 15 symbology control characters which are special non-data characters with no ASCII character equivalents, which have particular significance to the encodation scheme. These characters shall be used to instruct the decoder to perform certain functions or to send specific data to the host computer. These symbology control characters are found only in Code Sets A and B. The complete list of assigned symbology control characters in Code Sets A and B is as follows:

Function Name and Purpose	Short Name	Codeword Value in Code Set		
		A	B	
Latch: to switch and remain in a new code set	Latch A		63	
	Latch B	63		
Shift: to switch to a new code set for one character and to return	Shift A		59	
	Shift B	59		
	Shift C	60	60	
	Shift D	61	61	
	Shift E	62	62	
Double Shift: to shift for two characters	2 Shift A		56	
	2 Shift D		58	
Triple Shift: to shift for three characters	3 Shift A		57	
Numeric Shift: to compact numeric strings efficiently	N/S	31	31	
Code Page: to switch to a new Code Page interpretation	CP	27	27	

Numeric Shift

A Numeric Shift Character [N/S] should be used to switch all numeric data compaction from a character-based scheme to a binary scheme in Code Sets A and B. The next five codewords (equivalent to 30 bits) following [N/S] shall represent numeric data in binary format. Numeric Shift enables all 9 digit strings to be more compactly encoded. For longer numeric strings it is possible to mix numeric compaction using Numeric Shift and conventional encoding.

The [N/S] character shall immediately precede each binary string; and [N/S] may be used as often as required within a MaxiCode symbol. Subsequent character encodation shall revert to the code Set A or B defined prior to the Numeric Shift Character.

Code Page Character

A Code Page Character [CP] shall be used to change the default code page used to encode data. The [CP] character shall be followed by a codeword value (0-63), which indicates the code page used for encoding subsequent data. The new code page remains in place until the end of the MaxiCode data or until another [CP] is used to invoke another code page.

Field Separator

In MaxiCode data encodation, the ASCII control character, Field Separator [FS] (ASCII value 28), shall be used for syntax purposes to separate fields.

Group Separator

In MaxiCode data encodation, the ASCII control character, Group Separator [GS] (ASCII value 29), shall be used for syntax purposes.

It shall also be reserved to encode Function Character 1 [FNC1]. Codeword 29 shall be reserved to represent both the ASCII control character Group Separator (ASCII Value 29) and Function Character 1 [FNC1] when used to identify EAN/UCC Application Identifiers.

Record Separator

In MaxiCode data encoding, the ASCII control character, Record Separator [RS] (ASCII value 30), shall be used for syntax purposes. It is also used as part of the Structured Append function.

Bell Character

In MaxiCode data transmission, the ASCII control character Bell [BEL] shall be used as an 'escape' character to indicate that the following data has a particular Code Page interpretation.

Shift In Character

In MaxiCode data transmission, the ASCII control character Shift In [SI] shall be used as an 'escape' character to indicate the beginning or the end of a block of data conforming in format to the EAN/UCC Application Identifier Standard.

Structured Append

There may be application requirements where the number of MaxiCode symbols has to be restricted to one symbol, or a fixed or maximum number of symbols, or has the freedom to extend to the maximum of eight linked symbols. The limiting number of MaxiCode symbols shall be specified for an application. Up to eight MaxiCode symbols may be appended in a structured format. If a symbol is part of a Structured Append this shall be indicated by a sequence of two codewords in particular positions in the symbol, depending on the Mode.

For Mode 0, these shall be placed in the first two data codewords in the Secondary Message, i.e. codewords in position 31 and 32 of the codeword sequence (allowing for the preceding error correction codewords). For Modes 1 to 3, these shall be placed in the first and second codewords in the Primary Message.

The Structured Append indicator shall follow the following structure:

1. The first character shall be [R/S].
2. The second codeword shall indicate the position of the symbol within the set (of up to eight) MaxiCode symbols in the Structured Append format; i.e. in the format of **m of n symbols**.

The first three bits of the second codeword identify the position of the particular symbol. The last three bits identify the total number of symbols to be concatenated in the Structured Append format. The 3-bit patterns shall conform to those defined below:

Symbol Position	Bits 123	Total Number of Symbols	Bits 456
1	000	N/A	N/A
2	001	2	001
3	010	3	010
4	011	4	011
5	100	5	100
6	101	6	101
7	110	7	110
8	111	8	111

Note:

- A Mode 0 symbol shall only appear in the first symbol position in a Structured Append. Subsequent symbols may be Mode 1 or 2 or combinations thereof.
- Mode 1 and 2 symbols (i.e. representing different degrees of error correction) may be intermixed in any sequence.
- Structured Append shall not apply to Mode 3.

Message Structure

MaxiCode symbols shall be divided into blocks, each of which contains data and error correction codewords. The structure is used for the efficient calculation of error correction and shall not be a consideration when encoding data, which typically may occupy more than one block.

The Primary Message shall contain 20 codewords, represented by bits 1 to 120. Of these codewords:

- 9 shall be used to encode data.
- 10 shall be used for error correction.
- Part of one codeword (bits 57 to 60) shall be used to encode the mode, generally leaving 2 elements unused.

Only one level of error correction, Enhanced Error Correction, shall apply to the Primary Message.

The Secondary Message shall contain four Segments each of 31 codewords. One of two levels of error correction shall apply to the entire Secondary Message, i.e. shall consistently apply to each Segment: Enhanced Error Correction (EEC) or Standard Error Correction (SEC).

If EEC is used, data shall be encoded in 17 codewords and error correction in 14 codewords. If SEC is used, data shall be encoded in 21 codewords and error correction in 10 codewords.

A data string shall be encoded into codewords using the symbology control characters as appropriate to meet the requirements of the application. Particular structuring rules shall be followed for Mode 0: Structured Carrier Message.

The encoding process generates a sequence of codeword values defined as:

$$s_1 \text{ .... } s_n$$

where: s = codeword including all symbology control characters and mode value

n = total number of codewords

During the encoding process, a sequence of codeword values will be established. Like the original data itself, the most significant data shall appear first, for example textual and numeric data reads from the left to the right. The sequence of codeword values shall be that the most significant codeword value is the one designated s_1. The final codeword value is the one designated s_n.

Depending on the level of error correction selected for the Secondary Message, this sequence is subdivided as defined in Table K-2. This provides the capacity for the codewords used for error correction. Note that in MaxiCode, the error correction codewords precede the codewords encoding data from which they are calculated.

Table K-2
Codeword allocation in Messages and Segments

| Message Structure | Error Correction in Secondary Message | | | |
| | SEC | | EEC | |
	Correction	Data	Correction	Data
Primary message	$S_1 - S_{10}$		$S_1 - S_{10}$	
		$S_{11} - S_{20}$		$S_{11} - S_{20}$
Secondary Message Segment 1	$S_{21} - S_{30}$		$S_{21} - S_{34}$	
		$S_{31} - S_{51}$		$S_{35} - S_{51}$
Segment 2	$S_{52} - S_{61}$		$S_{52} - S_{65}$	
		$S_{62} - S_{82}$		$S_{66} - S_{82}$
Segment 3	$S_{83} - S_{92}$		$S_{83} - S_{96}$	
		$S_{93} - S_{113}$		$S_{97} - S_{113}$
Segment 4	$S_{114} - S_{123}$		$S_{114} - S_{127}$	
		$S_{124} - S_{144}$		$S_{128} - S_{144}$

The process for structuring the message is such that a symbology control character can appear at the end of the primary message or segment of the secondary message and its data character in the next. This shall have no material effect on the message.

There may not always be exactly the right number of codewords to fill up the symbol. Codeword 59 (Shift B in Code Set A) (Shift A in Code Set B) shall be used as a pad character for the remaining codewords. The pad character will therefore be encodable when resident in either Set A or B. The "toggle" effect between the two code sets will have no effect on data encoding.

Error Correction Characters

MaxiCode symbols shall employ Reed Solomon error correction at one of two levels.

The division of data into Primary and Secondary Messages and the subdivision of the Secondary Message into four segments is to enable error correction to be more easily applied. Error correction is applied separately to each of the five blocks. The error correction codewords shall be calculated from all the preceding codewords in the block used for data encoding. This is illustrated schematically as:

Primary Message	Secondary Message			
	Segment 1	Segment 2	Segment 3	Segment 4
EEC Data	SEC Data	SEC Data	SEC Data	SEC Data
EEC Data	SEC Data	SEC Data	SEC Data	SEC Data

The actual calculation of the specific error correction characters is a complex mathematical process.

Symbol Dimensions And Tolerances

L_N is the nominal width of the symbol measured from the center of the left-most element to the center of the right-most element in the top (or bottom) row of the symbol. The dimension and tolerance of L_N is given below:

$$L_N = 25.50mm \pm 1.47mm$$

H_N is the nominal height of the symbol measured from the center of the top row to the center of the bottom row. The dimension and tolerance of H_N is given below:

$$H = 24.38 \pm 1.40mm$$

Tolerances shall not accumulate across the width (L_N) or height (H_N) of the symbol.

The hexagonal elements in a MaxiCode symbol shall be nested in offset rows, containing 29 or 30 elements. Four measurements shall define the size and placement of the elements in relation to each other:

V is the vertical height of an element
W is the center to center distance between adjacent elements
X is the horizontal width of an element
Y is the vertical distance from the centerline of elements in one row to the centerline of elements in an adjacent row

The nominal dimensions and tolerances for an element are defined as:

Dimension	Relationships to Other Dimensions	Nominal Dimension (mm)	Tolerance (mm)
V	$V = (2 / Ö3)W$	1.02	± 0.13
W	$W = L/29$	0.88	± 0.05
X	$X = W$	0.88	± 0.13
			0.00
Y	$Y = (1.5 / Ö3)W$	0.76	± 0.05

The diameter of the central light area of the finder pattern shall equate to the vertical height (V) of a hexagonal element. The ring thickness (T) shall be given by the equation:

$$T = (D-V)/10$$
where D is the overall diameter of the finder pattern

An internal clear area surrounding the finder pattern is defined by the arrangement of the elements. This area should be kept free of all extraneous marks. The nominal dimensions and tolerances for the finder pattern are defined as:

Dimension	Nominal Dimension (mm)	Tolerance (mm)
D	7.75	±0.10
T	0.67	+ 0.15 −0.05
V	1.02	+0.13 −0.00

ArrayTag Specification

Formerly a proprietary symbology, the developers of ArrayTag decided to place this 2-D matrix symbology into the public domain just as the third edition of *The Bar Code Book* was being completed. The following preliminary specification is based on information provided to the author by Array Tech Systems in late 1994.

A single ArrayTag symbol consists of a hexagonal border pattern surrounding a hexagonally-shaped array of 91 packed circular cells. A single symbol can be used to encode short messages, or multiple ArrayTag symbols can be nested together to form a larger composite symbol encoding longer message strings. A summary of ArrayTag's main characteristics is as follows:

Character Set : Binary, decimal, C40, ASCII-128

Data Capacity : Single ArrayTag symbol—64 binary bits
19 decimal digits
12 C40 characters
9 ASCII characters
Composite symbol— Unlimited

Symbol Size : Single ArrayTag symbol—16.7 X is the largest dimension between opposite corners of the exterior border, and 14.3 X is the distance between the outer edges of two opposite sides.

Error Correction : Reed Solomon error correction and redundant border cells are used.

Other Features : No quiet zone is required.

Symbol Structure

Figure L-1 shows both an example ArrayTag symbol and the actual structure of the cells. The symbol has 91 inner circular cells and 24 peripheral cells. The 64 cells labeled D_1, D_2, ... D_{64} are used to encode a data stream $d_{64}d_{63}...d_1$. Cell D_{65} is black, and cells D_{66} and D_{67} are reserved for future use (but are normally colored black).

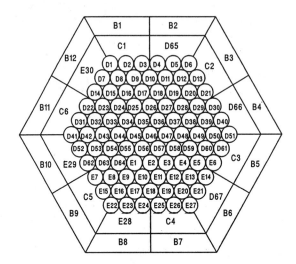

Figure L-1. ArrayTag Symbol and Structure. The symbol consists of 91 inner circular cells and 24 peripheral cells in a hexagonal arrangement.

The 12 border cells B_1, B_2 ... B_{12} are used to locate the symbol and to provide error control through border cell redundancy. The border cells are the opposite color of the adjacent inner cells. As an example, if C_2 is black, then B_2 is colored white. The cells E_1, E_2 ... E_{30} contain Reed Solomon error bits e_1, e_2, ... e_{30}. Cells C_1, C_2 ... C_6 are used to specify the type of data encoding on the tag as shown below:

Encoding Method	C_1	C_2	C_3	C_4	C_5	C_6
Binary	1	0	0	0	0	0
Decimal	1	1	0	0	0	0
C40	1	0	1	0	0	0
ASCII	1	1	0	0	1	0

Note that "1" represents a black cell, and "0" represents a white cell.

The unique cell color patterns defined by C_1, C_2 ... C_6 above also specify the "top" of the symbol.

Data Encoding
In the following discussion, string elements with smaller subscripts are less significant.

Binary Data
Binary data is encoded directly, without transformation. Up to 64 bits are encoded such that one cell represents one bit in the data string.

Decimal Data

A decimal digit string of up to 19 digits $\{s_{19}\, s_{18} \ldots s_1\}$ is mapped to the encoded string $\{d_{64}\, d_{63} \ldots d_1\}$ as follows:

$$\text{value}\{s_1\} = \text{value}\{d_4\, d_3\, d_2\, d_1\}.$$
$$\text{value}\{s_{3i+1}\, s_{3i}\, s_{3i-1}\} = \text{value}\{d_{10i+4}\, d_{10i+3} \ldots d_{10i-5}\} \text{ for } i = 1 \text{ to } 6.$$

For example, if $s_1 = 5$, then $\{d_4\, d_3\, d_2\, d_1\} = \{0101\}$.

As another example, for $i = 3$, if $\{s_{10}\, s_9\, s_8\} = \{567\}$, then $\{d_{34}\, d_{33} \ldots d_{25}\} = \{1000110111\}$.

C40 Data

The C40 characters are assigned the following values:

Character	Value
dash	0
period	1
comma	2
space	3
0 to 9	4 to 13
A to Z	14 to 39

A 12 character C40 string $\{s_{12}\, s_{11} \ldots s_1\}$ is mapped to the encoded string $\{d_{64}\, d_{63} \ldots d_1\}$ as follows:

$$\text{value}\{s_{3i}\, s_{3i-1}\, s_{3i-2}\} = 1600 \text{ value}\{s_{3i}\} + 40 \text{ value}\{s_{3i-1}\} + \text{value}\{s_{3i-2}\} \text{ for } i = 1 \text{ to } 4.$$
$$= \text{value}\{d_{16i}\, d_{16i-1} \ldots d_{16i-15}\} \text{ for } i = 1 \text{ to } 4$$

For example, if $1 = 3$ and the string $\{s_9\, s_8\, s_7\} = \{B,1\}$ then:

$$\text{value } \{B,1\} = (1600 \times 15) + (40 \times 2) + 5 = 24085.$$
$$\text{Therefore } \{d_{48}\, d_{47} \ldots d_{33}\} = \{0101111000010101\}$$

ASCII

A 9 character ASCII 128 string $\{s_9\, s_8 \ldots s_1\}$ is mapped to the encoded string $\{d_{64}\, d_{63} \ldots d_1\}$ as follows:

$$\text{value } \{s_i\} = \text{value}\{d_{7i}\, d_{7i-1} \ldots d_{7i-6}\} \text{ for } I = 1 \text{ to } 9. \quad d_{64} \text{ is unspecified.}$$

For example, for $i = 4$, if $s_4 = j$ then value$\{j\} = 106 = \text{value}\{d_{28}\, d_{27} \ldots d_{22}\} = \{1101010\}$.

Error Control

Referring to Figure L-1, the border cells B_1, B_2, ... B_{12} are the complement of the adjacent inner cells and hence provide redundancy.

Error control is provided by using a Reed Solomon (31,25) [as described in "Error Control Coding," Shu Lin and Daniel Costello Jr.] error control code shortened to a (19,3) error control code. The mathematics involved in determining the error correction bits are quite complex and will not be outlined here. The error bits are encoded in cells E_1, E_2, ... E_{30}, allowing up to 30 erroneous cells to be detected and 15 erroneous cells to be corrected.

Composite ArrayTags

ArrayTags may be packed together to form a Composite ArrayTag capable of storing any amount of data. The sequence of data stored within a Composite ArrayTag is encoded within the sequence of individual ArrayTags that make up the Composite ArrayTag. The data string from the next ArrayTag in the sequence is concatenated to the right of the current data string. Figure L-2 is an example of a Composite ArrayTag symbol.

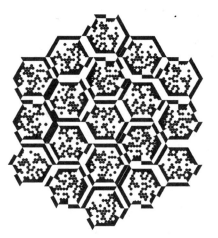

Figure L-2: Composite ArrayTag. Any length message can be encoded with a Composite ArrayTag symbol. The overall shape of the symbol can be varied to fit the available space.

The "top" of a single ArrayTag symbol is defined as the side containing the border cells B_1 and B_2. In a Composite ArrayTag symbol, the orientation of the individual symbols is such that the "top" of a symbol "points" to the symbol containing the next data to be concatenated. For a Composite ArrayTag symbol containing three or more individual ArrayTags, the last symbol in the sequence points back at the next-to-last symbol. Individual symbols in a Composite ArrayTag symbol containing only two individual symbols are oriented so that the first symbol points to the second symbol, and the second symbol does *not* point to the first symbol. Note that the term "point" refers to the fact that the "top" of a symbol is placed adjacent to a side of another symbol.

Postnet Specification

Postnet (Postal Numeric Encoding Technique) was developed by the U.S. Postal Service for encoding zip code information on mail. Postnet is a fixed length symbology using constant bar and space width. Information is encoded by varying the bar height between two values.

Three different length symbols are defined:

A Field: This is a 32-bar symbol encoding five digits of data.
B Field: This is a 37-bar symbol encoding six digits of data.
C Field: This is a 52-bar symbol encoding nine digits of data.

Postnet Symbol Description

Each Postnet symbol consists of:

1) A tall start bar.
2) Data digits consisting of groups of five bars for each digit to be encoded. Each digit contains two tall bars and three short bars.
3) A five bar check digit.
4) A tall stop bar.

|.|..|..||..||.||..||.||...||...|.|...||.|..|.|..|..||.|

Figure M-1: Example Postnet Symbol. The bar and space widths are constant throughout the symbol. Two bar heights are used.

Postnet Encodation

Each digit to be encoded is composed of five bars. Each bar is either tall (1), or short (0). The assigned patterns are as follows:

0	11000
1	00011
2	00101
3	00110
4	01001
5	01010
6	01100
7	10001
8	10010
9	10100

Note that every digit pattern has two tall bars and three short bars. The weighting of the five bars can be considered as 7,4,2,1,0, from left to right.

Check Digit

The last digit in a Postnet symbol is a check digit. Its value is chosen such that the sum of all data digits and the check digit is an integral multiple of 10.

Postnet Dimensions and Tolerances

The distance between the center lines of adjacent bars in a Postnet symbol is 47.5 mils, ±2.5 mils. The width of the bars in a Postnet symbol is 20.0 mils, ±5 mils. The height of short bars is 50 mils ±15 mils, and the height of tall bars is 125 mils ±15 mils. The bottom of all bars of a Postnet symbol shall be within ±5 mils from the average baseline of the symbol.

Postnet Optical Properties

Reflectivity measurements are made using an optical system with peak response centered at 650 nm, and having a 150 nm bandwidth at the 50 percent points.

Minimum background reflectance (MRD) is 50 percent.
MRD must be 30 percent or greater.
Print contrast signal (PCS) must be 40 percent or greater.

APPENDIX N

4-State Code Specification

The Royal Mail developed a height-modulated, variable-length alphanumeric symbology known as 4-State Code. For internal sorting and tracking applications, Royal Mail uses a version that employs error correction capability, but the typical postal customer will only be involved with the printing of what is referred to as the "4-State customer code." The Canadian postal system is considering the use of a version of this symbology that they call "PostBar 4-State Bar Code."

Four different types of bars are defined in the Royal Mail specification: short, full, ascender, and descender. These are illustrated in figure N-1.

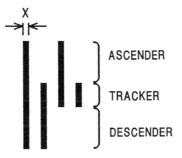

Figure N-1: 4-State Code. Four different bars are defined in this height-modulated symbology.

The Canadian PostBar specification describes the bars somewhat differently, although the end result is the same. They define three different elements of a bar as tracker (T), descender (D), and ascender (A). Every bar contains a T element, which is analogous to the "short" bar described above. A full height bar consists of A, T, and D elements.

Three different PostBar character sets are defined: Z (alphanumeric), N (numeric), and C (compressed). Each PostBar character from character sets Z and C contains three bars. The N character set (which only encodes numeric information) contains two bars. The bar patterns for the Z character set are shown in Figure N-2.

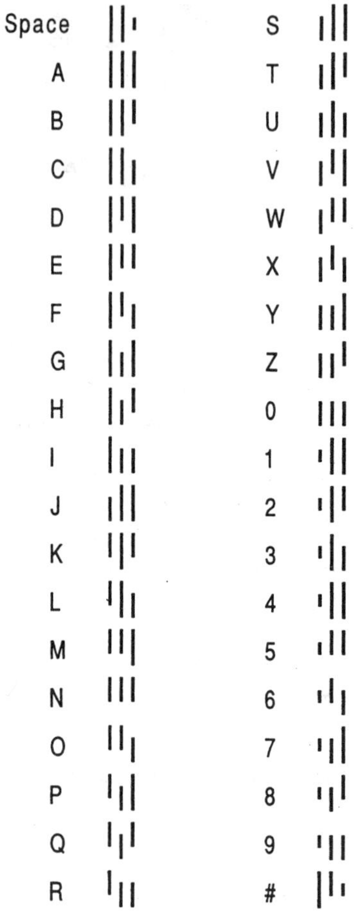

Figure N-2: 4-State Code Character Set.

The Royal Mail 4-State Code uses character patterns that each have four bars. Of these four bars, two are (or contain) ascenders, and two are (or contain) descenders. A complete 4-State customer code symbol consists of adjacent characters, such that there is a constant spacing throughout the clock track portion of the symbol. As shown in the example if Figure N-3, the symbol includes a simple start bit and stop bit.

Figure N-3: 4-State Code Symbol. The adjacent characters are arranged so that there is a constant spacing throughout the central clocking track.

For both of these 4-State symbologies, the nominal bar width and space width is 0.5 mm (0.02 inches).

APPENDIX O

Code 39 Printing Tolerance Derivation

The objective when specifying printing tolerances for any width-modulated bar code symbology is to ensure that elements will not be printed in a manner such that the reader makes an incorrect width determination. A Code 39 reader has only to determine if an element is wide or narrow, whereas a U.P.C. reader must differentiate between elements that are one, two, three, or four modules wide. Printing tolerances must include sufficient safety factors to allow for inaccuracies in the reading process.

When developing the printing tolerances for any symbology, the following approach can be used:

1. Determine the decode algorithm that will be used by the reader. This algorithm uses the raw perceived element widths and declares elements as either wide or narrow for a two-width symbology or outputs the number of module widths in the case of a multiple width symbology.
2. Analyze the operation of the decode algorithm, and determine the maximum width error E (as a fraction of X), which, when applied to one or several measurements, will result in the algorithm yielding the incorrect result.
3. Decide on an appropriate safety factor, S. The published printing tolerance is equal to E times (1-S), where S is a number less than one which represents the portion of breakdown tolerance that has been reserved for the reader. Choice of S will depend on code structure and the type of additional checking built into the symbology. Typical values are 0.4 to 0.5.

For Code 39, the recognized decode algorithm is the Factor R algorithm. This approach determines if an element is wide or narrow by comparing its width to a threshold value which is equal to one-eighth of the character width.

There are two types of Code 39 decode errors:

1. Case (A): Because of a printing error a narrow element is misinterpreted as being wide.
2. Case (B): Because of a printing error a wide element is misinterpreted as being narrow.

We will now examine both cases to determine which one is more vulnerable to printing defects of magnitude E. Figure O-1 shows case (A).

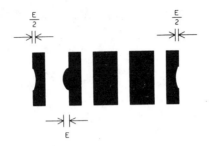

Figure O-1: Code 39 Decode Error Case (A). This illustration shows the case of a print error increasing the width of a narrow element so that it is perceived as a wide element.

The perceived character width is $(3N + 6)$X-E.

The perceived bar width is $X + E$.

The Factor R algorithm will break down when $(X + E)$ is equal to one-eighth of the character width, or:

$$\frac{(3N+6)X - E}{8} = X + E$$

solving,
$$E = \left(\frac{N}{3} - \frac{2}{9}\right)X$$

Figure O-2 shows Case (B)

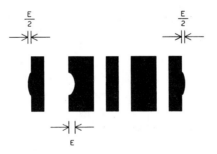

Figure O-2: Code 39 Decode Error Case (B). This illustration shows the case of a print error decreasing the width of a wide element so that it is perceived as a narrow element.

The perceived character width is $(3N + 6)X + E$.

The perceived bar width is XN-E.

The Factor R algorithm will break down when (XN-E) is equal to one eighth of the character width, or:

$$\frac{(3N+6)X + E}{8} = XN - E$$

solving,

$$E = \left(\frac{5N}{9} - \frac{2}{3}\right)X$$

Realizing that N is restricted to values between 2.0 and 3.0, Case (A) appears to be the most severe. Therefore, the printing tolerance for Code 39 is

$$(1-S)\left(\frac{N}{3} - \frac{2}{9}\right)X$$

The value of S for Code 39 was arbitrarily chosen to be 5/9 (0.555). This results in the published Code 39 printing tolerance:

$$\pm\frac{4}{27}\left(N - \frac{2}{3}\right)X$$

Code 39 Error Rate Derivation

If Code 39 symbols were printed in spec and scanning were performed carefully, there would be no errors. In the real world, however, bars and spaces do deviate from the published printing tolerances.

As outlined in Appendix O, bar code printing tolerances include a safety factor for the reader (often over 50 percent of the tolerance budget). As elements are printed that exceed the published printing tolerances, the reader reserve is consumed. If symbols are printed that are significantly out of spec, the reader will have a difficult time decoding the information, causing a low first read rate (FRR). If element width variations consume all of the safety factor, then certain combinations of printing errors will result in data substitution errors.

Any printing process is a random process. Even if the intention is to print all bars with a width of 10 mils, some will be printed at 9.9 mils, and some at 10.1 mils. The deviation from nominal element width can be described as a distribution function, as shown in Figure P-1. The distribution function indicates the probability that a given range of element widths will occur. The total area under the curve represents a probability of 1.0. In Figure P-1, the probability that an element width between 9.9 and 10.1 mils will be printed is equal to the cross-hatched area. In this example, the probability is approximately 0.6.

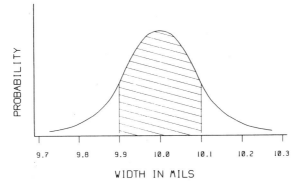

Figure P-1: Code 39 Element Width Deviation Distribution. This figure shows a probability distribution for the measured widths of elements in a typical Code 39 symbol printing process. The actual measured width of a bar varies at random around the nominal width intended. The shaded area in this distribution represents the probability that an element will be printed with a width between 9.9 and 10.1 mils.

All printing processes will have a characteristic width distribution about the nominal element widths. More precise printing processes will have a tighter width distribution.

In statistics, it is convenient to describe the relative width of a distribution by the term standard deviation. The standard deviation is that range of element widths that includes 68 percent of the area under the distribution curve. Good quality printing will have at least 95 percent (which corresponds to two standard deviations) of the element widths within the published printing tolerances. These are shown in Figure P-2.

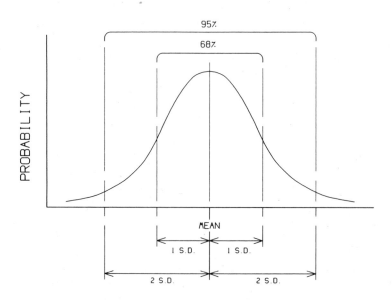

Figure P-2: Standard Deviation. From statistics, the probability distribution of a measurement such as an element width is characterized by its standard deviation. The standard deviation is a statistical measure of the range of element widths that includes approximately 68 percent of the area under the probability distribution curve. Approximately 95 percent of the element widths measured will lie within two standard deviations of the mean value.

First read rate (FRR) and substitution error rate (SER) will be affected by the relative position of the tails of the distribution function to the breakdown tolerances. (As described in Appendix P, these are the width deviations at which wide elements of a two-width symbology are inadvertently interpreted as narrow, and vice versa. In a multiwidth symbology, breakdown tolerance describes the width deviations that result in the element width's being misinterpreted as the incorrect number of modules.) Figure P-3 illustrates this concept for Code 39.

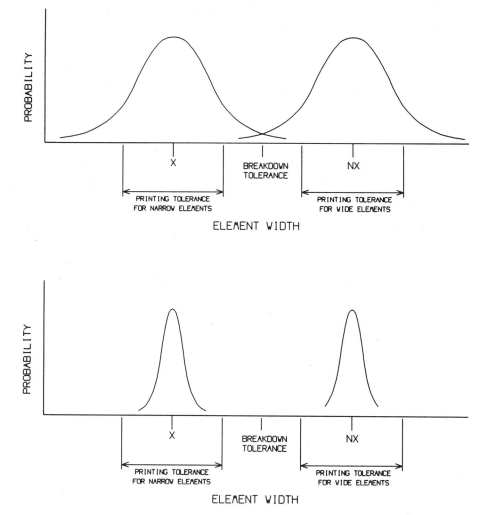

Figure P-3: Code 39 Element Width Distribution and Tolerances. For a symbology such as Code 39 with widths X(narrow) and NX (wide), the nominal widths used can be shown on a combined probability distribution. If the actual distributions of element widths are too wide, as at top, the overlaps of the distributions can lead to errors in decoding widths in the "Breakdown Tolerance" region. At bottom, where the actual distributions are narrower than the printing tolerances, there is little overlap.

In examining the top part of Figure P-3, we see that the positive tail of the narrow element width distribution curve extends well past the specified printing tolerance, and a significant part of the curve's area is beyond the breakdown tolerance. Likewise, a significant part of the area of the wide element width distribution curve lies to the left of the breakdown tolerance. This overlapping zone represents the probability that a wide element will be perceived as narrow, and vice versa.

The bottom part of Figure P-3 shows that tighter control of the printing process significantly reduces the probability of element width misinterpretation.

When a single Code 39 element's width is misinterpreted, the character will not transpose to another valid Code 39 character because of the symbology's self-checking feature. It takes two complementary errors in a Code 39 character to cause a transposition. If one or several element width errors occur in a character but do not result in a substitution error, the symbol will be unreadable.

Each Code 39 symbol has 10 edges (one on each side of each of the five bars). By examining each Code 39 bar/space pattern, it is possible to determine which edge errors will cause substitutions and which will result in unreadable symbols. Of the 20 possible single edge errors, 15 of them will result in an illegal width pattern, and five of them will still allow the character to be decoded correctly. The probability that a character will be unreadable in the presence of a single error is therefore 15/20 = 0.75. Of the 180 possible double errors in a character, 23 of them will result in character substitutions.

The probability that an edge will be in error will be called p. The probability p is a function of the extent to which the element width distribution curve extends beyond the breakdown tolerances.

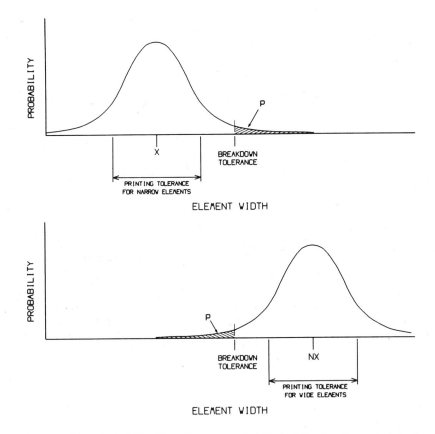

Figure P-4: Edge Error Probability. The edge error probability is defined as the area under the distribution curve beyond the breakdown tolerance.

Note that in both examples shown in Figure P-4, p is equal to the fraction of the total area under the curve that is represented by the shaded area.

Assuming that each error is statistically independent, it is possible to use the Binomial Distribution equation to determine the probability that one or more edges in a character will have an error:

Probability of zero edge errors, $P_0 = (1-p)^{10}$

Probability of one edge error, $P_1 = 10p(1-p)^9$

Probability of two edge errors, $P_2 = 45p^2(1-p)^8$

Probability of three edge errors, $P_3 = 120p^3(1-p)^7$

Practical bar code systems will have values of p that are well below 0.001. This will result in P_3 and higher orders being substantially less than P_2. For this analysis, we will therefore only consider P_0, P_1, and P_2. Note that $P_0 >> P_1 >> P_2$.

The probability that a character will be unreadable as a result of a single edge error is $0.75P_1$. The probability that a character substitution will occur as a result of two edge errors is $(23/180)P_2$. This is commonly referred to as the substitution error rate per character.

The ideal first read rate is called F and is equal to the read rate to be expected if scanning is always done carefully, excluding excessive acceleration or partial scans. Studies have indicated that F is approximately equal to the square root of the real first read rate. For a complete symbol:

$$F = \left(1 - 0.75P_1\right)^N$$

where

N = total number of characters

Through the above analysis we have now developed equations for substitution error rate and first read rate as a function of p, the probability of an edge error:

$$SER = \frac{23}{180}P_2 = 5.75p^2\left(1-p\right)^8$$

$$FRR = F^2 = \left(1 - 0.75P_1\right)^{2N} = \left(1 - 7p(1-p)^9\right)^{2N}$$

If we could measure p, we could predict SER and FRR. Unfortunately, it is not possible to measure p. Assuming smooth distribution curves of the type shown in FigureP-1, we can calculate p if we know the standard deviation of the printing process. Unfortunately, this is also impractical to measure.

The easiest parameter to measure for a symbol is the first read rate. What we would like to do is determine the relationship between SER and FRR. Examination of the equations, however, indicates that there is no closed solution that will express SER as a function of FRR. It is therefore necessary to use a numerical approach, assuming several different values of p, and observing the resulting values of FRR and SER. This is done in Table P-1.

FRR AND SER AS A FUNCTION OF p

p	FRR				SER
	N = 10	N = 15	N = 20	N = 25	
0.002	0.743	0.641	0.552	0.476	2.263×10^{-5}
0.001	0.861	0.800	0.742	0.689	5.704×10^{-6}
0.0005	0.928	0.894	0.861	0.829	1.432×10^{-6}
0.0002	0.971	0.956	0.942	0.928	2.296×10^{-7}
0.0001	0.985	0.978	0.971	0.963	5.745×10^{-8}
0.00005	0.993	0.989	0.985	0.981	1.437×10^{-8}
0.00002	0.997	0.996	0.994	0.993	2.300×10^{-9}
0.00001	0.999	0.998	0.997	0.996	5.750×10^{-10}

Using the data from Table P-1, Figure P-5 plots SER as a function of FRR for several values of N.

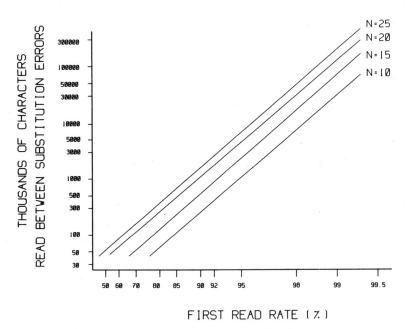

Figure P-5: Plotting Substitution Error Rate as a Function of First Read Rate. The axes of this plot are logarithmic. The lines shown are for messages of lengths N=10, 15, 20, and 25 characters.

Note that although Figure P-5 plots the data as straight lines, the axes are not linear. In particular, the Y axis is logarithmic, and the X axis is scaled as the logarithm of 1-FRR.

All of this analysis has presumed that printing errors have a distribution similar to that shown in Figure P-1. Unfortunately, the real world includes perceived printing defects that are not uniformly distributed. This can be due to actual printing errors, to scanning through the ragged ends of bars, or to using a contact scanner on a rough or irregular substrate. In these situations, the actual error rate can be significantly worse than predicted by the above analysis.

Note that this analysis was done for Code 39. Other relationships will exist for other symbologies, although the general shape of the SER vs. FRR curve will be similar.

APPENDIX Q

Federation of Automated Coding Technologies (FACT) Data Identifiers

The FACT organization has published a comprehensive document describing a system of data identifiers that denote the general category or intended use of the data that follows. The data identifier precedes the associated data, and consists of a single alphabetic character preceded by up to three numeric digits.

FACT has grouped the data identifier assignments according to 26 application categories. An abbreviated summary of these categories is as follows:

TABLE Q-1 FACT Data Identifiers

Category Number	Code Allocation	Description
0	All non-alphanumeric characters	Special characters not controlled by FACT
1	A-999A	Reserved
2	B-999B	Container information
3	C-999C	Field continuation
4	D-999D	Date
5	E-999E	Reserved
6	F-999F	Reserved
7	G-999G	Reserved
8	H-999H	Human resources
9	I-999I	Reserved
10	J-999J	Reserved
11	K-999K	Trading relationship transaction reference
12	L-999L	Location
13	M-999M	Reserved
14	N-999N	Industry-assigned codes
15	O-999O	Reserved (not recommended)
16	P-999P	Item information
17	Q-999Q	Measurements
18	R-999R	Miscellaneous
19	S-999S	Traceability number for an entity
20	T-999T	Traceability number for a group of entities
21	U-999U	Reserved
22	V-999V	Party to the transaction
23	W-999W	Activity reference
24	X-999X	Reserved
25	Y-999Y	Internal applications
26	Z-999Z	Mutually defined

The FACT Data Identifier Standard provides considerably more detail and guidance than this brief listing. Perspective users of data identifiers are strongly urged to refer to a current copy of the FACT document. Contact AIM-USA at 634 Alpha Drive, Pittsburgh, PA 15238.

AIM Symbology Identifiers

The symbology identifier is a string of characters prefixed to data messages by suitably equipped readers to indicate the symbology that had just been read. The prefix is a three character string:

] c m

where

] = the symbology identifier flag character

c = symbology identification

m = a modifier character

Symbology Characters

The characters assigned by AIM-USA as of late 1994 were as follows:

A	Code 39
B	Telepen
C	Code 128
D	Code One
E	EAN/U.P.C.
F	Codabar
G	Code 93
H	Code 11
I	I 2/5
K	Code 16K
L	PDF417
M	MSI Code
N	Anker Code
O	Codablock
P	Plessey Code
R	Straight 2 of 5 (with two bar start/stop codes)
S	Straight 2 of 5 (with three bar start/stop codes)
T	Code 49
X	Other Bar Code
Z	Non Bar Code Data

For further information on symbology identifiers, contact AIM-USA at 634 Alpha Drive, Pittsburgh, PA 15238.

Modifier Characters

Some symbologies have pertinent modifiers. The modifier character is determined by summing the option values listed below and referring to Table R-1:

TABLE R-1 Modifier Characters

Sum of Option Values	Modifier Character
0	0
1	1
2	2
3	3
4	4
5	5
6	6
7	7
8	8
9	9
10	A
11	B
12	C
13	D
14	E
15	F

Code 39 Option Values

0   No check character or Full ASCII conversion
1   Reader has performed mod 43 check
2   Reader has performed mod 43 check and stripped the check character
4   Reader has performed Full ASCII conversion

Telepen Option Values

0   Full ASCII mode
1   Double density numeric mode
2   Double density numeric followed by full ASCII
4   Full ASCII followed by double density numeric

Code 128 Option Values

0   Standard
1   Function code 1 in first character position
2   Function code 2 in second character position
4   Concatenation according to ISBT specification has been performed, and concatenated data follows.

Code One Option Values

0   Standard
1   Function code 1 in first character position
2   Function code 2 in second character position
4   Pad character in first symbol character position

EAN/U.P.C. Option Values

Note that symbology identifiers are not used with U.P.C.-A and U.P.C.-E unless the data is expanded to the full 13-digit EAN code. U.P.C. symbols with supplements are treated as two separate symbols, with separate data and identifiers for each. Data from these two symbols are transmitted sequentially, with the main symbol's data being first. Alternatively, they may be transmitted as a combined data message using modifier character "3".

0   Standard 13-digit EAN or U.P.C.
1   Two-digit supplemental data
2   Five-digit supplemental data
3   Combined data message consisting of 13 digits from EAN or U.P.C.
      symbol and 2 or 5 digits of supplementary data
4   EAN-8
8   U.P.C.-D1
9   U.P.C.-D2
A   U.P.C.-D3
B   U.P.C.-D4
C   U.P.C.-D5

Codabar Option Values

0   Standard
1   ABC concatenation has been performed

Code 93 Option Values

No options are specified for this symbology. The modifier character is 0.

Code 11 Option Values

0   Single check digit checked
1   Two check digits checked
2   All check digits stripped

Interleaved 2 of 5 Option Values

0   No check digit processing
1   Check digit has been checked
2   Check digit has been stripped

Code 16K Option Values

0   No special characters in first data position
1   Function code 1 in first character position (or implied due to starting character)
2   Function code 1 in second character position
4   Pad character in first position

PDF417 Option Values
No options are specified for this symbology. The modifier character is 0.

MSI Code Option Values
0   Single check digit checked
1   Single check digit stripped.

Anker Code Option Values
No options are specified for this symbology. The modifier character is 0.

Codablock Option Values
No options are specified for this symbology. The modifier character is 0.

Plessey Code Option Values
No options are specified for this symbology. The modifier character is 0.

Straight 2 of 5 (with two bar start/stop) Option Values
0   No check digit processing
1   Check digit has been checked
2   Check digit has been stripped

Straight 2 of 5 (with three bar start/stop) Option Values
No options are specified for this symbology. The modifier character is 0.

Code 49 Option Values
0   No special characters in first data positions
1   Function code 1 in first character position
2   Function code 1 in second character position
3   Function code 2 in first character position

Non-Bar Code Option Values
If data from non-bar code sources is directed through a bar code reader, the following options can be used to identify the source of data:
0   Keyboard
1   Magnetic stripe
2   RF tag
3-F   Other values as assigned by particular equipment manufacturers

EAN Prefix Identifiers

The European Article Numbering Association has defined the following country code prefix identifiers. For current information/changes, contact EAN at Rue des Colonies 54, Kolonienstraat, Bruxelles 1000, Brussels, Belgium.

Prefix	Assignment
00-09	UCC (USA + Canada)
20 to 29	In-store numbers
30 to 37	GENCOD (France)
40 to 43	CCG (Germany) *
440	Chamber of Foreign Trade (Germany) *
460 to 469	USSR CCI (USSR)
471	ANC of ROC (Taiwan)
49	Distribution Code Center (Japan)
50	ANA Ltd (UK) and ANA of Ireland
520	HELLCAN (Greece)
529	Cyprus Chamber of Commerce and Industry (Cyprus)
54	ICODIF (Belgium + Grand Duchy of Luxembourg)
560	CODIPOR (Portugal)
569	Iceland EAN-Committee (Iceland)
57	Dansk Varekode Administration (Denmark)
599	Hungarian Chamber of Commerce (Hungary)
600–601	SAANA (South Africa)
64	Central Chamber of Commerce (Finland)
70	Norsk Varekodeforening (Norway)
729	Israel Coding Association (Israel)
73	Swedish EAN Committee (Sweden)
750	AMECOP (Mexico)
759	CIP (Venezuela)
76	SACV (Switzerland)
779	CODIGO (Argentina)
789	ABAC (Brazil)
80 to 83	INDICOD (Italy)
84	AECOC (Spain)
859	Czechoslovak CCI (Czechoslovakia)
860	JANA (Yugoslavia)
869	Union of Chambers of Commerce of Turkey (Turkey)

87	STICHTING UAC (the Netherlands)
880	KOREA CCI (South Korea)
885	Thai Product Numbering Association Ltd (Thailand)
888	SANC (Singapore)
90–91	EAN-AUSTRIA (Austria)
93	APNA Ltd (Australia)
94	NZPNA Ltd (New Zealand)
955	Malaysian Article Numbering Council (Malaysia)
959	PNGPNA (Papua, New Guinea)
977	Periodicals (ISSN)
978–979	Books (ISBN)
98–99	Coupon numbers

*At the time of publication, no information was available to indicate whether or not any code assignment changes would be made to reflect changes caused by political changes associated with events in the former Soviet Union.

APPENDIX T

Sources of Symbology Standards Information

Following are the addresses and phone numbers for purchasing copies of symbology standards. Also included are personal contacts (data was valid as of mid 1994):

ANSI—American National Standards Institute, 11 West 42nd Street, 13th Floor, New York, NY 10036. The telephone number for ordering ANSI Standards is (212) 642-4900. Personal contact for X3.182 is Chuck Biss at (716) 265-1600. Personal contact for MH10.8M is Gary Ahlquist at (716) 477-1370.

AIM-USA—Automatic Identification Manufacturers, AIM-USA, 634 Alpha Drive, Pittsburgh, PA 15238. The telephone number for ordering AIM-USA Standards is (412) 963-8588. Personal contact is Dan Mullen. European Affiliate: AIM Europe, The Old Vicarage, Haley Hill, Halifax HX3 6DR, West Yorkshire, England. (011) 44 422 359 161. Personal contact is Christopher Swindin.

AIAG—Automotive Industry Action Group, 26200 Lahser Road, Suite 200, Southfield, MI 48034. The telephone number for ordering AIAG Standards is (810) 358-3570. Personal contact is Marilyn Sherry.

EAN—(International Article Numbering Association), Rue Royale 29, B-1000, Brussels, Belgium (011) 32 2 218 76 74. The EAN is the publisher of the International Article Number standard, formerly referred to as the European Article Number Standard. This standard specifies both symbology and application-specific details.

EIA—Electronics Industry Association, 2001 Pennsylvania Avenue N.W., Washington, DC 20006. Information about EIA Standards is available by calling (202) 457-4900. The telephone number for ordering EIA Standards is (800) 854-7179. Personal contact is Allan Gilligan at (908) 870-7902.

HIBCC—Health Industry Business Communication Council, 5110 North 40th Street, Suite 250, Phoenix, AZ 85018. The telephone number for ordering HIBCC standards is (602) 381-1091. Personal contact is Beverly Kieffer. European affiliate: EHIBCC (European Health Industry Business Communications Council), Boulevard Schmidt 87, Box 3, 1040 Brussels, Belgium (011) 322 732 4300. Personal contact is Anton Van Zijl.

UCC—Uniform Code Council, 8163 Old Yankee Road, Suite J, Dayton, OH 45458. The UCC is the publisher of the Universal Product Code specification

(U.P.C.). They have also published the U.P.C. Shipping Container Symbol specification, which includes a brief description of the Interleaved 2 of 5 symbology. Both of these standards include application-specific information. The Uniform Code Council also maintains the UCC-128 symbology. As described in Chapter 4, this uses standard Code 128 coding structures, but the particular format is treated by this group as a separate symbology. The UCC also publishes VICS Implementation Guidelines for EDI and maintains the EDI standard for the department store industry The telephone number for ordering UCC standards is (513) 435-3870. Personal contact is Tom Brady.

Other Industry Associations:

AA—Aluminum Association, 900 19th Street NW, Suite 300, Washington, DC 20006 (202) 862-5100.

ABC—American Blood Commission, 1600 Wilson Blvd., Ste. 905, Alexandria, VA 22209 (703) 525-1191.

API—American Paper Institute, 260 Madison Avenue, New York, NY 10016 (212) 340-0660.

DOD—Department of Defense, Naval Publications & Forms Center, 5801 Tabor Avenue, Philadelphia, PA 19120 (215) 697-2000.

GCA—Graphic Communications Association, 100 Daingerfield Rd., Alexandria, VA 22314-2804 (703) 519-8160.

IATA—International Air Transport Association, 26 Chemin de Boinville, CH-1216 Cointrin, Geneva, Switzerland (011) 41 22 98 33 66, ext. 465.

ISBN—International Standard Book Number, U.S. Agency—Bowker/Martindale-Hubell, 121 Canion Rd., New Providence, NJ 07974 (908) 665-6770.

MEMA—Motor & Equipment Manufacturing Association, 300 Sylvan Avenue, P.O. Box 1638, Englewood Cliffs, NJ 07632-0638 (201)569-8500.

NEMA—National Electrical Manufacturer's Association, 2101 L Street NW, Suite 300, Washington, D C 20037 (202) 457-8400.

NOPA—National Office Products Association, 301 North Fairfax Street, Alexandria, VA 22314 (703) 549-9040.

Relevant U.S. Patents

The following lists are by no means inclusive, but are intended to show the breadth and scope of intellectual property protection that was in place as of the beginning of 1995. In each section, the listings are organized by assignee. In many cases there are many patents assigned to a single organization that all have the same title: in this case, only one or two of the patent numbers are shown. There are many bar code patents assigned to organizations that are not included in this brief list. By the inclusion of certain patents in this summary, the author is not necessarily confirming the validity or uniqueness of the claimed inventions. In some cases the patent titles or assignee names have been slightly abbreviated in order to get them to fit into the available space. Note that these partial lists only include U.S. patents.

Symbology Patents (sorted by assignee)

5,202,552	Data Tag and Detecting Method	Array Technologies
5,260,556	Optically Readable Coded Target	Australian Meat R&D
3,916,160	Coded Label for Automatic Reading Systems	Bendix
3,808,405	Symmetrically Encoded Label for Automatic Label Reading Systems	Bendix
3,636,317	Machine Readable Code Track	Charecogn Systems
4,754,127	Method and Apparatus for Transforming Digitally Encoded Data into Printed Data Strips	Cauzin Systems
4,286,146	Coded Label and Code Reader for the Coded Label	Hitachi
5,070,504	Method and Apparatus for Providing Error Correction to Symbol Level Codes	IBM
4,794,239	Multitrack Bar Code and Associated Decoding Method	Intermec
5,329,107	Dynamically Variable Machine Readable Binary Code, Method for Reading and Producing Thereof	International Data Matrix
4,939,354	Dynamically Variable Machine Readable Binary Code, Method for Reading and Producing Thereof	International Data Matrix
5,124,536	Dynamically Variable Machine Readable Binary Code, Method for Reading and Producing Thereof	International Data Matrix
5,126,542	Dynamically Variable Machine Readable Binary Code, Method for Reading and Producing Thereof	International Data Matrix
3,985,293	Machine Readable Merchandise Marking Tag	NCR
5,395,181	Method and Apparatus for Printing a Circular or Bullseye Bar Code with a Thermal Printer	Microcom
5,357,094	Two Channel XOR Bar Code and Optical Reader	Minn. Mining & Mfg
5,189,292	Finder Pattern for Optically Encoded Machine Readable Symbols	Omniplanar
5,153,418	Multiple Resolution Machine Readable Symbols	Omniplanar
5,241,166	Low Resolution Target Acquisition	Omniplanar
5,262,623	Method and Apparatus for Distinguishing a Preferred Bar Code or the Like	Omniplanar
5,331,137	Machine Readable Code Combining Preprinted Indicia with Hand-Mark Data	Symbol Technologies
4,874,936	Hexagonal Information Encoding Article Process and System	United Parcel Service

4,896,029	Polygonal Information Encoding Article Process and System	United Parcel Service
4,998,010	Polygonal Information Encoding Article Process and System	United Parcel Service
5,337,361	Record with Encoded Data	Symbol Technologies
5,304,786	High Density Two-Dimensional Bar Code Symbol	Symbol Technologies
5,243,655	System for Encoding and Decoding Data in Machine Readable Graphic Form	Symbol Technologies
4,924,078	Identification Symbol, System, and Method	Veritec
4,972,475	Authenticating Pseudo-Random Code and Apparatus	Veritec
1,985,035	Card Sorter	Westinghouse
2,020,925	Card Sorting Machine	Westinghouse
3,044,696	Process for Data Recording	
4,926,035	OpticallyReadable Code and Method for Communication	
4,924,078	Identification Symbol, System, and Method	
4,776,464	Automated Article Handling System and Process	

Hardware Patents (sorted by assignee)

5,124,538	Scanner	Accu-Sort
5,028,772	Scanner to Combine Partial Fragments of a Complete Code	Accu-Sort
5,164,573	Optical Reading Device	Alps Electric
5,122,644	Optical Code Reading Device with Autofocussing	Alps Electric
5,406,062	Sensitivity Adjustment Circuit for Bar Code Scanner and Method Therefor	Alps Electric
5,401,949	Fuzzy Logic Barcode Reader	American NeuroLogix
5,192,856	Auto Focusing Bar Code Reader	An Con Genetics
4,916,318	Scan Type Optical Reader with Changing Beam Waist Position	Asahi Kogaku Kogyo
5,361,158	Multiple Source Optical Scanner	AT&T Global Info Systems
4,800,257	Optoelectronic Reading Pen	BBC Brown Boveri
5,155,344	Method and Apparatus for Reading a Bar Code of Variable Orientation on a Motionless Medium	Bertin & Cie
4,948,955	Barcode Location Determination	Boeing
5,064,222	Bar Code Applicator	Canada Post
4,886,957	Card Reader for Receiving a Card Bearing an Imprinted Data Strip, Scanning the Strip in 2 Directions	Cauzin
4,916,441	Portable Handheld Terminal	CliniCom
4,884,904	Bar Code Printer	Cognitive Solutions
5,149,948	Improved Bar Code Reader Sys. for Reading Bar Codes under High Specular Reflection Conditions	Computer Identics
5,177,346	Bar Code Reader Sys. for Reading Bar Code Labels with a Highly Specular, Low-Contrast Surface	Computer Identics
4,816,659	Bar Code Reader Head	Control Module
5,087,137	Ribbon Assembly Including Indicia to Identify Operating Parameters and Ribbon Depletion	Datamax
3,604,899	Mark-Detecting System	Dennison Manufacturing
3,662,362	Device for Printing and Coding Tickets	Dennison Manufacturing
5,128,528	Matrix Encoding Devices and Methods	Dittler Brothers
5,126,544	Bar Code Reader	Eastman Kodak
4,973,829	Bar Code Reading Method	Eastman Kodak
5,194,720	Method and Apparatus for Performing On-Line Integrated Decoding, Evaluation of Bar Code Data	Eastman Kodak
4,843,222	Bar Code Reader for Reading Bar Codes at Different Distances	Eastman Kodak
5,384,450	Bar Code Reader for a Singulated Product Strream	ElectroCom Automation
4,759,288	Printer for a Bar Code	Ecupan
5,268,565	Compact Type Bar Code Reader	Fujitsu
5,266,788	Laser Scanner for Bar Code Reader Having a Transparent Light Guide Plate	Fujitsu
5,068,520	Signal Processing Circuit of a Bar Code Reader	Fujitsu
5,206,491	Plural Beam, Plural Window Multi-Direction Bar Code Reading Device	Fujitsu
5,393,968	Method and Device for Reading Bar Code	Fujitsu
5,404,004	Bar Code Reader Having N counters and N-1 Composers	Fujitsu
5,047,615	Bar Code Printing or Reading Apparatus	Furuno
5,371,347	Electro-Optical Scanning System with Gyrating Scan Head	GAP Technologies
5,166,500	Barcode Reader Decoder System	Goldstar
4,999,482	Optical Scanning System for a Bar Code Reader	Goldstar

5,028,771	Bar Code Reader	Goldstar
5,281,800	Method and Apparatus for Low Power Optical Sensing and Decoding of Data	Hand Held Products
4,978,860	Optical System for a Large Depth-of-Field Bar Code Scanner	Hewlett Packard
4,963,756	Focused Line Identifier for a Bar Code Reader	Hewlett Packard
5,010,242	Sensor Array and Illumination System for a Large Depth-of-Field Bar Code Scanner	Hewlett Packard
4,775,967	Beam Spot Control Device Using a Thin Micro Lens With an Actuator	Hitachi
4,777,357	Bar Code Reader	Hitachi
4,992,650	Method and Apparatus for Barcode Recognition in a Digital Image	IBM
5,175,421	Dual Depth-of-Field Deflector for Bar Code Scanners	IBM
5,007,748	Printer for Bar Code Using Thin and Thick Bar Code Fonts	IBM
4,873,426	Technique for Reading Bar Codes	Image Business Systems
4,958,064	Bar Code Locator for Video Scanner/Reader System	Image Recognition
5,216,550	Optical System for Scanning Device	Intermec
4,675,695	Method and Apparatus for Temperature Control in Thermal Printers	Intermec
4,391,535	Improved Method and Apparatus for Controlling Thermal Print Medium Exposed by a Thermal Printer	Intermec
4,164,180	Impact Printer Including Hammer Bank Assembly	Intermec
5,319,184	Tip Assembly for a Bar Code Scanner	Intermec
3,866,851	High Speed Impact Printer	Intermec
4,335,301	Wave Shaping Circuit for Electro-Optical Code Readers	Intermec
5,389,770	Method and Apparatus for Decoding Unresolved Bar Code Profiles	Intermec
5,404,493	Method and Computer System for Processing Keycode and Symbol Code Data in a Bar Code Device	Intermec
5,059,773	Bar Code Reader Signal Processing Method and Device	Japan Steel Works
4,757,206	Bar Code Reading Method and Apparatus	Kabushiki Kaisha Sato
5,012,079	Bar Code Scanner Mirror Assembly	Lazerdata
5,132,524	Multidirectional Laser Scanner	Lazerdata
5,387,787	Scanning Device for Reconstructing a Complete Code from Scanned Segments	Lazerdata
4,969,038	Method for Scanning Image Information	Lemelson
4,965,829	Apparatus and Method for Coding and Reading Codes	Lemelson
3,735,350	Code Scanning System	Lemelson
3,918,029	Scanning System and Method	Lemelson
5,059,778	Portable Data Scanner Apparatus	Mars
5,010,242	Method and Apparatus for Variable Speed Scanning of Bar Codes	Mars
5,223,957	Optical Scanning Device	Matsushita Electric
4,866,258	Optical Pattern Detecting Apparatus	Matsushita Electric
5,349,171	Bar Code Reader	Matsushita Electric
5,304,787	Locating 2-D Bar Codes	Metamedia
5,019,714	Scanning System with Array of Laser Scanner Modules to Produce Complex Scan Pattern	Metrologic
4,960,985	Compact Omnidirectional Laser Scanner	Metrologic
4,805,175	Ultra-Compact, Handheld Laser Scanner	Metrologic
4,958,894	Bouncing Oscillating Scanning Device for Laser Scanning Apparatus	Metrologic
4,962,980	Laser Scanner Engine with Folded Beam Path	Metrologic
5,340,971	Automatic Bar Code Reading System Having Selectable Long and Short Range Modes of Operation	Metrologic
5,340,973	Automatic Laser Scanning System and Method of Reading Bar Code Symbols Using Same	Metrologic
4,855,581	Decoding of Bar Codes by Preprocessing Scan Data	Microscan
5,239,169	Optical Signal Processor for Bar Code Reader	Microscan
4,870,274	Laser Scanner with Rotating Mirror and Housing which Is Transparent to the Scanning Direction	Micro Video
5,239,622	Bar Code Identification System Format Editor	Monarch Marking
5,146,546	Printer with Hardware Symbol Data Accessing Scheme	Monarch Marking
5,061,946	Microprocessor Controlled Thermal Printer	Monarch Marking
4,980,009	Handheld Labeler and Method of Labeling	Monarch Marking
4,785,735	Label Printing and Applying Apparatus	Monarch Marking
4,327,640	Selective Printing Apparatus	Monarch Marking
4,199,677	Record Decoding System and Method Utilizing Logarithmic Techniques	Monarch Marking
5,402,528	Reconfigurable Printer	Monarch Marking

5,058,055	System for Printing Labels and Tags	Naiga Clothes
5,283,699	Micro-Bar Code Reader System	Neorex
5,276,316	Method for Reconstructing Complete Bar Code Signals from Partial Bar Code Scans	NCR
5,274,491	Dynamic Laser Diode Aperture for Optical Scanners	NCR
5,177,347	Axially Invariant Pattern Scanning Apparatus	NCR
5,173,603	Focus Changing Apparatus and Method for Optical Scanners	NCR
5,262,625	Multiple Bar Code Decoding System and Method	NCR
4,967,076	Optical Scanner Producing Multiple Scan Patterns	NCR
5,057,687	Detector Assembly with Plural Optical Axes	NCR
5,065,842	Removable Window Carrier for Mounting in a Scanner Checkout Counter	NCR
5,043,563	Portable Overhead Bar Code Scanner	NCR
4,794,237	Multidirectional Holographic Scanner	NCR
5,132,523	Dual Mode Optical Scanning System	NCR
4,868,375	Method for Changing the Functions of a Bar Code Reader	NCR
4,789,775	Optical Scanner	NCR
5,367,578	System & Method for Optical Recognition of Bar-Coded Characters Using Template Matching	NCR
5,221,832	Raster Variation Method for Omnidirectional Optical Scanners	NCR
5,384,452	Quasi-One-Dimensional Focal Plane Array for Vision Scanners	NCR
5,231,275	Bar Code Reader	NEC
4,818,856	Optical Information Reading Apparatus	Nippondenso
5,184,005	Non-Decoded Type Bar Code Reading Apparatus	Nippondenso
5,392,150	Optical Information Reading Device	Nippondenso
5,331,136	Handheld Data Capture System with Interchangeable Modules	Norand
5,180,232	Modular Printer System	Norand
4,882,476	Bar Code Reader with Enhanced Sensitivity	Norand
5,052,943	Recharging and Data Retrieval Apparatus	Norand
5,322,991	Compact Handheld RF Data Terminal	Norand
4,282,425	Instant Portable Bar Code Reader	Norand
5,359,185	Chromatic Ranging Method for Reading Optical Readable Information over Substantial Distances	Norand
5,347,114	Bar Code Symbol Reading Apparatus	Olympus Optical
5,369,265	Bar Code Reader Apparatus with an Automatic Read Starting Function	Olympus Optical
5,365,048	Bar Code Symbol Reading Apparatus with Double-Reading Prevention Function	Olympus Optical
5,124,537	Omnidirectional Bar Code Reader Using Virtual Scan of Video Raster Scan Memory	Omniplanar
5,155,343	Omnidirectional Bar Code Reader with Method and Apparatus for Detecting and Scanning a Symbol	Omniplanar
5,223,701	System Method and Apparatus Using Multiple Resolution Machine Readable Symbols	Omniplanar
4,841,129	Pattern Recognition Device	Opticon
5,196,684	Method and Apparatus for Improving the Throughput of a CCD Bar Code Scanner/Decoder	Opticon
5,365,049	Focusing Means for a Symbol Code Reader	Opticon
5,135,160	Portable Bar Code Reader Utilizing Pulsed LED Array	Opticon
5,387,786	Focussing Device for a Bar Code Reader	Opticon
5,384,453	Bar Code Scanner with a Scanning Pattern Divider	Opticon
5,406,061	Bar Code Scanner Operable at Different Frequencies	Opticon
5,406,060	Bar Code Reader for Sensing at an Acute Angle	Opticon
5,015,831	Scan Modules for Bar Code Readers and the Like in which Scan Elements Are Flexurally Supported	Photographic Sciences
4,820,911	Apparatus for Scanning and Reading Bar Codes	Photographic Sciences
4,652,750	Optical Device for Detecting Coded Symbols	Photographic Sciences
5,200,597	Digitally Controlled System for Scanning and Reading Bar Codes	Photographic Sciences
5,212,371	Handheld Bar Code Scanner with Improved Aiming Means	Photographic Sciences
5,231,293	Bar Code Reading Instrument which Prompts Operator to Scan Bar Codes Properly	Photographic Sciences
5,386,105	Diffractive Optical Beam Shaping Methods for Providing Enhanced Depth-of-Working Range	Photographic Sciences
5,389,917	Lapel Data Entry Terminal	Photographic Sciences

4,818,886	Method and Apparatus for Self-Referencing and Self-Focusing a Bar-Code Rreader	Quential
3,796,863	Optical Scanning Arrangement and Article Useful Therewith	RCA
4,822,986	Method of Detecting and Reading Postal Codes	Recognition Equipment
4,874,933	Ambient Illumination Bar Code Reader	Recognition Equipment
5,397,885	Handheld Barcode Label Reader with increased Depth of Field	Reflexion Plus
5,237,160	Barcode Scanner Having Hologram	Ricoh
5,285,056	Bar Code Reflectance Measurement Apparatus	RJS
5,051,567	Bar Code Reader to Read Different Bar Code Formats	RJS
3,801,775	Method and Apparatus for Identifying Objects	Scanner
4,916,298	Method for the Optical Reading of Bar Codes	SGS-Thomson
5,393,967	Method and Apparatus for Noncontact Reading of a Relief Pattern	Sensis
4,967,074	Scanner for the Detection of Bar Codes on Articles	Sick
5,385,416	Device for Identifying an Ink Ribbon Cartridge Used in a Printer	Sony
5,256,866	Handheld Scanner	Soricon
5,247,161	Bar Code Scanning Sys. with Converter Means and Microprocessor Means in an Integrated Circuit	Spectra-Physics
5,232,185	Method and Apparatus for Mounting a Compact Optical Scanner	Spectra-Physics
5,198,649	Bar Code Scanner and Method of Scanning Bar Code Labels with or without an Add-On Code	Spectra-Physics
4,866,257	Bar Code Scanner and Method	Spectra-Physics
4,963,719	Bar Code Scanner and Method of Scanning	Spectra-Physics
4,749,879	Signal Transition Detection Method and System	Spectra-Physics
4,861,972	Bar Code Scanner and Method of Programming	Spectra-Physics
5,144,118	Bar Code Scanning System with Multiple Decoding Microprocessors	Spectra-Physics
4,939,356	Bar Code Scanner with Asterisk Scan Pattern	Spectra-Physics
4,879,456	Method of Decoding a Binary Scan Signal	Spectra-Physics
5,298,728	Signal Processing Apparatus and Method	Spectra-Physics
4,786,798	Beam Forming and Collection Lens Assembly for Laser Scanner Systems	Spectra-Physics
5,347,113	Multiple-Interface Selection System for Computer Peripherals	Spectra-Physics
5,371,361	Optical Processing System	Spectra-Physics
5,347,121	Variable Focus Optical System for Data Reading	Spectra-Physics
4,396,303	Improved Bar Code and Alphanumeric Printer	Swedot
5,245,167	Bar-Code Reading Apparatus	Sumitomo Electric
5,177,343	Symbol Reader Using Differentiating Circuit for Light Beam Focusing	Sumitomo Electric
5,045,677	Combining Bar Code Read Data from a Plurality of Scanning Lines	Sumitomo Electric
5,340,982	Symbol Reading Device for Varying the Focal Point of a Scanning Laser Beam	Sumitomo Electric
5,319,181	Method and Apparatus for Decoding Two-Dimensional Bar Codes Using CCD/CMD Camera	Symbol Technologies
4,816,660	Portable Laser Diode Scanning Head	Symbol Technologies
5,324,924	Bar Code Decoder with Changeable Working Ranges	Symbol Technologies
5,311,001	Analog Waveform Decoder Utilizing Histogram of Edge Sizes	Symbol Technologies
5,302,812	Laser Scanning Device with Automatic Range and Spot Size Adjustment	Symbol Technologies
5,281,801	Low-Cost Low-Power Scanner and Method	Symbol Technologies
5,278,398	Decoding Bar Code Symbols by Determining the Best Alignment of Partial Scans	Symbol Technologies
5,302,813	Multi-Bit Digitizer	Symbol Technologies
5,280,162	Object Sensing System for Bar Code Laser Scanners	Symbol Technologies
5,266,787	Laser Scanner Using Two Scan Motors Independently Controlled by a Single Signal	Symbol Technologies
5,241,164	Method of Decoding Bar Code Symbols from Partial Scans	Symbol Technologies
5,235,167	Laser Scanning System and Scanning Method for Reading Bar Codes	Symbol Technologies
5,229,591	Scanning System with Adjustable Light Output and/or Scanning Angle	Symbol Technologies
5,218,190	Means and Method for Noncontact Bar Code Label Verification	Symbol Technologies
5,210,398	Optical Scanner with Extended Depth of Focus	Symbol Technologies
5,180,904	Bar Code Scanner with Automatic Deactivation of Scan Upon Bar Code Recognition	Symbol Technologies
5,168,149	Scan Pattern Generators for Bar Code Symbol Readers	Symbol Technologies
5,140,146	Bar Code Symbol Reader with Modulation Enhancement	Symbol Technologies
5,136,147	Light Emitting Diode Scanner	Symbol Technologies
5,021,641	Handheld Bar Code Scanner with Jointly Mounted Scanning Mirrors	Symbol Technologies

5,015,833	Scan Board Module for Laser Scanners	Symbol Technologies
4,871,904	Multidirectional Optical Scanner	Symbol Technologies
4,736,095	Narrow-Bodied, Single and Twin-Windowed Portable Laser Scan Head for Reading Bar Codes	Symbol Technologies
5,206,492	Bar Code Symbol Scanner with Reduced Power Usage to Effect Reading	Symbol Technologies
4,593,186	Portable Laser Scanning System and Scanning Methods	Symbol Technologies
4,354,101	Method and Apparatus for Reading and Decoding a High-Density Linear Bar Code	Symbol Technologies
4,471,218	Self-Contained Portable Data Entry Terminal	Symbol Technologies
4,354,101	Method and Apparatus for Reading and Decoding a High-Density Linear Bar Code	Symbol Technologies
5,243,655	System for Encoding and Decoding Data In Machine Readable Graphic Form	Symbol Technologies
4,160,156	Method and Apparatus for Reading Bar Coded Data wherein Light Source is Periodically Energized	Symbol Technologies
5,340,972	Hands-Free Bar Code Scanner with Finger-Activated Optical Control	Symbol Technologies
5,352,922	Wand Readers	Symbol Technologies
5,369,264	Reading Bar Codes with a Wide Laser Beam	Symbol Technologies
5,369,262	Electronic Stylus Type Optical Reader	Symbol Technologies
5,369,260	Bar Code Scanning with Correction for Spot Speed Variation	Symbol Technologies
5,367,152	Method of Reading Indicia from Either Side of Scanner Housing	Symbol Technologies
5,367,151	Slim Scan Module with Interchangeable Scan Element	Symbol Technologies
5,386,107	Scanning Arrangement in which the Focus Is Varied in Correlation with the Scanning Angle	Symbol Technologies
5,396,055	Handheld Bar Code Reader with Keyboard, Display, and Processor	Symbol Technologies
5,396,054	Bar Code Reader Using Scanned Memory Array	Symbol Technologies
5,396,053	Method of Adjusting Electrical Circuit Parameters during Manufacture of a Bar Code Scanner	Symbol Technologies
5,401,948	Mirrorless Scanners with Movable Laser, optical, and Sensor Components	Symbol Technologies
3,550,770	Method for Automatic Sorting or Recording of Objects and Apparatus for Carrying Out the Method	Svejsecentralen Glostruk
4,988,852	Bar Code Reader	Teknekron Transportation
5,334,821	Portable Point-of-Sale Terminal	Telxon
4,621,189	Handheld Data Entry Apparatus	Telxon
3,956,740	Portable Data Entry Apparatus	Telxon
5,343,031	Method of Decoding a 2-D Code Symbol Mark	Teiryo Sangyo Co.
5,229,587	Bar Code Label Printer and Bar Code Label Issuing Method	Tohoku Ricoh
5,183,343	Method of Printing Bar Codes by a Bar Code Printer	Tohoku Ricoh
4,833,309	Bar Code Reading Apparatus	Tohoku Ricoh
5,329,105	Method and Apparatus for Determining the Width of Elements of Bar Code Symbols	United Parcel Service
5,276,315	Method and Apparatus for Processing Low-Resolution Images of Degraded Bar Code Symbols	United Parcel Service
5,325,276	Lighting Apparatus for The Computer Imaging of a Surface	United Parcel Service
5,308,960	Combined Camera System	United Parcel Service
5,343,028	Method and Apparatus for Detecting and Decoding Bar Code Symbols Using 2-D Digital Pixel Images	United Parcel Service
5,384,451	Method and Apparatus for Decoding Bar Code Symbols Using Composite Signals	United Parcel Service
5,404,003	Method and Apparatus for Decoding Bar Code Symbols Using Byte-Based Searching	United Parcel Service
5,399,852	Method and Apparatus for Illumination and Imaging of a Surface Employing Cross Polarization	United Parcel Service
5,331,176	Handheld Two-Dimensional Symbol Reader with a Symbol Illumination Window	Veritec
5,308,962	Reduced Power Scanner for Reading Indicia	Welch Allyn
5,294,783	Analog Reconstruction Circuit and Bar Code Reading Apparatus Employing Same	Welch Allyn
4,013,893	Optical Bar Code Scanning Device	Welch Allyn
5,286,960	Method of Programmable Digitization and Bar Code Scanning Apparatus Employing Same	Welch Allyn
5,132,709	Apparatus and Method for Closed-Loop Control of Printing Head	Zebra

3,757,090	Machine Reading and Recognition of Information Displayed on Information Carriers	Zellweger
5,354,977	Optical Scanning Head	
4,920,255	Automatic Incremental Focusing Scanner System	
4,782,219	System and Method for Reading Specular Barcodes	
5,175,420	Bar Code Scanner Having a Light Source/Photodetector Movable iIn a Raster Pattern	
3,497,239	Label Reader with Tracking of Label Using Concentric Binary Code Rings and Modulated Circular Scan	
3,971,917	Labels and Label Readers	
3,414,731	Package Classification by Tracking the Path of a Circular Label and Simultaneously Scanning the Information	
3,418,456	Encoded Tag Reader	
3,453,419	Code Reading System	
5,349,172	Optical Scanning Head	
5,404,001	Fiber Optic Bar Code Reader	
5,396,840	Manual Bar Coder	

Application Patents (sorted by assignee)

5,245,533	Marketing Research Method and Sys. for Management of Manufacturer's Discount Coupon Offers	A. C. Nielsen
4,972,504	Marketing Research System and Method for Obtaining Retail Data on a Real Time Basis	A. C. Nielson
5,134,271	Bar Code System Used in Geophysical Exploration	Amoco
4,825,045	System and Method for Checkout Counter Product Promotion	Advance Promotion Tech.
4,970,655	Automatic Fee Collecting and Receipt Dispensing System	American Registration
5,397,133	System for Playing Card Games Remotely	AT&T
5,071,167	Shipping and Return Mailing Label	Avery
5,028,766	Automated Rental System	AVS
5,057,677	Transaction Monitoring and Security Control System	Avicom Intl.
5,225,990	Apparatus and Methods for Baggage Reconciliation and Location	Brals Limited
4,449,042	Redeemable Container with End Closure Redemption Code	Can & Bottle Systems
4,823,162	Method and Apparatus for Marking Photographic Orders	Ciba-Geigy
5,056,019	Automated Purchase Reward Accounting System and Method	Citicorp POS
5,053,956	Interactive System for Retail Transactions	Coats Viyella
5,273,392	Automated Work Center and Method	Computer Aided Systems
4,859,839	Point-of-Sale Terminal for Laundry or Dry Cleaning Establishments	Counter Computer
5,388,165	Method for Building a Database and Performing Marketing Based on Prior Shopping History	Credit Verification
4,760,330	Test System with Shared Test Instruments	Northern Telecom
4,978,305	Free Response Test Grading Method	Educational Testing
4,982,346	Promotion Network Apparatus and Method	Expertel Communications
5,287,414	Coded File Locator System	Esselte Pendaflex
5,291,399	Method and Apparatus for Accessing a Portable Personal Database as for a Hospital Environment	Executone Information
5,072,822	Article Sorting System	Fabri-Check
5,225,996	Emissions Monitoring and Tracking System	Fugitive Emissions Control
5,159,385	Total Photofinishing Laboratory System	Fuji Photo
5,053,955	Process and Apparatus for Administering Promotional Information	Fulfillment Systems
4,544,064	Distribution Installation for Moving Piece Goods	Gebhardt Fordertechnik
5,160,383	Tire Having Identification Label Affixed Thereto	Goodyear Tire & Rubber
5,269,522	Apparatus and Method for Promotional Contests	Graphic Technology
5,003,251	Bar Code Reader for Printed Circuit Board	Grumman Aerospace
5,262,954	Automated Manufacture Line	Hitachi
5,042,972	Toy Building Set Provided with Elements that Can Sense Bar Codes	Interlego
5,265,874	Cashless Gaming Apparatus and Method	Intl. Game Technology
5,038,023	System for Storing and Monitoring Bar Coded Articles	C. Itoh
5,103,737	Garment Transfer Apparatus	Japan Steel
5,262,597	System and Method for Processing International Priority Airmail	Johnson & Hayward
5,266,780	Human Error Preventing System Using Bar Code Reading Collations	Kansai Paint
4,929,820	Procedure and Label for Bar Code Marking on Vulcanizable or Vulcanized Rubber Products	Milliken Denmark

5,357,090	Copy Service Accounting Device and System For Printing a Copy Charge in Bar Code Form	Mita International
5,269,478	Bobbin Trace System	Murata Kikai Kabushiki
5,278,551	Meter Reading System	Nitto Kohki
5,272,318	Electronically Readable Medical Locking System	Novatek Medical
4,876,571	Copying Machine Having a Bar Code Reader	Ricoh
5,362,051	Entertainment and Promotional Method	RTC Industries
4,915,205	Apparatus for Dispensing and Receiving Rented Articles	Sovereign Technical Svcs.
4,879,540	Data Exchanging System Using Bar Code	Sanden
4,945,216	Wireless Bar Code Reader	Sharp
5,159,635	System for Encoding Data in Machine Readable Graphic Form	Symbol Technologies
5,393,965	Flexible Merchandise Checkout and Inventory Management System	Symbol Technologies
5,401,944	Traveler Security and Luggage-Control System	Symbol Technologies
5,399,846	Systems Utilizing a High-Density Two-Dimensional Bar Code Symbology	Symbol Technologies
5,007,641	Gaming Method	Take One Marketing
5,080,364	Gaming Method	Take One Marketing
5,362,053	Card Reader for Blackjack Table	Tech Art
5,169,155	Coded Playing Cards and Other Standardized Documents	Technical Systems
5,046,014	Automatic Tool Position Recognizing Device Recognizing Bar Code	Toshiaki Anjo
4,832,341	High Security Instant Lottery Using Bar Codes	UPC Games
4,905,080	Apparatus for Collecting Television Channel Data and Market Research Data	Video Research
5,003,472	Apparatus for Order Entry in a Restaurant	Wand Corp.
4,881,061	Article Removal Control System	3M
4,920,488	Physical Inventory System	
4,814,589	Information Transfer and Use, Particularly with Respect to Objects Such as Gambling Chips	
5,192,854	System for Electronically Recording and Redeeming Coupons	
5,362,949	Packing House Control System	
4,945,218	Mailing Device and Machine Readable Business Card	
4,228,112	Inspection Control System and Method	
5,091,727	Fully Optimized Automatic Parking Facility Management System	
5,168,961	Supermarket with Self-Service Checkout	
5,125,513	Apparatus and Method for Automatically Assembling Randomly Ordered Laundered Items	
5,111,927	Automated Recycling Machine	
5,169,061	Two-Way Envelope	
5,159,560	Automated Merchandise Dispensing and Retrieval System	
5,159,180	Litigation Support System and Method	
5,166,498	Procedure and Assembly for Drawing Blood	
5,165,726	Mailing Device and Business Card Combination	
5,059,126	Sound Association and Learning System	
5,047,614	Method and Apparatus for Computer-Aided Shopping	
4,887,208	Sales and Inventory Control System	
5,250,789	Shopping Cart	
5,245,162	Method for Determining Sequence of Arrival and Racing Time of Runners at Finish Line with Bar Code	
5,190,162	Sorting Machine	
4,857,713	Hospital Error Avoidance System	
5,171,976	Dynamic Coded Mechanical Metering System	
3,211,470	Coded Coupon	
3,478,316	Inventory Control System	
4,340,810	Method and Apparatus for Merchandise Distribution Control	
4,781,696	Method of Dispensing Medicine	
5,288,977	System for Imprinting Patient-Identifying Bar Codes onto Medical X-Rays	
5,290,033	Gaming Machine and Coupons	
5,273,281	Game Card and Associated Playing Method	
3,458,706	Tape Reel Identifying Arrangement Employing Light Reflective Coded Label	
5,389,771	Bar Coding	

Other Patents (sorted by assignee)

5,179,569	Spread Spectrum Radio Communications System	CliniCom
5,287,384	Frequency Hopping Spread Spectrum Data Communications System	LXE
5,386,435	Frequency Hopping Spread Spectrum Data Communication System	LXE
4,940,974	Multiterminal Communication System and Method	Norand
5,070,536	Mobile Radio Data Communication System	Norand
5,295,154	Radio Frequency Local Area Network	Norand
5,394,436	Radio Frequency Local Area Network	Norand
5,280,498	Packet Data Communication System	Symbol Technologies
4,914,700	Method and Apparatus for Scrambling and Unscrambling Bar Codes	
4,977,619	Distributed Infrared Communication System	

APPENDIX V

Glossary of Terms

Accuracy—The determination of whether any element width or intercharacter gap width (if applicable) differs from its nominal width by more than the printing tolerance.

AIM-USA—The Automatic Identification Manufacturers Inc., a U.S.trade association headquartered in Pittsburgh, PA.

Alignment—In an automatic identification system, the relative position and orientation of a scanner to the symbol.

Alphanumeric—The character set that contains letters, numbers, and usually other characters such as punctuation marks.

ANSI—The American National Standards Institute, a nongovernmental organization responsible for the development of voluntary standards.

Aperture—The opening in an optical system that establishes the field of view.

ASCII—The character set and code described in American National Standard Code for Information Interchange, ANSI X3.4-1977. Each ASCII character is encoded with seven bits. The ASCII character set is used for information interchange between data processing systems, communication systems, and associated equipment. The ASCII set consists of both control and printing characters.

Aspect Ratio—In a bar code symbol, the ratio of bar height to symbol length.

Asynchronous—In a data communication system, an arrangement whereby every character is transmitted independently and there is no associated clock.

Average Background Reflectance—Expressed as a percent; the simple arithmetic average of the background reflectance from at least five different points on a sheet.

Background—The spaces, quiet zones, and area surrounding a printed symbol.

Bar—The darker element of a printed bar code symbol.

Bar Code—An automatic identification technology that encodes information into an array of adjacent varying width parallel rectangular bars and spaces.

Bar Code Character—A single group of bars and spaces that represents a specific number (often one) of numbers, letters, punctuation marks, or other symbols. This is the smallest subset of a bar code symbol that contains data.

Bar Code Density—The number of data characters that can be represented in a linear unit of measure. Bar code density is often expressed in characters per inch.

Bar Code Label—A label that carries a bar code symbol and is suitable to be affixed to an article.

Bar Code Reader—A device used to read a bar code symbol.

Bar Code Symbol—See *Symbol.*

Bar/Half-Bar Code—An early attempt (about the late 1960s) at automatic identification as a two-track direct binary symbology. It was resurrected by the U.S. Postal Service in the late 1980s as the basis for its Postnet Code.

Bar Height—See *Bar Length.*

Bar Length—The bar dimension perpendicular to the bar width. Also called height. Scanning is performed in an axis perpendicular to the bar length.

Bar Width—The thickness of a bar measured from the edge closest to the symbol start character to the trailing edge of the same bar.

Bar Width Reduction—Reduction of the nominal bar width dimension on film masters or printing plates to compensate for systematic errors in some printing processes. Bar width reduction can have positive or negative values.

BCD—Binary coded decimal; see *Decimal, Binary Coded.*

Bi-directional—A bar code symbol capable of being read successfully independent of scanning direction.

Binary—The number system that uses only 1s and 0s.

Bit—An abbreviation for binary digit. A single element (0 or 1) in a binary number.

Character—1. A single group of bars and spaces that represents a specific number (usually one) of numbers, letters, punctuation marks, or other symbols. 2. A graphic shape representing a letter, numeral, or symbol. 3. A letter, digit, or other symbol that is used as part of the organization, control, or representation of data.

Character Alignment—The vertical or horizontal position of characters with respect to a given set of reference lines.

Character Set—Those characters available for encodation in a particular automatic identification technology.

Check Character—A character included within a string of data whose value is used for the purpose of performing a mathematical check to ensure the accuracy of that data.

Check Digit—A check digit serves the same purpose as a check character, but it may assume numeric values only.

Clear Area—See *Quiet Zone.*

Code—See *Bar Code.*

Concatenation—The ability of a reading system to join together the data from multiple symbols and interpret it as a single message.

Continuous Code—A bar code symbology where all spaces within the symbol are parts of characters, e.g., Interleaved 2 of 5. There is no intercharacter gap in a continuous code.

2-D Stacked Symbology—A symbology consisting of 2 or more adjacent and associated rows of varying-width parallel bars and spaces. All of the rows in a symbol are the same length.

2-D Matrix Symbology—A two dimensional arrangement of contrasting marks encoding information in accordance to specific rules. The resolution of the symbol's markings is substantially equal in two orthogonal axes.

Decimal, Binary Coded (BCD)—A numbering system using base 2, that represents each decimal digit by four binary bits, with the weighting values equal to 8, 4, 2, and 1, reading from left to right.

Decoder—As part of a bar code reading system, the electronic package that receives the signals from the scanner, performs the algorithm to interpret the signals into meaningful data, and provides the interface to other devices.

Density—See *Bar Code Density*.

Depth of Field—The distance between the maximum and minimum plane in which a code reader is capable of reading symbols of a specified X dimension.

Diffuse Reflection—The component of reflected light that emanates in all directions from the reflecting surface.

Discrete Code—A bar code symbology where the spaces between characters (intercharacter gap) are not part of the code, e.g., Code 39.

DSSG—Distribution symbology study group.

EAN—European Article Numbering system, the international standard bar code for retail food packages.

Element—In a bar code symbol, a single bar or space.

Film Master—A photographic film representation of a specific bar code or OCR symbol from which a printing plate is produced.

First Read Rate—The ratio of the number of successful reads on the first scanning attempt to the number of attempts. Commonly expressed as a percentage. Abbreviated as FRR.

Font—A specific size and style of printer's type.

Font-Independent OCR—Optical character recognition by generalized algorithms allowing wide ranges of character fonts. In the most general case, this extends to bar code patterns as well.

FRR—First Read Rate.

Guard Bars—The bars that are at both ends and center of a U.P.C. and EAN symbol. They provide reference points for scanning, serving a function similar to start/stop codes.

Helium-Neon (HeNe) Laser—A type of laser commonly used in bar code scanners. It emits coherent red light at a wavelength of 633 nanometers.

HIBCC—The Health Industry Business Communications Council.

Horizontal Bar Code—A bar code or symbol presented in such a manner that its overall length dimension is parallel to the horizon. The bars are presented in an array that looks like a picket fence.

Input Device—That portion of a bar code reading system that employs electro-optical techniques to determine the localized reflectivity of a symbol.

Intercharacter Gap—The space between two adjacent bar code characters in a discrete code. For example, the space between two characters in Code 39.

Interleaved Bar Code—A bar code in which characters are paired together using bars to represent the first character and spaces to represent the second, i.e., Interleaved 2 of 5 (See *Continuous Code*).

Ladder Code—See *Vertical Bar Code*.

Laser Diode—A semiconductor laser commonly used in bar code scanners.

Laser Scanner—An optical bar code reading device using a low energy laser light beam as its source of illumination.

LED—Light emitting diode. A semiconductor that produces light at a wavelength determined by its chemical composition. The light source often used in light pens.

Light Pen—In a bar code system, a handheld scanning wand that is used as a contact bar code reader held in the hand. (See *Wand Scanner*.)

Mil—One one-thousandth of an inch (0.001").

Misread—A condition that occurs when the data output of a reader does not agree with the data encoded in the bar code symbol.

Module—The narrowest nominal width unit of measure in a bar code.

Modulo Check Digit or Character—See *Check Character*.

Moving Beam Bar Code Reader—A scanning device where scanning motion is achieved by mechanically or electronically moving the optical geometry.

Multidrop—A network topology in which multiple devices, each with a unique address, are connected to a common set of data communication lines.

N—The ratio between the widths of wide elements and narrow elements in a two-width symbology.

Nanometer—A unit of measure used to define the wavelength of light. Equal to 10^{-9} meters.

Nominal—The exact (or ideal) intended value for a specified parameter. Tolerances are specified as positive and negative deviations from this value.

Non-Read—In a bar code system, the absence of data at the scanner output after an attempted scan due to no code, defective code, scanner failure, or operator error.

Numeric—A character set that includes only the numbers.

OCR-A—An abbreviation commonly applied to the character set contained in ANSI Standard X3.17-1981. A stylized font choice used for Traditional OCR printing.

OCR-B—An abbreviation commonly applied to the character set contained in ANSI Standard X3.49-1975. A stylized font choice used for Traditional OCR printing.

Opacity—The optical property of a substrate material that quantifies the show-through from the back side or the next sheet. The ratio of the reflectance with a black backing to the reflectance with a white backing. Ink opacity is the property of an ink that prevents the substrate from showing through.

Orientation—The alignment of a bar code symbol with respect to horizontal. Two possible orientations are horizontal with vertical bars and spaces (picket fence) and vertical with horizontal bars and spaces (ladder).

Overhead—In a bar code system, the fixed number of characters required for start, stop, and checking in a given symbol. For example, a symbol requiring a start/stop and two check characters contains four characters of overhead. Thus, to encode three characters, seven characters are required to be printed.

PCS—Print contrast signal. A measurement of the ratio of the reflectivities between the bars and spaces of a symbol, commonly expressed in percent. PCS is calculated as:

$$\frac{R_L - R_D}{R_L} \times 100 \text{ percent}$$

where
   R_L = reflectivity of the light elements
   R_D = reflectivity of the dark elements

Picket Fence Code—See *Horizontal Bar Code*.

Pitch—Rotation of a bar code symbol about an axis parallel to the direction of the bars.

Port Concentrator—A piece of data communication equipment that allows several different connected devices to transmit data to or receive data from a single master communication port.

POS—Point of sale.

Postnet Code—A height modulated, numeric symbology developed by the United States Post Office.

Preprinted Symbol—A symbol that is printed in advance of application either on a label or on the article to be identified.

Print Contrast Signal—See *PCS*.

Print Quality—The measure of compliance of a bar code symbol to the requirements of dimensional tolerance, edge roughness, spots, voids, reflectance, PCS, quiet zone, and encodation.

Quiet Zone—A clear space, containing no dark marks, that precedes the start character of a bar code symbol and follows the stop characters. Sometimes called the "clear area."

Reader—See *Bar Code Reader*.

Reflectance—The ratio of the amount of light of a specified wavelength or series of wavelengths reflected from a test surface to the amount of light reflected from a barium oxide or magnesium oxide standard under similar illumination conditions.

Resolution—In a bar code system, the narrowest element dimension that can be distinguished by a particular reading device or printed with a particular device or method.

Scanner—An electronic device that electro-optically converts optical information into electrical signals.

Self-Checking—A symbology is termed self-checking if a single printing defect will not cause a character to be transposed into another valid character in the same symbology.

SER—Substitution error rate. The rate of occurrence of incorrect characters from an automatic identification system.

Show-Through—The generally undesirable property of a substrate that permits underlying markings to be seen.

Skew—Rotation of a bar code symbol about an axis parallel to the symbol's length.

Space—The lighter element of a bar code usually formed by the background between bars.

Space Width—The thickness of a space measured from the edge closest to the symbol start character to the trailing edge of the same space.

Spectral Response—The variation in sensitivity of a reading device or the variation in reflectivity of a test surface to light of different wavelengths.

Specular Reflection—The mirror-like reflection of light from a surface.

Spot—1. The undesirable presence of ink or dirt in a space. 2. The area on a bar code symbol that is being examined by an input device at any given point of time.

STAC—Symbol Technical Advisory Committee to the Uniform Code Council, Inc. (see *Uniform Code Council*).

Start/Stop Character or Pattern—A special bar code character that provides the scanner with start and stop reading instructions as well as scanning direction indicator. The start character is normally at the far left end of a horizontally oriented symbol. The stop character is normally at the far right end of a horizontally oriented symbol.

Substitution Error—A misencodation, misread, or human key entry error where incorrect information is substituted for a character that was to be entered. Example: correct information—1, 2, 3, 4; substitution—1, 2, 3, 5.

Substitution Error Rate—See *SER*.

Substrate—The surface on which a bar code symbol is printed.

Symbol—A combination of bar code characters (including start/stop characters, quiet zones, data characters, and check characters required by a particular symbology), that forms a complete, scannable entity.

Symbol Density—See *Bar Code Density*.

Symbol Length—The distance between the outside edges of the quiet zones on the two ends of a bar code symbol.

Synchronous—A data communication scheme whereby data is transmitted in reference to a master clock signal. The clock may be a separate signal or may be part of the data.

TCS—Transport case symbol.

Tilt—Rotation of a bar code symbol about an axis perpendicular to the substrate.

Traditional OCR—The first form of 2-dimensional OCR developed, using the stylized OCR-A and OCR-B fonts.

UCS—Uniform Container Symbol.

UCC—Uniform Code Council, previously the Uniform Product Code Council; the organization that administers the U.P.C. and other retail standards.

U.P.C.—Universal Product Code, the standard bar code symbol for retail food packages in the United States.

U.P.C.—A A U.P.C. symbol encoding a number system character, 10 digits of data, and a check digit.

U.P.C.—E A U.P.C. symbol encoding 6 digits of data in an arrangement that occupies less area than a U.P.C.-A symbol. Also called a "zero-suppressed" symbol because a 10 digit U.P.C.-A code can be compressed to a 6 digit U.P.C.-E format by suppressing redundant zeros.

USS—Uniform Symbol Specification. The current series of symbology specifications published by AIM-USA; they currently include USS-Interleaved 2 of 5, USS-39, USS-93, USS-Codabar, USS-128, USS-49, USS-16K, USS-PDF417, and USS-Code One.

Vertical Bar Code—A code pattern presented in such orientation that the axis of the symbol from start to stop is perpendicular to the horizon. The individual bars are in an array that appears as rungs of a ladder.

Void—The undesirable absence of ink in a printed bar.

Wand—See *Wand Scanner*.

Wand Scanner—A handheld scanning device used as a contact bar code or OCR reader.

X Dimension—The nominal width dimension of the narrow bars and spaces in a bar code symbol.

Z Dimension—The achieved width of the narrow elements, calculated as the average of the average narrow bar width and the average narrow space width.

BIBLIOGRAPHY

Ackley, H. Sprague. *Verification—New Insight for an Old Debate*. Scan-Tech 1987.

Allais, Dr. David C. *An Analysis of the Substitution Error Rate of Code 39*. Intermec Corp., Document 601975, March, 1979.

_____*Bar Code Symbology*. Lynnwood, WA: Intermec Corp. 1984.

_____*Characteristics of Code 39 and Code 93*. Scan-Tech 1983.

_____*High Density—The Challenge of Identifying Miniature Objects*. Scan-Tech 1987.

_____*History and Overview of Automatic Identification*. Scan-Tech 1985.

_____*Industrial Symbology: A Deeper Understanding*. Scan-Tech 1983.

Automatic Identification Manufacturers, *USS-39*. Pittsburgh: AIM-USA, 1986.

_____*USS-93*. Pittsburgh: AIM-USA, 1986.

_____*USS-128*. Pittsburgh: AIM-USA, 1986.

_____*USS-Codabar*. Pittsburgh: AIM-USA, 1986.

_____*USS-I 2/5*. Pittsburgh: AIM-USA, 1986.

_____*USS-PDF417*. Pittsburgh: AIM-USA, 1994.

_____*USS-Code One*. Pittsburgh: AIM-USA, 1994.

Bravman, Richard. *Systems Models*. Scan-Tech 1986.

Brodheim, Eric, Sc.D. *The Use of Machine-Readable Codes as a Basis for Automating Blood Transfusion Services*. Scan-Tech 1983.

Callahan, Michael W. *Systems Models—An Overview for Users*. Scan-Tech 1985.

Coe, Edward S. *Inventory—Increasing Profitability with More Accurate Systems*. Institute for International Research Conference on Bar Coding, 1984.

Czaplicki, David J. *Contact Scanners and Supporting Devices*. Scan-Tech Europe, 1984.

Dooley, James A. *On-Site Bar Code Printing*. Scan-Tech 1986.

Eastman, Jay M. *Emerging Scanning Technologies*. Scan-Tech 1987.

Gilligan, Alan. *Bar Code Standards within ANSI Supported Committees*. Scan-Tech 1987.

Harmon, Craig K. *Specifications for the HIBC Symbol and Code*. Scan-Tech 1983.

Harmon, Craig K. and Russ Adams. *Reading Between the Lines*. Helmers Publishing, Inc. formerly North American Technology, Inc., 1984

Harmon, Craig K. *Lines Of Communication*. Helmers Publishing, 1994.

Harnick, Keith D. *Off-Site Printed Bar Codes*. Scan-Tech 1986.

Hill, Raymond. *A First Course in Coding Theory*. Oxford University Press 1986.

Huber, Greg. *Human-Involved Scanning, Pens and Guns*. Scan-Tech 1984.

Jones, Keith. *A Damage Resistant Bar Code For The Royal Mail*. USPS Advanced Technology Conference, 1993.

Klaisner, Lowell A. *Data Communications in Automatic Identification Systems*. Scan-Tech 1985.

_____*Data Communications Concepts for Data Collection Systems*. Scan-Tech 1984.

_____*Systems Implementation Concepts in a Fixed Asset Inventory Application*. Scan-Tech 1983.

Little, Warren. *Array Tags In Forestry*. IEEE Pacific Rim Conference On Communications, Computers, And Signal Processing, 1991.

Loeffler, J. R. *AIAG Shipping/Parts Identification Label*. Scan-Tech 1984.

_____*Lessons Learned in Establishing AIAG Standards*. Scan-Tech 1987.

MacWilliams, F.J. and Sloane, N.J.A. *The Theory of Error-Correcting Codes*. Elsevier Science Publisher B.V. 1977.

Meyers, Richard B. *What's My Line?* ID Expo 1988.

Nelson, Benjamin A. *On-Site Printing of Bar Code Symbols*. Scan-Tech 1983.

Noll, Michael W. *Lessons Learned from the Department of Defense LOGMARS Project*. Institute for International Research Conference on Bar Coding, 1984.

_____*LOGMARS—The Second Generation Department of Defense Bar Code Standards And Future Automatic Identification Initiatives*. Scan-Tech 1987.

Palmer, Roger C. *Bar Code Dimensional Tolerances*. Intermec Corp., Document 603154, March, 1984.

_____*Bar Code Scanning Technology in the Health Care Industry*. Health Care Material Management Society Seminar, 1988.

_____*Bar Code Standard Development*. Scan-Tech 1987.

_____*Bar Code Standards in the Health Industry*. Packaging Technology for Medical Devices and Pharmaceuticals (SME), 1985.

_____*Bar Code Technology and Manufacturing Applications*. AMS, 1987.

_____*Bar Codes, the Major Symbologies*. Scan-Tech 1985.

_____*Considerations in Implementing a Bar Code Shop Floor Data Collection System*. Scan-Tech 1984.

_____*Contrasting Approaches to Standard Development*, Scan-Tech 1986.

_____Printing Health Industry Bar Code. HIBCC Conference, 1984.

_____State of the Art and Future Trends in Bar Coding. Institute For International Research Conference on Bar Coding, 1984.

_____System Considerations for Implementing Factory Data Collection System Using Bar Code. Scan-Tech 1982.

_____The Evolution of High Density Symbologies. Scan-Tech 1990.

_____Area Scanning For Postal Applications. Jet Poste 1993.

_____ Two Dimension Symbologies. Scan Tech Japan 1994.

Pavlidis, Theo, Swartz, Jerome, and Wang, Ynjiun P. Fundamentals Of Bar Code Information Theory. IEEE Computer, 1990.

Penkar, Rajan C. A Two Dimensional Dense Code Symbology And Reader For The Package Handling Environment. USPS Advanced technology Conference 1993.

Sharkey, Frank M. Principals of Bar Code Scanning. Scan-Tech 1987.

Wray, Bruce. Bar Codes in Harsh Manufacturing Environments. AMS, 1987.

INDEX

Delta Distance, 45-46

Density, 14, 19, 22, 31-33, 37-40, 42-45, 50-52, 54, 62, 69, 139, 141, 154, 156, 183, 185, 211, 245, 251, 257, 263, 269, 275, 289, 306, 318, 354, 362, 372-373, 377, 379

Depth Of Field, 74, 89-91, 93, 100-104, 365, 373

Diodes, 90, 93, 97, 120

Direct Sequence, 210-211

Discrete, 18-19, 31-32, 34-35, 43, 45-46, 60, 105, 137, 251, 257, 373-374

Distribution, 29, 39, 75-76, 176, 232, 318, 343-347, 349, 357, 367-368, 373

Dot Matrix Printer, 138

Drum Printer, 140, 143, 152-153

EAN, 13, 20, 25, 27-29, 42, 44-45, 73, 80, 160, 223, 232-233, 243, 324-325, 353, 355, 357, 359, 373

Edge Contrast, 170-171

Edge-To-Edge, 79

EDI, 230, 232-233, 303, 306, 310, 360

Electrostatic, 8, 137, 147-150, 204

Element, 19-20, 24, 26, 29, 31-34, 37, 39, 43, 65, 80, 85, 92, 99-100, 104-105, 141-143, 159, 161-162, 164-166, 169, 171-173, 180-182, 184, 186, 188, 190, 245-248, 252-253, 258, 260, 266-267, 273-274, 290, 319, 328-329, 337, 339-340, 343-346, 366, 371-373, 376

Emulate, 206, 218

Erasures, 194, 301

Error Rate, 3-5, 9-10, 77, 111, 139, 159, 161, 163, 179, 189-191, 193, 243, 343-345, 347-349, 376-377, 379

Ethernet, 200-201

ETSI, 209-211

Face Material, 156-157

FACT, 3, 19, 43, 54, 67, 76, 85, 148, 155, 222, 226, 233, 243, 334, 351-352

Factor R, 181-183, 339-341

Film Master, 132, 373

Fixed Beam, 88-89

Fixed Mount, 88, 95, 110, 117-120, 123-126, 207, 212, 221

Flash Lamps, 97

Flexography, 131, 134, 137

Formed Bar, 142-143

Frequency, 7, 10, 83, 95, 108-110, 128, 198, 201, 207-213, 236, 369

Frequency Hopping, 210-211, 369

Galois Fields, 194

Grade, 77-78, 164, 170-177, 228

Guard Bar, 289, 294

Helium-Neon, 83, 90, 97, 120, 374

Hexagon, 319

Hexagonal, 57, 175-177, 319, 328-329, 331-332, 361

HIBCC, 37, 76, 189, 359, 374, 381

Hot Stamping, 131, 136, 155

I2/5 (Interleaved 2 of 5) 13-14, 29-31, 42-44, 63, 75, 80, 113, 160, 182, 188-189, 192-193, 234, 243, 245-249, 290, 355, 360

IEEE, 175, 201, 212, 380-381

Illumination, 90-94, 96, 104, 124, 126, 168, 363, 365-366, 374, 376

Incandescent, 89, 91, 94, 97, 241

Inking Wheel, 131, 135, 137

Input Devices, 87-89, 93, 95-97, 113

Interleaved 2 of 5, See I2 of 5

Inventory, 44, 106, 117, 215, 226-228, 231-232, 234-235, 368, 379-380

Ion Deposition, 149-151

ISO, 195, 313-314, 317-318, 323

Label, 5, 9-10, 13, 15, 26, 54, 68-69, 73-74, 75, 85, 97, 129, 136, 141-146, 149-157, 169, 225, 230-231, 233, 235, 240, 253, 295-296, 301-302, 361, 363, 365-368, 372, 376, 380

Laminators, 152

Laser Diode, 90, 364-365, 374

Laser Etching, 131, 154

Laser, 65-66, 69, 82-83, 90-91, 94, 97, 101, 117, 120-121, 123, 129, 131, 136, 138, 140, 147-148, 150, 153-155, 225, 233, 240, 362-366, 374

LED, 9, 11, 13, 67, 89, 91, 94, 110, 124, 147, 364, 374

Letterpress, 131-133, 135, 137

Local Area Networks, 195, 200, 204

Machine Vision, 1, 7, 54, 123

Magnetics, 6, 207

Magnetographic, 137, 150-151

MAP, 86, 200, 206, 276

Masterless, 201

Matrix 2 of 5, 45

MaxiCode, 14, 55-57, 69-70, 243, 319-329

Measuring Geometry, 168-169

Media, 132-133, 135, 139, 141, 146, 149, 153, 156, 195, 198, 201

MICR, 5-6, 10

Modem, 197-198, 209, 226

Modulation, 16-17, 46-47, 77, 148, 154, 170-171, 186, 198, 200-202, 208, 210-212, 365

Module, 48, 52-53, 56, 63, 69, 104-105, 181, 185-186, 270, 276, 284, 286, 290, 295-296, 302, 306, 339, 362, 366, 374

Moving Beam, 88, 90-92, 100, 113, 117-120, 155, 189, 225, 234, 374

MRD, 164, 167-168, 247, 253, 259, 266, 272, 286, 336

MRP, 5, 228-229, 232

MSI, 44-45, 353, 356

Multidrop, 116, 199-201, 203, 217, 374

Network, 106, 116, 195-196, 198, 201, 204-207, 211-213, 215, 228, 367, 369, 374

Nixdorf Code, 45

Numbering Association, 28-29, 264, 292, 357-359

OCR, 4-5, 7, 10, 237, 373, 375, 377-378

Offset, 3, 85, 92, 131, 133-134, 137, 319, 328

Omnidirectional, 5, 26, 92, 94, 120-121, 123, 125-126, 129, 237, 303, 313, 363-364

Open Systems, 195-196, 223, 246, 249, 252, 255, 258, 262, 264, 267, 270, 274

Orientation, 7, 22, 55, 58, 60, 92, 95, 99, 117-118, 120, 123, 138, 143, 237, 303, 313, 320, 334, 362, 371, 375, 377

OSI, 195-196, 206

Package Sensor, 119

Painting, 154

Parity, 43, 48-49, 203, 276

Patent, 11, 13, 56, 61, 72-73, 92, 241-242, 361

PCMCIA, 108, 212

PDF417, 14, 20, 52-54, 63, 67-70, 75-76, 105, 160, 174, 190, 194, 243, 295-302, 353, 356

Plessey, 13, 44-45, 234, 353, 356

Point-To-Point, 115-116, 196

Port Concentrator, 116, 375

Portable, 7-8, 44, 105-111, 115, 144, 198, 201, 207, 212, 221, 226-227, 232, 235, 362-367

Postnet, 14, 19, 46-47, 73, 236-238, 243, 335-336, 372, 375

Protocol Converter, 218

Protocol, 108-109, 196, 200-203, 206, 212, 218

QR code, 58-59

Quiet Zone, 48, 53, 57, 69, 89, 180, 245-246, 249, 251-252, 255, 257-258, 262-264, 267, 269-270, 274-275, 284, 289, 296, 301, 311, 313, 319, 331, 372, 376

Radio Frequency, 7, 110, 201, 207, 210, 369

Radio Reader, 110, 235

Readability Grade, 175, 177

Receiving, 99, 108-109, 117, 198, 200, 203, 210, 229-230, 233-236, 362, 368

Redundancy, 9, 35, 50, 56, 91, 94, 108, 119, 179, 189, 194, 203, 313, 317, 332-333

Reflectivity, 76, 78, 80, 82-85, 87, 94-96, 98-99, 154-155, 159, 162, 164-168, 172, 175-176, 247, 253, 259, 266, 272, 286, 336, 374-376

Resolution, 18, 69, 76, 79, 81, 84-85, 99, 123-128, 136, 140, 148-150, 154, 163, 180-181, 185-186, 361, 364, 373, 376

Retail, 1, 5, 11, 13, 23, 29, 39, 44, 223, 231-234, 367, 373, 377

Rotogravure, 131, 134-135, 137

RS-422, 115-116, 199

RS-449, 199

RS-485, 199-200

SDLC, 202-203

Security, 7-9, 19, 21, 29-30, 37, 40, 43, 45, 62, 83, 95, 105, 109, 113, 125, 179, 181, 183, 185, 187, 189, 191, 193, 203, 221, 225, 235, 247, 259, 367-368

Shipping, 13, 75, 117, 231-235, 239, 360, 367, 380

Signaling, 195-197, 199-200

Spot, 1, 80-85, 87, 89-90, 92-94, 99-100, 102, 104-105, 123, 162-164, 166, 180, 363, 365-366, 376

Spread Spectrum, 110, 209-212, 221, 369

Standard Deviation, 175, 344, 347

Standards, 13-14, 42, 47, 65-66, 74, 75-77, 96, 126, 163, 165, 169, 195, 200, 209, 212, 218, 223-224, 233, 243, 359-360, 371, 377, 379-380

Start Code, 29, 32, 34, 37, 39, 42-43, 48

Stop Code, 29-32, 34-35, 37, 39-41, 43-44, 48, 257

Symbol Contrast, 96, 170

Synchronous, 202, 377

System Analysis, 215

System Design, 194, 215, 218

Take-Up, 152

Thermal Printer, 141-143, 156, 361, 363

Thermal Transfer Printer, 155

Threshold, 84-85, 104, 142, 145, 169-170, 173, 175-176, 184, 339

Tilt, 26, 50, 53, 118-119, 179, 377

Tolerance, 12, 19, 34, 53, 62, 119, 159-161, 165, 180-188, 243, 247, 249, 252-254, 258-259, 261, 265, 271-272, 274, 285, 328-329, 339, 341, 343-346, 371, 376

Topology, 201, 217, 374

U.P.C., 11-13, 20, 23-29, 42, 60, 63, 73, 80, 104, 184-185, 187, 189-190, 223, 232-234, 289, 339, 353, 355, 360, 377

U.P.C.-A, 27-28, 189-190, 355, 377

U.P.C.-E, 27, 189, 355, 377

Uniform Code Council (UCC), 28, 76, 264, 292, 324-325, 357, 359-360, 376-377

Verifier, 75, 161

VICS, 360

Voice Recognition, 6

Voids, 76, 78, 99, 159, 162-164, 166, 180, 186, 376

Waist, 94, 100-103, 362

Wands, 65, 88-89, 97, 100, 180, 222, 233

Warehousing, 235

Wavelength, 77-78, 83-84, 95-97, 101-103, 134, 166, 169, 173, 207-208, 223-224, 247, 253, 259, 266, 272, 286, 374, 376

Waveshaper, 79, 84-85, 88, 104

Wedge, 114-115

WIP, 227-228, 235